M000209157

The Politics of Disgrace

The Politics of Disgrace

The Role of Political Scandal in American Politics

Nancy E. Marion
UNIVERSITY OF AKRON

CAROLINA ACADEMIC PRESS
Durham, North Carolina

Copyright © 2010
Nancy E. Marion
All Rights Reserved

Library of Congress Cataloging-in-Publication Data

Marion, Nancy E.
 The politics of disgrace : the role of political scandal in American politics /
Nancy E. Marion.
     p. cm.
 Includes bibliographical references and index.
 ISBN 978-1-59460-508-6 (alk. paper)
 1. Scandals--United States. 2. Misconduct in office--United States. 3. Politi-
cal corruption--United States. 4. Corruption investigation--United States. 5.
Scandals--United States--History. 6. Misconduct in office--United States--
History. 7. Political corruption--United States--History. 8. Corruption inves-
tigation--United States--History. I. Title.

 JK2249.M37 2009
 364.1'3230973--dc22

                               2008048735

                    CAROLINA ACADEMIC PRESS
                          700 Kent Street
                    Durham, North Carolina 27701
                     Telephone (919) 489-7486
                        Fax (919) 493-5668
                        www.cap-press.com

          Printed in the United States of America

29.75   364.132
          Mar

*This book is dedicated to
my parents and the JAM-D Club*

Contents

Cases Cited

The Politics of Disgrace

Chapter 1

Introduction: The Role of Scandals in Government

Introduction

On the day before Valentine's Day 2008, Client-9 arranged to meet with a prostitute named "Kristen" in the Mayflower Hotel in Washington, D.C. To meet him, Kristen needed to travel from New York City to Washington. Client-9 agreed to pay for the travel and hotel expenses, including train tickets, cab fare, and even reimbursement for travel time. The final bill for Client-9 was $4,300, including a $1,100 deposit for a future meeting, all paid in cash. Over the past few years, Client-9 had many liaisons with prostitutes, with his costs totaling about $80,000.[1]

In bringing Kristen to Washington for the evening, Client-9 may have violated the Mann Act, a federal law that bans interstate transportation of women to engage in prostitution.[2] Moreover, he may have committed money laundering, as he made payments to the prostitution service's shell corporations to conceal the real purpose of the payments.[3] There was also evidence that he used political campaign funds to pay for the hotel.[4]

Client-9 turned out to be New York Governor Eliot Spitzer, who, up to then, had a promising political career. He served six years as a prosecutor in the Manhattan district attorney's office where he set up a sting operation intended to break organized crime's hold on trucking in the garment district.[5] He was the state's attorney general for eight years, during which time he pursued wrongdoing on Wall Street.[6] During his campaign for governor, he promised to clean up state politics and became known as "Mr. Clean."[7] He had been elected to the office with a record margin of victory. After calls for his impeachment, Spitzer resigned from office on March 12, ending a potentially long and successful political career.

Another long and successful political career ended in January 2009 when the Illinois State Senate voted to remove Governor Rod Blagojevich from office and banned him from ever holding public office in the state. Governor Blagojevich was arrested in December 2008 on federal corruption charges involving conspiracy to commit mail and wire fraud and solicitation of bribery. The Justice Department alleged that he tried to sell Barack Obama's vacated United States Senate seat to the highest bidder.[8]

Blagojevich was arrested and appeared before a federal judge to answer the charges,[9] but returned to work the next day.[10] There were numerous calls for his resignation, one even coming from then-president-elect Obama himself.[11] A panel set up to investigate the possible impeachment of the Governor began proceedings in mid-December,[12] and the House voted to impeach Blagojevich in January 2009.[13] Just a few days later, on January 29, the Illinois Senate voted to remove him from office.[14]

Scandals such as this one are not a new phenomenon on the American political scene. On the contrary, public scandals are one of the most pervasive elements of our history,[15] and there have been an unprecedented number of scandals in national politics in recent years.[16] Such scandals have become a common element of the modern political system. They are now a constant occurrence, but at the same time an unknown. We almost expect them, and are certainly not surprised by them, but we are never sure when they will happen and to whom. Most people see scandals as part of politics, often initiated by the other party, with unknown consequences.

Oddly enough, this recent proliferation of scandals has happened at a time when Congress has imposed stricter ethics rules on its members than ever before. There is new legislation banning honoraria (monetary gifts for speeches), placing limits on gifts, implementing strict reporting standards for campaign contributions and spending,[17] putting restrictions on postgovernment employment, creating new forms of investigations, and tightening scrutiny of political figures' private lives. Other legislation increases the potential penalties for existing offenses.[18] All in all, legislation concerning personal behavior of politicians has become dramatically stricter in the post-Watergate era.[19] If someone violates one of the numerous laws, we have the Office of Independent Counsel set up and ready to investigate allegations of wrongdoing.[20] Nonetheless, American politics continues to be dominated by scandal.[21]

These scandals are a reflection on the culture, values, and political processes of society as much as the people directly involved in them.[22] Although many people argue that our attitudes toward politicians' private lives have changed, others still believe that politicians ought to set an example of a solid private morality.[23] It might be argued that scandalous behavior by politicians demonstrates the moral character (or lack thereof) of those who are involved more so than conventional politics.[24] In that sense, scandals point to a person's flawed character and exacerbate it for all to see.

Scandals attract and excite media interest and public attention in ways that few other political events can match. They dominate newspaper headlines and television news bulletins, sometimes for long periods.[25] American journalists now devote extraordinary amounts of time to controversies surrounding the moral and ethical behavior of politicians, sometimes at the expense of real news. Instead of debating the meaning of good and bad policy or who provides effective and ineffective leadership, Americans often debate about personal wrongdoing.[26]

The impacts of scandals can vary tremendously, but on the whole, there does not seem to be a great deal of correspondence between the degree of controversy generated by scandals and the gravity of the misdeeds. Some of those involved in scandals pay a heavy price, whereas others escape with only minor damage, if any at all. The effects can range from a damaged reputation or resignation to heavy fines or even imprisonment.[27] The impact of a political scandal often depends more on factors outside of the scandal than on the seriousness of the misdeeds themselves or the culpability of individuals. The ultimate seriousness of an ethics breach is determined by the public's reaction to the charges.[28]

In many cases, the impact of a scandal can reach beyond the individual involved. Scandals often result in an enormous amount of wasted time and attention.[29] They can easily take over the agenda of politicians and the government. If the scandal is serious enough, the process of government is disrupted as attention is diverted from the task of governing. In the long run, the government may become unable to deal with crisis. In some cases, the scandal can even paralyze those involved, making it impossible for politicians to be effective at their jobs as they must respond to the allegations.

For citizens outside of the government, scandals cause cynicism and alienation.[30] For many Americans, the recent proliferation of scandals has resulted in a culture of mistrust, or a suspicion of political leaders and a willingness to believe the worst about them.[31]

American society today is not the only place where scandal exists. Political scandals exist in every country; at all levels of government; in different social, economic, and political systems; and in all political parties.[32] But the substance of what is considered scandalous behavior changes political morality and societal norms vary enormously from one country to another or from one era to another.[33] It is important to note that there is a great deal of diversity and variety in the values, norms, and moral codes that exist in any society. Therefore, what is considered a scandal in one context may be considered acceptable or normal elsewhere.[34] A good example of this is Thomas Jefferson's relationship with his slave Sally Hemings. During that time period, it was acceptable behavior for a slave owner to have an affair with a slave. Today, if a president had an affair with a housekeeper, it may be considered an abuse of political power. However, many of the things that were considered scandalous in older days would be considered scandalous today, too, such as sexual or financial misconduct.[35]

It is easy to see that scandals are not new. Hundreds of years ago, there were political scandals in Rome, Babylon, and the Spanish Empire. In the United States, James Wilkinson, the governor of Louisiana Territory in George Washington's administration, was involved in an early scandal. It was thought he was being paid by the Spanish, but nothing came of it at the time.[36] However, his questionable behavior continued into the Jefferson administration, when it was discovered that Wilkinson was paid 12,000 pesos by the Spanish in 1804 in return for information about American boundary policies, military readiness, and diplomatic plans.[37]

Political scandals occur outside of the United States. For example, in Mexico City in 2000, Raul Salinas, the brother of the former Mexican President, stashed away $100 million for his personal use. He did this at a time when there was a devaluation of the peso and millions of Mexicans had their life savings wiped out. Pictures were published of Salinas frolicking on a yacht with women, and there were even allegations of murder. In the end, he went to prison for the murder of a rival, and former President Carlos Salinas was exiled to Ireland.[38]

Other examples of scandals in other countries abound. For example, in Tokyo, Hidenao Nakagawa, one of Prime Minister Yoshiro Mori's top advisors, admitted to accepting millions in yen in questionable donations. Nakagawa was the chief cabinet secretary and the government's top spokesman. He acknowledged receiving 8.5 million yen from two people in 1997 when the maximum legal donation an individual could make to a politician was 1.5 million yen. Nakagawa denied any legal violations.[39] At about the same time, the chairman of the Financial Reconstruction Commission in Japan resigned after acknowledging that he received 230 million yen for advisory work for the Mitsubishi Trust and Banking Corporation over a period of thirteen years. He also accepted 100 million yen from a condominium developer.

In China, a former central government official was executed for taking almost $5 million in bribes.[40] Cheng Kejie was one of nineteen vice chairmen of the National People's Congress[41] at the time of his scandalous behavior. In Peru, a videotape of the President's top intelligence aide giving a bribe to an opposition lawmaker emerged causing a stir in that country.[42]

One of the most publicized scandals in Britain was the Profumo scandal in 1963, where the minister of War, John Profumo, had been sharing a prostitute with the naval attaché at the Russian embassy. When questioned by the House of Commons about it, he lied and was forced to resign.[43] Later, the prime minister resigned, and eventually the Conservative government was swept from power.

In France in 1985, Greenpeace sent its ship *Rainbow Warrior* to harass the French military because they were blowing up small islands in the Pacific with nuclear weapons, upsetting environmentalists. When the *Rainbow Warrior* was preparing to set sail for another journey, there was a large explosion on board that killed one person. It was discovered that the explosion was caused by a bomb. When two men were arrested, it turned out that they were French agents named Alain Mafart and Dominique Prieur, who had been sent to get information about Greenpeace and their intentions. It was also discovered that the French were responsible for the bombing.

Some political systems are more prone to scandal than others. In those countries where there is a single source of power, where the press is limited, and where there are no controls or checks on those who hold power, it is possible for political leaders to behave with impunity. Conversely, in a more democratic political system with a free press, political competition, decentralized authority, and multiple access points, the opportunities and incentives for scandal to flourish are numerous.[44] Moreover, those countries that have more visible public leaders are more vulnerable to scandal.[45]

In the United States, it seems that no politician is immune to scandal. No branch of government or political office is protected from the scandal plague that has hit the nation.[46] There have been scandals on the federal level surrounding the president, Congress, and the courts. In fact, three of the last five presidents (Richard Nixon, Ronald Reagan and Bill Clinton) have undergone major investigations into their behavior and that of their advisors or close associates.[47] In Congress, two of the last speakers of the House have had similar troubles. Speaker Jim Wright was forced to resign from office, and the following speaker, Newt Gingrich, escaped with censure and a large fine for his unethical behavior. In addition, speaker-elect Bob Livingston in 1998 resigned his seat rather than endure an apparently minor scandal about an extramarital affair.[48] Many judges have found themselves embroiled in political scandal as a result of taking bribes for lower sentences or for misdeeds in their personal affairs.

Scandals also impact state officials. Many governors have found themselves the center of scandal, some of whom are described in Table 1.1. One who paid the price for unethical behavior was Maryland governor Marvin Mandel, who, in the early 1970s, was having an extramarital relationship with Jeanne Dorsey. He sometimes visited her late at night using an unmarked state police car. One night, just a few minutes after midnight, he was returning home after visiting her house. Mandel was in a serious accident that caused the death of a man in the other car. On investigation, the Governor refused to say what he was doing out at that time in a chauffeur-driven unmarked police car, claiming that he had been attending a "secret political" meeting. Not too long after this, Mandel and his wife separated. His wife refused to leave the Governor's mansion, claiming that Mandel needed psychiatric help.[49] Meanwhile, Mandel got remarried. He and his new wife flew to Jamaica in a plane owned by an oil company that was seeking state and local government permission to build and operate an oil refinery in southern Maryland. Later, Mandel admitted to ten free trips in four years on private jets as the guest of friends who did extensive business with the state.[50] In 1975, Mandel was indicted by a federal grand jury of charges that he participated in a "corrupt relationship" designed to defraud the citizens of Maryland. He was charged with ten counts of mail fraud and two separate counts of violating the bribery laws in Maryland.[51] He was convicted and served nineteen months in prison.

There are many other examples of state official scandals. In 1974 in Baltimore County, State Attorney Samuel A. Green was convicted of sixteen counts of obstruction of justice, misconduct in office, and attempted subordination of perjury after it was alleged that he had sexual relations with at least nine of his secretaries in 1968. It was also alleged that he had sexual relations with women who were accused of crimes in exchange for criminal charges being dropped.[52]

Another example of political scandal on the state level occurred with Arizona's Evan Mecham in 1987–88. Governor Mecham began his term by rescinding the Martin Luther King, Jr. holiday, obviously antagonizing many people. He then appointed someone to serve as tax commissioner who did not pay his own taxes. In the end, Mecham became the seventh governor to be removed from office by impeachment.[53]

More recently, in 2008, a Pennsylvania state senator was acquitted of perjury surrounding allegations that he lied about where he stored a gun that was used by a fourteen-year-old neighbor boy to commit suicide. The boy had been housesitting while the Senator's family was on vacation. Senator Robert T. "Bob" Regola had been charged with perjury, reckless endangerment and allowing a minor, his son, to illegally possess a 9 mm Taurus pistol. The son, the prosecution claimed, was allowed to keep the gun in his bedroom, where the victim found it.[54]

Table 1.1: Gubernatorial Scandals

William Barstow: Governor of Wisconsin from 1854–56: He was implicated in massive bribery during his tenure. He resigned due to possible election improprieties in the 1856 state election but was never tried.

Leonard Blanton: U.S. Representative from Tennessee and Governor of the state from 1975–79: He was removed from the governorship because of allegations that he sold pardons and profited from them.

Edwin Washington Edwards: Governor of Louisiana from 1972–80, 1984–88, and 1992–96: He was convicted in 2000 of using his influence to sell boating licenses in exchange for kickbacks.

Harold "Guy" Hunt: Governor of Alabama from 1987–93: He was convicted of misusing campaign funds and removed from office. Hunt was one of the few governors in the United States to be removed from office for corruption.

Edward Jackson: Governor of Indiana from 1925–29: He was put on trial for accepting a bribe while governor, but acquitted because the statute of limitations had expired.

John Symington: Governor of Arizona from 1991–97: He was convicted of fraud and resigned from office, but was later cleared by a federal court and pardoned by President Clinton.

Jim "Guy" Tucker: Governor of Arkansas from 1992–96: He was implicated along with President Clinton in the Whitewater affair, in which Tucker was found guilty of bank fraud.

Local government officials are not immune from scandal. In Akron, Ohio, a serious judicial scandal emerged in the 1980s. Judge James Barbuto was accused of taking bribes and receiving sexual favors for lighter punishments. He was also involved in illegal gun sales.

One of the most well known local public officers to be involved in a political scandal was Marion Barry, who served as the mayor of the District of Columbia from 1983–90. He was accused of using illegal drugs on many occasions. Barry was caught in a 1990 FBI sting where he was arrested in a hotel after he bought and smoked crack cocaine with an FBI informant. Barry was only convicted of a single misdemeanor charge of cocaine possession but was sentenced to jail.[55] More details about Mayor Barry are provided in Table 1.2.

Table 1.2: D.C. Mayor Marion S. Barry

Marion Barry was born 1936 in Itta Bena, Mississippi. He moved to Memphis, and graduated from LeMoyne College in chemistry. He started graduate studies in chemistry at Fisk University, but quit to join the civil rights movement. In 1965, Barry was elected as the first chairman of the Student Nonviolent Coordinating Committee. In the 1970s, he served on Washington's first elected school board and first elected city council. While serving as city councilman in 1977, he was shot at the District Building by Hanafi Muslim extremists as he was getting off the elevator. They were holding thirteen hostages. Barry was made to look like a hero for taking the bullet near his heart during a two-day hostage crisis. He said that he was attempting to defend the District Building from radical black Muslim terrorists.

In 1978 Barry was elected mayor of D.C., only the second person ever elected to that position. He served as mayor for twelve years until a 1990 drug arrest and misdemeanor conviction forced him to step down. He was reelected into office in 1994.

There were many controversies surrounding Barry's administration. In December 1981, Barry went to an adult club that was known for nude dancers called the *This Is It* nightclub. Barry went to the party and either used cocaine or was present while others did. He admitted to being there but denied using drugs, and said that it was a mistake to go to the party.

In August 1984, Barry acknowledged that he was "visiting" a woman, Karen K. Johnson, who was known for selling cocaine and was eventually convicted of it. He "visited" her for over a year. In March 1987, he was accused of another womanizing scandal. He admitted to visiting a part-time model, Grace Shell, who was twenty-three. The mayor and his legal counsel stated that Barry had no romantic interest in Shell and had merely been calling to set up a time to meet her three-year-old son. However, Johnson claimed that Barry kept harassing her.

After an investigation that lasted several weeks, Barry was arrested at the Vista Hotel. He was videotaped while smoking cocaine with his "longtime friend" Hazel Diane "Rasheeda" Moore. Moore had agreed to work with the FBI during the investigation. She had been arrested on narcotics charges prior to this. After his arrest, Barry tried to say that he was set up. The jury at the trial was divided. Of the fourteen charges presented in the trial, only one produced a verdict of guilty. He was sentenced for that misdemeanor charge to six months in prison and ordered to pay a $5,000 fine for cocaine possession. Barry was required by federal law to serve his full six months.

Ten of Barry's top officials were also convicted, including his wife, who was charged with defrauding the government and selling cocaine. After serving his sentence, he reentered the political scene. He used his conviction and sentence as a tool to show that he was no different than anyone else. He admitted that he had made many mistakes and that he learned from these mistakes, but it was time to move on. He won back a council seat in 1992, and in 1994 he was reelected mayor, but allegations again surfaced about women and drugs.

The mayor of Providence, Rhode Island, Vincent A. Cianci Jr. (1991–2002) was indicted and then convicted in a federal court of racketeering conspiracy, extortion, money laundering, and tampering with a witness for his role in corruption that was uncovered in city contracts. In September 2002 he was sentenced to sixty-four months in prison and fined $100,000.[56]

These examples show that scandals are prevalent in every time period and in many different places. Additionally, the social and economic conditions in any particular society at a given time vary as to the extent to which they are conducive to corruption. Nonetheless, each of these behaviors involved particular acts that are now, or were then, considered to be scandal.

Scandal: Definition

Because every scandal is, to some extent, dependent on the cultural mores, the public's reaction, and the time and place of the behavior, it is difficult to provide an exact meaning or definition of a political scandal. However, some generalizations about scandals can certainly be made. One is that a political scandal involves a political leader or figure.[57] Second, a scandal involves an action or event that involves some kind of social or behavioral transgression. Third, the offending behavior must become known to others. Fourth, the offending behavior must be sufficiently serious to elicit a public response.[58] This definition, then, includes three major elements: an action or event, publicity, and a public response.

A. Action

First, for a scandal to exist, there must be an action or behavior, and that behavior must offend public expectations of acceptable moral conduct. In other words, the action or event must involve a breach of public morality. The act must involve a transgression of societal norms, moral codes, or values or be a behavior that is disgraceful, shameful, or discredits someone.[59] It can be sexual behavior, illicit acts, or corrupt wrongdoing.[60] Under this definition, a behavior that involves a minor criminal offense, such as jaywalking, would not necessarily be a scandal because it does not violate a moral code. An action such as a sexual offense is more objectionable to a society's moral code. Many times the offending behavior may have had no bearing on the performance of the officeholder's professional responsibilities,[61] but nonetheless it is considered scandalous.

B. Publicity

To be a scandal, the offensive behavior must become known to others. There must be public knowledge of the event. If people are not made aware of the behavior, then there can be no outrage, and thus no scandal. President John F. Kennedy's numerous affairs did not create scandal because the journalists and editors who knew about the acts chose not to report them and because the women involved did not kiss and tell until after his death.[62] However, many of President Clinton's numerous affairs were made public, resulting in at least some public outrage.

The media's disclosure and condemnation of these types of actions may damage the reputation of the individuals responsible (although this is not always or necessarily the case). The individual may also face criminal charges or prosecution. Of course, those involved in the scandal may make an effort to defend their reputations or clear up their names by launching a counter-attack rejecting the allegations or denying the charges. In some cases, they may claim that the ends justified the means.[63] President Reagan attempted this in the Iran-contra affair.

Sometimes, emerging scandals are dominated by the efforts of public officials to suppress or withhold information.[64] The cover-up is sometimes more scandalous than the act itself. The lies and actions to get others to lie can be more offensive than the act itself.

C. Public Response

Finally, to be a scandal, the behavior must elicit a public reproach or public concern, indignation, or outrage.[65] The public must demand a punishment of some kind, whether it is a mild one like a public apology or a harsher penalty, such as imprisonment. Sometimes this is left up to a court to decide.

In some cases, what is shocking about a scandal is not the behavior in question but the identities of those involved. No one is surprised by members of a rock band who use illicit drugs and have many affairs, but if the President engaged in such behavior, it would probably be a major scandal. This means that it is not necessarily the behavior that causes the scandal, but the behavior in relation to a public figure and the attendant expectations of that role that matter.[66] Some societal members who represent certain values or beliefs as part of their position or affiliation may be more vulnerable to scandals: for example, religious leaders, teachers, police officers, or politicians. These groups are sometimes held to a higher standard than others and are usually in a position of trust in the community.

It is not necessary for an investigation to take place for a behavior to be considered a scandal. Although the appointment of a special prosecutor or independent counsel signifies the high probability of scandal, there does not have to be an investigation for media coverage and public outcry over illicit behavior. It is also not necessary for a behavior to be illegal to be a scandal. A scandal can be a criminal act but does not have to be.[67] Many scandals involve illegal behavior, but others are misjudgments made by those involved. When a politician is charged with illegal behavior, a thorough and nonpartisan investigation can determine the exact nature of that behavior.

Scandals are often defined by political cultures. What behaviors are scandalous vary from place to place and over time. As attitudes change, behavior that was once tolerated becomes unacceptable, and behavior that was once seen as deviant becomes accepted. For example, Senator Bob Packwood discovered that his behavior toward women in his office, which he thought was normal, was in fact no longer acceptable.[68]

Some political scandals involve the use of public office for private benefit. This happens when politicians use their power to gain some advantage. Some use their positions for monetary gains.[69] A large proportion of scandals relates to the cost of elections and the raising of campaign finance. Politicians can also use their power for policy goals or personal goals.[70] Watergate and Iran-contra were used for personal gains, not monetary or policy ends.[71] These scandals all involve allegations of violations of the political process and the illegitimate exercise of power.[72] In this case, there is a breach of the legally binding rules and procedures that govern the exercise of political power.[73]

In most scandals, there are two distinct phases. The first involves the actual breach or deviation from customary standards, and the second refers to the subsequent efforts made to conceal, coverup, or minimize the breach.[74] The first phase, which Lowi called the substantive stage, involves an element of secrecy or concealment. The offending party tries to hide the offensive or criminal behavior. Often, the offending behaviors are known to or strongly believed to exist by other individuals (nonparticipants). There is a breach of a norm, such as taking money, giving money, or entering into a conspiracy to gain or maintain power without playing by the rules. The offender attempts to prevent this from becoming widely known.[75]

At some point, there is a news break and the corrupt conduct is revealed. This is the start of the second stage of the scandal, known as second-order transgressions or procedural scandal. This refers to efforts to keep the substantive conduct concealed, more commonly known as the cover-up. This includes all of the forms of political response that serves to conceal, justify, deny, or mitigate the behavior.[76] This is where the attention is shifted from the original offense to a series of subsequent actions that are aimed at concealing the offense.[77]

Obviously, the substantive scandal must take place prior to the procedural one. The attempts to cover up scandalous behavior may involve deception, obstruction, false denials, and lies, which may become more harmful than the original transgression.[78] In many cases, the procedural scandal can and often does outweigh the substantive. This happened in the Watergate scandal in which the President and his aides attempted to cover up the president's knowledge of the initial break-in of the Democratic National Committee headquarters. Eventually, the cover-up led to the resignation of the President.

Those who are aware of the behavior (the nonparticipants) typically disapprove of the actions or events and may be offended by the transgression. For example, the public will disapprove of the behavior. In some cases, they may even be offended or shocked by it, while others are amused.[79] Some non-participants may express their disapproval by publicly denouncing the actions or events. Without public discussion, there is no scandal. Observers often engage in moral discussions in which they can express their disapproval. This often lends itself well to the media.[80]

Other Terms

There are many other terms that are related to scandal, that have different meanings. They include corruption, political crimes, gossip, rumors, and mistakes.

A. Corruption

Corruption can be defined as the abuse of public office for personal gain or advantage. It can include performing official public duties through bribery or favor. It can also be acquiring forbidden benefits by officials or employees that bring into question their loyalty to their employers. The underlying problem is the injury done to the public's interest. If the actions result in benefits to the public, they may not be corrupt but instead considered devious.

Corruption typically involves two elements. One is the infringement of rules or laws concerning the proper exercise of public duties for the purposes of private or personal gain, and the second is the perversion or undermining of the standards of integrity associated with public office.[81]

Corruption is sometimes associated with bribery. In fact, many consider bribery to be a form of corruption. Making and accepting bribes involve the exchange of inducements that are intended to influence decisions or outcomes in favor of the giver. This can be as simple as a large campaign contribution, which is given in hopes of favorable legislation or even an appointment to a job. But acts that are considered corrupt in one administration may be permitted in another.

Corruption may be caused by a person's character. Personal honesty plays a great role in opposing corruption and maintaining the integrity of the governmental process. Most times, sanctions against corrupt behavior are weak and the penalties minor. Because of this, most corruption probably goes undetected and unpunished. Reform may require psychological insight and moral inquiry.

Corruption can give rise to scandal. All occurrences of corruption are scandalous, but not all scandals involve corruption.[82]

B. Political Crime

Another closely related term is political crime. These are politically moti-vated law breaking behaviors by altruistic individuals. In other words, the term refers to illegal actions that are carried out by public officials to maintain and enhance the existing economic and political power structure or to change the structure of economic and political power. Typically the offenders are mem-bers of groups or organizations that are attempting to improve or maintain their relative positions with regard to other groups or organizations. This means that the political crimes are part of an on going social process.

C. Gossip

As opposed to scandal, gossip is a form of talk or communication that takes place between friends and acquaintances. It is often small talk or idle chatter about relatively trivial matters. It typically implies a degree of familiarity or intimacy between the participants. Gossip often serves to reaffirm social rela-tionships by demonstrating trust and friendship.[83]

The difference between gossip and scandal has to do with truth. Gossip may or may not be true, whereas scandal generally is. Gossip often remains at the level of private communication among friends or acquaintances, but scandal is public. Gossip can fuel scandal, and gossip can turn into scandal, but not always. There can be gossip that does not turn into scandal.

D. Rumors

Much like gossip, rumors are talk or hearsay that are not based on definite knowledge. They are an unauthenticated report of behavior, which may very well be untrue. Gossip tends to be small talk about other people or relatively unimportant matters, whereas rumors can be about almost anything, includ-ing very serious issues, both can have far-reaching consequences. Many times, scandals are preceded by rumors that turn out to be true, but there can be ru-mors without scandal alongside.

E. Mistakes or Errors

Like normal every day people, politicians often misspeak or make mistakes that are not scandals. There are many examples where public officials make erroneous statements or misjudgments that do not turn into scandals. One of those was in 1968 when Spiro Agnew described a Japanese American campaign reporter from the *Baltimore Sun* as a "fat jap." He had known that journalist for many years and said it was a joke, but some saw it as an example of ethnic insensitivity.[84] It was a mistake, but not scandalous.

Another mistake occurred during the 1976 presidential campaign when candidate Jimmy Carter, in an interview with *Playboy* magazine, admitted that he had "lust in my heart," that he had "looked on a lot of women with lust," and that he had "committed adultery in my heart many times."[85] He also said he did not care if "people say fuck."[86] His comments were damaging because Carter had stressed his high level of morality throughout the campaign. He portrayed himself as religious, honest, and boring, but when these comments appeared in a pornographic magazine, it shocked people. His responses were not what most people expected from a presidential candidate. The prospect of him as president shocked many people.

Other politicians have made similar faux pas. In 1976, during a debate with Carter a month before the presidential election, Gerald Ford said that "there is no Soviet dominance of Eastern Europe." After, Ford's chances of being elected president were diminished considerably. In 1984, Jesse Jackson referred to Jews as "Hymies" and to New York City as "Hymietown" during a conversation with a black *Washington Post* reporter, Milton Coleman. Apparently, Jackson thought the references would not be printed because Coleman was also black, but Coleman allowed another reporter to use the quotes in an article about Jackson's rocky relations with American Jews. At first, Jackson denied the remarks, but later apologized while meeting with national Jewish leaders in a New Hampshire synagogue.[87]

In 1995, Congressman Dick Armey, the second most powerful member of the House, called fellow Congressman Barney Frank "Barney Fag." He later claimed it was a slip of the tongue.[88] This was not a scandal per se, but a mistake.

Why Study Scandals?

Despite the long history of scandals and their influence on the political scene and society, political scandals have received surprisingly little academic attention.[89] There is no doubt that scandals are viewed by many academics as a subject too frivolous to warrant serious scholarly attention.[90] Some major political scandals, notably Watergate, have been extensively discussed, focusing on what happened rather than on the causes, consequences, and character of those involved.[91] However, an intensive focus on the causes and impacts of political scandals, to date, has been lacking. At the same time, the study of political scandals has recently become more widely recognized, as is acceptance of the idea that there are broader social and political significances of scandals.[92]

Lowi has termed the emerging field "scandology." He cites many reasons to study scandals. One is that through studying political scandals, we improve our grasp of society and the polity at large and get a more thorough understanding of mores and laws, as well as changes in them. Studying scandals helps us understand current laws and why they are written in a particular fashion. For example, new laws regarding special prosecutors were implemented after Watergate but allowed to lapse after the Whitewater investigation. By studying those scandals, one can understand why the laws were written and why they were allowed to lapse.

We can learn how and why an event becomes a scandal, whereas other events do not. We can get a better understanding of the media's role in society and their effect on politics and the people who serve in the political system.

Third, an understanding of scandals can provide more knowledge about the aftermath of inappropriate behavior by people in the public eye. This can include both long- and short-term impacts. In the short term, for example, political careers can be affected. In the long term, there may be serious effects on the political system, such as new laws. There may also be effects on the media and how they report on corruption and illicit affairs to the public.

Fourth, by studying scandals, we can learn about society as a whole. Scandals help define what is acceptable behavior and the expectations of people who live in different societies. We can learn about mores and customs held by the majority of people in society. In short, scandals tell a lot about society, and they help reaffirm the social order.[93]

Why Do Scandals Happen?

The causes of political scandals are not entirely clear.[94] But it is important to understand why they occur, because in this way, it may become possible to prevent future scandals. Many theories exist that help explain why political crimes occur.

A. Max Weber

Max Weber describes the "red tape" that is a recognized element of bureaucracies. However, in some cases, the red tape becomes so overwhelming that informal relationships and unofficial routines become important. These relationships can be used to manage workloads, reduce delays, or even get things done. All bureaucracies develop informal relations that make the bureaucrats' lives easier and also enhance efficiency. In some cases, a bond of goodwill and friendship may develop. But when the attention given to one client is greater, or dependent on a returned favor, corruption may formally develop. Corruption may occur when a client and a bureaucrat turn into friends and exchange gifts, or when attention is greater to one than the other.

B. Emile Durkheim

Emile Durkheim presents another theory of political corruption. He claims that amoral actions are functional to society. By violating a shared belief, a transgression helps reaffirm the belief by the general population. In the long run, transgressions are normal and necessary to maintain order because, according to Durkheim, political scandals strengthen the community's "collective conscience." They create scapegoats and enemies that are needed in all communities. The public's investigation, discussion, and punishment of wrongdoers helps reinforce shared norms and values held by society and help reaffirm the social order. Scandals sometimes challenge the norms and values of a community to help redefine acceptable behaviors.

C. James Q. Wilson

Wilson presents three major theories of political corruption. One is that a political culture exists that gives low value to impersonal efficiency of bureaucracies and governments and high value to favors, personal loyalty, and private gain. In such a system, people must use favors to get something from government. The secret, informal, or "covert" government is the way to get things done. However, those in government will produce irresistible demands for favoritism and thus for corruption.

Another idea presented by Wilson is that political corruption is the result of ordinary men facing extraordinary temptations. In many political situations, there are great prizes at stake, including power, wealth, and status. Many elected officials face frequent temptations when it comes to sex, money, legislative favors, or even drug abuse.[95] Often, politicians are corrupt because businessmen bribe them. Political crimes are committed because politicians yield to temptation and will continue to do so if not checked. The solution thus becomes consistent inspection, audits, and double-checks on individual choices.

The third idea presented by Wilson revolves around the separation of the branches in government as the cause of corruption. Because the branches of government are separate, each branch can paralyze the other, so each becomes unable to function. To prevent such action, the members turn to an exchange of favors to get things done. The solution to scandal is to bring the branches together constitutionally.

D. Psychiatric Theory

Under this idea, politicians need constant nourishment and reinforcement from others. They are people who are often overcompensating for deep-rooted insecurities, so they seek constant external approval. They will often translate the roar of the crowd and votes into "love."[96] Many psyches of politicians are damaged, so they are egotistical, preoccupied, and absorbed with themselves.[97] They often make choices thinking they will not be caught, or they will not be punished like the average person.

E. RIP

A new theory of political scandals was developed by Ginsberg and Shefter (1999). They point to a major change in the conduct of politicians in recent years, particularly their willingness to use investigations against their political opponents as a political weapon. The choice to use accusations of wrongdoing against members of the opposing party reflects the declining role of elections in the United States. They show that in past years, debates about policies and battles for power used to take place during a campaign, and elections decided who would control government. However, in today's world, the significance of elections has decreased to the point that they do not decide who will have power. Instead, those decisions take place outside the electoral arena.[98] Politicians must now rely on "politics by other means" to achieve and maintain power.

During a modern political campaign, candidates know that it is often a risk to talk too much about specific policies because they may offend potential voters. Instead, both parties rely on undermining and disrupting the institutions controlled by the opposing party once in office. For example, when Democrats controlled the Congress, they launched a number of major legislative investigations aimed at embarrassing or discrediting Republican presidents and other officials in the executive branch. This included Watergate and Iran-contra. In similar fashion, when the Republicans won control of Congress in 1994, the investigations were turned around and the Republicans used their power to launch inquiries into allegations made against the Clintons. Throughout his administration, the Republicans used the investigative process to harass Clinton and prevent him from pursuing any serious legislative agenda.[99] The Republicans, in effect, were getting revenge for what the Democrats did to Nixon earlier.[100]

Ginsberg and Shefter also point out that the courts have become a major battlefield among politicians. They show that there has been a tenfold increase in the number of indictments brought by federal prosecutors against national, state, and local officials, including many prominent political figures. There has been a sharp increase in the number of major policy issues that have been fought and decided in the judicial arena rather than through the campaign process.[101] Many indictments were initiated by Republican administrations against Democrats, and others were initiated by Democrats against Republicans. At the same time, they point out that there is no reason to believe that the level of political corruption has increased tenfold during this same time.[102]

Their theory, revelations, investigation, and prosecution (RIP), is based on the expanded political roles of the news media and the federal judiciary in political environments. Opponents of presidential administrations have used RIP to attack and weaken their enemies in the executive branch. The RIP process became institutionalized when Congress adopted the 1978 Ethics in Government Act that created an independent counsel. Now politicians seek to undermine and disgrace one another in the media, sometimes forcing their competitors to resign from office or even send their opponents to prison.[103]

The recent prevalence of scandals represents "politics by other means."[104] At any opportunity, parties will seize on their ability to punish opponents or even end their careers.[105] Those in both the liberal or conservative parties are likely to reveal, investigate, prosecute, or even impeach their opponents for matters that have nothing to do with crimes.[106] The process of RIP has made the national press and the courts grow in importance.[107]

Why Are There More Scandals Today?

The apparent surge in scandal in the years after Watergate can be explained in a variety of ways.[108] One is simply that there has been a decline in moral standards of political leaders. Most people would probably disagree with this, as there is little evidence to support the idea that politicians are more corrupt than before.[109] Another possible reason is that the federal government has grown enormously. Because there are more people employed in the government, there are more chances of seeing criminal or unethical behavior by someone.

Another explanation is that the number of political scandals has grown because society has changed its views about how much politicians' personal characters and conducts mattered to their public lives and how much the public had a right to know about their private behavior.[110] There was a change in the overall moral codes that are used to assess the behavior of politicians and a growing salience of these codes in the conduct of political life. Behavior that would have been condoned in the past is more likely to be censured today. For example, the acceptance of gifts may have been tolerated in the past, but not today.[111]

Additionally, there is now an unprecedented number of federal prosecutors who are making use of existing criminal laws to prosecute acts that in past years would have been civil cases.[112] As more cases come to court, more attention is given to them in the media, resulting in more public attention.

At the same time, there has been a change in the journalistic culture that has gradually eroded the informal norms and conventions, which had previously discouraged journalists from publishing details of private lives.[113] These changes in the media have led to the discovery of more scandals, which in years past may have gone unnoticed. There are also more female journalists who no longer accept the adage "that's the way men are." There are no more "men's clubs" to protect the men in charge.[114]

The national press has become more active in finding and publicizing official malfeasance.[115] This means that political scandals have proliferated, maybe not because of an increase in corruption but because of a growing interest in political scandal by the public and the media.[116] People enjoy watching scandals unfold, so the media is more likely to present them. There are also many more types of media that can report, analyze, and discuss the scandal over and over again. What was once private is now public, and the media today is more vigilant in its detection and pursuit of officials who give the slightest hint of misbehavior.[117] The media is also becoming more sophisticated and more widely available than in the past. It is better able to record, process, and transmit information to the nation very quickly.[118] What may have once remained local now goes national.

The Media and Scandal

The media plays a fundamental role in political scandals.[119] Without the media informing the public about events, there could be no public outrage, and thus no scandal. Thus, a free press that is permitted to publish information is needed for scandals to thrive. Societies in which there are no institutionalized means of exposure have few scandals.

Today, there are many types of media sources that provide news to those who are interested. Citizens now have a larger and more diverse range of political media options available to them than at any time in history. The traditional type of media is print media, which includes newspapers, journals, and magazines. Broadcast media refers to radio and television. This type of "old media" is alive and well. It remains the news source that most Americans trust and on which most continue to rely for their news.[120]

These traditional media organizations are no longer the only gateways of information. An emerging media, called "new media," includes the Internet, cable, and satellite technology. New media has significantly altered the way news is reported. With new technology, people can get news much faster and from just about anywhere. Online resources give the nontraditional media national reach. This means that scandals (and rumors) are made public much more quickly than before.[121]

This new information technology also assists reporters in getting background information more quickly than in the past. During Watergate, reporters made phone calls and searched through library cards to get information. Now, journalists can get the same information almost instantly through cyber sleuthing. Journalists can find direct phone numbers for news sources, their e-mail address, criminal background, and other general background information about them, like their activities and affiliations.

The same technology that is changing the way the press covers politics is also changing the way politicians behave. Such things as free online databases make it easier to get information on the opposition's voting record, public statements, and personal lives. Candidates and their political consultants, especially a new breed of "opposition researchers," make extensive use of these information sources to quickly develop comprehensive data profiles of opponents that can be used against them in an investigation or to make allegations.

New media actors such as talk show hosts, tabloid reporters, and Internet gossip columnists have entered the political communications scene.[122] These new media outlets often thrive by treating politics and political events as entertainment and tend to be driven more by scandal reporting than other media sources.[123] They tend to rely on political rumors because they are quick, simple stories that can be framed in dramatic, personal terms that are easy to understand.[124] New, alternative news sources such as Bloomberg and MTV provide news stories that tend to be specialized, so the listener can pick the news he or she wants and not have to be exposed to what does not interest him or her.

Once the story is put on the Internet, it can take on a life of its own. The new media played an important role in shaping the Monica Lewinsky story.[125] Virtually anyone could post information, whether it was factual or not. This contributes to saturation coverage of the story. Unfortunately, new media covered the Clinton/Lewinsky matter as a sex scandal rather than an event with important political consequences. Citizens may have discounted the seriousness of the allegations against Clinton because the media trivialized the situation.[126]

Another one of the problems associated with new media is that it is not accountable to established journalistic rules or authorities.[127] Some established mechanisms of quality control used by old media, such as fact-checking and sourcing, have largely been abandoned by new media. This means that the political news agenda is often set by rumor and innuendo and emphasizes personal drama without solid proof.[128] It has become an increasingly common practice to publish or air rumors for which a convincing body of evidence does not exist.[129] The media now covers extramarital affairs, office romances, divorces, drug use, drinking, sexuality, illegitimate children, and other rumors on a regular basis. As new media relies more on gossip than news, their coverage of real news suffers. At times, more vital and revealing information is ignored.[130] This might lead some to argue that with these changes, there has been a decline in the standards of broadcast journalism.[131] There have been many unethical practices, uncorrected errors, and invasion of innocent individuals' privacy.[132]

Scandal coverage in the media is no longer restricted to misuse of public office, incompetence in the exercise of public responsibilities, or some other inadequacy or malfeasance in a public role. Instead, media coverage now sometimes extends to purely private misbehavior and offenses, some of them trivial, even those that had been committed long before an individual's emergence into public life.[133]

Scandal-related stories are an integral part of media because they sell. Simply put, scandal sells and scandal pays.[134] Scandals and sex sell well in the media—much better than discussions of policy issues. The more tantalizing the offense, or the more volatile the mix of vices, the more irresistible the subject is for the news media. When scandals are in the headlines, the viewers/buyers increase. MSNBC and talk radio stations found that scandal coverage increased their ratings.[135] We may not like to admit it, but scandal is entertaining and it sells. In today's competitive world, ratings and circulation increasingly matter.[136] Today's media has a financial interest in maintaining or increasing the sale of its products, and scandals provide the stories that can help achieve this goal.[137] Because the main goal of media companies is to make a profit, scandal becomes a staple of news.

This has led to fierce competition between media outlets and reporters for new stories. The hunt for bad deeds has become a business, and large numbers of people have developed personal stakes in its continuing.[138] Those politicians involved in illicit behavior of some type are trying to conceal, and the media are trying to expose. We have seen a rise in "adversarial journalism," in which the media adopts a hostile posture toward public officials. The media has a stake in finding and revealing damaging information about prominent politicians and to do so before anyone else. New technologies make the decision-making process faster. Decisions over which a newsroom might have previously deliberated for weeks are sometimes made in minutes or even instantly. Editors who hesitate run the risk of having a rival run the story first. In their push to be the first to run a story, media today is more likely to rely on rumors, claims, and charges that may not be true. Sometimes, high standards are lowered in the heat of competitive battle.[139] If one newspaper prints or one broadcaster airs a story, however questionable or poorly documented it may be, other media outlets will then publish or broadcast the news without independently verifying it. At times, partial truths and distortions of reality may be published. Those accused may feel compelled to rebut the charges, thereby prolonging the life of the story. The competition for readers/viewers/surfers puts more stories out there, some of which are true, others are not.

A. History

Scandal reporting is nothing new to the press. The first newspaper published in America in 1690 carried a report that the king of France used to "lie with" his son's wife. Since then, the media has played many roles and assumed many postures in U.S. history. Moreover, like every other American institution, its power, promise, and performance have varied greatly from one era to the next. The breadth, depth, and influence of the news media have expanded enormously, as political journalism has passed through three phases in its recent development: (1) lapdog, (2) watchdog, (3) junkyard dog.[140] Some say that we have even moved from poodles to watchdogs to Rottweilers.[141]

The first phase, lapdog journalism, is where the media rarely challenged prevailing orthodoxy. Instead, they accepted at face value much of what those in power told them. The reporters protected politicians by revealing little about their nonofficial lives, even if their private vices affected their public performance. This type of journalism peaked under the Kennedy administration.[142] During this time, the press knew about indiscretions, but did not report them. The information was used behind closed doors by the political parties, not by reporters, editors, and producers.

The second phase of the media is watchdog journalism. This was between 1966–1974, during which time reporters scrutinized and checked the behavior of politicians by undertaking independent investigations into statements made by public officials. This was stimulated by the Vietnam War and Watergate.[143]

Third was the period of junkyard dog journalism. This refers to political reporting that is often harsh, aggressive, and intrusive, and where gossip reaches print. Every aspect of private life potentially becomes fair game for scrutiny. It is almost an "anything goes" philosophy.[144]

Some would argue that now we have "pack journalism," whereby reporters move on a story together in essentially the same direction.[145] They report on the same stories, providing the same information as the majority of other media outlets.

The shift from watchdog to junkyard dog journalism was the result of many changes. One was increased competition between media outlets. The sometimes fierce competition between media outlets sometimes drives the press to cover the private lives of politicians. In an effort to sell more copies or increase viewership, the press began to scrutinize even the most private sanctums of public officials. This shifted the orientation of journalism away from mere description of events to focusing attention on the politicians' shortcomings and social problems. The media asks questions and demands answers like never before.[146]

Another reason for the change was the emergence of the character issue after Watergate. The character issue leads the media to cover scandal more. Because of Watergate, journalists now feel they can look into the character of politicians.

There was also a loosening of libel laws. This began in 1964 when the Supreme Court decided *New York Times v. Sullivan* (376 U.S. 254). The Court decided that simply publishing a defamatory falsehood was not enough to incur a libel judgment. Now a public official has to prove "actual malice" to prove libel. They must prove that the publisher either believed the challenged statement was false or at least entertained serious doubts about its truth and acted recklessly in publishing it in the face of those doubts. This has made it very hard for a politician to prevail in a libel case. The loosening of libel laws have provided journalists with a safer harbor from liability in their reporting on elected officials and candidates.[147] The laws no longer restrain the media from reporting on a politician's "character" or private life.[148]

Another event that influenced the role of the media was the events at Chappaquiddick in 1969, when a young woman drowned after a car driven by Ted Kennedy ended up in a pond. This was the first occasion where the private conduct of a prominent politician was extensively discussed in the public domain.[149] After Chappaquiddick, many journalists began to believe that private life and individual character traits had such profound effects on politics and public policy that politicians' personal lives could no longer be ignored. The new rule for political coverage: Since any aspect of private life is potentially relevant to an official's public performance, everything is fair game. This includes personal relationships, private behavior, and any matter exhibiting an official's character or judgment. In addition, anything that affects the political players and outcome—including unproved rumor and innuendo, can be made public in the process.

There was also a change in the public's ethics. Many years ago, the media would not have published information about someone's affair. Now the media is much more willing to publish rumors and gossip, whether or not there is truth to it. Where a figure like the president of the United States is concerned, the national media's standards of "proof" are lower than the standards considered for other stories.[150]

B. Presidents and Media

The press's relationship with the President is important because the public's image of the nation's leader is a critical ingredient in his political power.[151] How the President and other officials construct their image with the public, and how the media portray the president may influence how other officials and the public think about him and his policies.[152]

Early on, journalists knew about the private sexual practices and personal secrets of prominent political figures but did not print them. The media did not make public the dalliances of Warren Harding, Franklin Roosevelt, and John F. Kennedy, so their infidelities did not become publicly known until after their presidencies.[153] The hesitancy to print private information extended beyond sexual behavior. Although John Kennedy's private life, Lyndon Johnson's investments, and other presidents' activities prior to becoming chief executive had raised questions during election campaigns, they never became the subject of congressional investigations once the public had cast its votes.[154] This implies that the press believed that the president's sexual behavior was not relevant to his public office or a fundamental moral issue worthy of their stories.[155] At the time, it was believed that the private life of a public figure should stay private and undisclosed unless it seriously impinged on his or her public performance. Unpleasant personal vices were ignored completely, but presidents and other politicians are much more visible today than they were in the past. It is much more difficult for them to throw a veil of secrecy around activities or events that they would prefer to keep out of the public eye.[156]

Many politicians react badly to the treatment they receive from the press. They are convinced that the media have one goal: to hurt or destroy them. They may react by restricting journalists' access except under highly controlled conditions. Despite being denied access, the press is expected to provide visibility for the politician. This makes reporters strike back at the first opportunity. A slip of the tongue or a scandal is especially welcome so that reporters can freely release pent-up emotion on a nonideological subject.

Every president used the media in his own way to develop a relationship with the media while in office. Each of those relationships was different. Some presidents worked to deceive the press. Woodrow Wilson suffered a massive stroke in 1919 that paralyzed the left side of his body. Reporters were told that he had a nervous breakdown. The truth about his health did not come out for months. Dwight Eisenhower had a serious heart attack in 1955, and the press was told he had suffered a digestive upset. Jimmy Carter's press secretary, Jody Powell, told the *LA Times* that a rescue mission to free the American hostages in Iran would make no sense. Two days later, they tried it, and it was a disaster. Reagan's spokesman, Larry Speakes, said in 1983 that an American invasion of Grenada would be "preposterous." The marines landed the next day.

1. Harding

Harding had a great relationship with the press. He was honest in confessing his limitations to them. But neither Harding nor the White House Press Corps were always completely happy with their relationship.[157] The press wanted more information from Harding, but he was never happy with the coverage he received.

2. Roosevelt

Franklin Roosevelt believed that the private life of a public figure should stay private and undisclosed unless it seriously impinged on his or her public performance.[158] He told reporters that he did not want to be quoted directly but would provide "background" and "off-the-record" information to them. They respected that and printed largely only what he told them to print. Roosevelt set strict ground rules that enabled him to shape the news agenda.[159]

The relationship that developed between Roosevelt and the media was one of respect. Journalists treated him with deference and affection. No one would think of telling the public that he was confined to a wheelchair because of polio or in a poor state of health. If he fell in public, no reporter would take his picture. No reporter wrote of his affair with Lucy Mercer, who lived in the White House at times and was with him in Warm Springs at his death. At that time, any unpleasant personal vices were ignored completely.[160]

3. Kennedy

It is public knowledge that Kennedy shared the company of many female companions during his stay in the White House.[161] But he also got along well with the media.[162] He was the first president to hold live, televised press conferences. This was a new idea that permanently changed the nature of White House communications. Kennedy personally befriended reporters who gave him positive coverage throughout his term in office. He reached every American living room. Because of his good relationship with the press, he received positive coverage.[163]

4. Johnson

Johnson's lack of couth was legendary. He was known to be a hard drinker[164] and chased women around the office. LBJ is reported to have said that he bedded more women in Texas than Kennedy had in his lifetime.[165] For the most part, this went unreported. President Johnson made an effort to get along with the press. He sent military aircraft to pick up press and bring them to his house for private meetings and dinners. But over time, the press became disillusioned with him, as did the public.[166] But he still enjoyed the full private-life protections.

5. Nixon

Nixon had trouble with the media. He had a general dislike of the press, even ordering wiretaps and tax audits of selected journalists. Nixon had CBS's Daniel Schorr investigated by the FBI, demanded an immigration probe of household help employed by *Los Angeles Times* publisher Otis Chandler, and moved to revoke television licenses held by the *Washington Post* Company.[167] Nixon told his press aides that it was important to stay on the offensive against the press. He had strategies for handling both friendly and hostile journalists.[168] Nixon was convinced that the nation's media was hostile[169] and said, "The media are all shits."[170] In the end, it was the media who brought down Nixon, forcing him to resign from office.

6. Clinton

President Clinton also had issues with the press. He thought the media lied a lot and had their own agendas. He often blamed the press for his setbacks. He spent less time talking to the media than other presidents, which only served to anger the press. During his first term, his efforts to control the press were clumsy, and he had trouble fashioning a consistent media message. Clinton himself was unfocused and error prone.[171] He began to work to generate favorable headlines and deflect damaging ones. During his second term, they imposed some order. He invited some journalists for tea and cookies at the White House.[172] For a short time before the Lewinsky scandal, Clinton's spin team enjoyed success. They leaked proposals and policy tidbits to select news organizations to create a sense of momentum. Clinton's approval rating was around 60 percent. The media seemed to have grown comfortable with him.[173]

C. What Role Should the Media Play?

Many would argue that the media should publish the facts surrounding the good and bad deeds of public officials, as the public has a right to know about the character of their elected officials. Private situations can significantly influence politics, it is necessary to know if an official is taking part in illicit or illegal acts. [174] At the same time, should a politician's personal life be fair game for media coverage?[175] How much privacy can a politician reasonably expect to maintain for himself and his or her family?

The right of an official's privacy often conflicts with the public's right to know.[176] The news media's focus on the personal lives of politicians is gradually erasing the line between a public and personal life. This can make the price of public life enormously high.

Some media outlets still struggle with where to draw the line between what should be made public and how to do that. During the Clinton scandal, for example, the media struggled with how to handle references to oral and anal sex, presidential ejaculation, and sexual behavior involving a cigar.[177] According to Sabato and Lichter,[178] there are certain types of behavior that generally should and should not be covered by the press.[179] They write that the things that should be made public about a candidate include their personal and professional finances, their health (as it may affect performance in office), any criminal or civil charges, sexual activity when it coincides with their professional lives (e.g., relationships with staff members) or is compulsive, any addictive behavior such as alcohol or drug use, and illegal drug use as an adult. Moreover, it is important for the press to discuss a politician's character, management skills, and how he or she handles stressful situations.

At the same time, Sabato and Lichter also present those behaviors that should remain out of the press. These include things like nonlegal family matters, discreet extramarital sexual activities, sexual orientation, and experimental drug use that occurred many years ago.

Conclusion/This Book

Political scandals are now an important part of the political environment. They have been around for many years and occur at all levels of government, to members of all political parties. The definition of what constitutes a political scandal varies, depending on the mores and norms in society. That means that what is considered a scandal in one administration may be permitted in another. What is required, though, is some kind of offending behavior, media publicity, and a negative public response. This means that the media, whether a traditional source or a type of new media, is key to scandal. The impacts of scandal vary, depending on a variety of factors, but can range from public embarrassment to resignation.

In the following chapters, the exact nature of scandals is discussed, as well as the impacts they have on the individuals involved, the political process, and society as a whole. Although it is not possible to provide an exhaustive analysis of every political scandal, many presidential, legislative, and judicial scandals are explored. Chapter 2 presents an analysis of special prosecutors/independent counsels and the impeachment process. These investigators play a key role in scandals, because they are responsible for discovering the truth about allegations made against a politician. In doing so, they often bring scandals to light that may otherwise go unknown. In Chapter 3, some early political scandals are described to show that such behaviors have been around for many years and are not a new phenomenon in our government. The next chapters focus on presidential scandals. Often, the focus of an investigation is on a president, as it is much easier to cover a single individual than many people.[180] In Chapter 4, the focus is on the Nixon scandals, primarily Watergate, one of the most significant political scandals in United States history. The scandals that emerged in the Ford, Carter, Reagan and Bush administrations are described in Chapter 5. The primary focus is another major scandal, the Iran-contra affair. The scandals that almost brought down the Clinton administration are analyzed in Chapter 6, including the scandal that led to his impeachment. Because presidents are not the only politicians involved in scandal, Chapter 7 focuses on congressional scandals and Chapter 8 on judicial scandals. Together, these will provide a thorough analysis of political scandals.

Review Questions

1. What are the elements included in the definition of a scandal?
2. What are some terms related to scandal?

3. Name the stages in a scandal.
4. Why study scandals? Why is it important?
5. Describe the different theories that help us understand scandals.
6. What role do the media play in scandals?
7. Why is it important to study public opinion toward political scandals?

Important Terms

Scandal

Corruption

Political Crime

Gossip

Rumor

RIP

New Media

New York Times v. Sullivan

Lapdog Journalism

Watchdog Journalism

Junkyard dog Journalism

Pack Journalism

Discussion Questions

1. As morals change over time, do the behaviors we consider "scandalous" change?
2. To what extent is the personal life of the president "no business of ours," or do some very private matters still have public consequences? Where should the line be drawn between a person's private and public life?
3. What behaviors and characteristics do you think are important to know about a presidential candidate?
4. Is it important to study political scandals?
5. Can rumors and gossip be as damaging to a political candidate or office-holder as a full-fledged scandal? Or are they simply rumors and gossip?
6. Why has there been such a dramatic increase in scandals in recent years?

Chapter 2

Special Prosecutors/ Independent Counsels and the Impeachment Process

Introduction

When allegations of misconduct occur, whether it be criminal or unethical, members of Congress and the public often demand a thorough investigation to determine if the charges are true and require punishment, or if they are simply political attacks or rumors. For most of our history, there has been a mechanism for conducting an investigation, called a special prosecutor or special investigator. This person is given the responsibility to question those involved, examine relevant documents, and otherwise determine whether there is enough evidence to substantiate the charges. If so, the special prosecutor/investigator can take that evidence either to criminal court or to Congress. At that point, the evidence is presented to the House of Representatives, which determines if enough evidence exists to impeach the accused. If they vote affirmative, the person is impeached. The next step is that the charges are brought to the Senate, which can choose to examine the evidence. If there is enough evidence of wrongdoing, the Senate votes to remove the accused from office.

There have been very few cases of presidential impeachment in the United States, and no cases of removal from office. President Andrew Johnson was impeached in 1868 by the House but not removed from office by the Senate. Impeachment charges were brought against Richard Nixon in 1974, but he resigned before the process could proceed. Most recently, Bill Clinton was impeached by the House for charges of perjury and obstruction of justice, but he was not removed from office by Senate members.

The existence of an institutionalized process for appointing a special prosecutor or investigator has evolved over time. Although the impeachment process itself has not changed, the willingness of Congress to bring charges has become more acceptable. This chapter presents a history of the special prosecutor and investigator and the impeachment process.

Special Prosecutor/Special Investigator

Before the Watergate scandal, special prosecutors were rarely used against members of the executive branch, and they were used only in the most serious matters. When one was needed, the president had the responsibility to appoint one.[1] There are only a few cases in which special prosecutors were appointed. In 1875, a special prosecutor, General John Brooks Henderson, was called in to investigate whether President Ulysses S. Grant's personal secretary, General Orville E. Babcock, was involved in a ring of tax-evading whiskey distillers. In the 1920s, Congress passed a joint resolution calling for a special prosecutor to probe charges of corrupt leasing of oil reserves by Warren Harding administration officials, called the Teapot Dome Scandal. During the Harry S. Truman administration, officials from the Justice Department and the Bureau of Revenue were accused of fixing tax cases. Truman appointed his own former attorney general, J. Howard McGrath, to conduct a cleanup campaign, but the House Judiciary Committee objected, claiming a conflict of interest because McGrath was attorney general when the offenses occurred.

Special prosecutors reached a peak of prominence during Watergate. In the spring of 1972, there was massive support for a special prosecutor to investigate the burglary of the Democratic National Committee headquarters by men with ties to Nixon's reelection committee. At that time, Nixon had named Elliot Richardson as attorney general. The Senate Judiciary Committee blocked his confirmation until he promised to appoint a special prosecutor to look into the burglary. When he was confirmed, Richardson chose Harvard law professor Archibald Cox to serve as special prosecutor. But when Cox demanded that Nixon provide him with the secret tape recordings of conversations made in the Oval Office, Nixon refused and ordered Richardson to fire Cox. Richardson would not do so and resigned as attorney general. Richardson's deputy, William Ruckelshaus, also refused to carry out Nixon's order to fire Cox and was also fired (or resigned). Finally, Solicitor General Robert H. Bork fired Cox. These events, dubbed the Saturday Night Massacre, outraged the American public. They began to wonder why Nixon wanted to fire the investigator and what he was trying to hide.

Nixon also questioned the constitutionality of the special prosecutor as it was then instituted. Part of the problem was that the investigator was appointed by the president to investigate the president or his associates. Questions arose about the ability of the investigator to be truly independent in this precarious position. It had become apparent that special prosecutors appointed by presidents could not be truly independent and that the Department of Justice could not be trusted to investigate allegations against high-level executive colleagues.[2] On review, the Supreme Court decided that the office of the independent counsel was constitutional.

After Watergate, Congress began to consider how it might write legislation that would create independence for future special prosecutors. They wanted to make the independent prosecutor really independent so that he or she would not answer to the president, the subject of the investigation. In the spring of 1974, many proposals were considered, and there was much debate about the best way to place a special prosecutor. Senator Sam Ervin proposed legislation to create an "independent" Justice Department with an attorney general appointed by the president for a six-year term and not subject to removal by the president. Archibald Cox, among others, testified against this proposal. Senator Alan Cranston proposed a commission to study the need for a permanent special prosecutor. Not long after, the Senate Watergate committee issued its final report that included a recommendation for the establishment of a permanent Office of Public Attorney entrusting the courts, not the attorney general, with the power to appoint and dismiss.[3] The public attorney would be appointed for a five-year term by a panel of retired Court of Appeals judges selected for this purpose by the chief justice of the Supreme Court.[4]

Congress realized that they needed to make the investigator more independent by removing the president's power to appoint a special investigator and placing it with the judiciary.[5] In 1978, Congress passed the Ethics in Government Act of 1978 (PL 95-521), and President Jimmy Carter signed it into law. Among other things, the law set up a mechanism for court appointment of a temporary special prosecutor to probe allegations against high government or campaign officials. This meant that special prosecutors would be appointed by a panel of federal judges to investigate possible misconduct in the executive branch, including the president, vice president, heads of executive departments, and other high-ranking executive officials.[6] Under the law, if the independent counsel found any credible information that constituted grounds for impeachment, he or she would advise the House of Representatives of it. The independent counsel could, if needed, suggest that Congress consider impeaching the president.[7]

Further, the attorney general could remove the special prosecutor only for what the law called "extraordinary impropriety," a phrase that was later changed to "good cause." The law also set up the Office of the Special Prosecutor for a five year period. With this new law, Congress sought to ensure that politics did not interfere when an investigation was necessary against the president, his Cabinet, and other senior officials. This was probably the single most important legislative response to Watergate.[8]

A. 1982 Reauthorization

The provisions of the 1978 law were subject to reauthorization every five years. The first reauthorization occurred in 1982. The Ronald Reagan administration opposed congressional reauthorization of the law, pointing out that it unconstitutionally involved the judiciary in the enforcement of laws, an executive branch function under the Constitution. Nonetheless, Congress passed the reauthorization with a few changes.[9]

One of the changes made in the new version was a switch in the name from special prosecutor to independent counsel. Critics of the Ethics in Government Act felt the term "special prosecutor" had a stigmatizing effect on those who were subjected to the investigations, so the reauthorization of the statute changed the name to independent counsel.[10]

Another change made in the 1982 revision was a tightening up of the standards for triggering the appointment of an independent counsel. The power to appoint an independent counsel was placed with a specially constituted judicial panel made up of Courts of Appeals judges. However, the ultimate decision about whether an appointment was even necessary to begin with was left with the attorney general. The new law gave more discretion to the attorney general to trigger an investigation. Under this system, any allegations of misconduct against anyone in the executive branch would go first to the Department of Justice (i.e., the attorney general), which would determine if the charges were legitimate. If so determined, a preliminary investigation would be conducted by the attorney general. If that preliminary investigation showed some evidence of misconduct and the need for further investigation, the attorney general would then ask the court panel to appoint an independent counsel. After the panel named the independent counsel, it would also define his or her jurisdiction. The power to remove the special prosecutor remained with the attorney general, although limits were placed on the causes for removal. Any decisions to remove a special prosecutor were subject to judicial review.[11]

The 1982 law also shortened the list of officials covered by the law, and provided for reimbursement of legal fees incurred by those under investigation who were not indicted after an investigation.

B. 1987 Reauthorization

In 1987 the Ethics in Government Act was again reauthorized by Congress.[12] This time, Congress changed the procedures for the initial determination for an independent counsel by the attorney general. Under the new legislation, the attorney general had only fifteen days after receiving allegations against an official to determine if there were sufficient grounds to investigate any further. If within that fifteen-day period the attorney general determined that the information was not credible, he or she could close the matter. Otherwise, the attorney general would begin a preliminary investigation and determine, over the next ninety days, whether to ask the panel of judges to appoint an independent counsel. If necessary, the attorney general could request an extension of not more than sixty days.[13]

The 1987 reauthorization of the Ethics in Government Act made some other revisions as well. One change extended the period of time individuals subject to independent counsel investigations were covered by the statute after they left their office or position from two to three years. The new law also expanded the independent counsel's jurisdiction, as defined by the court, to include the authority to investigate and prosecute all federal crimes, other than petty offenses, and created restitution for attorney's fees if the investigation did not result in an indictment.

C. 1988 Supreme Court Review

In 1988, the constitutionality of the Ethics in Government Act was brought into question and reviewed by the U.S. Supreme Court. The independent counsel statute was challenged as unconstitutional on the grounds that it vested part of the power of law enforcement in an officer not appointed by the president, stripping the executive branch of its constitutional power to enforce the laws.[14] President Reagan argued that all prosecutions were exclusively an executive branch function. The Supreme Court examined the act in light of these arguments in the case of *Morrison v. Olson* (487 U.S. 654 (1988)).

The case began when Theodore Olson, an assistant attorney general, was accused of lying to Congress during a scandal in the Environmental Protection Agency in 1982–83. Olson had appeared before a House subcommittee in March 1983 and was asked if the department had given the House all the documents relevant to the issue. He replied, "I'm not sure we included everything." The committee was not satisfied with the response, so they asked for an independent counsel to be appointed. Alexia Morrison was appointed to serve as independent counsel in the case in April 1986. On December 27, 1988, five and a half years after the alleged offense, Morrison submitted a final report on her investigation. In the report she announced that she would not seek prosecution of Olson for lying because what he had told Congress was not a lie,[15] and his response probably did not constitute a prosecutable offense because it was literally true.

Opponents of the independent counsel law used the situation to try to have the legislation declared unconstitutional.[16] The case was heard in the Supreme Court in April 1988. In June, by a seven-to-one majority, the Supreme Court justices upheld the constitutionality of the law.[17] The court declared that Congress did not take away the president's power to enforce the law because the independent counsel could be removed by the attorney general for cause and was empowered to perform only certain functions.[18] Moreover, the office was limited in jurisdiction and tenure.[19] The court also said that the independent counsel had no authority to formulate policy for the government or the executive branch. Since the counsel had limited jurisdiction and was temporary, it was constitutional.[20] One justice, Antonin Scalia, dissented, arguing that the statute had an "intimidating effect" on the president and his aides.

D. 1992 Expiration

In 1992, after the investigation of the Iran-Contra affair, Congress did not reauthorize the 1987 Ethics in Government statute. The independent counsel law had become very controversial by then. Congress simply allowed the statutory authority for appointment of independent counsels to lapse,[21] and it formally ended on December 15, 1992.[22]

E. 1994 Reauthorization

On June 30, 1994, Congress reauthorized the independent counsel law for another five years. This version placed new restrictions on expenditures by independent counsels and clarified the attorney general's authority to use independent counsels in cases involving members of Congress.[23] The new law required the attorney general begin a thirty-day review when allegations of criminal wrongdoing were raised about any of the more than fifty top-level government officials covered by the law, including the president, vice president, and the president's Cabinet. The new law also provided that the attorney general could choose to appoint an independent counsel if there was a conflict of interest between the target of the allegations and the Justice Department. The initial thirty-day review was to be narrow in scope and conducted by the Justice Department to determine if the charges against an official were credible and further action was warranted.

F. 1995 Supreme Court Review

In 1995, the Supreme Court struck down part of the Ethics in Government Act as unconstitutional. In the law, members of Congress and other federal employees are prohibited from accepting an honorarium for making a speech or writing an article, even if the person or group paying for the honorarium has no connection with the official's public duties. In the case of *United States v. National Treasury Employees Union* (115 S.Ct. 1003, 513 U.S. 454 ((1995)), the Supreme Court examined the question if the ban abridged freedom of speech. In their decision, the Court held that yes, any type of flat ban such as the one in this provision of the law violated the First Amendment of the Constitution because honoraria allow for free speech.[24]

G. 1999 Expiration

The Ethics in Government statute was once again up for congressional renewal in 1999, but by then it had made enough enemies on both sides of the aisle that most agreed the law had caused more problems than it had solved. At that time, the attorney general, Janet Reno, told the Senate Governmental Affairs Committee that the independent counsel statute was "structurally flawed" and should be abandoned. She said there were serious prosecutorial abuses committed during the Starr investigation as well as others. Starr also testified that the statute should not be reaffirmed. But the independent counsel in the Iran-Contra scandal, Lawrence Walsh, testified that the law should not be allowed to expire, but that it needed to be narrowed. He argued that the law gave credibility to investigations of presidents and other top officials, and that it would not work if the attorney general oversaw inquiries, because the attorney general is appointed by the president. The statute was again allowed to expire in June 1999.[25]

H. OIC: Pro and Con

The provisions of the original 1978 Ethics in Government Act provoked a debate among legal practitioners and scholars about the best way to control the executive branch's exercise of law enforcement power.[26] The special prosecutors appointed during the Watergate scandal were appointed by members of the executive branch for the executive to exercise its power over law enforcement. Later, the independent counsels appointed under the statutory arrangement were appointed by members of the judiciary and were less accountable to any of the three branches.[27] They are supposed to look into allegations of high-level wrongdoing. However, there are a lot of questions and concerns about special investigators and independent counsels.

It has been argued that the independent counsel appointed by a judicial panel has much more independence than one appointed by the president. He/she does not have to answer to the president, who in turn has less power over the investigator. For example, Nixon's ability to control the criminal investigation of Watergate was severely hampered by the appointment of a special prosecutor who is independent of the executive branch.[28] Judicial appointment of the special prosecutor in the long run helps the special prosecutor investigate charges more effectively.

Opponents of the law point out that the independent counsel can be a powerful figure with few checks on their power. First, there are almost no limits to the funds that an independent counsel can spend in an investigation.[29] His or her budget is often unlimited. Because the independent counsel is funded by Congress, more than ample funds are often provided. Second, there are no time limits on the special investigator.[30] The independent counsel is under no obligation to show results within a given period.[31] Third, it is almost impossible to remove an independent counsel. Fourth, the independent counsel is not appointed to investigate a specific crime that has taken place but is assigned to determine if any crime has been committed. This is very vague, and allows the independent counsel to look into events that may look suspicious but are not necessarily criminal. The process is such that an individual from the executive branch may be identified and chosen as a suspect, and then the special prosecutor tries to identify a crime that this person may have perpetrated.[32] Such an investigation could not be performed on an average individual prior to charges being made.[33] Fifth, the independent counsel has broad leeway to expand the scope of investigation from its initial focus to seemingly unrelated matters. This is something that ordinary prosecutors cannot do. They have to confine themselves to the initial subject matter of an investigation. The independent counsel can expand the investigation (with judge's approval) any time he or she uncovers evidence of other crimes.

In fact, there are fewer checks on the behavior of an independent counsel than on almost any other government official wielding comparable power.[34] Because of that almost unlimited power, the Office of Independent Counsel (OIC) has been described as an office that was simply designed to find criminal acts.[35]

Despite these limits, the use of independent counsels has proliferated in recent years. During the Clinton administration, there were many counsels that investigated possible crimes of all types. People began to question if there was a need for so many investigators, or if the Republicans were using special prosecutors as a form of RIP against the Democrats.

I. Recent Investigations by Special Prosecutors

Despite all the problems, there have been many independent counsels appointed since 1970, in accordance with the Ethics in Government Act provisions. In many of these investigations, the evidence proved insufficient to warrant prosecution, but some of them led to indictment and prosecution.[36] Some recent special prosecutors are described below and others in Table 2.1.

1. Carter

During the Carter administration, his chief of staff, Hamilton Jordan, was investigated for possibly using cocaine on a social occasion. After an investigation, the independent counsel concluded there was insufficient evidence to prosecute.[37] Another one of Carter's top aides, Tim Kraft, was also investigated for drug use, but there was no criminal indictment.[38]

2. Reagan

During the Reagan administration, there were multiple independent counsels appointed. For example, in 1981, an investigation was conducted of Raymond Donovan, Reagan's secretary of Labor, for alleged ties to organized crime and racketeering. Before working for the Reagan administration, Donovan was executive vice president of the Schiavone Construction Company in New Jersey. There were allegations that he had contact with organized crime and made payoffs to them. The investigator concluded that there was insufficient credible evidence to warrant prosecution,[39] and thus there was no criminal indictment.

Reagan's nominee for attorney general, Edwin Meese, was investigated in 1984 and 1987 for irregularities with his personal finances. During his confirmation hearings in March 1984, investigators looked into the records on the sale of his home in San Diego and claimed that the financial dealings were unethical. They said that Meese's wife had taken a $15,000 interest-free loan from a man who became Meese's White House deputy, and the loan was not listed on Meese's financial disclosure form. Mrs. Meese had used the money to buy stock for the Meese children in a company called Biotech, and documents showed that a Biotech subsidiary had been given a special exemption to make it eligible for a Small Business Administration loan.[40]

Moreover, the White House was forced to admit that Meese, after a trip to Korea, had kept a set of jade cufflinks given to him by the South Korean government. Rules said a federal official could accept only gifts worth less than $140, but the cufflinks were said to be worth $375.[41] Then the army's inspector general charged that Meese had gotten an improper promotion in the army reserve. So Meese himself called for an independent counsel to clear his name. The independent counsel was Jacob A. Stein. After his investigation, Stein's report claimed that there was no evidence to warrant criminal prosecution.[42]

An independent counsel was appointed in 1990 to investigate Samuel Pierce Jr., Reagan's HUD secretary, about allegations of fraud and favoritism in the awarding of contracts. The investigation wrapped up in 1999 after almost a decade.[43] Pierce was never charged with any offenses.

There were many other investigations during the Reagan administration. They are included in Table 2.1.

3. Clinton

One of the independent counsels appointed during the Clinton administration was Donald Smaltz, appointed to investigate Secretary of Agriculture Mike Espy, who was accused of accepting improper gifts from companies regulated by his department. In 1999 a jury acquitted Espy of all of the charges brought against him after a four-year, $17 million investigation. In the end, Smaltz did get fifteen convictions and $11 million in fines from other offenses related to the original charges.

Table 2.1: Other Recent Independent Counsels

Independent Counsel	Year	Scandal/Person
Arthur Christy	1978–80	Illegal drug use by Carter's aide Hamilton Jordan
Gerald Gallinghouse	1980–81	Cocaine use by Timothy Kraft, an aide to Jimmy Carter
Leon Silverman	1981–84	Raymond Donovan and possible ties to organized crime
Jacob Stein	1984	Financial improprieties by Edwin Meese III
Whitney North Seymour, Jr.	1986–89	White House deputy Chief of Staff Michael Deaver for lobbying a foreign client in violation of the Ethics Act[42]
Alexia Morrison	1986–88	Theodore Olson, a Justice Department Official in the Office of Legal Counsel; for obstruction of Justice and lying to Congress during Superfund

Lawrence Walsh	1986–94	Multiple politicians involved in the Iran-Contra affair
James Harper	1986–87	Assistant Attorney General Lawrence Wallace for income tax violations[43]
James McKay	1987–90	Edwin Meese and White House aide Lyn Nofziger for involvement in Wedtech scandal, an affair involving a New York City defense contractor under investigation by the U.S. attorney for the Southern District of New York; Nofziger was accused of illegal lobbying in behalf of the defense contractor[44]
Arlin Adams and Larry Thompson	1988–98	Samuel Pierce and U.S. Department of Housing and Urban Development for financial improprieties
Joseph DiGenova and Michael Zeldin	1992–95	Improper search of passport records
Donald Smaltz	1994–2001	Corruption against Mike Espy
David Barrett	1995–2006	Henry Cisneros' payments made to a mistress
Daniel Pearson	1995–96	Ron Brown, Secretary of Commerce, for financial improprieties
Curtis Emery von Kann	1996–97	Americorps Chief Eli J. Segal for conflict of interest
Carol Bruce	1998	Bruce Babbitt, Interior secretary, for lying to Congress
Kenneth Starr	1994–2001	Vince Foster, Whitewater, Travelgate, Filegate, and Lewinsky scandals
Ralph Lancaster	1998	Labor Secretary Alexis Herman for influence peddling

Clinton and Starr

In 1993, amid allegations that the Clintons had potentially engaged in wrongdoing in association with a 1980s real estate deal called Whitewater, there was a renewed interest in the independent counsel arrangement. Before Congress could reauthorize the statute, Attorney General Janet Reno used her own regulatory authority to appoint a special prosecutor to investigate the Whitewater allegations and the death of White House aide Vincent Foster.[44] On January

20, 1994, she named Robert B. Fiske Jr., a moderate Republican, to investigate the charges.[45] Not too long after, in June 1994, the independent counsel provisions were reauthorized by Congress with a special provision that allowed for Fiske to be reappointed. However, the special court panel responsible for choosing the independent counsel decided that Fiske could not be sufficiently impartial because he had been appointed by Reno. The panel replaced Fiske with Kenneth W. Starr.[46] The Clinton administration did not like Starr and waged a silent war against him. At the same time, no official would come out and attack him because he had the power to bring charges against anyone.

Starr was born in Texas in 1946, the son of a Church of Christ minister. He was raised to abstain from alcohol or tobacco. After high school he went to Harding College, a Christian school in Arkansas. But after criticizing the school's spending priorities, he transferred to George Washington University in Washington, D.C., and then attended Duke University law school. He clerked for Supreme Court Chief Justice Warren Burger until 1977 and then went to work for a Washington law firm based in Los Angeles. There he met a friend of Ronald Reagan, William French Smith. When Reagan was elected president, Smith went to D.C. and took Starr with him. Reagan named Starr to the D.C. Federal Appeals Court, which he left in 1989 to become George Bush's solicitor general, who is typically the lawyer who argues administration positions before the Supreme Court. When Bush lost the election to Clinton, Starr joined a law firm in D.C. He was appointed as a special prosecutor in August 1994. Starr taught Sunday school, prayed before every courtroom appearance, and sang hymns on morning jogs. He has been reported as saying that he considers lies under oath, on any subject, to be intolerable because lies and half-truths corrode our system of justice.

Starr was originally appointed to investigate the Whitewater land deal. Later, he got the authority from Attorney General Reno and a three-judge panel to expand his jurisdiction. This was expanded to encompass the firing of White House travel office employees, the gathering of FBI files on Republican White House aides, the possible perjury of Clinton's former White House counsel, and the mysterious reappearance in the White House of Rose Law Firm billing records two years after they were subpoenaed. He then investigated a possible cover-up of an affair with a White House intern, Monica Lewinsky. This led to a criminal investigation and depositions, where it was discovered that Clinton lied under oath. Clinton was then impeached by the House of Representatives, but not removed from office by the Senate.

Starr also obtained a criminal conviction of Jim Guy Tucker, the former governor of Arkansas who was charged with conspiring while a lawyer in private practice. Starr also got convictions of Webb Hubbell, the former associate attorney general of the United States, for bilking his own law firm and clients. Moreover, Starr got convictions of Jim and Susan McDougal, Clinton's friends and former business partners.

As special prosecutor, Starr had offices in Washington and Little Rock, Arkansas, and a staff of twenty lawyers who work in both places. He had an unlimited budget and unlimited time frame for his investigation. Starr's critics claimed that these powers allowed him to push people to say things they did not believe or knew were not true. They said that Starr's use of subpoena powers was overkill. There were concerns over leaks during the investigation. Some were upset that he continued his private law practice while being special prosecutor, earning over $1 million a year. Clinton said Starr was out to get the president at any cost.

Special Prosecutors/Independent Counsels: Conclusion

The question of whether the country should to have a method to investigate wrongdoing on the part of high-level government officials remains unanswered. Congress originally chose to have investigations by independent counsels rather than by the Justice Department because the independent counsel would help ensure that politics do not influence the course of the investigation or the decision about a possible indictments or other action.[47] They decided to give the power to appoint a special prosecutor to the attorney general. But appointment by the attorney general causes potential conflict. If the power to appoint a special prosecutor remains with the attorney general, problems may arise. The attorney general is supposed to be a trusted and loyal member of the president's Cabinet, a person in whom the president can turn to for advice. That same person is also the nation's highest law enforcement officer, and the one who decides if the president will be the focus of an investigation and possible prosecution.[48] It would be difficult to force anyone in that position to investigate and prosecute the president or other officials while at the same time serving the president. Moreover, there would always be a perception of unfairness, no matter the decision.[49] The public will simply not trust a process in which the subjects of an investigation have the power to hire, fire, promote, and demote those who decide the course of the investigation.[50]

Congress attempted to solve that problem by putting the power to appoint an independent counsel with the courts.[51] But that system still leaves the attorney general with a prominent role in the process. Moreover, once appointed, the independent counsels create other problems. The subjects of the investigations are often hounded throughout the investigation and bankrupted in the end.

There is little accountability of the special prosecutor. Additionally, the procedure for appointing an independent counsel is too easily triggered so that frivolous cases are often pursued, wasting taxpayer dollars to damage reputations where there is little or no significant evidence.[52] Almost everyone agrees that the independent counsel law is a problematic piece of legislation as it currently exists.[53]

One suggested method to solve the problem is to have a permanent office of prosecution that is outside of the political system, similar to what exists in other countries.[54] Or, on charges being made, a special prosecutor could be appointed immediately to conduct a full investigation and to report his or her findings to the American public.[55] If charges are brought, then impeachment becomes a possibility.

Impeachment

Impeachment refers to the constitutional process of bringing charges against a public official for specified illegal or unethical conduct while in office, before the end of their designated term of office. It applies to all federal officeholders, including presidents and their cabinet members, judges, and members of Congress. If there are allegations made against a president, the House of Representatives has the sole power of impeachment. According to the Constitution, the impeachment trial of a president takes place in the House. If they vote to impeach, the managers or prosecutors then present the evidence in the Senate. The second stage of the process occurs in the Senate, with 100 senators acting as a jury. The chief justice of the U.S. Supreme Court presides over the trial. There must be a two-thirds vote to convict that person and remove him or her from office.

According to Article II, Section 4 of the U.S. Constitution, the president can be impeached for "treason, bribery or other high crimes and misdemeanors."[56] There is a general consensus that "high" modifies both crimes and misdemeanors. But to many, that is still unclear. President Gerald Ford once tried to address the problem in 1970, when he was involved in impeachment proceedings against Supreme Court Justice William O. Douglas. When asked "What, then, is an impeachable offense?" Ford responded by saying: "The only honest answer is that an impeachable offense is whatever a majority of the House of Representatives considers it to be at a given moment in history." It seems to be that impeachment is to a great extent discretionary and dependent on a variety of circumstances.[57] In some cases, the standards for impeachment remain rather broad.[58]

For some, to impeach a sitting president, there must be an act that is a high public violation of official duty, as opposed to a low, private sex scandal, even if it may have included acts that might technically be criminal.[59] In other words, to be removed from office, a president must be guilty of criminal conduct. The high crime and misdemeanor must rise to the level of treason, bribery, or a similar betrayal of the nation's interest. Some would further argue that the criminal conduct should be related to matters of state as opposed to private conduct.[60] Under this definition, the crimes committed by Nixon fit within the definition of a removable offense as a high crime and misdemeanor because they involved a criminal cover-up of matters of state, including the burglary of opponents' offices.[61]

But in recent years, attitudes toward impeachment have evolved,[62] and the impeachment process has become a powerful constitutional weapon for waging political combat.[63] During the past fifty years, the role of impeachment in American political culture expanded substantially.[64] Each of the presidents who were elected to a second term between 1960 and 2008 had impeachment charges proposed against them. Two of the four, Nixon and Clinton, actually confronted congressional impeachment proceedings; a third, Reagan, may have faced similar charges had he not left office.[65] There had also been calls to impeach G. W. Bush over controversies with the Iraq War.

Judges can also be impeached and removed from office. Similar to the presidency, this has not been used very often. Between 1789 and 1960, only thirteen judges had impeachment proceedings formally initiated in the House of Representatives. In thirty-one other cases, there were resolutions introduced into the House against judges and other federal officials, but they did not move forward for one reason or another, such as the resignation of the accused. These cases are only a small percentage of the officials who held impeachable positions during that time frame.[66]

For most of the history of the United States, impeachment has rarely been employed or even mentioned.[67] In 1841, John Tyler became president after William Henry Harrison died a month into his term. Tyler was a Democrat but accepted the position on a Whig ticket. The Whigs were angry that they won the election but then lost control of the White House to Tyler. They wanted nothing to do with him, but instead wanted Henry Clay to be president. Tyler continued to antagonize the Whigs by vetoing a bill to revive the national bank and a bill to give money from land sales to the states and to raise the tariff. A House committee chaired by former president John Quincy Adams declared that Tyler deserved impeachment because he was weak and wavering. A Whig, John M. Botts from Virginia, proposed a resolution to impeach Tyler. In 1843 the impeachment resolution failed in the House by a vote of 127 to 83.[68]

In 1868, President Johnson was impeached and was one vote short of being removed from office. Johnson removed Edwin M. Stanton from the position of secretary of War, and Congress accused him of violating the Tenure of Office Act of 1867. Congress had passed the law over Johnson's veto. Congress impeached Johnson for eleven charges, one of which was saying nasty things about Congress. Johnson ultimately escaped conviction in the Senate by one vote and was not removed from office. Once the Congress used the impeachment process against President Johnson, they were less reluctant to use impeachment against other presidents.[69]

Impeachment proceedings were considered against President Herbert Hoover after he lost the election of 1932 and became a lame duck president. There was a motion to impeach Hoover in 1932 for twenty-six offenses, including reducing Germany's war debt, and misadministering the Federal Reserve Board, but Congress tabled the vote and nothing was done on it.

Impeachment proceedings had begun against President Nixon for his role in the criminal break-ins of the Democratic National Committee and the subsequent cover-up. However, he resigned in 1974 and was pardoned by President Ford, so no hearings took place.

The most recent, and only successful, presidential impeachment was against President Clinton. He was impeached in 1998 for lying under oath in a sexual harassment case brought against him by Paula Jones.

Censure

A lesser punishment than impeachment is a censure. This is when a congressional member is formally reprimanded in public for inappropriate behavior. This punishment is not found in the Constitution or in the rules of the House or Senate. Instead, it comes from the power of each body to punish its members. Censure has not been used often. In 1954, Republican Senator Joseph McCarthy was censured for not cooperating with the subcommittee that was investigating him. In 1983, Representatives Dan Crane and Gerry Studds were censured for their involvement in a congressional page scandal. If a president is censured, it serves as a public condemnation of his behavior but has no direct effect on his presidency. He remains in office with the same powers as before. President Andrew Jackson was censured, but it was later expunged from the record.

In some cases, a member could be expelled from the House or Senate. Typically for more serious or continuing unacceptable behavior, the members of the individual bodies may vote to remove a member from office. This is a rare occurrence, however.

Conclusion

Investigations by special prosecutors and independent counsels are essential to scandals. The investigations help discover the facts of the allegations and who is responsible. The need for some type of a special prosecutor to look into charges of illegal or unethical behavior on the part of executive level officials has been recognized by Congress, but the exact process for appointing that person and how an investigation should be carried out are still unclear.

What is important to recognize is that the investigations can lead to impeachment and removal from office for some officials. The crimes for which an official may be impeached are vague and unclear, and change from one time period to the next. More presidents and other officials are being investigated and impeached more than ever before, and the trend is only likely to continue.

Review Questions

1. What is the role or purpose of the special prosecutor or independent counsel?
2. Describe the impeachment process.
3. What is censure and for what offenses would it be used?
4. Explain why we have a special prosecutor or independent counsel. How has this changed over time?
5. Why is the Ethics in Government Act significant?
6. Describe the process by which an independent counsel is appointed.
7. What is the current status of the Independent Counsel Law?
8. List some recent independent counsels and the focus of their investigations.
9. What has the Supreme Court decided about the Independent Counsel Law?

Special Terms

Independent Counsel
Ethics in Government Act
1982 Reauthorization
1987 Reauthorization

United States v. National Treasury Employees Union
Impeachment
Censure

Discussion Questions

1. Should Congress pass a new Independent Counsel Law? If so, what would it include? How would it be different from previous laws?
2. Is the Independent Counsel Law a good idea?
3. Do independent counsels have too much power?
4. Why is the impeachment/removal process separated into two distinct phases?
5. Is the Independent Counsel Law constitutional?
6. Why was Independent Counsel Law allowed to expire?
7. What are the pros/cons of the Independent Counsel Law?
8. Is Congress more willing to use impeachment as a political attack than in the past?

Chapter 3

Early Presidential Scandals

Introduction

Even though there has been a proliferation of political scandals in recent years, politicians of yesteryear were not immune to scandal. There is nothing new about Washington scandals—they are not by themselves a new phenomenon in American politics.[1] Political scandals have been part of the scene in the United States for over two centuries. Even the earliest politicians in America, the Founding Fathers, were accused of being involved in illegal or unethical behavior of different kinds. Sometimes, those scandals resulted in harsh, long-term, or permanent effects, whereas others involved only had to endure minor consequences. In this chapter, early political scandals are described. It is easy to see that scandals were a fairly common event to those holding office, even 200 years ago.

George Washington (1789–97)

George Washington became America's first president in 1789 and served two terms, with no official political party affiliation. Throughout his service, there were many allegations that he was involved in scandalous behavior, many of which were not true. For example, Washington was accused of excessive drinking and having an affair with a British mistress by the name of Mary Gibbons, who allegedly stole secret documents.[2] But there was no valid proof of such. It turns out that some of the rumors were spread by the British, who wanted to keep Americans loyal to England after the war and wanted Washington to appear as an unfit leader.[3]

Moreover, it was falsely alleged that Washington had several illegitimate children,[4] including an illegitimate son with a woman in Barbados. As the story goes, the son's name was Lawrence Posey. Lawrence's father, Captain Thomas Posey, supposedly received money from Washington as the result of an agreement, whereby Thomas would raise Lawrence as his own son.[5] Washington was also supposed to have had an Indian squaw as a lover, which was probably not true.[6]

Another popular but untrue rumor was that Washington contracted syphilis in early manhood and allegedly died as a result of a cold he got while sleeping with his overseer's wife on a cold December day.[7] There is no proof that either of these allegations have any truth to them.

At the same time, some of the scandalous allegations made against the first president were true. Washington wrote love letters to a married woman, Sarah "Sally" Cary Fairfax, his friend's wife.[8] She was his first love and he was captivated by her.[9] After he was engaged to Martha Custis, he continued to write letters to Mrs. Fairfax, expressing his love for her, but she did not return his love. Historians agree that there is no proof of a sexual relationship between them.[10]

During the Revolutionary War, Washington agreed to forgo a salary and be reimbursed for expenses. Oddly enough, his expense account included travel for his wife and others to visit him, charges for keeping his slaves and other aides. In the end, he received more money by being reimbursed for expenses than his salary would have been.[11]

Others accused Washington of using intermediaries to purchase land for him. He realized if he identified himself as the party interested in the land, the price would increase because of his wealth. In 1770, Washington purchased 3,000 acres of land. While he was away, squatters moved onto the land. Even though Washington was formally recognized as the rightful owner, the squatters remained. He attempted to have them removed, but there was a disagreement over the squatter's rights to the property. Washington had to take out newspaper space explaining his side of the story and challenged anyone who could prove that his story was not true to come forward. When no one did, the squatters were forced to leave.[12]

Alexander Hamilton (1789–95)

Hamilton was a Founding Father whose face is currently on the $10 bill. Hamilton served as Secretary of the Treasury and was Washington's principal adviser for many years, but this did not protect him from scandal. He had an affair with Maria Reynolds,[13] whose husband, James, blackmailed Hamilton, demanding money and a job in the Treasury Department.[14] Hamilton paid hush money to Reynolds but refused to give him a job. Reynolds then accused Hamilton of speculating with government funds, but there was no proof and the issue was dropped.[15] Opponents in Congress found out about the cover-up in 1792, leaked the story to the press, and nearly ruined Hamilton's career.

Most historians agree that many of the scandals concerning Hamilton were political charges led by Thomas Jefferson, particularly because of his ideas for creating a national bank and solving the national debt.[16] Hamilton came up with a way to solve the nation's debt by taking loans from foreign governments at 5 percent interest and paying off loans to the government that were at 6 percent. Even though the plan was legal, some members of Congress pursued an investigation of it, arguing that Hamilton violated the law by mixing two separate loans into one pool. Rep. William B. Giles of Virginia introduced nine resolutions that called for further investigation of how the money was handled and called for Hamilton's removal from office. The resolutions were defeated by large majorities.[17]

Thomas Jefferson (1801–09)

Thomas Jefferson was the third U.S. president, elected in 1800 and serving until 1809 as a member of the Democratic-Republican Party. He was also appointed Secretary of State under Washington. It was said that he had sexual relations with many of his slaves and then sold some of the resulting children at auction, even selling one into prostitution in New Orleans. Others claimed that Jefferson embezzled money, was a drunkard, and was profane. It was also claimed that he was a plagiarist, lifting many ideas from John Locke. It is fairly clear that some of the phrases used by Jefferson are similar to those of Locke.[18]

Many of the scandals of which Jefferson was accused revolved around his relationships with women. In 1768, he allegedly had an affair with Betsey Moore Walker, the wife of his neighbor, John Walker.[19] Some also said he had an affair with James Madison's wife, Dolly, after his own wife died. Others said Jefferson was "close friends" with Maria Cosway, whom he met while serving as an ambassador to France.[20] At the time, Cosway was married and a member of the Catholic religion, leaving her no options for a divorce.[21] He also allegedly had an affair with Angelica Schuyler Church.[22] Jefferson denied the allegations, but only privately. Most authorities on him have found many of these stories to be untrue.

Jefferson is most widely known for his long-term relationship with his slave, Sally Hemings, one of the 187 slaves he inherited from his and his wife's families. Jefferson had married his wife, Martha, in 1772, but she died in 1782 after giving birth to six children, only two of whom survived into adulthood.[23] Before she died, Jefferson promised her that he would never re-marry. But seven years after she died, he began a relationship with Hemings. Hemings had three white grandparents and was allegedly the daughter of Jefferson's father-in-law, John Wayles, making Sally Martha's half-sister.[24] Hemings was the maid for Jefferson's ten-year-old legitimate daughter, Maria. Over their thirty-eight-year relationship, Jefferson and Hemings had seven children,[25] only five of whom lived into adulthood.[26] Her children reportedly all resembled him.[27]

Their relationship started when they were in France. In 1784, Washington had sent Jefferson to France as a representative of the new government. His oldest daughter, Patsy, accompanied him. A year after he arrived in France, Jefferson sent for the other daughter, Maria, and her personal maid, fourteen-year-old Hemings.[28] While there, Jefferson took Hemings as his mistress.[29] When Jefferson and his daughter returned to the United States, Hemings could have stayed in France where they did not recognize slavery and she would have been legally free. Nevertheless, she decided to return to Virginia with Jefferson, after getting a promise from him that he would free her children when each reached the age of twenty-one.[30]

Allegations of their relationship were printed in a newspaper at the time called the Richmond Reporter.[31] The editor of the paper, James T. Callender, did not like Jefferson because Jefferson refused to appoint him to a political office.[32] Callender was known to drink frequently and had many enemies, so when he was found dead in three feet of water, no one could tell if he was killed or if it was an accident. [33]

It is important to note that sexual relations between white plantation owners and their slaves were common in Jefferson's era. It was not necessarily a behavior that was approved, but nonetheless it was quietly accepted as a natural part of life. At the same time, Jefferson despised mixing of races. His writings show that he abhorred slavery, but felt that blacks and whites should remain separate and even suggested that blacks should lead a separate existence in unsettled areas of the United States, Africa, or even the Caribbean. He thought this would allow slaves to have a fresh start as a separate, free, and independent group of people.

On his plantation, Jefferson was considerate of his slaves even though he did not believe that most were sufficiently educated and trained to survive outside the plantation on their own. He believed that a life of slavery had made most of them incapable of taking care of themselves. At the same time, though, he relied on his slaves to keep Monticello going. He was not a rich man, as through most of his public service he was paid only for his expenses. Despite this, Jefferson often gave huge parties, sometimes ordering 500 bottles of wine at a time. He died penniless, and his relatives had to sell Monticello and everything in it to pay for his debts.

James Monroe (1817–25)

James Monroe was the fifth president of the United States. In 1814, before he became president, British troops burned the White House and all of the furnishings. In response, Congress established a fund of $20,000 to refurnish the president's home, but it took a long time to get the furniture. So Monroe suggested that he loan his personal furniture to the White House without requesting immediate compensation. Eventually, Congress gave him $9,000 for his furniture, money that Monroe then used for a trip across the country. On his return, Monroe repaid $6,000, but had briefly used public funds for his own use and used the furniture fund as a personal loan. Some felt that while he was being less than candid with Congress, he was not doing anything illegal.[34]

John Quincy Adams (1825–29)

John Quincy Adams, our sixth president, was elected in 1824. In that election, there was no winning candidate, as no one achieved the necessary 131 votes in the Electoral College. Andrew Jackson received 41 percent of the popular vote; John Quincy Adams received 31 percent of the popular votes; Henry Clay received 13 percent, and William Crawford received 11 percent. Therefore, the election went to the House of Representatives, where each state had one vote to choose the next president. After Clay was dropped from the ballot, only three candidates' names were up for consideration. Clay decided to support Adams, resulting in Clay's Electoral College votes going to Adams. In return, Clay was given the position of Secretary of State. This agreement between Adams and Clay was later called the "corrupt bargain." The charges of a corrupt bargain between the two men crippled the Adams's administration.[35] Adams's opponents also argued that Adams' was amoral because he installed a billiard table in the White House and swam nude in the Potomac. There is strong evidence that both of these allegations were indeed true.[36]

Andrew Jackson (1829–37)

Andrew Jackson was the seventh U.S. president, elected in 1828 as a member of the Democratic Party. Before he was president, Jackson was a successful attorney, becoming the first person from Tennessee to be elected to the House.[37] He married Rachel Donelson Robards in 1791. Some say he invested in land speculation, and was a liar, drunkard, gambler, slave trader, and murderer.[38] People also said he was an adulterer, since his wife was married to two men at one time. It was well known that he bet on racehorses and cockfights. In fact, his winnings from dice games helped him attend school and establish his law practice in Tennessee.

Some of the allegations made against Jackson were true. He really was a slave trader, owning many slaves that served on his plantation, and he had killed a man in a duel,[39] a common practice for the time. The allegations about being an adulterer were also true. Before marrying Jackson, his wife was first married to Captain Lewis Robards, but she left him because he did not treat her well. Robards told Rachel that the Virginia Courts had agreed to an annulment when in actuality, the divorce petition had been denied.[40] Assuming that the marriage had been annulled, Rachel married Jackson. Both Jackson and his wife believed that she had been legally divorced from her first husband.[41] This meant that Jackson was "living openly" with a married woman. When the Jacksons found out, Rachel got a divorce and they remarried.[42] This mistake led to claims that Jackson married a bigamist,[43] and he dueled to defend their honor.

Throughout his life, Jackson had a deep hatred for Indians.[44] In 1813, settlers had taken refuge at Fort Mims. Some Indians overcame the Americans and butchered the white settlers.[45] The massacre of Fort Mims angered Jackson and prompted him and other Americans to seek revenge. The Indians did not submit easily to American domination. Therefore, at Creek Village of Talluschatchee, 1,000 of Jackson's troops encircled 200 Indians and slaughtered every one of them. Jackson said it was retaliation for the assault on Fort Mims.[46] Afterward, many people decided that his behavior was murderous.

There were many accusations made against Jackson as president. In 1832, he vetoed rechartering the Second Bank of the United States. He considered it to be mismanaged and believed it was the cause for the nation's first prolonged economic depression.[47] He decided to remove the funds from the bank, something he had no authority to do. Jackson approached his Cabinet members and informed them of his plans for the bank, but the secretary of the Treasury, William J. Duane, refused to remove the funds. At that point, Jackson fired Duane and replaced him with someone who would remove the funds. The Senate argued that under the Constitution, Congress had control of public funds. They adopted a resolution to censure the president. The House made no move to impeach him.[48]

There was also a scandal involving the Secretary of War, John Henry Eaton, during Jackson's administration. He and his wife, Peggy O'Neale Eaton, allegedly had "criminal intercourse" prior to their marriage. The resulting scandal, called the Petticoat War by many, caused quite a few wives to refuse to attend functions if Mrs. Eaton was in attendance. They also refused to meet with her or be seen with her, or even for their husbands to be seen with Secretary Eaton.

Martin Van Buren (1837–41)

Martin Van Buren was elected to the presidency in 1836, making him the eighth president of the United States. He served only one term as a member of the Democratic Party. It was said that he was illegitimate and really the son of Aaron Burr, the vice president during Jefferson's administration.[49] However, he was really the third child (of six) for Abraham Van Buren and his wife, Maria Hoes.[50] As president, Van Buren was accused of spending too much money to redecorate and entertain at the White House, but he actually spent far less than other presidents.[51] Van Buren's wife died eighteen years before he entered the White House and he never remarried, prompting some to accuse him of being a homosexual.[52] But again, there was little evidence to support that claim.

John Tyler (1841–45)

When President John Tyler vetoed an economic bill from the Whig Congress, the House appointed a select committee to investigate a possible pattern of presidential vetoes. Their report claimed Tyler's vetoes had upset the balance where the president was to be responsible to Congress and concluded that he deserved to be impeached. In the end, articles of impeachment were not recommended because there were not enough votes.[53]

President Tyler's wife died while he was in the White House. He became a fifty-four-year-old widower and decided to marry a twenty-four-year-old model. This led to many scandalous rumors that he was a cruel husband. Despite this, during their marriage, they had seven children together.[54]

Franklin Pierce (1853–57)

Elected in 1852, Franklin Pierce was a Democrat who served one term as president. Charges made against him included that he was a drunkard and a coward in the Mexican War. Records indicate that he actually did have a drinking problem. Just weeks before he was to move to Washington, his eleven-year-old son died in a train wreck while his parents watched. Pierce's wife remained in mourning for two years and did not serve as hostess at the White House, often repeating that they were being punished by God for moving to Washington. Though it is fairly well known that Pierce sometimes turned to alcohol to cope with the loss of his son, there is no evidence that the behavior made him unable to perform his job.[55]

James Buchanan (1857–61)

James Buchanan was a Democrat who was elected to one term in office in 1856. He was a lawyer and a member of the Pennsylvania House of Representatives. It was said that he had a mistress, while at the same time being engaged to a young girl, Caroline Coleman. At one point, he and his fiancée had a fight and she broke off the engagement, later committing suicide.[56] Buchanan wrote her father a letter and asked to come to the funeral, but his letter came back unopened. His friends said he was so heartbroken he vowed never to marry.[57] Instead, he used his niece as First Lady. Throughout his term in office, women tried to get his attention, but he was not interested. There was some thought the he was involved in a homosexual relationship with William R. King, a member of Congress, but this appears unlikely.[58]

Another scandal revolved around allegations that Buchanan directly funneled large sums of government money into Democratic coffers in New York for his campaign.[59] It was also alleged that his close friend George Plitt was promised naval contracts in return for campaign contributions. The naval contracts were later awarded.[60] It was also alleged that in the days prior to a government printing office, Buchanan gave government printing jobs to his friends rather than to the lowest bidders.[61]

Abraham Lincoln (1861–65)

Abraham Lincoln was elected to be president in 1860 and served until 1865 as a Republican. It was said that he was in love with Ann Rutledge before Mary Todd. The story came from Lincoln's law partner, who Mary disliked, so it may have been false. The partner said that when Mary and Lincoln were to be married, he did not show up to the wedding. At first, Mary was forced to call it off, but they married later.[62] There is some evidence that he had an illegitimate daughter, but no real proof of that exists.

Early on, it was alleged that Lincoln had an affair, which made his wife's migraines and "chills and fever" worse. Much criticism was lodged against his wife for having lavish parties in the White House during the Civil War. She allegedly spent too much money to refurbish the White House for their administration and was accused of firing many people on the White House staff, then performing many of the duties herself to collected the salary.[63] In the end, many of the allegations against Mary Todd were simply because she was from the South and not well liked because of it. Her family was from Kentucky, and some of her relatives supported the Confederacy, whereas others supported

the Union. It was said that Mary Lincoln remained in contact with her Confederate family members and that she may have passed information on to Lincoln. A congressional committee met in secret to draw up impeachment charges
against the president. One day, Lincoln himself turned up at the hearings and
read a statement saying that the rumors were untrue. The investigation was
immediately stopped.[64]

Lincoln's administration was plagued with allegations about his staff as well.
His secretary of War, Simon Cameron, was responsible for spending an enormous amount of money to supply the Union army. He often gave grants to
state governors and private citizens, but there was little record keeping and it eventually became chaotic. When Congress demanded that Cameron provide specific information on all government contracts that were awarded, he refused. The
House established a committee to investigate Cameron's spending. They found
that contracts had gone to his favorite middlemen and suppliers, who had provided rotten blankets, tainted wine, uniforms that fell apart, and diseased and
dying horses. So Cameron was fired and replaced by Edwin Stanton.[65]

Andrew Johnson (1865–69)

When Lincoln was assassinated in 1865, Andrew Johnson became president
and served until 1868. He was accused of being a drunk and that by late in the
day he would be too drunk to speak coherently and he could not perform the
duties of his office.[66] Some say he was even drunk at his inauguration, but
there is nothing to support this rumor.[67]

Johnson was a Tennessee Democrat who was on Republican Abraham Lincoln's national unity ticket for the election of 1864. After only a short time as
vice president, he became president and had a difficult relationship with Congress. As a Democrat, he was at odds with the Republican Congress from the
start, and he obstructed the enforcement of any laws he opposed.[68] When Congress passed a bill renewing the Freedman's Bureau, Johnson vetoed it. Congress then approved the Civil Rights Act of 1866 that declared blacks as citizens
and made the Black Codes unlawful. Johnson vetoed this bill, but this time
Congress overrode the veto. Members of Congress then approved the Four-
teenth Amendment to the Constitution that provided equal protection of the
law to all citizens regardless of race. Although he could not veto an amendment, Johnson advised states not to ratify it.

Then Congress passed the Tenure of Office Act that prohibited the president from removing officeholders appointed during his term without Senate
approval.[69] It was designed to stop the president from sacking Northern car-

petbaggers who had seized federal posts in the South under the authority of Congress after the Civil War. Johnson argued that the act violated the concept of separation of powers and refused to acknowledge it. He considered it the constitutional responsibility of the chief executive to deal with the errant states. The Republican congressional majority believed that it held constitutional authority over conquered territory as well as the right to set the terms for readmitting the former Confederate states to the Union. Johnson was accused of violating the Tenure of Office Act by Congress[70] because he fired the secretary of War Edwin Stanton. Stanton refused to step down, and Congress rallied behind him.

Additionally, as a Southerner, Johnson sought reconciliation between the states after the war. He wanted to carry out Lincoln's plans to be lenient with the South. As such, he fought for the conciliatory treatment of the states that seceded from the union. Johnson continued to grant pardons to prominent Confederates, and refused to require Southern reform.[71] The Republicans were opposed to Johnson's gentle treatment of the Confederacy. Most of Congress favored reconstruction that would provide black suffrage and more equality for former slaves. Johnson disagreed with Congress on issues of race and reconstruction.[72] He denounced congressional actions designed to protect black rights as unfair.

The clash between Johnson and Congress was fundamentally constitutional in nature.[73] The president insisted that the national government had no power to compel state action, and Congress disagreed.[74] Congress took advantage of the disagreement and used it to attempt to impeach the unpopular president who had undertaken policies with which they disagreed.[75] The impeachment resolution charged Johnson with "high crimes and misdemeanors" for violating the Tenure of Office Act.[76] Congress also charged him with using undignified utterances, declarations, and threats against Congress.[77] He lacked sophistication and was generally crude.[78] The impeachment trial against Johnson was in 1868, and there were eleven charges of impeachment. The vote to impeach Johnson was thirty-five to nineteen, just one vote short of the two-thirds majority required to impeach.

Ulysses S. Grant (1869–77)

Ulysses S. Grant succeeded Johnson in 1869 and served two terms as president. He was a Republican. The media said he had a problem with alcohol and that he was on a "drunken tear" during the Vicksburg campaign. For the most part, his wife kept him from drinking too much.[79] Others deny any real proof of a drinking problem exists.[80]

During the Grant administration, his brother-in-law Abel Corbin wrote to him asking him not to sell some of the government's supply of gold to keep the price down. Despite his pleas, Grant decided to sell $4 million worth of gold and the price fell. Many speculators lost millions, and it seriously affected the economy at the time.[81]

Although Grant was innocent of personal wrongdoing, many in his administration were corrupt. His supervisor of internal revenue, General John A. McDonald, extorted more than $2.5 million from various liquor distillers. When his involvement in the Whiskey Ring was discovered, McDonald was indicted by a federal grand jury and resigned.[82] The Whiskey Ring was the largest in the nation's history up to that date. In the end, 238 men were indicted and 110 were convicted.[83]

Grant's secretary of War (1869–90), William W. Belknap, resigned instead of being impeached after he was accused of bribery for accepting payments in return for giving out an appointment to a lucrative army post tradership. At that time, a post trader had a monopoly over providing provisions to soldiers at a fort.[84] On his wife's request, Belknap assigned the Fort Sill post tradership to her friend, Caleb Marsh. However, the post operator at the time, John Evans, did not want to leave the position because he made a great deal of money there. The nominee Marsh and the post operator Evans came to an agreement whereby Evans would remain in the position but pay the appointee large sums of money (around $12,000), which he then split with Mrs. Belknap.[85] After an investigation, Mr. Belknap was impeached in the House. He resigned from his office in the morning of March 2, 1876, but the House impeached him in the afternoon for corruption by a unanimous vote.[86] He narrowly won acquittal in the Senate, not because senators thought he was innocent but because they were unsure if they had jurisdiction over the case once Belknap resigned.[87]

Another scandal during the Grant administration was the Credit Mobilier scandal. This scandal revolved around members of Congress who accepted money or stock from a railroad company in exchange for enacting legislation favorable to that company. In the end, the vice president and several congressmen and senators were implicated, but not Grant himself.[88]

Credit Mobilier was a corporation established in the early 1860s in connection with the construction of the Union Pacific Railroad, a transcontinental railroad. Headed by Congressman Oakes Ames,[89] it received huge appropriations from Congress to subsidize the building of the Union Pacific. By 1864, Ames and Thomas Durant, then the vice president of the Union Pacific Railroad Company, profited significantly from the venture, but as time went on it became apparent that they were building the railroad at a ridiculously high cost. Durant and Ames were fearful that Congress would question their profits in light of the high costs and subsidies, so they began to sell Credit Mobilier stock to individual members of Congress at less than its market value, even giving some away, to forestall an investigation.[90]

Durant's payments to various congressmen continued for many years, effectively inhibiting calls for an investigation. But when the Union Pacific Railroad began to lose significant profits, Congress began to question their increased appropriations. Throughout, Durant continued to give money to members of Congress.[91] Eventually, a list of people who received money was printed in the New York Sun.[92] Shortly thereafter, an investigation was held in the House of Representatives to determine if any of the people who received the stock could be held liable. It was discovered that Ames and others, acting as representatives of Credit Mobilier, spent the congressional subsidies on construction contracts and other companies they controlled. In all, it was estimated that they received profits of over $20 million.[93]

The congressmen involved all received censures,[94] but no charges were brought against them. Vice President Schuyler Colfax was also exposed for having accepted shares of stock while he was Speaker of the House in 1867–68. The House considered impeachment, but his act was viewed as a nonimpeachable offense because it took place before he became vice president.[95] Nothing could be pinned on Grant.[96]

Rutherford B. Hayes (1877–81)

The election of 1876 was, according to many, one of the most corrupt elections in U.S. history. There were many questionable activities on the part of Rutherford B. Hayes' supporters. In the state of Florida, both parties engaged in so much fraud that historians have never settled who actually won.[97] Hayes did almost no campaigning, but attained the White House in exchange for ending Reconstruction and withdrawing federal troops from the South.[98] Once in office, Hayes rewarded many of his supporters with government jobs.[99]

James A. Garfield (1881)

Before becoming president, James A. Garfield was engaged to marry a woman named Lucretia, but at the same time was dating another girl, Rebecca Selleck. The two girls were friends, but when Lucretia found out about Garfield's behavior with Rebecca, she was angered. Garfield married Lucretia out of a sense of duty, not love.[100] Once married, he was not faithful to his wife. It was rumored that he visited a prostitute in New Orleans after being elected,[101] although both he and his wife denied it. He also strayed with a New York Times reporter, Mrs. Lucia Gilbert Calhoun. His wife knew about the relationship but forgave him.[102]

President Garfield was also implicated in the Credit Mobilier scandal but never formally charged.[103]

Chester Arthur (1881–85)

In 1881, when Garfield was shot, Chester A. Arthur became president but was not reelected. His wife died before he became president, and he put flowers next to her picture each day.[104] As a single man, he was pursued by women regularly, but did not seem interested. His widowed sister was his designated official hostess for formal events. It was said that he used government funds to cover his personal expenditures, but it did not result in any significant public outcry or scandal.

Grover Cleveland (1885–89; 1893–97)

Grover Cleveland was elected in 1885 and then again in 1893, serving two nonconsecutive terms as a Democratic president. He had a reputation for overindulging in food and drink. It was said to be a response to his pattern of working himself into exhaustion, relieved by an evening of heavy eating and beer drinking at a nearby tavern.[105]

Cleveland was very proper and sometimes unconfident with women of his own social class.[106] However, he did have an affair with Maria Crofts Halpin, during which she became pregnant.[107] An article in the Buffalo Evening Telegraph accused him of leading her to believe he was going to marry her, but instead forcing her to commit the baby to an orphan asylum and then forcing her to leave town.[108] In reality, Maria Halpin was a young widow who left her children in Pennsylvania and traveled to Buffalo where she found a job in a dry goods store. She dated Cleveland, and they had a baby boy.[109] When the child was very young, Halpin began to drink heavily and neglect her son. Cleveland arranged for her to be committed to Providence Asylum, an institution for mentally deranged people run by the Sisters of Charity, and the boy was sent to the Protestant Orphan Asylum.[110] After a short time, Cleveland persuaded Halpin to leave town and helped her get established in Niagara Falls.[111] Halpin was disappointed that Cleveland would not marry her, so she returned to Buffalo and kidnapped the boy. He was eventually returned and adopted by a respectable family in New York.[112]

After Cleveland became president, Halpin wrote to him and asked for support. He accepted responsibility for the child and contributed financially to both Halpin and her son for many years.[113] However, questions arose as to whether he was the real father. Halpin claimed Cleveland was the father, and he never denied it.[114] However, paternity was uncertain because Halpin had been intimate with many of Cleveland's friends. In the presidential campaign of 1884, the Democrats tried to use this against him, with the cry "Ma! Ma! Where's My Pa?"[115]

When Cleveland was forty-nine he married a twenty-seven-year-old lady named Frances Folsom, the daughter of his law partner.[116] There was some gossip that he was cruel to his wife, but nothing came of it.

William McKinley (1897–1901)

William McKinley was a Republican who was elected to the presidency in 1896 and 1900 but was shot and killed in 1901. The media tried to invent gossip about him, but they found that all they could say was that he smoked a lot. In 1871 he married Ida Saxton, and she suffered convulsions during child labor. This may have caused some brain damage and been the cause of her epilepsy.[117] Both of his daughters died as young children.[118] He served in office during the day but stayed at home in the evening to take care of his wife's needs.[119] He was often admired for the time and attention he devoted to her.[120] Despite this, some Democrats claimed he beat his wife and ran after women, none of which was true.[121]

Theodore Roosevelt (1901–09)

Theodore Roosevelt was president in the early years of the 20th Century. There were many scandals in his administration. It was alleged that his administration swindled the Creek Indians of their land and accepted bribes. There were also accusations over the amount of money Roosevelt paid for the Panama Canal.[122] He successfully sued a Michigan newspaper for libel after the editor charged that Roosevelt was drunk all the time. He won the suit, and the jury awarded him damages of six cents.

Woodrow Wilson (1913–21)

Woodrow Wilson was elected in 1912 and again in 1916 as a member of the Democratic Party. It was said that he was a womanizer. On a trip to Bermuda, Wilson met Mary Peck, wife of Thomas D. Peck. After she separated from her husband, Wilson and Peck met when they could, but the affair ended before he was elected governor of New Jersey in 1910. His wife discovered the affair, but forgave him.[123] Wilson's wife died less than a year and a half after becoming First Lady. Less than one year later Wilson started dating Edith Bolling Galt and eventually married her.[124] People were critical of Wilson, accusing him of poisoning his first wife and pushing her down the stairs. They then said he let her grave overgrow.

Warren Harding (1921–23)

Republican Warren Harding was elected in 1920. He is best known as America's worst president.[125] He was a very attractive man who was well dressed and had a reputation as being nice. Many women were attracted to him, and even though he was a married man, he sometimes pursued them. Harding had numerous affairs with a variety of women before and during his presidency. Secret Service agents assisted Harding in his assignations with numerous women while he was in office. His friends set up secret bank accounts for payments to women threatening to reveal their relationships with him. On occasion, his laxity in his personal behavior spilled over into the rest of his administration.[126]

When he got married, Harding's father-in-law did not like him. At that time, Harding was the editor of the local newspaper.[127] His wife took over the circulation department and ran it well, but people did not give her credit for her good business sense. Instead, they said that she hung around the newspaper office just to watch over Harding.

There may have been reason for her to do so. Harding had an affair with Carrie Fulton Phillips, wife of Jim Phillips. The affair went on for fifteen years, beginning in 1905.[128] The two couples often vacationed together. Carrie told many people about the affair and kept hundreds of his letters that detailed their relationship.[129] She started to demand that Harding leave his wife and marry her, but he would not. When her husband found out about the affair, he demanded a payoff from Harding to keep quiet. To get away, Carrie decided to move to Germany with her daughter for three years, but when she returned at the beginning of World War I, their affair began again. In 1920, Harding's campaign manager offered her $20,000, a trip around the world, and $2,000 a month to stay away.[130] Carrie and her husband stayed abroad until after Harding's death.

After Phillips left for Germany, Harding began a long-term affair with his secretary, Nan Briton. As a young child, Nan began writing to him when he ran for governor in 1910. She got pregnant, and Harding sent her money every month. During Harding's campaign for presidency and his time in office, he continued to meet her.[131] Their favorite place to meet was a closet reached through a secret passage from the Oval Office. Briton got pregnant and had a baby daughter who later wrote a book about the affair and her childhood. The book was published in 1927 and was called *The President's Daughter*.[132]

The Harding administration was the first since Prohibition began. Harding supported Prohibition when serving as a member of Congress, but enjoyed fine liquor, playing poker, and beautiful women. There was a lot of drinking in the White House during the Harding administration. Some said that much of the whiskey came from raids led by Prohibition agents.[133]

Some enemies of Harding said that he had African American blood, a statement that he denied.[134] Reports emerged before the convention that nominated him to be the presidential candidate indicating that Harding did not have only white ancestors and that he could be traced to a "West Indian Negro of French Stock."

Teapot Dome

One of the worst political scandals in the nation's history, referred to as Teapot Dome, occurred during Harding's administration. It revolved around the illegal leasing of oil reserves in Wyoming by Interior Secretary Albert B. Fall to wealthy oil men, who profited immensely.[135] The reserves are shaped like a teapot, thus giving the scandal its name.[136] The scandal may have led to Harding's impeachment had he not died in 1923.[137] The major participants involved in Teapot Dome are listed in Table 3.1.

Table 3.1: Primary Actors in the Teapot Dome Scandal

Albert Fall: Secretary of the Interior

Harry Ford Sinclair: President of the Sinclair Consolidated Oil Corporation

William Bryce Thompson: One of Sinclair's directors and largest shareholder; also a New York banker and treasurer of the Republican Party and a delegate to the convention

Warren G. Harding: President of the United States

Edward L. Doheny: Wealthy oil man and a Democrat

Colonel Robert W. Stewart: Chairman of Standard Oil of Indiana

Edwin C. Denby: Secretary of Navy under Harding

Thomas J. Walsh: Led the Senate Inquiry

Robert Stewart: Prominent wealthy oil man

Jake Hamon: Prominent wealthy oil man

The scandal began when the nation's most prominent oil men, Jake Hamon, Robert Stewart, Edward L. Doheny, and Harry Sinclair, sought a new U.S. president who would support their quest to drill for oil in parts of the West.[138] These areas included Naval Petroleum Reserve No. 1, a 38,969-acre field in Elk Hills, California; Naval Petroleum Reserve Number 2, consisting of 29,341 acres at Buena Vista, California; and Teapot Dome, about 45 miles north of Casper, Wyoming.[139] In 1912 and 1915, these three fuel reserves had been set aside as U.S. Naval Petroleum Reserves by the Taft and Wilson administrations to provide the navy with oil in case of war or a national emergency.[140] They were also important reserves because the demand for oil had increased markedly after both British and U.S. navies converted their fleets from coal to oil during World War I.[141] Additionally, automotive travel in the United States had increased dramatically.[142] As a result, there was a perceived shortage of oil.

With oil prices rising along with demand, the naval reserves could generate revenues of several billion dollars to those oil producers who could develop them.[143] But since the oil fields were seen as vital to the nation's defense,[144] to some, opening the fields to the public was an act of treason.[145] Nonetheless, Sinclair, Doheny, and Stewart were hopeful that a new administration would open these reserves to commercial drilling.[146] The men worked to get Harding elected to the presidency in 1920. Sinclair himself borrowed $3 million to pay for the Republican campaign.[147] Although much of the money contributed to Harding's campaign was legitimate campaign funds, much of it was so-called black money that was donated by the oil men and went unreported by the Republican Party.[148]

Since the men donated to Harding's campaign, they hoped he would return the favor and open the reserves to them. To do that, Harding needed to appoint an Interior secretary who was in favor of drilling.[149] The oil men supported Jake Hamon for the job. Sinclair and Hamon had privately agreed that if Hamon took over Interior, he would then lease the Teapot Dome reserves to Sinclair in return for one-third of the earnings.[150] But Hamon was shot by his girlfriend before Harding was elected, leaving Harding to choose another Interior secretary who would agree to the wishes of the oil men.[151] He chose Albert Bacon Fall, a Republican senator from New Mexico. Fall and Harding were close friends and had served in the Senate together, often playing poker late at night.[152] Fall had been one of Harding's early backers and had served as his principal campaign adviser.[153] As secretary of the Interior, Fall did not support the conservation movement in America. He wanted to open up Alaska's resources—primarily timber, oil, and coal—to development. He also wanted to open up the naval oil reserves at Teapot Dome and Elk Hills.[154]

Originally, Fall agreed to take the Interior post for only a year, at which point he would need another job. He knew that one potential employer was oil man Doheny. Fall understood that if he helped Doheny while secretary of the Interior, then he could secure a job when he quit. He also knew that the oil men could barely wait to get their hands on the naval reserves, which were strictly off-limits as long as the navy controlled them. In 1921, oil prices were the highest in history. If Fall managed to transfer the oil fields to the Department of the Interior, the oil crowd would be eager to bid for the drilling rights. However, there was one more obstacle they had to face. The oil reserves were under the control of the navy, so before the Interior Department could lease the fields to the oil men, they would have to be transferred to the Interior Department. The move had to be approved by the president on the recommendation of U.S. Attorney General Harry Daugherty.[155] Luckily for the oil men, Harding had appointed a naval secretary who supported the move. Edwin Denby, a lawyer, was a former Michigan congressman and U.S. Marine captain during World War I. Denby quickly proved amenable to just about anything Fall wanted.[156]

Fall moved on the naval reserves within just a few weeks after taking office. On April 1, 1921, he met with Naval Secretary Denby to discuss the transfer. Denby told Fall that oil wells adjacent to the reserves were tapping into or draining navy oil. He thought that the Department of the Interior would be better able to deal with the drainage issue than could the navy.[157] Harding indicated he approved of putting the oil reserves under control of the Interior Department. Fall then drafted an executive order for the president to sign that authorized the transfer and drew up a cover letter to be signed by Denby requesting the change.[158] With these documents, Fall had complete authority to lease the reserves.[159]

Six weeks after Harding signed the transfer order, Fall awarded Doheny the lease for the offset wells.[160] At first, Doheny complained that the royalties he had to pay on the oil taken from the offset wells at Elk Hills were too high. So Fall offered to give him additional leases on the Elk Hills reserves and preferential leases on any additional California naval reserves. In other words, the entire California naval oil reserves, an estimated 300 million barrels of oil, was Doheny's.[161]

Fall divided up the reserves into two fairly equal parcels, each containing millions of barrels of oil. Doheny was given the California reserves, and Sinclair was given Teapot Dome.[162] But another oil field adjacent to Teapot Dome, Salt Creek, was at the time the richest oil field in the world.[163] Salt Creek was not a naval reserve but was owned by the federal government, which meant that Fall could decide who could mine it. Sinclair and Stewart hatched a plan by which Sinclair would gain Teapot Dome and Stewart would take over Salt Creek and then build a pipeline linking the fields to a refinery owned by Standard Oil of Indiana.[164]

In addition to Salt Creek, the oil men also wanted access to a reserve called Four Corners. Because this reserve was situated on the Navajo reservation, any outsiders who wanted to drill there had to get the approval from the tribal council and provide the Navajos with a share in the royalties. Fall agreed to intercede on the behalf of the oil companies and designate millions of acres of Navajo reservation land as public lands. This meant that the oil companies had the right to drill there. It also meant that royalties from any drilling had to be shared with the states where the drilling took place, including New Mexico and Arizona, as well as the federal government.[165]

Fall also convinced Harding to develop vast tracts of Alaskan wilderness. He sent a team of geologists to Alaska to study its oil potential. He subsequently sent along their findings to his future boss, Doheny, before making them public, so that the Californian could have the first crack at the Alaskan fields.[166]

Throughout this time, Fall received secret payments as reciprocity for the Teapot Dome contract from Doheny and Sinclair. He spent the money to improve his ranch.

The investigation into possible illegalities with the leasing of the oil reserves began in 1922.[167] On April 28, Wisconsin Senator Robert "Fighting Bob" M. La Follette introduced a resolution in the Senate calling for an investigation, and the Senate unanimously passed it the following day.[168] Fall wrote a report on June 7, 1922, in which he justified the Teapot lease as necessary to eliminate drainage. He claimed to have repeatedly informed President Harding and members of the Cabinet of his activities leading up to the leases. Harding then sent the report to the Senate, with a statement attached in which he agreed that the naval reserve plan "was submitted to me prior to the adoption thereof, and the policy decided upon and the subsequent acts have at all times had my entire approval." It was in this statement that Harding linked his name to the Teapot Dome scandal.[169]

Fall resigned from the Cabinet in January 1923, effective March 4.[170] But before leaving Washington, he gave Sinclair a five-year renewable contract to buy all the oil from the Teapot Dome fields that had originally been given to the U.S. Shipping Board. This amounted to close to two million barrels of oil a year.[171]

The hearings began on Monday, October 23, 1923, by the Senate Committee on Public Lands and Surveys.[172] The first witness was Fall, followed by Denby, Sinclair, and Doheny. The committee members wanted to know whether money given to Fall to improve his ranch was a bribe or a loan. They also questioned Sinclair's role in Harding's election into the presidency and if the million dollars raised was followed by an understanding that Fall was to be made secretary of the Interior.[173] During the hearings, there were letters presented that were written by Harding and Fall that clearly indicated the entire Cabinet had conferred and approved the leases. Experts explained how the reserves had been transferred from the Navy Department to Interior, the fallacy of the leakage arguments, how Fall had given the leases out secretly and without competitive bids to Sinclair and Doheny, and how the oil men had rewarded him.[174] Many of the people scheduled to testify in front of the committee got ill. Others refused to answer questions. When they did answer, the responders seemed to ramble on endlessly, were difficult to follow and sometimes confusing.[175]

The new president, Calvin Coolidge, did his best to distance himself from the hearings. He believed that if there had been any crime committed concerning the naval leases, it should be prosecuted. Further, if there had been any property of the United States illegally transferred or leased, it should be recovered.[176] Coolidge decided to turn over the investigation to two special counsels, the former Democratic Ohio Senator Atlee Pomerene and Republican Owen J. Roberts.

On July 1, 1924, former Secretary Fall, Sinclair, Doheny, and Doheny Jr. were criminally indicted for fraud.[177] On September 28, 1926, the U.S. Circuit Court of Appeals declared the Teapot Dome lease invalid because it was negotiated and executed under fraudulent circumstances. This meant that after four years, the U.S. Naval Reserves were once again property of the U.S. government.[178] Other outcomes are provided in Table 3.2.

Table 3.2: Outcomes of the Teapot Dome Scandal

Stewart: Was acquitted on contempt charges arising from his refusal to answer questions. He never went to prison, but was ousted as chairman of Standard Oil of Indiana.

Sinclair: Went to prison and served almost seven months for contempt of the U.S. Senate.

Fall: Was the first Cabinet member in U.S. history ever to be convicted of a felony. He was sentenced to a year in prison and ordered to pay a $100,000 fine. Fall served nine months and one day, and died on November 30, 1944.

Doheny: Was acquitted on charges of bribery. He lived another five years and died on September 8, 1935.

Source: McCartney 2008.

As a result of the events of Teapot Dome, Congress passed the Leasing Law of 1920. The new law altered the way public lands were leased for developing natural resources such as coal, oil, and gas. Under the law, the right to mine or process resources on federal land is secured for ten-year periods by competitive bidding.

Harding's health was failing in the spring of 1923, so he and his wife went to Alaska to relax. During the trip, he collapsed, went into a coma, and died on August 2. He was three months short of his fifty-eighth birthday. Mrs. Harding did not allow an autopsy on her husband. Some doctors signed a statement saying it was a cerebral hemorrhage. A book called *The Strange Death of President Harding* came out in 1931 that claimed that Mrs. Harding poisoned him. Other rumors said that he committed suicide over Teapot Dome.

There are many Harding supporters and biographers who argue that the president knew nothing of the leases until after the fact, and that he was not part of it in any way.[179] There is no evidence that Harding financially profited from Teapot Dome. However, others acknowledge that had he lived, he more than likely would have been impeached, despite there being no evidence that he was aware of the leases or financially profited.

Calvin Coolidge (1923–29)

Calvin Coolidge was elected in 1924 to the presidency as a Republican and served only one term. During his administration there were no scandals, except once when his wife went for a short hike with a Secret Service agent. They were gone all day, and there was some innuendo that they had a romantic tryst. However, Grace Coolidge was known to be honest and faithful, so no one paid it much attention. It was noted that Coolidge himself symbolized purity in government.[180]

Franklin Delano Roosevelt (1933–45)

As president, Franklin Roosevelt ran an informal White House, but that did not make him immune from scandal. It was said he had numerous affairs, one of which was with his wife Eleanor's social secretary, Lucy Page Mercer.[181] He was infatuated with Mercer,[182] but Eleanor found out and stopped it.[183] Later, Lucy was a frequent guest at the White House when Eleanor was away.[184] Lucy was also at Warm Springs, Georgia, when Roosevelt died, but she was quickly sent away when Eleanor showed up.[185]

FDR's private secretary was Marguerite (Missy) LeHand,[186] who helped him, traveled with him, and entertained with him when Eleanor was out of the country. There is some thought that he had a sexual relationship with her, too.[187] He was also linked to Crown Princess Martha of Norway, but nothing has been substantiated.[188]

There was also scandal revolving around Eleanor Roosevelt. It was said that she had earned more than $3 million in fees for her work as a radio commentator, lecturer, and newspaper columnist. Some concerns were raised about her tax returns, but no one could find anything wrong.[189] It was also said that she had an affair with Associated Press reporter Lorena Hickok, who lived in the White House with her.[190] She was close friends with lesbians Nancy Cook and Marion Dickerman.[191] Some thought that she had an affair with her bodyguard, Earl Miller, but others say it was not sexual.[192]

Roosevelt's son, James, was said to have used his father's name and influence to develop a lucrative insurance business. He used his famous name to attract corporate clients to his business, but there was no proof that he did that.[193]

Harry Truman (1945–53)

Harry Truman became president in 1945 when FDR died, then was elected in 1948 as a Democrat. His conduct as a faithful husband was never questioned. However, as with other presidents, many in the administration engaged in scandalous behavior. For example, Truman's attorney general, J. Howard McGrath, was fired after he tried to dismiss a special investigator appointed to inquire into possible improprieties at the Justice Department.[194] Truman's appointments secretary, Matthew J. Connelly was indicted and convicted in 1956.[195] Connelly accepted gifts from Irvin Sachs in exchange for pressuring the IRS and the Justice Department not to investigate him and to limit his sentence. Sachs was later found guilty of evading income tax and fined $40,000. Connelly was convicted of conspiracy to defraud the government and commit bribery and perjury, knowingly making false statements, and violating the Internal Revenue Code. He was sentenced to two years in prison. After serving only six months, he was pardoned by President John F. Kennedy in 1962.[196]

Dwight Eisenhower (1953–61)

Dwight Eisenhower, a Republican, was elected in 1952 and again in 1956. Before he became president, during World War II, it was alleged that had an affair with a British WAC, a young Irish divorcee named Kay Summersby.[197] Summersby was a former fashion model in Paris.[198] She was Eisenhower's driver while he was in London and later one of his secretaries while he was commanding general of the U.S. forces in Europe. Although they were often seen and photographed together in public,[199] they were seldom alone together.[200] She often joined him for dinner and played bridge with other couples.[201] She accompanied him to meetings,[202] joined him on a five-day vacation in Cannes,[203] went horseback riding with him, and generally just relaxed with him.[204] She wrote that they had fallen in love[205] and that they began a romance that included everything but sex[206] because he was unable to perform.[207] Kay eventually wrote two books about their alleged affair: *Eisenhower was my Boss*[208] and *Past Forgetting: My Love Affair with Dwight D. Eisenhower.*[209]

Eisenhower acknowledged to his wife, Mamie, that Kay was often part of his daily routine, but denied that anything happened between them.[210] Not even Kay ever claimed they had a genuine love affair.[211] There is no evidence they ever consummated a physical relationship.[212] Even all of his advisers, who were around him most of the time, denied the allegations.[213] However, there is no doubt that he was extremely fond of Kay and valued her company.[214]

John Fitzgerald Kennedy (1961–63)

John Kennedy, a Democrat, was elected to the presidency in 1961 and served until his assassination in 1963. During his time in the White House, he had numerous extramarital affairs.[215] He was also sick and taking many prescription and nonprescription drugs.[216] He allegedly had affairs with Inga Arvad,[217] a stripper named Tempest Storm and a stripper Blaze Starr, numerous call girls, Joan Lundberg, Pamela Turnure, Florence Prichett Smith (the wife of the U.S. ambassador to Cuba), Priscilla Wier (his secretary), Jill Cowan (another secretary), Judith Campbell Exner (who had ties to organized crime boss Sam Giancana of Chicago),[218] Mary Pinchot Meyer (the sister-in-law of *Washington Post* executive editor Ben Bradlee, who was said to introduce JFK to LSD and marijuana),[219] Jayne Mansfield,[220] Angie Dickinson,[221] and Marilyn Monroe.[222] There were accusations that he was married before he married Jackie Bouvier, but he always denied it. There were also allegations that he had links to organized crime, some of which were based on his relationship with Judith Exner, others based on his father's alleged links to organized crime.

Kennedy was reckless and irresponsible in his sexual exploits while in office. He was increasingly worried about disclosures detailing his much-rumored womanizing. Almost everyone in the press corps knew about or at least suspected his philandering, but the mainstream press resisted publishing the stories for the general public.[223] Thus, most people were unaware of his numerous affairs and they did not become scandalous.

Lyndon Baines Johnson (1963–69)

Democrat Lyndon Johnson became president in 1963 when Kennedy was assassinated, and was then reelected in 1964. Like Kennedy, Johnson also had numerous sexual relationships outside of his marriage.[224] He had affairs with Alice Glass, the common-law wife of Texas millionaire Charles Marsh,[225] and Madeleine Brown, with whom he had a son.[226] Johnson kissed every lady, danced with every lady, and was a woman's man.[227]

In 1964, questions were raised about the source of the Johnson family wealth, which was very large. He was born poor and served his entire life in public office. But his wife, Lady Bird, had a radio-TV station that was the only television station in the area, so she had a total monopoly in the market.[228] Their radio and television properties were successful when he became vice president.[229] It is alleged that he used the Federal Communications Commission (FCC) to assure his financial success in his broadcast stations. After he left the White House in 1972, the FCC ruled against owning both a television and a cable company in the same market, and he was forced to sell the station.[230]

Conclusion

American scandals have been strikingly similar to one another across the years. Yet in a few periods of our history, the politics of scandal have come to play a dominant role in public life.[231] From this chapter, it is easy to see that most U.S. presidents have been alleged to have been involved in some form of scandal. Some, like the Teapot Dome scandal, have been more serious and have had more intense, long-term results. Other allegations, such as those lodged against President McKinley or President Coolidge, were accepted then and now to be trivial or even false. In any event, the scandals listed here show clearly that political scandals in the United States are not new and have been around since our Founding Fathers were our political leaders.

Review Questions

1. Are political scandals new to government?
2. Describe some early political scandals.
3. What was the Credit Mobilier scandal and why was it important?
4. Describe the Teapot Dome scandal and its effects.

Special Terms

Credit Mobilier
Teapot Dome

Discussion Questions

1. How do ethics and mores affect scandals over time? Would some of the early political scandals be considered a scandal today?
2. How do behaviors we consider "scandalous" change over time?
3. Which was worse: Teapot Dome or Credit Mobilier?
4. Is it important to study early political scandals?
5. Why did the media not report on President Kennedy's many relationships?

Chapter 4

Nixon Scandals and Watergate

Introduction

President Richard Nixon was involved with one of the most well-known and infamous political scandals in American history. Called Watergate after the office complex where the original criminal acts occurred, the scandal resulted in the only resignation of a U.S. president, who had just two years earlier won the Electoral College votes from forty-nine of fifty states.[1] Throughout the scandal, Nixon denied having any involvement with the alleged criminal activities, and then denied covering up the scandal. It is often the case that what is done after an alleged offense creates more culpability than the act itself,[2] which seemed to happen here.

This chapter describes the scandals that happened during the Nixon administration, beginning with some earlier, small scandals, through the resignation of Nixon's vice president, and then ending with the Watergate scandal. This analysis will cover the criminal break-in of the Democratic headquarters in the Watergate complex and the ensuing cover-up by Nixon and his associates. The scandal had some short- and long-term impacts on the actors involved, on the media, on public opinion, and on the political process as a whole, which are discussed.

Liu and Arab Gifts

There were many scandals that impacted the Nixon administration. One involved allegations that he had an affair with Marianna Liu while serving in Hong Kong. This was especially interesting because it was thought that Liu was a Chinese spy.[3] Nixon also allegedly accepted $1 million in jewelry from Arab leaders in violation of federal law that prohibits accepting gifts valued at $50 or more.[4] Later in his administration, allegations were made that Nixon did not pay his taxes. The Internal Revenue Service (IRS) audited his income tax returns and found that most of his deductions were not justified. The IRS assessed him nearly half a million dollars in taxes and interest.

Spiro Agnew

Spiro Agnew was governor of Maryland from 1967–69 and then served as vice president from 1969–73 under Nixon. He often criticized the press and the Vietnam War protesters. Even as he was running for reelection, he was being investigated for bribery, conspiracy, tax evasion, taking kickbacks from milk producers, and other charges.[5] It was alleged that from the time he was county executive in 1966 through his time as governor and even as vice president he was taking bribes.[6] He also failed to pay income tax on his kickbacks.[7]

Agnew was born in Baltimore, the son of Greek immigrants. He fought in World War II and Korea, then married and settled in Baltimore. He attended law school at night to become an attorney, but struggled to get by. He defended insurance companies and other small civil actions. In his forties he started to volunteer on political campaigns. This earned him a spot on the zoning board, and later he became the county executive. Two years later, in 1966, when the Republican Party did not have a candidate for governor, Agnew threw his hat into the ring and won.[8] He was only the fifth Republican governor in Maryland history. He served twenty months as governor of Maryland.

Agnew made a name for himself in 1967 when rioting broke out in the suburbs of Baltimore. He called black leaders into his office and berated them on live television. This caught Nixon's attention, and when Nixon won the Republican presidential nomination, he chose Agnew as his running mate. Agnew served as vice president under Nixon, rising from an unknown in only six years. He also made enemies along the way. He contributed to an increasingly bitter political climate in the country at the time[9] by calling protesters dissident and destructive elements.[10]

In February 1973, his attorney, George White, called Agnew and told him that two men had gone to him threatening to turn Agnew over to the U.S. Attorney for Maryland if Agnew did not get them a presidential pardon for related crimes. Lester Metz, a professional engineer, and Jerome Wolff, a former chairman of the State Roads Commission under Agnew, were former associates when he was governor of Maryland. Metz and Wolff were prepared to say that Agnew took bribes and kickbacks in return for giving contractors and engineers state development jobs.[11]

Wolff and Metz reached a plea agreement that would incriminate Agnew. Wolff told the story that he had donated money to and worked on several of Agnew's political campaigns. He said Agnew promised him a job when he got elected, and Wolff became the chairman of the State Roads Commission. Soon after Wolff started, a man by the name of Bud Hammerman approached him and said that he was an old friend of Agnew. Hammerman said that he needed the names of contractors who were up for state jobs so he could contact them and ask them for money even though it was not an election year. For the next eighteen to twenty months Wolff and Hammerman worked together, splitting their share of the kickbacks, taking 25 percent each and giving 50 percent to Agnew.

Wolff was able to back all of his testimony up by giving the prosecutors little notebooks in which he kept notes. He had kept every single notebook from the years Agnew was governor of Maryland.

Attorney General Elliott Richardson told them it was the strongest kickback case he had ever seen. Agnew did not think the country could have two scandals simultaneously, as Watergate was also being investigated, so although he professed his innocence, he considered turning himself in to the House of Representatives so they could hold impeachment hearings against him. This way, if they found him guilty, he would not have been able to be indicted in criminal courts. Instead, he decided to resign. On October 10, 1973, one of his aides delivered his resignation letter to secretary of State Henry Kissinger[12] while Agnew was in court pleading no contest to one count of tax evasion for 1967 and falsifying his tax returns by not reporting the bribes.[13] The courts also said he willfully evaded paying $13,551.41 in taxes and sentenced him to three years' probation and a $10,000 fine.[14]

Later, the citizens of Maryland sued Agnew. In 1983, ten years after his resignation, the people of Maryland won their case and Agnew was forced to pay back $368,482 to cover kick backs and interest on the $87,500 he took while he was county executive, governor, and vice president. He became the first sitting vice president to resign from office for personal scandal.

Watergate

A. Introduction

Watergate is a complex political scandal that involved many people and continued for a long time. Table 4.1 indicates only some of the major actors in the scandal. There were many others involved in some fashion. Table 4.2 presents a brief timeline. It can be broken down into two parts. The first part of Watergate, the criminal offenses and abuse of power by executive-level personnel in the White House, began during Nixon's first term in office. This included illegal campaign contributions, money laundering, the break-in of the Democratic headquarters and a psychiatrist's office, political spying and sabotage on opponents, illegal wiretaps, and the use of the IRS to harass enemies.[15] The second part of the scandal surrounded Nixon's attempts to cover up the criminal acts and his involvement with them. These activities included hiding and destroying evidence, payoffs from a secret slush fund (especially to keep people from testifying against Nixon), suborning perjury, and attempts to halt an FBI investigation.[16] These activities eventually led to a grand jury naming Nixon an "unindicted co-conspirator" for his involvement in possible criminal acts. After an investigation and televised hearings, the House Judiciary Committee voted to approve three articles of impeachment against Nixon, who chose to resign rather than face impeachment. In the end, Nixon became the only popularly elected president to resign his office rather than face a great likelihood of being impeached and removed from office.[17] A month later, his successor in office, Gerald Ford, granted him a full pardon.[18]

Table 4.1: Selected Actors in the Watergate Scandal

Alexander Butterfield: Deputy to Haldeman 1969–73

Charles Colson: Member of Plumbers and Nixon's own special counsel 1970–73

Archibald Cox: First special prosecutor

John W. Dean III: White House counsel 1970–73

John D. Ehrlichman: Chief Domestic Policy adviser 1969–73; head of Plumbers

Sam Ervin: Democratic senator from North Carolina; chairman, Senate Watergate Committee

Gerald Ford: House Republican minority leader; became vice president

L. Patrick Gray III: Acting director of FBI 1972–73

Alexander Haig: White House Chief of Staff 1973–74

H. R. (Bob) Haldeman: White House Chief of Staff 1969–73: controlled access to the president

E. Howard Hunt: Ex-CIA officer; White House consultant; member of Plumbers; involved in break-in of Ellsberg's psychiatrist's office and DNC

Leon Jaworski: Second special prosecutor

Richard G. Kleindienst: Attorney General 1972–73

G. Gordon Liddy: Ex-FBI agent; general counsel for the Committee to Reelect the President (CREEP); involved in break-in of Ellsberg's psychiatrist's office; member of Plumbers

James W. McCord Jr.: CIA security officer; arrested for Watergate break-in

John N. Mitchell: Attorney General 1969–72; director of CREEP

Richard M. Nixon: President of the United States, 1969–74

Lawrence O'Brien: Chairman of Democratic National Committee

Elliot L. Richardson: Attorney General of the United States 1973

Peter Rodino Jr.: Democratic congressman from New Jersey; chairman, House Judiciary Committee

Donald Segretti: White House attorney; responsible for campaign "dirty tricks"

John Sirica: Chief Judge, District Court for the District of Columbia

Rose Mary Woods: President Nixon's secretary

Table 4.2: Major Events in the Watergate Scandal

June 1971: Publication of the Pentagon Papers in the *NY Times*

September 3, 1971: Break-in of Ellsberg's psychiatrist office

December 1971: CREEP is formed

June 17, 1972: Liddy, Hunt, and Cubans break into the DNC and are arrested

June 20, 1972: In a phone call, Nixon and his campaign manager, John Mitchell, discuss the arrests; also, Nixon meets with Haldeman to discuss the arrests; The tape of this conversation was later erased to create an 18.5 minute gap

May 1972: J. Edgar Hoover dies; replaced with L. Patrick Gray

September 15, 1972: Hunt, Liddy, and five burglars are indicted on federal charges

November 1972: Nixon reelected as president

January 8–30, 1973: Trial of seven men indicted for the Watergate burglary; all plead guilty except Liddy and McCord, both of whom are found guilty

February 7, 1973: Senate votes 70–0 to set up a committee under Sam Ervin to investigate irregularities during the presidential campaign

March 23, 1973: Judge Sirica hands down sentences on Watergate Seven

April 27, 1973: L. Patrick Gray resigns

April 30, 1973: Nixon appears on TV and admits there was a cover-up and takes responsibility for the break-in; accepts the resignations of Haldeman, Kleindienst, and Ehrlichman; and announces Dean's dismissal

May 17, 1973: The Senate Watergate Committee begins its nationally televised hearings

May 18, 1973: Archibald Cox is named special prosecutor

June 25–29, 1973: Dean testifies in front of the Watergate Committee and implicates the president

July 16, 1973: Butterfield tells the committee that Nixon had a taping system

July 23, 1973: Cox subpoenas the tapes of nine presidential conversations

July 25, 1973: Nixon refuses to turn over the tapes

August 29, 1973: Judge Sirica rules that the president must turn over the tapes

October 10, 1973: Agnew resigns; is replaced by Ford

October 12, 1973: The U.S. Court of Appeals upholds Judge Sirica's order that the tapes be surrendered

October 20, 1973: Saturday night massacre

November 1, 1973: Leon Jaworski is named special prosecutor

March 1, 1974: The grand jury indicts Haldeman, Ehrlichman, Mitchell, Mardian, Colson, and others in the cover-up; Nixon is named an unindicted co-conspirator by the grand jury

April 11, 1974: The Judiciary Committee subpoenas 42 tapes

April 30, 1974: Transcripts of the tapes are released

July 24, 1974: The Supreme Court rules 8–0 that the president must turn over the 64 tapes sought by Jaworski

July 27, 1974: The House Judiciary Committee passes first article of impeachment, 27–11, charging the president with obstruction of justice in attempting to coverup Watergate

July 29, 1974: The second article of impeachment passes

July 30, 1974: Third and final articles of impeachment pass

August 5, 1974: The White House releases transcripts of the three conversations of June 23, 1972

August 8, 1974: Nixon announces his resignation in a televised address

August 9, 1974: Nixon's resignation becomes effective and Ford becomes president

September 8, 1974: Ford grants Nixon a full and absolute pardon

B. Nixon's Background

Before Watergate, Nixon had a long and extensive political career. He was elected to the House of Representatives in 1946 and again in 1948.[19] While serving in the House, he sat on the Committee on Un-American Activities, which made him nationally known.[20] He was elected to serve in the Senate in 1950,[21] where he continued to make a name for himself fighting communists, especially Alger Hiss.[22] The nation's voters chose Nixon to serve as the country's vice president alongside Eisenhower in 1952.[23] During that campaign, Nixon faced a personal attack, the "fund crisis," where he was accused of using a slush fund set up by corporate benefactor of $18,000 for his own personal use.[24] He addressed the allegations in a televised speech and explained that the fund was not secret and that he only used the money only for political expenses such as traveling. At the end of the speech, with his voice cracking, Nixon described how his family did accept the gift of a small cocker spaniel that his six-year-old daughter Tricia named Checkers.[25] In the end, Nixon was able to quell the fears that people had about the secret account, and he became the second youngest vice president in American history.

Nixon had a much more active role in diplomatic and foreign policy than had previous vice presidents, and he was the first vice president to travel extensively abroad.[26] As a result, he ran successfully for reelection in 1956. In 1960, he ran for the presidency but failed when he was defeated by John Kennedy by only 112,000 votes.[27] After leaving national politics, Nixon ran for governor of California in 1962 and lost.[28]

One of the major issues in the country was Vietnam. The president at the time, Lyndon Johnson, pursued the war, making him increasingly unpopular with the electorate, many of whom were becoming dismayed at the mounting casualty list. The number of American soldiers in Vietnam had grown from 184,000 at the end of 1965 to 385,000 by end of 1966. When Johnson decided not to run again for the presidency in 1968, Nixon seized the opportunity.[29] Throughout his campaign, he told voters that he could get the United States out of Vietnam peacefully.[30] In the end, he was elected by a margin of less than 1 percent of the votes cast. He received 43.4 percent of the votes, while 42.7 percent went to the Democratic nominee, Hubert Humphrey, and 13.5 percent being cast for the third-party candidate George Wallace.[31] Nixon was inaugurated on Monday, January 20, 1969.

C. Presidency

Once president, Nixon immediately created a Cabinet that included some powerful and experienced staff members.[32] The Chief of Staff position was filled by Bob Haldeman.[33] Haldeman was the president's closest adviser and was almost obsessed with pleasing the president. Haldeman then recruited John Ehrlichman to serve as Domestic Affairs adviser. Ehrlichman also became a confidant of the president and of Haldeman. John Dean was brought in to serve as counsel to the president, and the attorney general's position was filled by John Mitchell, later replaced by Kleindienst.

Nixon had to deal with the Vietnam issue almost immediately on taking office. During the campaign, he had promised the voters he would bring the soldiers home. To do that, he first had to build up the South Vietnamese, both militarily and politically, so they could defend themselves. Nixon believed that a stronger South Vietnam would compel the North to negotiate more seriously, and the United States could withdraw. Nixon agreed to a plan whereby the United States would secretly begin bombing the supply routes to North Vietnam in order to block supplies going there. Thus, as it turns out, while the United States was in peace talks with the North Vietnamese, the military were also bombing them.[34]

To keep it a secret, Nixon did not inform Congress of the bombing. Congressional members found out when the *New York Times* published the information on May 9, 1969, on the front page.[35] Nixon was angry that the bombing was made public, and he wanted to know who leaked the information to the press. He ordered the FBI to place wiretaps on the telephones of members of the National Security Council, the White House, the State Department, the Department of Defense, the Pentagon, and several newspaper reporters.[36] At that time, wiretaps had been declared illegal by the Supreme Court when placed without a court order, except in cases of national security.[37] The attorney general at the time, John Mitchell, supported Nixon, and both of them claimed the wiretaps were in the interest of national security.

On April 30, 1970, Nixon went on television and told Americans of his decision to invade Cambodia and destroy North Vietnam and admitted to secretly bombing them for fourteen months. This revelation angered many Americans. There were multiple protests, especially in colleges and universities. There were hundreds of takeovers of buildings, riots, and fires, all in an effort to protest Nixon's policies and stop any continued bombings.[38] Nixon was convinced that the protests were backed by the communists. To investigate that idea, the CIA was given power to investigate campus unrest because a possible "foreign enemy" was involved. In the end, they found no enemies and no evidence of financial support by communists to protestors.

One college protest at Kent State University in Ohio ended when eight national guardsmen opened fire on students, killing or injuring thirteen of them. Afterward, members of seven intelligence agencies met to discuss the administration's policy on student protests and domestic security concerns. The committee was chaired by J. Edgar Hoover, then head of the FBI. The committee came up with a plan to use methods to get more information on "left wingers."

The plan was put together by Charles Huston, a White House staffer.[39] Among other things, the plan recommended:

1. Monitoring of communications of U.S. citizens using international facilities;
2. Intensifying coverage of individuals and groups in the United States who posed a major threat to international security by means of electronic surveillance;
3. Modifying restrictions to permit the use of surreptitious entry (breaking and entering) against urgent security targets;
4. Expanding surveillance on violence-prone campuses and student-related groups;
5. Increasing CIA coverage of American students (and others) traveling abroad.

The plan did not have the support of all of the committee members. In fact, Hoover and Mitchell wanted nothing to do with it, claiming that much of it was clearly illegal.[40] Some said the plan plainly ignored the Constitution.[41] Even though Nixon was warned that parts of the plan were illegal, it was nonetheless implemented and in effect for five days.[42] After that short period, the president withdrew his official support, but it may have continued unofficially. It appears as if Nixon wanted to crush his enemies, including the media, intellectuals, elites, political opponents, hippies, and any others who protested the war and his policies.[43]

D. Reelection

Between 1970 and 1972, the last two years of Nixon's first term in office, his popularity was decreasing. Demonstrations against the war continued. He was facing reelection with his opinion polls showing an all-time low. To get him reelected, the Citizen's Committee for the Reelection of the President (CREEP) was secretly formed.[44] Some of its members included those people listed in Table 4.3. CREEP had no ties to the Republican National Committee. Instead, many members were also administration officials who reported to the White House. All decisions made by CREEP had to be cleared by Mitchell, the attorney general.

Table 4.3: Members of CREEP

E. Howard Hunt: Former CIA agent

Egil Krogh Jr.

Fred LaRue: Chief deputy to Mitchell

G. Gordon Liddy: Finance counsel for CREEP; former FBI agent

Jeb Stuart Magruder: Deputy director of CREEP

Robert Mardian

James McCord: Head of security for CREEP; a former FBI agent and CIA agent

John Mitchell: Attorney General who resigned to be director of CREEP

Hugh Sloan Jr.: Treasurer of CREEP

Maurice Stans: Had been Secretary of Commerce; became chair of Finance Committee of CREEP

During Nixon's reelection bid, there were major changes in the election laws. The old law, called the Corrupt Practices Act of 1925, forced contributions to nominated candidates to be identified, but at the point in the campaign where someone was not formally nominated for president yet was a front-runner, any political contributions could remain anonymous. This meant that fundraising and spending for candidates in primaries escaped any kind of reporting.[45] In addition, a political donor could remain anonymous regardless of the size of the contribution.

A new law was passed, the Federal Election Campaign Act of 1972, that put limits on a candidate's expenditures of personal funds in a campaign. Donors were limited to $50,000 for president or vice president; $35,000 for senator; $25,000 for representative. The new law also required detailed accounts of all contributions and expenditures with receipts. All contributions in excess of $10 had to be listed with the contributor's name, address, occupation, and place of business. Anonymous contributions were now illegal.[46] The new laws were intended to limit the wealthy from buying their way into office.

The old law was set to expire on March 10, 1972. But the new law became effective sixty days after the president's signature, which was on April 7, 1972. So there was a period of twenty-seven days with no law governing campaign funds. After April 7, campaign contributions and expenditures would have to be declared and contributors identified.[47]

Nixon and CREEP used the campaign finance laws to their advantage. They had $1.6 million left over from the 1968 campaign,[48] and they continued to collect new funds from private citizens and corporations.[49] The president had Haldeman skim $350,000 off the top of the contributions and hold it in a private safe-deposit box in the White House for "emergencies."[50] They used the money to create a "slush fund" controlled by Haldeman that was used to pay for dirty tricks.[51] It was alleged that CREEP received illegal campaign contributions from Howard Hughes that went into the secret fund.[52] There was no need to report any money that was donated to CREEP before April 7. This money was simply added to the slush fund with no record made.[53] By the April 7 deadline,

Nixon had raised over $20 million.[54] The campaign coffers were so overflowing with dirty funds that there was hush money in abundance.[55]

About that time, Daniel Ellsberg, a Pentagon analyst who was opposed to the war,[56] stole and published the "History of the United States Decision-Making Process in Vietnam," better known as the Pentagon Papers. The top-secret report was an in-depth history of American involvement in Southeast Asia. The report revealed how much the administration had lied to the public about military and political actions in these areas.[57] Portions of the Pentagon Papers were published in the *New York Times* on June 12–14, 1971.[58]

The White House was once again outraged and responded by obtaining a court order restraining the *New York Times* or any other newspapers from publishing any further portions of the Pentagon Papers. Although some argued that such a policy would be considered censorship, the White House defended their stand by arguing that halting any further publication was in the interest of national defense.[59] The administration appealed its case to the U.S. Supreme Court in *United States v. New York Times* (403 U.S. 713 (1971)). The Court said that the *New York Times* broke no law by publishing the report, and that publishing the papers did not pose a direct and immediate threat to national security.[60] This was a major victory for the press, and a major loss for Nixon.

As before, Nixon was eager to learn who leaked the information to Ellsberg. Less than a week after the Pentagon Papers were published,[61] Nixon created a group later nicknamed the Plumbers, who were asked to fix the leaks of information from the White House.[62] The Plumbers, who reported to Ehrlichman, included E. Howard Hunt, G. Gordon Liddy, and James McCord. They were headed by Egil Krogh Jr.

In essence, Nixon had set up, without statutory or congressional oversight, a secret police squad in the Plumbers.[63] Their first job was to find the source of the leaked Pentagon Papers. They decided to break into the office of Daniel Ellsberg's psychiatrist, Dr. Lewis Fielding, on September 1, 1971 to find out more about Ellsberg, in particular any damaging personal information they could use to discredit him.[64] The burglary was carried out by Hunt, Liddy, and others. Once in the office, they found only an empty file.[65]

E. Break-In

The Republicans were convinced that the Democrats had some dirty tricks planned for the 1972 presidential campaign.[66] To get information on their plans, members of CREEP decided to break into the Watergate office of Larry O'Brien, head of the Democratic National Committee (DNC), and put a bug on his telephone.[67] They first tried to break in on Friday, May 26 and again on

Saturday, May 27 but failed.[68] On Sunday, May 28, they succeeded and entered the office to put wiretaps on three phones. It was later discovered that the tap on O'Brien's phone did not work, so the burglars decided to go back one more time.[69] They tried for the fourth time on June 17, 1972.

That night, a security guard in the Watergate Complex found that a door leading to the parking garage had been taped open. He removed the tape and did not think much of it. Fifteen minutes later, he came back and found the door taped open again.[70] This time, he called the police. Three officers responded in an unmarked car and found that the suite of the DNC was open. On entering, they found five unarmed men dressed in business suits, wearing surgical gloves and carrying lock picks, teargas guns, bugging equipment, cameras, and film. Each man was also carrying a bundle of consecutively numbered $100 bills.[71]

The police arrested five men for breaking and entering.[72] They also arrested two other men in the Howard Johnson's hotel across the street who had been directing the burglars.[73] All of the men were informed of their rights and given the option of calling a lawyer, but they declined. They were charged with felonious burglary and possession of implements of crime (burglary tools). Each had given aliases to the police, but their true names were soon discovered.

It was determined that the leader of the team was James McCord, who had served in the FBI for three years and in the CIA for over twenty.[74] Three of the burglars were Cubans who were employed by CREEP.[75] G. Gordon Liddy and E. Howard Hunt were the men in a command post across the street, communicating with the burglars via walkie-talkie.[76] Further investigation showed that Liddy had been in the FBI[77] and Hunt had been in the CIA.[78] Within twelve hours of the break-in, investigators linked the burglars with Haldeman and Ehrlichman, the president's closest advisers at the White House.[79]

It is now known that Nixon learned of the connection between CREEP and the burglars on June 20 and three days later, began to take steps to cover up the relationship.[80] An elaborate cover-up was organized.[81] The White House began by denying any knowledge of the break-in, calling it a third-rate burglary attempt and dismissed it as a "caper."[82] Any documents that could prove ties to the burglars were destroyed.[83] Mitchell denied publicly that McCord was part of the White House staff. White House counsel Dean devised complex cover stories to prevent the operation from being traced. Hush money was paid to the burglars so they would not tell who hired them. Liddy, Hunt, and McCord were fired.[84]

Shortly after the break-in, the FBI investigated the charges that the burglars had some connection to the White House. Nixon, fearing that his role would be discovered, attempted to have the investigation stopped by ordering the CIA to inform the Washington, D.C., police and the FBI that the break-in was a "national security" operation and they should not pursue it.[85] Thus, Nixon used a federal agency—the CIA—to halt the FBI investigation of the break-in.[86] The order to the CIA to stop the FBI investigation was clearly an obstruction of justice.[87]

Despite Nixon's order, the CIA and FBI both continued to investigate the allegations. Some inside the White House were concerned about how far the investigation would go.[88] They were able to convince then acting director of the FBI, L. Patrick Gray, to put a hold on giving their information and leads to the prosecutor. Gray also ordered that FBI interviews of White House staff be delayed.[89] Gray later testified that he gave Dean information about the FBI investigation, so that the White House not only learned what the agency had done but also what it planned to do.[90] After a while, Gray was under pressure from the U.S. attorney's office to investigate the charges.[91] He also faced a near mutiny from his top officers, who were unwilling to accept the delays he was imposing on them. The second-in-charge at the FBI, Mark Felt, insisted that Gray go ahead with the investigation.[92]

While he was attempting to stop the formal investigations of the Watergate break-in, Nixon told the American public that he had John Dean investigate the allegations. Nixon informed Americans that Dean's investigation found that no one in the White House or employed by the administration was involved in any criminal activity.[93] He also declared that there had been a full investigation by the FBI and the Justice Department, which also found no wrongdoing.[94]

The information about the investigations was not reported in most newspapers. The majority of papers across the nation did not pursue stories related to Watergate, especially in the beginning. However, two reporters for the *Washington Post*, Bob Woodward and Carl Bernstein, continued to investigate the story and keep it alive.[95] They were able to make a connection between the Watergate burglars and the Nixon administration[96] with the help of an anonymous source they nicknamed "Deep Throat," who was a source high up in the administration.[97] Deep Throat met with Woodward in the middle of the night in a parking garage. Their meetings were arranged by the position of a flowerpot on a windowsill. The information provided by Deep Throat was always a bit vague and he usually gave no names, but he gave leads and encouraged the reporters.[98] The source turned out to be Mark W. Felt Jr., deputy FBI director.[99]

Eventually, news reports by Woodward and Bernstein clearly linked the burglars with the White House and CREEP.[100] They reported that the burglars had been paid hush money out of a secret fund controlled by White House staff to keep them quiet and willing to accept jail sentences.[101] The money had come from the illegal campaign donations that were sent to CREEP.[102] Dean was involved in setting up hush money payments, which he never denied.[103] Payoffs would eventually reach nearly half a million dollars.[104] Woodward and Bernstein also reported the White House destroyed evidence about the break-in and lied to investigators.[105]

Woodward and Bernstein reported that the Watergate break-in was only part of a wide program of electoral dirty tricks carried out by the Republicans.[106] The dirty tricks were also funded through the secret fund in the White House. The money was used to fund information gathering on certain Democrats who were perceived to pose a threat to Nixon.[107] Donald Segretti was hired to carry out the dirty tricks, which including spying on the Democrats, making false statements to the press, disrupting Democratic political rallies, stealing files, forging letters, and making false accusations to discredit Democratic candidates.[108]

One of the more famous dirty tricks by Segretti was when he attacked the Democratic candidate for president.[109] Segretti forged a letter on Edmund Muskie letterhead in which Muskie appeared to call French Canadians "canucks." After, Muskie stood in front of a New Hampshire newspaper office and read a statement about the false letter, crying in rage.[110] This seriously harmed his campaign for president.[111] Segretti also used fake Muskie stationery to mail a Harris poll reprint dealing with Senator Ted Kennedy and the incident at Chappaquiddick to Democratic members of Congress. In other instances, the Republicans followed members of Democratic candidates' families to collect information about them and harass them.[112] Additionally, Segretti

- ordered flowers, cakes, pizzas, and entertainers "cash on delivery" at a Democratic fundraiser;[113]
- distributed a flier on Muskie stationery a few days before the Florida primary, accusing Senators Hubert Humphrey and Henry Jackson of illicit sexual conduct;[114]
- canceled hotel reservations;[115]
- called voters in the New Hampshire primary campaign in the middle of the night identifying themselves as canvassers from the Muskie committee, urging that they cast their ballots for Muskie "because he'd been so good for the black man";
- twice stole raw polling data from the desk of the Muskie polling expert at campaign headquarters;
- monitored events after Chappaquiddick and tried to get dirt on Ted Kennedy;[116]
- handed out posters in Florida that read "HELP MUSKIE IN BUSSING MORE CHILDREN NOW"; a hugely unpopular position in Florida at the time;[117]
- distributed cards at a Wallace rally that said "IF YOU LIKED HITLER YOU'LL LOVE WALLACE";[118]

- scheduled fake meetings and stole shoes that were put out for cleaning;[119]
- dropped white mice at a press conference with ribbons on their tails that said "Muskie is a rat fink";[120]
- planted embarrassing signs in campaign crowds, changed schedules to create confusion, and generally spread disruption;[121]
- hired a plane to fly over Miami during the Democratic convention trailing a sign that read: "PEACE POT PROMISCUITY VOTE McGOVERN";
- printed fliers on April Fool's Day inviting people to an open house with free lunch and drinks at Humphrey's headquarters in Milwaukee; and,
- paid people to carry "Kennedy for President" signs outside Muskie meetings.[122]

Despite all of these acts, Nixon's reelection bid was moving forward. Since he was successfully covering up his involvement in the Watergate break-in, the investigations were all moving slowly, and the whole thing was not an issue in the campaign.[123] This was the case despite the indictment of the five men arrested at the DNC and Hunt and Liddy on criminal bugging charges on September 15, just prior to the campaign.[124] After the voters cast their ballots, Nixon was reelected by a landslide, carrying forty-nine of fifty states, losing only Massachusetts and D.C.[125]

After the election, the Senate formed the Select Committee on Presidential Campaign Activities (otherwise known as the Senate Watergate Committee) to investigate the allegations surrounding the burglary[126] in February 1973, by a vote of seventy-seven to zero.[127] It was chaired by Samuel J. Ervin from North Carolina.[128] The committee was comprised of members of both parties, including four Democrats and three Republicans.[129] The committee members were given the formal task of investigating the extent, if any, to which illegal, improper, or unethical activities were used by any persons in the presidential election of 1972 or any campaign activity related to it. Informally, the committee wanted to know, "What did the president know and when did he know it?"as asked by Senator Howard Baker Jr., a Republican from Tennessee.[130]

On January 8, 1973, the trial of the Watergate Seven began in federal court.[131] At the trial, McCord and Liddy both pleaded not guilty (although they were both eventually convicted). Hunt and the other burglars pled guilty to charges of breaking and entering. The judge presiding over the case was Judge John "Maximum John" Sirica, a tough law-and-order Republican judge.[132]

At their sentencing on March 20, 1973, McCord handed Judge Sirica a letter in which he said there was political pressure applied to the defendants to plead guilty and remain silent, and that perjury had occurred during the trial.[133] He claimed that there were others involved in the Watergate operation that were not identified and revealed that the Watergate break-in was not a CIA operation concerning national security issues.[134] McCord also told Sirica that the "overall boss" of the operation was the attorney general, John Mitchell.[135]

Three days later, on March 23, 1973, Sirica read McCord's letter in open court,[136] then handed out maximum sentences to all defendants. The five defendants who pled guilty expected light sentences, but Sirica believed the trial was a sham. He was dissatisfied with the lack of answers[137] and had a growing discontent with prosecutors.[138] He gave out heavy sentences, the maximum provided by statute.[139] He gave a provisional sentence of thirty-five years in jail to Hunt and forty years to each of the other four. Liddy, who had already been cited for contempt because of his refusal to talk about the burglary to investigators, was given a final sentence: six years and eight months to twenty years in jail and a $40,000 fine.[140] He said he would reduce the sentences of those convicted if they would cooperate with other investigations.[141] Eventually, Sirica reduced the sentences to all but Liddy, who still refused to testify.[142]

Throughout all of these events, Nixon denied any involvement. On April 30, 1973, he gave a speech to the American public on national television, which has come to be known as the Watergate Address. It was the first time he addressed the American people specifically on Watergate.[143] In the speech, he accepted responsibility for what had happened, but still denied knowing of the break-in in advance. He announced the resignation of Attorney General Kleindienst, his Chief of Staff Haldeman, his chief domestic adviser Ehrlichman, and counsel Dean.[144] He also announced the nomination of Elliot Richardson to replace Kleindienst as attorney general.[145]

Many times, people asked Nixon to appoint a special prosecutor. He refused, saying that the White House had conducted its own investigation and found that no one did anything wrong.[146] During the confirmation hearings for his nominee for attorney general, Richardson, the Senate Judiciary Committee refused to approve him until he agreed to appoint an independent special prosecutor. Richardson agreed and was confirmed by the Senate.[147] He immediately began conducting a search for a special prosecutor. It took him two weeks and several refusals before he finally selected Professor Archibald Cox of the Harvard Law School.[148] Cox was appointed on May 18, 1973.[149] He was authorized to determine the extent to which Nixon's reelection committee had been involved in the burglary and cover-up.[150]

In the meantime, Nixon had nominated Gray to be head of the FBI. During his confirmation hearings, Gray admitted that he destroyed files related to Watergate,[151] that Dean sat in on FBI interviews during the investigation of the break-in, and that Dean had received copies of FBI investigation reports.[152] Because of this, his nomination was withdrawn.[153]

F. Hearings

On May 17, 1973, the Ervin committee opened its televised hearings into Watergate.[154] This marked the first time in history that presidential assistants and others on the White House staff were brought before a committee of the Congress on television to account for their conduct.[155] In the beginning, Nixon said that no White House staff member could testify because of executive privilege. Ervin warned that if they failed to comply with subpoenas, he would recommend that the Senate issue warrants for their arrest. Eventually, the staff appeared before the committee.

McCord was one staff member to testify.[156] His testimony opened up a floodgate of confessions[157] as other White House officials told one incredible story after another and exposed one illegality after another. The key witness turned out to be Dean, the White House counsel.

Dean testified in June and was the first in the White House inner circle to level charges directly against Nixon.[158] Feeling that he was being set up to be the fall guy, he decided to testify and tell all, especially after being given immunity for his testimony.[159] He spoke softly, reading continuously for a full day from a 245-page prepared statement in which he described the president as deeply involved in the cover-up.[160] He said he and Nixon had discussed the cover-up on at least thirty-five separate occasions beginning in September 1972.[161] His testimony revealed widespread wiretapping, the existence of the Plumbers, and an intelligence plan that was in violation of the Constitution. He also implicated Haldeman in the hush-money payments and Ehrlichman in the destruction of incriminating documents.[162] Dean testified that Nixon had an enemies list made up of people who would be targeted for harassment by the FBI and IRS.[163] He told the committee that Nixon had authorized the payments of hush money to the men charged in the burglary.[164] Afterward, Dean was allowed to plead guilty to a single felony charge of conspiracy to obstruct justice in exchange for his testimony.[165]

Lesser known assistants also testified in front of the committee.[166] One of those was Alexander Butterfield, a former White House communications aide. On July 16, 1973, when questioned out of the Senate chamber, Butterfield revealed accidentally that since 1971 Nixon had taped himself and all conversations in the Oval Office.[167] The system triggered automatically when the president entered the room.[168] At first, microphones were placed in the Oval Office and the Cabinet room. Two months later, more microphones were installed in Nixon's office in the Executive Office Building. The president's office telephones and a telephone in the Lincoln sitting room were also wired. In May 1972, a taping system was placed in the president's study in Camp David. Altogether, more than 5,000 hours of conversations were taped.[169]

When Butterfield made the existence of the tapes known, it was thought that finally the American people would be able to find out if Nixon knew about Watergate and what his role was. Immediately, both the Senate and the special prosecutor subpoenaed the tapes.[170] Nixon refused the request.[171] He claimed that presidential conversations with advisers were constitutionally protected by executive privilege,[172] an implied power that enables presidents and high-level executive branch officers to withhold information from Congress, the courts, and ultimately the public.[173] But Cox found no justification for executive privilege and believed that Nixon was using it to conceal evidence of criminal conduct.

Nixon announced that he would make summaries of the tapes available to the courts and the Ervin committee.[174] He said that John Stennis, a Democratic member of Congress, would verify their authenticity.[175] Although the Ervin committee agreed to the arrangement,[176] Cox did not accept the offer on the grounds of inadequacy and inadmissibility of transcripts as evidence.[177] Cox then approached Judge Sirica to get a subpoena ordering Nixon or any subordinate officer to provide nine particular tapes and other documents.[178] Two days later, Nixon, "with the utmost respect for the courts" again declined to obey the subpoena's command.[179] He said that a president's papers and thoughts were his personal property.[180]

On August 29, 1973, Judge Sirica ruled against the president, saying that Nixon should supply the tapes not to Cox and the grand jury but to the judge himself. Then, sitting in chambers, he would listen and rule on the claims for privilege, and where he found conversations relevant to the investigation, he would turn them over to the grand jury.[181] Nixon appealed Sirica's ruling.[182] On Friday, October 12, the U.S. Court of Appeals for the District of Columbia upheld Sirica's order by a vote of five to two, directing Nixon to turn over the nine requested tapes to the special prosecutor.[183]

G. Saturday Night Massacre

On Saturday, October 20, Nixon directed Cox to accept the Stennis arrangement and cease seeking any further tapes. But Cox refused that direct order, outraging Nixon.[184] Cox appeared on a televised afternoon press conference and called for the president to comply with the court's decision to hand over the tapes. Moreover, he declared that he would not resign,[185] reiterating that only the attorney general, Richardson, could fire him.[186] Nixon told Richardson to fire Cox,[187] but Richardson reminded the president that he had promised Cox independence when he accepted the special prosecutor's position, and that he would be forced to resign rather than fire Cox.[188] Nixon then turned to Deputy Attorney General William D. Ruckelshaus to dismiss Cox, but he also refused and was fired. At that point, Solicitor General Robert Bork, as acting attorney general, fired Cox. The press began calling this the Saturday Night Massacre.[189]

After the Saturday Night Massacre, Nixon was forced to act quickly to gain control of the situation. First, he agreed on October 23 to turn over the nine tapes.[190] He also gave in to public demands for a new special prosecutor, and on October 31, agreed to appoint Leon Jaworski, a Texas Democrat.[191] Nixon thought this was a safe choice.[192] Jaworski easily stepped into the investigation.[193] He investigated many issues, including the Watergate break-in and cover-up by White House employees (the Plumbers), illegal campaign contributions for the Nixon reelection campaign, and Nixon's evasion of income taxes and questionable tax returns.[194]

Through October and November, 1973, Nixon handed over seven tapes to Judge Sirica.[195] It was soon announced that one of the tapes had an 18.5-minute gap.[196] Nixon's longtime secretary, Rose Mary Woods, suggested she may have erased the tapes by accident when answering the phone while transcribing them.[197] The missing tapes were believed to have conversations from June 20, 1972, three days after the break-in (the first working day), which contained a conversation between Nixon and Haldeman.[198] For the most part, the tapes showed Nixon's conversations to be rambling and disjointed, petty and mean-spirited, and laced with profanity.[199]

H. Indictment

By early 1974, Jaworski's grand jury was ready to bring indictments against high-level members of the administration.[200] On March 1, 1974, the grand jury handed down a fifty-two-count indictment naming Ehrlichman, Haldeman, Mitchell, and others for conspiracy in a cover-up and on charges of obstruction of justice and giving false testimony, perjury, and making a false declaration.[201] All pleaded not guilty.[202] Nixon was named an unindicted co-conspirator by the grand jury.[203] It was necessary to do that prior to a trial to make his statements in the tape recordings admissible as evidence at the trial of those indicted in the cover-up case. Without naming the president in the indictment, some of his statements in the recordings would not be admissible as evidence.[204] Then, on March 7, Ehrlichman, Liddy, and others were indicted for the break-in at the office of Ellsberg's psychiatrist.[205]

On July 24, 1974, the Supreme Court ruled unanimously that Nixon had to surrender the tapes, including the June 23 tape.[206] In *U.S. v. Nixon* (418 U.S. 683 (1974)), the Supreme Court voted eight to zero that Nixon had to surrender sixty-four tapes subpoenaed by Jaworski.[207] The justices decided that Nixon had to give up the tapes because they were needed as evidence in a criminal prosecution.[208] They ruled that he had to produce the tapes for Sirica to conduct an in-chambers inspection.

Nixon had argued that the courts lacked the power to compel him to produce the tapes. He asserted that because the dispute was an internal disagreement between the president and the special prosecutor, it was purely an internal fight between himself and his subordinate and therefore not subject to judicial resolution. Moreover, as president, he could assert absolute presidential privilege. The need for executive confidentiality justified the application of privilege.[209]

The Court's decision was written by Chief Justice Warren Burger. In it, he said this controversy was appropriately before the Supreme Court because it is the duty of the Court to say what the law is.[210] Further, the regulations that established the special prosecutor had intended for it to be an independent position and to act without the president's approval, therefore the Court was justified in resolving the conflict.[211]

Moreover, the justices addressed the question of whether the president has an absolute executive privilege from being forced to provide evidence relevant to the prosecution of a criminal trial.[212] The justices upheld the legitimacy of the principle of executive privilege while striking down Nixon's particular exercise of that power. They recognized the need for presidential secrecy and confidentiality, but determined that this need was subject to a balancing test.[213] The burden was on the president to prove a compelling need to withhold information and not on Congress to prove that it has the right to investigate.[214] In this specific case, the requirements of criminal justice were more compelling than Nixon's claimed need for secrecy.[215]

Nixon decided to jump the gun and release the tapes himself so he could put the best possible spin on the information. On August 5, 1974, he released the three tapes that linked him to the cover-up of his involvement of the Watergate burglary.[216] One of the tapes was the "smoking gun" audiotape of June 23, 1972, which revealed his involvement in the cover-up just days after the arrests of the men at the Watergate complex.[217] This tape clearly refuted the president's defense that he had not learned about the cover-up until March 21, 1973, when he admitted to having been warned of its potentially dangerous consequences.[218] In the conversation, Haldeman explained to Nixon about the events, that the hush money could be traced back to CREEP, and that the FBI would eventually make the connections.[219]

I. Impeachment

If that particular conversation did not undercut his defense, there were plenty of others that did.[220] The evidence of his deep involvement in the cover-up was overwhelming.[221] The tapes showed that the president was indeed pre-occupied with covering up the illegal acts he claimed to know nothing about, and also often showed criminal intent.[222] At times, Nixon was heard telling his staff how to commit perjury,[223] or even ordering the payment of hush money to the burglars.[224] A tape from March 21, 1973, showed that Nixon, himself a lawyer, coached Haldeman on how to testify untruthfully while not commit-ting perjury.[225]

Many in Congress were beginning to call for Nixon's removal.[226] After the Saturday Night Massacre, twenty-two resolutions of impeachment had been in-troduced into the House of Representatives.[227] It then fell to the House Judi-ciary Committee to decide on impeachment. In those times, the presidency was a highly revered office, and removing a president was an almost frighten-ing thing to consider.[228] The committee had no real precedent to draw on and they faced many questions.[229] First, could they compel the president to deliver documents? Second, if the president refused to comply with their requests, what could they do? Additionally, what rights did Nixon have? Did he have the right to be present, to cross-examine witnesses, or call rebuttal witnesses?[230]

The hearings began May 9, 1974.[231] The committee was comprised of twenty-one Democrats and sixteen Republicans, and was chaired by Peter Rodino Jr. (D-NJ).[232] He tried to show that his committee was free of partisanship.[233] Draw-ing up the specific articles of impeachment was a challenge to the committee members because if they made any accusations that could be seen as petty or po-litical, they would probably not be persuasive and might undermine support.[234]

The first eleven weeks of hearings were not open to the public or televised.[235] At first, the debate centered on what was an impeachable offense. The mem-bers agreed that grounds for impeachment need not be criminal but must be a substantial breach of public trust and improper performance of constitu-tional duties. After that, Rodino presented evidence of a pattern of Nixon's misuse of presidential power.[236] The public hearings began on July 24, 1974.[237] They were the first televised House hearings in twenty years.[238] The commit-tee passed three articles of impeachment related to Nixon's involvement in Wa-tergate. The exact articles are listed in Table 4.4.

The first article charged that Nixon engaged in a "course of conduct" designed to obstruct the investigation of the Watergate case.[239] The article passed on July 27 by a vote of twenty-seven to eleven.[240] The second article, passed on July 29, charged that Nixon committed an impeachable offense by abusing the powers of the presidency, including the use of government agencies against individuals. It contained a number of different charges relating to an alleged attempt to use the IRS for political purposes (to harass his enemies) as related to the 1969 na-tional security wiretaps.[241] The article passed by a vote of twenty-eight to ten.[242]

Article III passed on July 30. It charged that Nixon committed an impeachable offense by failing to comply with the committee's subpoenas for tapes and documents. The committee charged that he refused to comply with Watergate-related subpoenas issued by the Judiciary Committee.[243] The vote was twenty-one to seventeen.[244]

The House Judiciary Committee also found that some campaign contributions had been "laundered" through Mexico. Just prior to the new campaign finance laws taking effect, Maurice Stans, the treasurer for CREEP, went on a fundraising swing to collect donations from large corporations, labor leaders, and special interest groups. The contributions were taken to Mexico, converted into cash, and then sent to Washington. Anyone with a favor to be granted gave money.

The committee voted down two other articles of impeachment—one dealing with Nixon's failure to inform the Congress of secret bombing raids in Cambodia, and the other concerning personal taxes he owed to the government.[245]

Once the House Judiciary Committee approved the three articles of impeachment, Nixon's downfall came swiftly.[246] Calls for his resignation came from everywhere. Newspapers demanded that he step down. The most powerful people in the House and Senate from both parties called on him to resign.[247] At first, Nixon decided to fight the charges,[248] but after coming down with phlebitis and fatigue,[249] he changed his mind. It had become clear to him that he would probably be impeached in the House and convicted in the Senate, and after much debate, he chose to leave.[250] He announced his resignation on Thursday, August 8, effective the following day.[251] Gerald Ford was sworn into office.

On September 8, 1974, President Ford found Nixon in bad shape both physically and emotionally, and had thoughts that he might not live out the year.[252] Ford believed that a pardon was the right thing for the country.[253] He believed that Nixon would have been indicted, probably convicted, and have a long tortuous appeal, at which point he would probably be sent to prison.[254] Ford questioned the usefulness of that and instead, chose to pardon Nixon for all federal crimes he "committed or may have committed or taken part in" during his presidency.[255] Because of the pardon, formal charges were never brought against Nixon.[256]

Conversely, some of Nixon's closest associates were either convicted or plead guilty to various Watergate-related offenses and sentenced to prison. Ford's failure to pardon any of these men underscored the impression that Nixon eluded conviction and punishment for his acts.[257] The outcomes of the criminal actions of some of Nixon's associates are listed in Table 4.5. Many criminal acts were committed throughout the affair. These are described in Table 4.6.

Nixon himself claimed that he did not want to accept the pardon, but said that it was needed so that those remaining in government would not continue to suffer from being unable to devote their full attention to the urgent problems at home and abroad. Further, he claimed that the attorneys' fees and other costs associated with defending himself would more than likely bankrupt him. Finally, Nixon claimed that he had taken as much physically, mentally, and emotionally as he could, and it was necessary to accept the pardon for his own well-being and that of his family. He said, "Next to the resignation, accepting the pardon was the most painful decision of my political career."[258]

J. Outcomes

Nixon never admitted any guilt for his involvement in Watergate.[259] In accepting the pardon, he did not admit to or apologize for the abuses of power and the obstruction of justice with which the articles of impeachment charged him. He acknowledged only that he made "mistakes and misjudgments" in handling Watergate[260] and called the episode a "tragedy of errors."[261] He blamed partisan opposition and media hostility for the scandal.[262] After leaving office, Nixon continued to deny ordering the break-in at the Democratic headquarters, ordering the payment of money to the burglars to keep them silent, ordering the CIA to stop the FBI from investigating the break-in, and that he (or his staff) erased 18.5 minutes of incriminating conversation from the tapes. He also denied ordering the IRS to audit his political adversaries, that he "sold" ambassadorships to major political contributors, that he lied throughout the Watergate period in his press conferences and speeches, that he ordered massive illegal wiretapping and surveillance of political opponents, members of the House and Senate, and news media reporters, that he ordered members of the White House staff to arrange the break-in of the office of Ellsberg's psychiatrist, that he cheated on his income taxes, or that he profited from his time as president.[263]

In the time after service as president, Nixon worked diligently to repair his image and reputation.[264] He published his memoirs in 1978, titled *RN: The Memoirs of Richard Nixon*. In 1981 he led the American delegation to Egypt for the funeral of President Anwar Sadat.[265] He wrote numerous best-selling books, traveled extensively abroad, spoke out on global and domestic politics, advised world leaders, and repaired his relationships.[266] A Gallup poll ranked Nixon among the ten most admired men in the world.[267] He died on April 22, 1994, and was buried in California. Presidents Ford, Carter, Bush, and Clinton all attended his funeral.

Table 4.4: Articles of Impeachment

Article 1: In his conduct of the office of the President of the United States, Richard M. Nixon, in violation of his Constitutional oath faithfully to execute the office of President of the United States and, to the best of his ability, preserve, protect and defend the Constitution of the United States, and in violation of his constitutional duty to take care that the laws be faithfully executed, has prevented, obstructed, and impeded the administration of justice.

In all of this, Richard M. Nixon has acted in a manner contrary to his trust as President and subversive of constitutional government, to the great prejudice of the cause of law and justice, and to the manifest injury of the people of the United States.

Wherefore Richard M. Nixon, by such conduct, warrants impeachment and trial, and removal from office.

Article 2: Using the powers of the office of President of the United States, Richard M. Nixon, in violation of his constitutional oath faithfully to execute the office of President of the United States and, to the best of his ability, preserve, protect and defend the Constitution of the United States, and in disregard of his constitutional duty to take care that the laws be faithfully executed, has repeatedly engaged in conduct violating the constitutional rights of citizens, impairing the due and proper administration of justice and the conduct of lawful inquiries or contravening the laws governing agencies of the executive branch and the purposes of these agencies.

In all of this, Richard M. Nixon has acted in a manner contrary to his trust as President and subversive of constitutional government, to the great prejudice of the cause of law and justice, and to the manifest injury of the people of the United States.

Wherefore Richard M. Nixon, by such conduct, warrants impeachment and trial, and removal from office.

Article 3: In his conduct of the office of the President of the United States, Richard M. Nixon, contrary to his oath faithfully to execute the office of President of the United States and, to the best of his ability, preserve, protect, and defend the Constitution of the United States, and in disregard of his constitutional duty to take care that the laws be faithfully executed, has failed without lawful cause or excuse to produce papers and things as directed by duly authorized subpoenas issued by the Committee on the Judiciary of the House of Representatives on April 11, 1974, May 15, 1974, May 30, 1974, and willfully disobeyed such subpoenas.

In all of this, Richard M. Nixon has acted in a manner contrary to his trust as President and subversive of constitutional government, to the great prejudice of the cause of law and justice, and to the manifest injury of the people of the United States.

Wherefore Richard M. Nixon, by such conduct, warrants impeachment and trial, and removal from office.

Source: House Committee on the Judiciary, *Impeachment of Richard M. Nixon, President of the United States*, 93rd Congress, 2d session, 20 August 1974, House Document 93-339, 1–4.

Table 4.5: Criminal Penalties of Watergate Offenders

Colson: Pled guilty March 9, 1974 to obstructing justice by attempting to defame Daniel Ellsberg. In return, all charges were dropped. He was disbarred from practicing law in Virginia and sentenced to a one- to three-year sentence. Colson was sent to Holabird federal prison for seven months. While there, he started a prison fellowship ministry. He won a million-dollar prize for Progress in Religion in March 1993. He was awarded his civil rights in October 2000, including the right to vote, to serve on a jury, to run for office and practice law. He also wrote many books.

Dean: Pled guilty on October 19, 1973, to one count of violation of conspiracy to obstruct justice. He was sentenced August 2, 1974, to a prison term of one to four years, serving four months. For much of the time, he was in Holabird prison during the night, but spent his days in Washington preparing to give testimony or on the witness stand. Sirica ordered him released on January 8, 1975, at which time he went on a $175,000 speaking tour.

Ehrlichman: Indicted on one count of conspiracy to obstruct justice, one count of obstruction of justice, one count of making false statements to the FBI, and two counts of making a false statement to a grand jury. He was found guilty on all counts but one. Sirica sentenced him to two and a half to eight years in prison, but he served less than two years. Additionally, he was suspended from practicing law in California and became an environmental consultant.

Haldeman: Indicted on one count of conspiracy to obstruct justice, one count of obstruction of justice, and three counts of perjury, He was found guilty on all counts. Sirica sentenced him to two and a half to eight years in prison, but he served only eighteen months.

Hunt: Sentenced to thirty-five years in prison, but served only thirty-three months. Since then he has written more than seventy spy novels.

Kleindienst: Pled guilty to a misdemeanor for not having testified fully to the congressional committee. He received a suspended one-month jail sentence.

Liddy: Because he would never confess, repent, or give evidence, he was sent to the tough D.C. jail. He was convicted of conspiracy, burglary, and illegal wiretapping and sentenced to twenty years, serving fifty-two months. Today he is a radio talk show host.

McCord: Sentenced to one to five years for burglary, wiretapping, and conspiracy, and served four months.

Mitchell: Found guilty of conspiracy to obstruct justice, one count of obstruction of justice, two counts of making false statements to a grand jury, and one count of perjury. He was sentenced by Sirica to two and a half to eight years in prison, but served nineteen months. He died in 1988.

Nixon: Wrote many books, and passed away in 1994.

Sirica: Passed away June 1992.

Table 4.6: Criminal Acts That Occurred During Watergate Scandal

Burglary: Initial illegal entry into the DNC, authorized by CREEP; burglary of office of psychiatrist of the Pentagon Papers defendants, authorized by White House; plots to burglarize embassies, Brookings Institute, authorized by White House; stealing campaign documents from Muskie's file

Campaign Funds: Secret cash funds of amounts up to $700,000 kept by the president's personal lawyer; illegal cash campaign contributions; contributions through banks in foreign countries to guarantee anonymity; illegal and anonymous contributions from corporations; massive bookkeeping errors (up to $800,000); distribution of large amounts of cash for "unknown reasons" by CREEP

Espionage: Spying on opposing candidates and their families during the presidential election, authorized by CREEP; electronic surveillance authorized by CREEP

Obstruction of Justice: Giving of false names at the time of initial Watergate arrests; payment of money for "living expenses and legal fees," also called "hush money"; perjury in testimony in grand jury investigations; deletion of details from tapes; offer of directorship of FBI to judge handling Ellsburg burglary trial

Violation of Federal Election Law: Dirty tricks illegal campaign practices hidden by White House staff, paid by the president's personal lawyer; destruction of records; failure to keep records, use of cash

Forgery: Campaign letters forged on candidate letterheads without knowledge of candidates; forged cables from State Department files implicating President Kennedy in the assassination of the president of South Vietnam in 1963

Slander: False press releases, newspaper advertisements; false accusations about candidate's personal lives

Perjury and Coverup: Payments for guilty pleas

Violation of Personal, Civil, and Human Rights: Listening and recording private conversations; following candidates' families for info on personal lives; investigation of private lives of members of press and Congress; wiretaps

Implications of Watergate

A year after Nixon left office, CBS political correspondent Bruce Morton told viewers that Watergate "didn't change much."[268] Many people would disagree, pointing out many long-term implications and impacts of the Watergate scandal.[269] Watergate had a profound effect on the nation, both in the long and short-term.[270] Even Nixon himself agreed that "Watergate turned out to be a very damaging thing to the country."[271] Following is a discussion of some of the effects of the Watergate scandal.

A. Effects on Careers

The Watergate scandal affected many careers in both positive and negative ways. After Watergate, the political careers of many simply ended.[272] Nixon's political career was permanently over. Although he was able to salvage his reputation to some degree, his public life was finished. President Ford's continued political career was also negatively affected. His unsuccessful bid for reelection in 1976 was, to some degree, because of the pardon he gave to Nixon. Many have argued that if it were not for the pardon, Ford probably would have been elected to another term as president.[273]

Twenty Nixon associates and subordinates were also impacted by their involvement in Watergate. Many went to prison, which led to the end of their political careers (see Table 4.5). They served prison sentences ranging from a one-month suspended sentence for Nixon's attorney, Richard G. Kleindienst, to a term of over four years for G. Gordon Liddy. The former attorney general who later became head of CREEP, John Mitchell, served nineteen months in prison. He was the only U.S. attorney general to spend time in prison.[274]

For a few people, Watergate actually helped them succeed in their careers. For example, John Ehrlichman wrote many novels, both fiction and nonfiction, and made numerous public appearances that might not have been possible without Watergate. John Dean, also obsessed with Watergate, did the same for a decade.[275] Charles Colson went on to head a successful prison ministries program, and claims that Watergate was the best thing that ever happened to him. Many people who were involved in the scandal wrote books about their experiences, including Cox, Gray, Hunt, McCord, Liddy, Magruder, Jaworski, Dean, and Haldeman, among others. Many of the witnesses who told the Watergate story became public personalities, such as Liddy, who is now a conservative talk-show host.[276]

A few years after the scandal, a little known politician from Georgia, Jimmy Carter, was elected to be president. During his campaign, he ran against the Washington establishment and the corruption there and successfully made character one of his chief issues. He was able to corner the market on trust, reaching out to those voters who were tired of the Watergate affair. In an interesting twist, it was Peter Rodino, chair of the Watergate Committee, who put Carter's name into nomination for the office.[277] Carter's election to the presidency is often linked to the Watergate scandal.[278]

Watergate also helped spur the careers of the two journalists often given credit for continually following the story and exposing Nixon's involvement.

Woodward and Bernstein were unknown reporters before Watergate, but became household names afterward. They wrote and published a book, *All the President's Men*, that detailed how they exposed the events of Watergate. It became a successful movie starring Dustin Hoffman and Robert Redford. After Watergate, Woodward took an editorial position at the *Washington Post*, and wrote many books, some of which were with Bernstein. Both have appeared on news shows and talk shows to discuss many events or issues with the public.[279]

Some might also argue that Bill Clinton's career was impacted by Watergate, specifically that his impeachment was another aftershock.[280] After Nixon was impeached, the House was more willing to deal with the process of impeaching a president. They had a model to follow, and knew how and why to do it. They were not reluctant to use impeachment against a sitting president, and were more willing to do so against Clinton.

B. New Legislation

Another impact of Watergate was a succession of new laws aimed at preventing such a scandal in the future. During the Watergate cover-up, it was discovered that Nixon abused the IRS, CIA, and FBI for political purposes, approved illegal wiretaps for government employees, and secretly bombed Cambodia without telling Congress. There were many new laws enacted to increase congressional oversight of or participation in executive policymaking so the presidential abuses found in Watergate could never happen again.[281]

Some of the new legislation affected the powers of the presidency and its relation to Congress. The new regulations sought to reign in some of the president's powers and help rebalance the three branches of government.[282]

One new law that was passed in the aftermath of Watergate was the Ethics in Government Act of 1978. This new law created the Office of Special Prosecutor (subsequently renamed the Independent Counsel) to investigate cases of alleged wrongdoing by senior officials in a presidential administration.[283] The special prosecutor would be appointed by a three-judge panel that would specify the jurisdiction of the investigator.[284]

Both houses of Congress also passed new ethics codes for their members. The House and Senate expanded financial disclosure requirements, limited the gifts and outside income a member could accept, and forbade the commingling of a congressman's personal financial accounts with political and public ones.[285]

Another new law related to campaign finance reform. In 1974, Congress amended the existing 1971 law and set more stringent limits on how much money an individual could contribute to a campaign for national office.[286] It incorporated contribution limits and a revised public financing plan and created a bipartisan Federal Election Commission to supervise campaigns.[287] The law set contribution limits of $1,000 per candidate per election, severely restricted untraceable cash gifts, compelled public reports of political donations by recipients, provided public funding for presidential campaigns, and established oversight and enforcement. The bill was signed by President Ford on October 15.[288]

Other new laws passed after Watergate include:

1. Foreign Corrupt Practices Act of 1977: passed in response to the special prosecutor's discovery of corporate slush funds maintained to buy political influence abroad.[289]
2. Foreign Intelligence Surveillance Act of 1978: required the government to secure warrants from a three-judge panel before investigating anyone suspected of espionage. It also legalized the use of electronic surveillance in the United States where foreign espionage was suspected.[290]
3. The Freedom of Information Act amendments: originally passed in 1966 and then amended in 1974, the law allowed citizens to inspect documents previously deemed secret. Many executive branch personnel resisted providing requested documents so the law was ineffective. President Ford vetoed the amendments because he argued they were unconstitutional and unworkable, but Congress overrode the veto.[291]
4. Intelligence Oversight Act of 1980: required that the president report "findings" in a "timely" manner for any covert action in which the CIA engaged.
5. Presidential Recordings and Materials Preservation Act of 1974: mandated government retention of the Nixon materials and called for the administrator of General Services Administration (GSA) to take custody of Nixon's presidential materials and have them screened by government archivists. Any personal and private papers that were found would be returned to Nixon. Those having historical value would be preserved.[292] This new law was passed even though a president's papers had always been regarded as his property.[293] The law marked a significant assertion of congressional authority against the gradual accretion of presidential power.[294] It established the rule that any records created by presidents as part of their official duties were owned by the public.[295]
6. War Powers Resolution of 1973: an effort to curtail the military authority of the president while asserting congressional authority over him.[296] The law

limited or specified executive power in foreign policy and required the president to consult with Congress before committing troops whenever possible. It also required the president to notify Congress within forty-eight hours of committing U.S. troops to combat, and that congressional permission be obtained to maintain troops beyond sixty days. Nixon's promised veto of the measure came four days after the Saturday Night Massacre. Congress voted to override the veto two weeks later.[297]

7. Privacy Act of 1974: required federal agencies to limit personal data they collect, limit disclosure of that data, and report on the personal data record systems.[298]

8. Tax Reform Act of 1976: restricted governmental use of tax information for other than tax collection purposes. This grew out of the revelations that the Nixon administration had used the IRS to harass political enemies.[299]

9. Budget and Impoundment Control Act: restricted presidential power to overturn congressional decisions by impounding funds. It required the president to notify Congress of any proposed impoundment. The impoundment could only go forward if Congress gave its approval within forty-five days. Either house in Congress could block a presidential impoundment.[300]

C. Lack of Trust in Government

After Watergate, according to Senator Sam Ervin, Americans developed a lack of trust in government.[301] Although mistrust probably already existed prior to Watergate, the scandal accelerated those feelings.[302] One result of this is a permanent contempt for politics and politicians. There is no doubt that presidents and other politicians are not as trusted as they once were. No longer are the words of a president taken at face value, either by journalists or the American public.[303] Instead, there is a general disdain for and suspicion of most political figures.[304] Further, people are more likely to be outraged over even the smallest impropriety or the appearance of one.[305]

D. Media

The role of the media changed dramatically after Watergate. In the short term, many reporters were inspired by Woodward and Bernstein.[306] Immediately after the scandal, journalism schools were filled with eager students hoping to be the next Woodward or Bernstein.[307] Everyone wanted to be a reporter who could pursue wrongdoers at the highest levels of government.[308] No journalist wants to miss the next big story.[309] Reporters became more inclined to search for, seize on, and make allegations concerning the private lives of public officials.[310]

In the longer term, the press became more adversarial in its coverage of public officials. Members of the media began to investigate and report on activities that previously had been considered private.[311] Before Watergate, the extramarital affairs of Franklin Roosevelt and John Kennedy were not reported in the media. Now the media digs up not only extramarital affairs but past drug use, divorces, criminal charges, and any other behavior that may be seen as immoral or unethical.[312] The new reporters have turned to "peeping Tom journalism" and character assassination.[313]

The press has put a new emphasis on the character of a candidate. Although the character issue has always been part of American politics, it became more important from 1976 onward.[314] At the same time, as the media grew more powerful, the public approval of their actions diminished. The media were viewed as being intrusive and insensitive.[315]

E. "-Gate"

One of the contributions of Watergate to the political scene is the addition of the suffix "-gate" to designate a scandalous events.[316] This has led to scandals termed Billygate, Lancegate, Koreagate, Irangate, Troopergate, Travelgate, Filegate, Monicagate.[317] Even internationally the suffix is used, in scandals such as Muldergate in South Africa; Collorgate in Brazil; SIDE-gate in Argentina.[318]

F. Crippled Administration

Watergate crippled the Nixon administration.[319] During the scandal, the president's ability to lead was compromised. He was distracted by spending so much time on Watergate that he had difficulty dealing with problems and issues in the country and was not paying close attention to national and international affairs. He was tired, distracted,[320] and preoccupied.[321] Congress, as well, was spending many hours on Watergate. This left the government largely paralyzed for at least a year and a half.[322]

Internationally, Watergate was "shattering the illusion of American strength … and with it, American foreign policy."[323] The affair had broad implications for American foreign policy. Nixon said that the events prevented him from carrying out a Middle East initiative he was planning that year to prevent the Yom Kippur War and the subsequent oil embargo.[324] Many foreign leaders, both friends and enemies alike, were confused by Nixon's inability to deal with his own troubles and make them go away.[325]

G. Power Realignments

The Watergate crisis involved significant issues regarding separation of powers. After the scandal ended, there were some major changes to the political and power relationships.[326] For many years, the powers of the presidency had been expanding. Early limits on executive power had slowly dissolved, and the presidential powers had expanded as he became the center of power, with little congressional oversight.[327] Along with that came a greater secrecy in which presidents cloaked their actions.[328] This was a frightening trend, as a president could misuse this power for his own political ends. Some say that is what Nixon did in April 1969 when he ordered large, secret bombing raids in Cambodia to slow the shipment of supplies and men from North Vietnam to the South.[329]

Questions arose about the role of the federal courts and Congress in the investigation of a president's misconduct. Specifically, can a court order a president to disclose his personal tape recordings of his private conversations? Further, can Congress enact new laws that deprive a president of the records of his administration?[330]

Nixon did not leave the presidency weaker, but instead, the power of the Congress and judiciary expanded. For example, the new Independent Counsel Act allowed Congress to ask the attorney general to call for a special panel of judges to appoint an independent prosecutor to investigate the president, vice president, Cabinet and subcabinet, as well as members of the White House staff, on a simple suspicion of misconduct.[331]

H. Morality

After Watergate a newly stringent set of norms about the appropriate behavior of the men and women in public life emerged, sometimes referred to as a "post-Watergate morality."[332] We now hold politicians to high standards; some say even too high standards.[333] Now, a candidate's character is just as important as the direction he or she promises to lead the nation.[334] Many times, voters tend to focus on the politics of personality, rather than on policy choices or competing partisan programs.[335]

I. Executive Privilege

Nixon's presidency marks the beginning of the modern understanding of executive privilege and presidential impeachment.[336]

Conclusion

Watergate was a major scandal in American politics that saw the only resignation of an elected president to date. The president abused his office in many ways. The scandal had many short-term effects, such as ending the political careers of many, but there were also long-term effects, such as new laws and a new attitude toward government. Even today, these changes remain part of American culture. Watergate set a tone for future scandals, particularly related to the investigation of alleged misdoing and media coverage of it.

Review Questions

1. What was Watergate and why was it called that?
2. What were the long- and short-term impacts of Watergate?
3. What was the role of the Supreme Court in Watergate?
4. What is the role of executive privilege?
5. What criminal acts may have been committed as part of the Watergate scandal?
6. What was the significance of the 1972 campaign finance law?
7. Describe some "dirty tricks" used by CREEP.
8. Why were Woodward and Bernstein important in this scandal?

Special Terms

Watergate	Saturday Night Massacre
CREEP	Executive Privilege
Plumbers	Watergate Seven
Pentagon Papers	*United States v. New York Times*
Dirty Tricks	*United States v. Nixon*

Discussion Questions

1. Is Watergate "old news" and no longer important to study and understand?
2. Was Ford's pardon of Nixon a good decision or a poor one?
3. Was Nixon guilty of criminal acts? If so, which ones? Should he have had to face a trial for his involvement in the scandal?
4. What should Nixon's punishment have been, if any?
5. Was Watergate a case where the cover-up was more damaging than the original offenses? If Nixon would have admitted his involvement in the affair early on, would he have been impeached?

Chapter 5

Ford, Carter, Reagan, and Bush Presidencies

Introduction

The four presidents in this chapter include one Democratic president, one nonelected president, and one who served two terms. Both the Ford and Carter presidencies were obviously influenced by Watergate. Ford became president only after Nixon's resignation, and probably lost his reelection bid in part because of granting a pardon to Nixon. Carter was elected on the premise of being a Washington "outsider" and promising an honest and ethical administration. These two administrations were relatively free of major political scandal. Reagan's administration, however, found itself immersed in an international affair that put a damper on the last few years of his presidency. President Bush, formerly Reagan's vice president, then served four years as president and, like Ford, chose to grant pardons to those involved in the previous administration's scandals. This chapter describes the political scandals related to presidents Ford, Carter, Reagan, and Bush.

Ford

President Gerald R. Ford was not in office for very long, and the nation was still reeling from Watergate. As a result, there were few political scandals during his administration. One "mistake" that occurred, as opposed to a full-fledged scandal, was in 1976, during a second critical debate with Carter a month before the election, Ford was asked if détente benefited the Soviet Union more than the United States. To that, he declared that there was no Soviet domination of Eastern Europe, and there never would be under his administration.[1] What he said was obviously incorrect and Ford appeared to not be knowledgeable about current events. To make it worse, 100 million people watched him say it on live television. Even when given the opportunity to retreat from the misstatement, he only dug himself in further. He said that he did not believe that the Yugoslavs, Romanians, or Poles considered themselves dominated by the Soviet Union.[2] With those remarks, Ford's chances of being elected president were diminished considerably. The press talked about little else for days.[3]

Ford's wife, Betty, also had some issues while she was First Lady. She admitted to abusing alcohol and drugs, mostly pain pills. Later, she founded the Betty Ford Center to help others addicted to drugs and alcohol.

Carter

Jimmy Carter ran for the presidency against Ford in 1976 on a theme of honesty, promising that there would be no scandal in his White House as we had experienced in the Nixon administration.[4] Even though he entered office with hopes of avoiding political scandals, this did not happen, and scandal undermined much of his presidency. His power depended on his ability to maintain his reputation as a man who could and would provide an honest government. The numerous scandals in his administration brought this into question and undermined the moral foundation of his presidency. This has been attributed to his loss in 1980 when he ran for reelection.[5]

It has been argued that the numerous scandals during the Carter administration (and any to follow, for that matter) were not necessarily the result of more unethical behavior. Instead, they were the aftereffects of Watergate and the changed role of the media. Carter came into office at a time when the American media and public in general were not as trusting of the presidency as they had been in the past. They were more willing to delve into questionable behavior, or even rumors thereof. Carter promised a higher ethical standard in politics,[6] and the media wanted to ensure this was happening. Therefore, it may not have been a more "unethical" administration per se, but instead a result of a change in the media in the post-Watergate era that haunted Carter.

Nonetheless, there were plenty of scandals during the Carter years. Some are described below.

A. Billygate

One of the major scandals to affect Carter was the result of his brother, Billy Carter, who came under investigation and brought embarrassment to the administration by developing relations with Libya and making offensive anti-Semitic remarks. The scandal was nicknamed "Billygate."[7]

Before becoming involved in politics, Jimmy Carter ran a peanut warehouse in Georgia. Billy took over managing the warehouse with great success when his brother was elected governor of the state in 1970. But when Jimmy became president, he transferred the warehouse over to a private trust so he would not be forced to give it to Billy, knowing that Billy had problems with excessive drinking. Billy owned a gas station but was mostly unemployed and out of money. He frequently visited alcoholic rehabilitation centers.

When Carter was president, beginning in 1973, relations between the United States and Libya were strained. The United States believed that Libya was involved in terrorist activity, which it sought to quell. But at the same time, a relationship developed between the two countries as the United States relied on Libya for about 10 percent of its imported oil, and Libya relied on U.S. oil payments to finance its domestic development. Some time around 1978, the leader of Libya, Muammar Qaddafi (Muammar Abu Minyar Al-Gaddafi), began searching for a way to increase Libya's economic interests in the United States and improve the relationship between the countries. Qaddafi believed that Billy, being the president's brother, was in a position to influence Carter's position on foreign policy. Therefore, Qaddafi called on Billy to help improve his image among the American public.

In the late summer of 1978, Billy traveled to Libya. While there, he was asked by the Libyans to set up a group in the United States to help establish and maintain a more positive relationship between the two countries. He attempted to establish the group, but the organization was never formalized. Billy continued his attempt to improve U.S. and Libyan relations. He made numerous public statements in favor of Qaddafi. He criticized the behavior of the American Jewish community, suggested that Americans ought to pay more attention to Arabs (because there are more of them than there are Jews), and accompanied a Libyan delegation on a "goodwill tour" of the United States.

Several days after the tour, the Justice Department sent a letter to Billy requesting that he register as a foreign agent. Under the 1938 Foreign Agents Registration Act, anyone trying to influence U.S. policy toward another country must register and fully disclose the nature of his or her activities and any compensation received from that country. For almost eighteen months, Billy refused to register with the Justice Department.

Billy then returned to Libya for a month in fall 1978. After that visit, he received two separate payments totaling approximately $220,000 from the Libyans. When questioned about it, Billy explained that it was a loan. In response, in April 1979, the Justice Department launched a formal investigation into Billy Carter's relationship with Libya. In June of that year, Billy admitted to the Justice Department that he had received money from Libya as part of a larger $500,000 loan and that he had also received four gold bracelets.

On June 17, 1979, Attorney General Benjamin Civiletti met with President Carter to discuss Billy's actions and his refusal to register as a foreign agent with the Justice Department. He told Carter that Billy would not be prosecuted if he registered at that time. He decided to register as a foreign agent on July 14, 1980, and the Justice Department dropped the investigation. Congress was skeptical about Billy's action and why the investigation was dropped, so they set up a Senate subcommittee to look into the case. The Senate members looked into how Billy Carter could arrange a $220,000 loan from the Libyans at 10 percent interest rate, and what he did with the money. They also wanted to know what the Libyans expected in return[8]. Other questions arose in the hearings, such as if Billy lied to Justice Department officials about the payments and the point at which the White House first learned of the loan. Others wanted to know if anyone alerted Billy that the FBI knew of the loan, prompting him to register as a foreign agent after eighteen months of declining to do so.

On November 4, 1979, militants in Tehran stormed the U.S. embassy, seizing American hostages. Libya's foreign ministry called on the leader of Iran, Ayatollah Khomeni, to release the Americans. Apparently, Carter's National Security Advisor Zbigniew Brzezinski asked Billy to intervene and use his friendship with Qaddafi to try to persuade Khomeini to let the hostages go free. Brzezinski actually held a meeting in the White House between himself, the Libyan foreign ambassador, and Billy Carter. The meeting signified to Libya that Billy was an authorized agent of the U.S. government.

On August 21–22, 1980, Billy Carter testified for ten hours in front of the Senate committee. He presented a twenty-seven-page opening statement in which he portrayed himself as an ordinary small businessman who had suffered simply because he was the brother of the president. He denied that he was a "buffoon, a boob or a wacko." He claimed that he explained to Libyan officials that he had no influence over American foreign affairs. He also explained to the senators that the money he received from Libya was part of a $500,000 loan given to him merely as a friendly gesture, not as a payment to influence any official U.S. policy. Last, he also claimed that he was not forewarned of the Justice Department's investigation of him and his relationship with Libya.

The hearings lasted several weeks, but in the end, the committee determined that Billy's conduct was inappropriate but not illegal. The members declared that there was no evidence that Billy influenced U.S. policy toward Libya, or that the president did anything worse than show poor judgment. The panel also put partial blame on the president and some of his aides both for asking Billy to enlist Libyan assistance in the Iranian hostage crisis, and for other acts that might have given Libyan officials a false impression of Billy's influence with his brother. No serious charges were made against Billy or anyone in the administration.

Nonetheless, the Billygate scandal negatively affected Carter's reelection bid. At the 1980 Democratic Convention, Carter was chosen as the Democratic nominee for president. He tried to campaign while the Senate subcommittee's hearings into Billygate continued. The hearings concluded before the election ended. The Republicans on the subcommittee reported that the manner in which the White House handled Billy's actions toward Libya should create serious doubt among voters about Carter's capability to be president, but the Democrats reported that the subcommittee found nothing illegal concerning Billy's actions. Many Americans questioned his relationship with Libya as well as the White House formally using him as a go-between in their attempts at freeing the hostages in Iran.

In November 1980, Carter was defeated in the election by Ronald Reagan. Most voters denied that Billy's conduct had an effect on their opinion of Carter. There were many issues facing the Carter administration that plagued his reelection bid. Although no illegal activity was ever formally linked to Billygate, Carter's handling of his brother increased voters' doubts about his ability to be president. Although the scandal may not have been the primary reason for the defeat, it certainly did not help.

B. Bert Lance

Bert Lance was Carter's budget director and a close friend.[9] He was accused of engaging in questionable financial practices while he was a bank president in Georgia,[10] prior to becoming part of the administration. When he was undergoing the confirmation process for Office of Management and Budget (OMB) in January 1977, it was discovered that he owned stock in the National Bank of Georgia. In keeping with the higher standards of ethics promised by Carter, Lance promised the Senate committee that he would sell the stock by the end of the year. When the announcement was made that he was selling the stock, its value dropped sharply. To avoid a huge loss and an "undue financial burden," Lance returned to the committee to ask for more time to sell his holdings. The committee gave him more time. In the meantime, investigators found that Lance had received a deal on the original loan he took out to purchase the stock. On further questioning, Lance convinced the Senate it was all fair. However, a new comptroller at the Treasury Department opened a new investigation into Lance's financial affairs, and even though the investigation found nothing, there was a lot of media attention and new questions raised.[11] Lance decided to resign in September 1977.[12] He was later indicted on ten counts of misapplication of bank funds in loans to relatives and friends and two counts of false financial statements. He was tried in a federal court in Atlanta, but none of the allegations against him led to a conviction.[13]

Reagan

President Ronald Reagan had a lot of charisma and great communications skills that made him one of the most popular presidents of all time.[14] Nonetheless, there was a great amount of scandal to plague his administration. As with Carter, it is difficult to say whether the increased number of scandals was due to more inappropriate behavior, or simply more media investigation and coverage of those involved. More than likely, it was the latter.

The scandals began before Reagan was even elected into office. During the 1980 presidential campaign, a copy of Carter's presidential debate briefing book found its way into the Republican campaign, and Reagan used the book to help prepare for the debate.[15] Carter said the book was stolen, but some in the Reagan camp said that someone in the Carter campaign gave it to them. The Justice Department said there was no evidence that the transfer of the document violated any criminal law.[16]

The scandals did not stop there. In 1982, Reagan's National Security advisor, Richard Allen, was forced to resign amid allegations of financial wrongdoing, including an accusation that he had accepted a gift of $1,000 from a Japanese reporter.[17] News stories charged that Allen accepted money from a Japanese journalist who had interviewed Nancy Reagan. Investigators found that Allen received an envelope with the money from the reporter, and then gave the money to his secretary and asked her to store it until they could give it to the Treasury Department. Instead, everyone forgot about it. When Allen later moved offices into the White House, the new officeholder found an envelope with $1,000 in a filing cabinet fitted with a combination lock. The money was identified as the gift given to Allen from the reporter, which was intended to be given to Reagan as a thank-you. The FBI believed that there was no dishonesty,[18] and Allen was cleared.[19]

There were many other scandals to hit the Reagan administration. Deputy Security of Defense Paul Thayer resigned in January 1984 over charges brought against him by the Securities and Exchange Commission of insider trading. In September 1984, Secretary of Labor Raymond Donovan was indicted on charges of defrauding the New York City Transit Authority on a subway construction project in 1979–80. He was eventually acquitted, but he resigned in March 1985, ending his political career. Reagan's first attorney general, William French Smith, resigned in January 1984 amid allegations of tax wrongdoings.[20] However, these scandals were all minor in comparison to the one major scandal that occurred during Reagan's administration: the Iran-Contra affair.

A. Iran-Contra Affair

One of the major scandals to hit the United States occurred during the second term of Reagan's administration. The Iran-Contra scandal began when it was discovered that Reagan's administration secretly sold arms to Iran in exchange for the release of American hostages and used the proceeds to back the Contra rebels who were attempting to overthrow the Marxist government in Nicaragua. These activities were at odds with policies passed by Congress, which prohibited the sale of weapons to Iran or support of the Contras.

The first public allegations of any wrongdoing came on November 3, 1986, when a Lebanese magazine published a story alleging that the United States had secretly sold weapons to Iran to secure the release of seven American hostages. The sale of weapons violated a number of policies that executive departments had been articulating, such as neutrality in the Iran-Iraq war, an embargo on arms sales to Iran, and the policy of not paying ransom to hostage takers.[21] Throughout subsequent investigations, Reagan denied any knowledge of the weapon sales or funding of the Contras. Although there were calls for his impeachment, Reagan left office with only his reputation damaged.

Like Watergate, the Iran-Contra scandal was complex and involved many different people in many different offices. Some of the actors in the scandal are listed in Table 5.1. Also like Watergate, the events leading up to the scandal went on for a long time before being discovered. Unlike Watergate, however, the president was not involved in a serious cover-up of the activities, which has been attributed to the decision not to impeach him.

Table 5.1: Actors in the Iran-Contra Affair

William Casey: Head of the CIA 1981–87

Carl R. (Spitz) Channell: Political fundraiser on behalf of the Nicaraguan resistance; founder of the National Endowment for the Preservation of Liberty

Manucher (Gorba) Ghorbanifar: Iranian arms merchant; intermediary in arms sales to Iran and the United States

Fawn Hall: Oliver North's secretary

Robert McFarlane: Reagan's National Security Advisor October 1983–December 1985; resigned

Edwin Meese: Counsel to President Reagan 1981–84; Attorney General 1985–96

Oliver North: Marine Lieutenant Colonel; staff member of NSC

John M. Poindexter: National Security Advisor December 1985–November 1986

Donald Regan: White House Chief of Staff 1985–86

Richard Secord: Retired Air Force Major General; head of Contra resupply effort, 1984–86

George Shultz: Secretary of State 1982–88

Caspar Weinberger: Secretary of Defense 1981–88

1. Introduction

As the name suggests, there were two parts to the Iran-Contra affair. The "Iran" part of the scandal involved the exchange of weapons for American hostages being held in Iran. The "Contra" part of the scandal was related to the Nicaraguan Contras who were supporting a democratic movement in that country. The formal U.S. policy toward the rebels varied between funding them and limiting or refusing funding altogether. In the end, the two parts of the scandal came together when U.S. officials sold weapons to Iran and make a profit. The money from the arms sales was used to support the Nicaraguan Contras. Unfortunately, the officials involved in both stages of the scandal, possibly even the president, may have committed criminal acts. Below is a discussion of the two parts of the scandal and how they came together in the end.

2. Nicaragua

The Sandinistas were a Marxist government that was formed in 1961 in Nicaragua.[22] The United States had cut aid to that country when the Sandinistas came into power because it feared the creation of a Soviet base in the Atlantic. In late 1981, Reagan authorized the CIA to help form a paramilitary force of about 500 fighters to harass the Sandinista government.[23] Reagan agreed to allocate $20 million in secret funds to supply and train the Contras.[24] Even though the United States was financially and militarily supporting the Contras, the administration insisted that it was not trying to overthrow the Sandinistas.[25] At that time, the financial assistance was legal, based on a law passed in 1980 that stipulated that such CIA covert action was permissible if the president found it important to national security and reported such a "finding" in writing to the House and Senate Intelligence Committees "in a timely fashion."[26] The CIA continued to fund the Contras through 1982 and 1983, providing a total of about $90 million.[27]

By November 1982, rumors were circulating around Washington that the Reagan administration was providing clandestine support for the Contras. The House decided to send a message of disapproval to the administration, and Representative Edward Boland (D-MA), chairman of the Intelligence Committee, proposed an amendment to the annual defense appropriation bill to prohibit the spending of federal funds "for the purpose of overthrowing the government of Nicaragua." The 1982 Boland Amendment did not deny all funding for all clandestine activity, but instead forced Congress to trust the president that the aid to the Contras was intended to stop the flow of weapons from the Sandinistas to El Salvador.[28]

In December 1983, Congress decided to place further limits on the president and halt U.S. spending for the Contras at $24 million.[29] However, it was discovered in early 1984 that U.S. mines were laid in Nicaraguan harbors.[30] This angered Congress, because the members of the Senate Intelligence Committee had not been informed of the continued military support of the Contras.[31] When it became obvious that the CIA was still supporting Contra actions against the Nicaraguan government, both houses of Congress rejected an administration request for further funds to support the Contras. Instead, they attached a second Boland Amendment to another defense appropriations act, leaving no doubt that it wanted an end to all U.S. assistance to the rebels.[32] The intent of the amendment was to cut off all U.S. support.[33]

Then Congress passed a third Boland Amendment in October 1984 that was even more restrictive. The law precluded military aid to the Contras from funds available to the CIA, the Department of Defense, or any other agency or entity of the United States involved in intelligence agencies.[34] Congress intended to prohibit all executive assistance to provide military support to the Contras.[35]

Reagan continued to assert his desire to support the Contras,[36] and by 1985 he persuaded Congress to restore $27 million of aid, to be used specifically for nonlethal purposes only. This was the fourth Boland Amendment.[37] In June 1986 Congress went further, approving $100 million for the Contras, including $70 million in military aid beginning in the next fiscal year.[38]

Probably more important than his public statements about the Contras were Reagan's private directives to his staff. He wanted to ensure that the Contras were supported both financially and militarily.[39] Thus, despite congressional legislation, the Reagan administration secretly continued its efforts to unseat the Sandinista government in Nicaragua.[40] It has been argued that he made a clear distinction between the National Security Council (NSC) and the intelligence agencies that were forbidden from assisting the Contras in the Boland Amendment. Reagan also differentiated between the Boland Amendment's prohibition on using U.S. government funds to aid the Contras and using private or foreign funds for that purpose.[41] Later, Oliver North joined him in these interpretations.

At that point, since there was much disagreement about funding, administration officials found it easier to do their work through informal, private channels.[42] Even though Congress blocked further aid to the Contras, the administration remained supportive of them. To provide funding, the administration began seeking out alternative sources of financing. Lt. Colonel Oliver North, a marine who was assigned to work for the NSC,[43] privately began recruiting others to help the rebels. One of his first recruits was retired Air Force Major General Richard Secord.[44] North also worked with the director of the CIA, William Casey, to provide the Contras with intelligence information and advice on military tactics. North arranged for the Contras to buy several major covert shipments of arms from China, Poland, and other countries. The Contras paid cash for those arms, using money supplied by the Saudis.[45]

The United States approached other countries for support. Robert McFarlane approached Saudi Arabian King Fahd, who eventually agreed to provide $1 million per month. Fahd later upped his contribution and by 1985 had provided nearly $32 million.[46] The Saudis also made a sizable contribution after the king's U.S. visit in 1985 (between $15–30 million).[47] Additionally, the administration approached Taiwan, which gave $2 million to the Contras.[48] Brunei agreed to donate $10 million, but the money was sent mistakenly to the wrong Swiss bank account and never reached the Contras.[49]

North soon began working closely with a group of conservative activists in Washington who were experts at raising money. North could tell the Contras' story compellingly, and he was able to raise several million dollars in contributions from wealthy Americans.[50] His fundraising activities were fairly well known in Washington, even being the subject of several newspaper stories in 1986. When the House Intelligence Committee questioned him, North testified that he always complied with the Boland Amendment. He said he justified his actions on the grounds that the Boland Amendment barred involvement with the Contras only by U.S. intelligence agencies, not by the NSC staff or private individuals.

3. Involvement with Iran

The second part of the Iran-Contra affair involved the U.S. relationship with Iran. The leader of Iran, Shah Mohammed Reza Pahlavi, left Iran on January 16, 1979, for an "extended vacation" after ruling Iran for thirty-seven years. At the time he left, there had been several months of civil disturbances and mass demonstrations in the country.[51] Within several months of his leaving, his monarchy was replaced by Islamic Republic, led by a seventy-seven-year-old Shiite Moslem, Ayatollah Khomeni.[52] The ayatollah had gone into exile in Iraq following anti-shah protests in 1963. In 1978, the Iraqi government, concerned with maintaining good relations with Iran, expelled Khomeni, who went to France, where he orchestrated a campaign of opposition to the shah and became a symbol of rebellion. Khomeni had made it known publicly that he wanted to eradicate Western influence from his country. On February 1, 1979, Khomeni returned to Iran to lead the revolution against the shah. Ten days later, on February 11, armed revolutionaries and sympathizers overthrew the shah's government. Three days later, leftist guerrillas stormed the U.S. embassy in Tehran and held seventy employees hostage. The American personnel were freed later the same day.

Toward the end of 1979, two key events occurred. First, the exiled shah received permission to enter America the United States for medical treatment. He flew to New York to undergo surgery.[53] On November 1, Khomeini denounced the shah's admission to the United States and ordered Iranian students to "expend with all their might" their attacks to force the United States to return the shah to Iran to stand trial for his "criminal" actions. Three days later, on November 4, a mob stormed the U.S. embassy in Tehran, taking sixty-six diplomatic personnel hostage. Over time, fourteen were released, but others were held for over fourteen months.

The Iranian militants demanded the extradition of the shah from the United States in exchange for the release of the American hostages. President Carter refused to give in to their demands. Meanwhile, the shah was granted permanent asylum in Egypt in March 1980, where he died in July. Carter ordered deportation proceedings against any Iranian students who were in the United States illegally, halted the imports of Iranian oil, and froze an estimated $12 billion in assets held by Iranians in U.S. banks.[54] Carter tried to negotiate, but all attempts failed. His administration attempted a helicopter rescue mission, which ended tragically on April 25, 1980, when eight Americans were killed as the mission was attempting to leave the Iranian desert.

Many Americans were frustrated with Carter's inability to free the hostages, and Reagan used that issue in the 1980 presidential campaign. Reagan was elected partly because of the hostage issue. Minutes after he was sworn into office, the hostages were freed, with no active involvement by Reagan.[55] Throughout his administration, Reagan tried to ignore Iran. He refused to make concessions to terrorists, saying he would not negotiate with or pay ransom to the hostage takers.[56] However, pro-Iranian groups continued to kidnap Americans, and Reagan could do nothing to prevent further kidnappings. He began to fear appearing helpless, reminiscent of Carter.

About that same time, Israel was also struggling with its relationship with Iran. Like the United States, Israel had close ties to Iran before the shah left and began "selective arms sales" to gain favor with conservative military elements there.[57] In 1981, Israel began supplying spare parts and other military gear to the Iranian army in hopes of improving their relationships with the faction opposed to Khomeini. However, some of the parts Israel was providing were American made, and U.S. law required Israel to get permission from Washington before sending American-made weapons to a third country. It is unclear whether the Reagan administration gave formal approval for the move, but many intelligence officials in the United States knew that Israel was supplying military items to Iran, and they seemed to support the move.

The primary reason Reagan wanted to improve U.S. relations with Iran was to get the American hostages released. The possibility that the moderates in Iran might be willing to help gain the release of American hostages proved irresistible to Reagan, who was apparently willing to take extraordinary steps to get the hostages home.[58] At that point, it was decided to work through Israel and Iranian intermediaries to sell American arms to Iran and possibly get the hostages released.[59] The principal mediator between the United States, the Israelis, and the Iranians would be Manuchar Ghorbanifar, an Iranian and former secret policeman. American officials had labeled Ghorbanifar as not trustworthy, but it was believed that there were few people who were as well connected as he was.[60]

The sale of arms was organized by a variety of means and through a number of different organizations and intermediaries. To conceal American involvement, arms were initially shipped to Iran by Israel. In August 1985, Reagan approved Israeli shipments of TOW antitank missiles to Iran.[61] As a result, two shipments were sent in August and September totaling 508 missiles[62] and resulted in the release of one American hostage, Reverend Benjamin Weir.[63] Iran paid more than triple the market price for the missiles, so the shipments also produced profits for the arms dealers who handled them.

Three months later, in November 1985, Israel proposed and the White House approved a shipment of Hawk antiaircraft missiles to Iran. The shipment became so fouled up that only eighteen missiles arrived, and then only because the CIA provided one of its aircrafts for the task. The White House expected that five Americans would be freed, but no hostages were released in exchange for that shipment. Iran claimed the missiles were inadequate and demanded that the United States take them back, which it did in 1986.

The shipments of Hawk missiles later took on great legal and political significance. Reagan had not given the legally required advance approval of CIA involvement and Congress had not been told, as required by law, that Israel had transferred U.S.-made weapons to another country. To cover the CIA's tracks, it was suggested that a presidential finding be drafted retroactively, authorizing the CIA's participation in the shipment. John Poindexter later testified that Reagan signed the finding on December 5, 1985, but that he destroyed the document a year later because its stated focus on releasing hostages might prove "embarrassing" to the president if ever revealed. The Hawk shipment was important in another respect because it marked the first involvement in the Iranian deals by North and Secord.

Eventually, the arms sales developed into direct sales to Iran.[64] The Department of Defense would sell arms to the CIA, which would then resell them to an armaments company controlled by Secord and his partner, Albert Hakim. Hakim was raised in Tehran and became a U.S. citizen in 1984.[65] Secord and Hakim would in turn sell the arms to Ghorbanifar and finally, Ghorbanifar would sell them to Iran.[66] Thus, Secord, Hakim, and Ghorbanifar each made a significant amount of money from the transactions.

On December 7, 1985, about ten days after the Hawk shipment was complete, Reagan and his top aides held their first serious discussion about the Iran initiative. George Shultz and Caspar Weinberger argued against proceeding with additional arms deals that were being planned by Israel, but Reagan approved more sales. McFarlane then flew to London for meetings with Ghorbanifar. McFarlane said he was shocked by Ghorbanifar's lies and misrepresentations, and he returned to Washington convinced that the Iran initiative should be ended. But North argued for continuing the initiative, and in January 1986, Israel sent a representative to Washington who was able to convince officials to carry on with the arms deals through Ghorbanifar. Poindexter later testified that he assumed Israel wanted the United States to give formal approval to the arms sales it had been making to Iran, because to date the approval had been informal, if any was granted at all.

B. Presidential Finding

On January 17, 1986, Reagan had another meeting with his top aides and signed a finding that authorized the CIA, working through third parties, to sell arms to Iran. The sales would be done in secret, so that not even Congress would be informed.[67] The third parties turned out to be Ghorbanifar and Secord.

The presidential finding resulted in more negations between the United States and Iran concerning arms deals. Throughout the early months of 1986, North and Ghorbanifar met secretly at various places in Europe to arrange arms sales, supposedly to be followed by the release of hostages. There was a sale of 1,000 TOW missiles in February, but no American hostages were released. Ghorbanifar continued to assure the United States that Iran was ready for better relations, so the White House moved ahead with plans for the next step up: a direct meeting in Iran between high-level U.S. and Iranian officials.

In May 1986, McFarlane, North, and an Israeli official traveled to Tehran using Irish passports. They carried with them gifts, a Bible signed by Reagan, and a chocolate cake made by a kosher baker in Tel Aviv. McFarlane took with him a pallet of spare parts for Hawk missiles that Iran already owned.[68] They spent three days negotiating with mid-level Iranians. The negotiations about a larger shipment of parts collapsed because Iran was willing to release only two hostages and McFarlane insisted on the release of all five Americans then being held in Lebanon. The failed mission dimmed White House enthusiasm for the Iran initiative, but only for a while. Iran arranged on July 26, 1986, for the release of another hostage, Reverend Lawrence Jenko. In response, Reagan approved the shipment of twelve pallets of Hawk spare parts to Iran.[69]

C. More Secret Talks/Sales

Secord and Hakim began searching for an alternative to Ghorbanifar to act as a middleman.[70] After several months they made contact with another person who led an Iranian delegation to Washington for more secret talks with North and others in mid-September. These discussions led to one final arms sale in October. This time, 500 more TOW missiles were sent to Iran by Israel in exchange for release of hostage David P. Jacobsen.[71] As part of the deal, the White House agreed to a plan, negotiated by Hakim, that included a promise to seek release of seventeen terrorists imprisoned in Kuwait for attacking Western embassies. Poindexter later testified that Reagan approved the plan, but the White House denied that the president ever gave his approval.

Overall, the arms sales were very profitable because the Iranians were asked to pay two or three times the normal price for the weapons. By the end of February 1986, Swiss bank accounts were filled with millions of dollars generated by the sales. At some point, it was suggested to use these profits to fund the Nicaraguan Contras. North testified that in January 1986, Ghorbanifar proposed aiding the Contras with some of the profits from arms sales to Iran.[72] Others said it was North's idea to link the Contras with the arms sales. [73] Poindexter said he approved the idea, but said he never told Reagan. McFarlane, the national security advisor, claims to have proposed the initiative to Bill Casey.[74] In any event, it was decided that the profits were to be used to support the Nicaraguan Contras.[75] This way, Congress would not have to appropriate any funds and violate the Boland Amendment.[76]

Secord testified that he spent about $3.5 million aiding the Contras. He used some of the money to rent and buy airplanes and to hire pilots and support crews for operations to deliver supplies to the Contras inside Nicaragua.[77] The drops began in April 1986 and continued through the summer and into the fall. The supply operations continued for a short time, but came to a stop when Nicaraguan troops shot down an American supply plane on October 5, 1986. All on board were killed except loading specialist Eugene Hasenfus, a U.S. civilian, who was captured by the Nicaraguans. He later claimed the Contra-aid network was run by the CIA.[78]

About that same time, on November 3, 1986, the arms sales to Iran were made public in *Al Shiraa*, a pro-Syrian magazine in Lebanon. The news report revealed a pattern of trading arms for hostages, even revealing McFarlane's trip to Tehran and the supplies of military equipment to the government.[79] The media reports described how the U.S.-made weapons and other military equipment had been shipped to Iran, using the rationale of gaining freedom for American hostages. The report was confirmed the following day, when Iranian officials insisted that Iran had rejected the U.S. overtures.[80] U.S. officials at first refused to comment but provided details and speculation that kept the issue on the front pages. It quickly became apparent that the Reagan administration had been secretly selling arms to Iran to secure the release of Americans held hostage in the Middle East.[81]

The source of the information was not revealed, but many officials in Washington felt Ghorbanifar had something to do with it. The thought was that he was upset about losing the profits from the weapons sales. The U.S. decision to get rid of Ghorbanifar as a middleman may be the reason the arms sales were made public.[82] Tehran University was papered with leaflets providing details that could only be revealed by Ghorbanifar. The downing of the supply plane in Nicaragua and the revelation of the arms sales to Iran ultimately led to exposure of the private Contra-aid network.[83] In the beginning, Reagan issued fumbling denials of an arms-for-hostages deal.[84] The administration denied that it had been dealing with Iran at all.[85] White House spokesman Larry Speakes said the U.S. arms embargo against Iran remained in effect. However, congressional leaders, none of whom had been informed about the U.S. ties to Iran, demanded explanations from Reagan.

Reagan and his advisers knew that it was important to respond to such a major embarrassment quickly and thoroughly.[86] After Watergate, they understood that most people thought that an attempt at a cover-up might be more serious than the offense itself. Since the operation had already been exposed in *Al-Shiraa*, the administration's strategy was to disclose the story.[87] On November 10, Reagan told his aides that they had to say something about the relationship, but to keep it simple. White House officials later said he feared that publicity would kill any chance of winning the release of any more hostages. Additionally, they had kept few formal records, so they had little hard evidence. There were conflicting recollections about what happened and when.

D. Chronology

In mid-November, North and others began working on a chronology of events they could give to the press. By November 20, the NSC staff had produced at least a dozen versions. Some had numerous essential facts and were labeled "maximum versions," whereas others just skimmed the surface. None of the versions mentioned Reagan's approval of the 1985 Israeli shipments, and none reported that money from the Iranian arms sales had been diverted to Secord's Contra-aid network. None of the versions mentioned Secord at all.[88]

E. Reagan's Response

Reagan made two attempts to explain the arms sales. The first was in a nationally televised speech from the oval office on November 13 where he first officially acknowledged that the United States directly shipped weapons and other military equipment to Iran.[89] However, he also said that the reports that he had supplied the arms in direct exchange for cooperation from Iran in the release of three hostages were "wildly speculative and false."[90] In this speech he offered no apologies and attacked the news media for revealing and speculating about the rationale behind the arms sales. He said the administration was attempting to seek an end to the Iran-Iraq war, eliminate state-sponsored terrorism, and achieve the safe return of American hostages. He also admitted he had authorized the transfer of only "small amounts of defensive weapons and spare parts."

Reagan's second attempt to explain the arms sales was in a news conference on November 19. He still insisted the arms deal was a good policy, and that the shipments were intended to signal his good faith to moderates in Iran. Immediately after the speech, the White House had to release a correction to his assertion that no third country had taken part in the arms transfer. They admitted that Israel had been involved.[91]

From a political standpoint, both efforts to explain the events were disasters. They only raised more questions. The news of selling arms to Iran, apparently in exchange for American hostages, and arming the Contras, possibly in violation of the Boland Amendment, triggered calls for an investigation. Other problems were raised, too. At the time, the United States had a policy of refusing to negotiate with terrorists for the release of hostages, which was possibly breached. The appearance of trading arms directly for the lives of American hostages was a blatant contradiction of stated American policy. There was also a U.S. arms embargo in effect against Iran since 1979. It appeared as if the president sought to bypass Congress by illegal and unconstitutional means.[92]

The White House ordered Attorney General Edwin Meese to conduct an investigation.[93] As a longtime confidant and loyal friend of the president, he conducted a hasty inquiry.[94] There was no written report of the result of the investigation. Instead, he simply told the president some of what he had learned.[95] Meese insisted he was trying only to straighten out conflicts in the recollections of top officials, and that he had no reason to look for criminal wrongdoing. Some say he actually destroyed or altered incriminating evidence. Meese did not seal North's office during the investigation, so North and his secretary, Fawn Hall, shredded dozens if not hundreds of documents, memos, telephone logs, and reports. They also altered some documents and removed others from the office.

However, Meese's investigation did turn up at least one damaging document: a memo written by North the previous April saying that $12 million from a proposed Iranian arms sale would be used to aid the Contras.[96] North acknowledged that he had written it and that money had been diverted to the Contras. He pleaded with Meese to keep it a secret, but Meese claims to have taken the information to Reagan on November 24. At that point, Reagan agreed the information should be made public.

On November 25, 1986, it was disclosed that some profits from the sales had been diverted to aid the Contras.[97] The attorney general reported that officials of the NSC had arranged the clandestine sale of TOW missiles to Iran in return for Iran's assistance in negotiating the release of the American hostages in Lebanon. The missiles had passed through Israel so that the United States would merely appear to be replenishing an ally's arsenal. After the $12 million cost of replacing Israel's missiles had been deducted from the $30 million sale to Iran, an extraordinary $18 million profit had been placed in a Swiss bank account, from which funds were being sent to the Contras.[98]

At a White House press conference that day, Reagan announced that he had not been "fully informed" about that aspect of the arms deal, and that as a result, Poindexter had agreed to resign and North had been fired.[99] Meese took over the press conference and revealed the diversion and estimated it at between $10 million and $30 million. Meese said that no other top U.S. officials knew about the transfer of Iranian money to the Contras.[100] Reagan also announced that he would appoint a special commission to examine the situation.[101]

The commission he established was a three-man board headed by former Senator John Tower (R-TX).[102] Other members were former Democratic senator from Maine and Secretary of State Edmund Muskie, and former national security advisor and retired Lt. General Brent Scowcroft.[103] The Tower Commission was asked to complete their inquiry within forty-five days. Reagan personally met with the commission on January 26, 1987, and told them that he had approved the initial Israeli arms transfers to Iran in August 1985, as well as U.S. replenishment of Israel's weapons stocks. This contradicted earlier testimony by White House Chief of Staff Regan. The commission was surprised at Reagan's limited memory and confusion about events.[104]

The commission had no legal power to subpoena documents, compel witnesses to appear, or grant immunity from prosecution in return for testimony and only had a staff of a few people. Collecting evidence was difficult. Central figures, such as North, received sufficient advanced warning from the initial Meese inquiry to be able to destroy critical files documenting their activities. Key witnesses proved unavailable. William Casey suffered a stroke days before the commission's appointment, and McFarlane attempted suicide hours before he was to testify a second time.[105] All in all, the Tower Commission did not have the ability to complete a thorough investigation.

The commission issued a 304-page report on the Iran-Contra scandal. The commission admitted that they had been unable to unravel the Iran-Contra affair because they had limited access to information and because those interviewed were either not forthcoming or gave contradictory answers. Nevertheless, the commission blamed the president but at the same time forgave him.[106] It concluded that serious errors had been made, laws had been broken, and there were major faults in the foreign policy making process. Furthermore, the report indicated that the White House decision-making process was "too informal" and the NSC was "very unprofessional." Reagan, it declared, had been motivated by "intense compassion for the hostages" but was unaware of how his subordinates were dealing with the matter. Although he "must bear primary responsibility" for the outcome, the president was principally faulted for his management style that gave too much authority to his staff.[107] His detached style allowed Reagan to avoid personal culpability, to appear frank when he admitted mistakes had been made in the implementation of policy, and to sound credible when he pledged to get to the bottom of this matter.[108] Additionally, the commission saw the president as out of touch with what his subordinates were doing.[109] The commission portrayed Reagan as a hands-off manager, one who asked few questions about what was being done in his name and who had little understanding of how his policies were being implemented. In the end, the Tower Commission did not accuse the president of illegal conduct, but found fault with almost all his senior staff and advisers.[110]

While introducing the Tower Commission at a press conference minutes after getting the report, Reagan was clearly stunned and confused. He stumbled in reading a prepared statement and rushed from the room to avoid questions from reporters. The next day he fired his chief of staff, Donald T. Regan, whom the Tower panel had criticized for allowing "chaos" to descend on the White House following the disclosure of the Iranian arms sales. Reagan appointed former Tennessee senator Howard Baker to replace Regan. Baker immediately launched another investigation, this one much more rigorous. They satisfied themselves that no evidence existed that could tie the president to any illegal acts.[111]

The appointment of the Tower Commission did not quell demands on Capitol Hill for separate inquiries. So on December 2, Reagan agreed to request appointment of an independent counsel, and a two-judge panel chose retired federal judge Lawrence Walsh.[112] He was appointed on December 19, 1986.[113] Walsh had worked under Thomas Dewey and served in the Eisenhower and Nixon administrations. For many years he was a federal district court judge, and then practiced law on Wall Street. He even served as president of American Bar Association.

Congress began its own investigation. In December, the House and Senate Select Committees on Intelligence conducted hearings. The meetings were closed to the public because of the national security issues involved. This frustrated the committee members because North and Poindexter refused to testify, claiming their Fifth Amendment rights against self-incrimination.[114] Late in July 1987, the committee made public a summary of its findings. There was a partisan battle over the timing of the report. It was crammed with details, but contained no conclusions and was of limited help in advancing public understanding of what happened and why.

On January 6, 1987, the Senate decided to form the Select Committee on Secret Military Assistance to Iran and the Nicaraguan opposition. At the same time, the House of Representatives was only one day away from creating its own select committee to conduct a parallel investigation. This was to be named the House Select Committee to Investigate Covert Arms Transactions with

Iran.[115] The Senate had an eleven-member committee, headed by Daniel Inouye (D-HI).[116] The House had a fifteen-member committee headed by Lee
Hamilton (D-IN) and Dick Cheyney (R-WY).

The need for so many separate investigations was questioned. Both the House
and the Senate wanted to share the spotlight, so the House agreed to allow the
Senate to take the initial risk of investigating an apparently popular president.
The outgoing Republican majority leader, Robert Dole, and the incoming Democratic leader, Robert Byrd, agreed to combine the Senate and House committees into one,[117] which would be headed by Inouye.[118] Inouye did not want to
inflict further damage on the presidency if he could avoid it.[119] The consequence
was that the committee investigating Iran-Contra was a large joint committee.[120]

The special joint committee found it difficult to obtain testimony from participants in the Iran-Contra affair, because they risked criminal prosecution
on the basis of information they provided.[121] In addition, the independent
counsel, Lawrence Walsh, was still conducting his investigation and warned
that he might issue indictments based on any testimony given. Walsh could
only use information gathered before a grant of immunity, and so he wanted
Congress to delay taking action as long as possible.[122] If the independent counsel indicted them, he would not be able to use their congressional testimony
to build a criminal case against them.[123] The immunity question caused the
joint committee hearings to be delayed until mid-May, and the testimony of
the key witnesses, Poindexter and North, to be put off even further.[124]

To reduce partisan feuding in the committee, congressional leaders agreed
to limit the agenda and implement tight time schedules for the investigations.
There were twelve weeks of hearings from thirty-two witnesses, several of
whom received limited immunity against prosecution for their testimony. The
hearings filled in many of the details of the affair and showed covert operations run by the NSC staff and private agents with little supervision by either
the president or his senior foreign policy advisers.

Some of the testimony was given in private, whereas other parts were televised.
The witnesses included Secord, Meese, Shultz, Weinberger, Regan, McFarland,
Fawn Hall, Poindexter, and others.[125] Poindexter testified in private that he never
told Reagan about the diversion of arms and money. His testimony probably
prevented the president from being impeached. North spent nearly six days at
the hearings. He portrayed himself as a loyal soldier who had done only what
he was authorized to do and who sought only to serve the president. His image
on television was good. People clearly liked what they heard as well as what they
saw. He depicted himself as a pawn in a struggle among higher-ups.[126]

On March 4, Reagan made another attempt to explain the Iran initiative, this
time in a prime-time televised speech. He acknowledged that the United States

had traded arms for hostages and accepted responsibility for any failures, but did not apologize.

F. Findings

The congressional joint committee issued two reports: one by the majority and one by the minority. The majority report found that the Iran-Contra scandal occurred because of the deficiencies of individuals and not the result of deficiencies in the law.[127] In part, the committee declared that the ultimate responsibilities for the events in Iran-Contra must rest with the president and that there had been a failure in leadership and supervision.[128] The committee stressed the dangers of bypassing standard procedures, allowing unelected aides to have too much power, and putting public policy in the hands of private agents. They also said that Congress shared a measure of blame and the hearings demonstrated the need for cooperation between the legislative and executive branches of government. Overall, the committee leaders more or less ignored Reagan's role in the affair. They said that the president's loose control over the White House meant that his aides had free rein to carry out what they perceived as his ideological stance.[129] The committee did not suggest that impeachment proceedings be brought against Reagan. The majority of committee members believed that impeachment was too severe a punishment for the offense committed.[130]

Even after the main investigations were completed, it was not clear that Reagan fully understood what had happened. Although he said on several occasions that he accepted responsibility for what had gone wrong, he appeared to accept personal blame on only one count: allowing his emotional concern about the hostages to override his judgment that making concessions to Iran was wrong. He never acknowledged that the White House pursued the arms sales in hopes of getting the hostages released before congressional midterm elections. It appears that McFarlane and Poindexter, in their daily briefings to the president, only gave him partial information. The formal procedures for making and implementing decisions were bypassed. Key actors, such as Shultz and Weinberger, were excluded when they voiced objections, and there were no periodic reviews to determine whether the adopted policies were working.

G. Special Prosecutor

In 1994, after a seven-year investigation and a cost of $37.6 billion, Walsh's report was made public. It concluded that the policies behind the Iran-Contra affair were fully reviewed and developed at the highest levels of the Reagan administration. The Iran operations were carried out with the knowledge of Reagan, Bush, Schultz, Weinberger, Casey, McFarlane, or Poindexter. Furthermore, U.S. policy toward Iran and Nicaragua was turned over to private people, who were outside the scrutiny of Congress and the public. Those people who did know lied to Congress.

The report concluded that Reagan broke no laws, but that he knowingly participated in covering up the scandal. Walsh claimed that Reagan knew of the arms-for-hostages swap from the beginning and was repeatedly warned that the plan was illegal. Reagan did not ensure that the laws were executed. Walsh noted that Reagan and his administration misled Congress and the public.[131] Moreover, according to Walsh, there was no evidence that the vice president, George H.W. Bush, violated any laws. At the same time, Bush was fully aware of the arms sales and he withheld evidence. In the end, the report concluded that neither Bush nor Reagan knew of diversion of money to the Contras.

However, the sales of arms to Iran may have violated the Arms Export Control Act, and the coordination of support to the Contras violated the Boland Amendment. Walsh implied that he would have been justified in bringing before Congress a case for the president's impeachment.[132] Although he did not do that, he was successful in prosecuting fourteen individuals, winning eleven guilty pleas or jury verdicts.[133]

When he became president, Bush viewed the Iran-Contra affair as a policy failure, not a crime. He believed several of Reagan's advisers had been unfairly prosecuted for doing what they thought was in the best interest of the nation. So, on December 24, 1992, he pardoned six people involved in the scandal, including Weinberger, McFarlane, Elliott Abrams, D. Clarridge, Alan Fiers, and Claire George.[134] By doing so, he guaranteed that no trials would be held. Some say he did that because without a trial, no evidence of his own conduct or misrepresentations would be made public.[135]

H. Outcomes

Many of the actors in the Iran-Contra affair were punished criminally for their actions. Secord pled guilty on November 8, 1989, to one count of "making a false statement to Congress" and received a $50 fine and two years' probation. The statement had to do with a new security fence placed at North's home.[136] On June 16, 1992, a grand jury indicted Weinberger, the former secretary of Defense. He was charged with five felonies, including one count of obstructing a congressional investigation, two counts of making false statements, and two charges of perjury.[137] McFarlane pled guilty to a misdemeanor count of supplementing North's salary, for which he received a $5,000 fine and two years' probation.[138] Poindexter was given immunity from prosecution for anything he said. He went out of his way to protect the president by accepting responsibility for Iran-Contra.[139] He was convicted on five counts of false testimony to Congress[140] and sentenced to six months in prison. Both men successfully appealed their convictions.[141]

In 1989, North was tried on twelve charges.[142] He was found guilty on three relatively minor charges: preparing false chronologies about Iran-Contra, destroying evidence, and accepting an illegal gratuity. He was acquitted on nine other counts. North's defense contended that he believed that in deceiving Congress and other actions he was merely carrying out the president's wishes.[143] North was under investigation for a new security system that had been installed in his home after he and his family had received credible death threats. As a response, Secord had someone put a security system in.[144]

Walsh immediately ran into a problem with the conviction. North had been granted immunity for his congressional testimony.[145] Although Walsh tried to immunize his case from North's prior testimony, an appeals court ruled that the case was tainted by the public statements that North had made. As a result, North's conviction was overturned.[146] Poindexter's conviction was also overturned on appeal.[147] These and other outcomes are presented in Table 5.2.

I. Illegal Acts

There is little doubt that many laws were broken during the Iran-Contra affair. The administration had failed to keep Congress informed of its actions. They were not notified in a "timely" fashion of covert actions.[148] In fact, throughout most of the Iran-Contra affair, Congress was not notified at all, a clear violation of the law. The diversion of funds from the Iran arms sales to the Contras was also a violation of the Boland Amendment.[149] Many involved committed perjury in their attempts to deceive Congress.[150]

Other laws were broken as well. In the 1970s, after the Vietnam War, Congress enacted several laws requiring the administration to report on covert operations overseas. PL 93-559, passed in 1974, required the president to tell Congress "in a timely fashion" about covert operations by intelligence agencies. It also required the president to sign a finding stating the justification and goals for each action. When Carter complained that reporting covert operations to multiple congressional committees would increase the risk of leaks, Congress revised the law (PL 96-450) so that notice need only be given to the House and Senate Intelligence Committees. Under certain circumstances, that notice could be limited to a few senior leaders. If the administration did not notify the committees before an operation began, the president would have to do so afterward "in a timely fashion" and explain why the advanced notice was not provided.[151]

In 1985, Congress again amended the notification law to require the Intelligence Committees to be told whenever an intelligence agency provided weapons or defense service (training) to any entity outside the U.S. government (PL 99-569). However, it noted that this was necessary only when the weapon or defense service was worth $1 million or more. None of the items reportedly sold to Iran—including spare parts for antiaircraft missile batteries—cost more than $1 million apiece.

The Arms Export Control Act (PL 90-629) enacted in 1968 and amended often after that, required the administration to report to Congress all major arms sales to foreign countries made through regular channels. This also included third party transfers and shipments of U.S.-originated arms from the country that first purchased them and sent to another country.[152] The 1976 amendment prohibited the transfer of arms by countries purchasing them from the United States and selling them to third parties to which the United States would not itself sell.[153] Sources say that Reagan provided no arms sales notices about Iran to Capitol Hill.[154]

Moreover, the supplying of weapons to Iran defied the directives of the first and second Boland Amendments and even to some extent the third. The failure to inform Congress about these transactions, not to mention lying when asked specific questions about the transfers, may have represented further offenses.[155]

Reagan could have been charged with high crimes and misdemeanors for his own acts or, if subordinates had taken these actions, for violating his oath of office to see that the laws were faithfully executed.[156]

PL 99-399 was signed into law on August 27, 1986, by President Reagan. This law toughened the restriction on arms sales to terrorist countries (Export Act). The bill increased funding for the security of U.S. embassies overseas and included a ban on military exports to countries on the list of those in support of terrorism. The president could waive the prohibition only by determining that such an export was "important to the national interests of the U.S." If he did so, however, he had to report to Congress within ninety days, justifying his decision.

Table 5.2: Outcomes of the Iran-Contra Scandal

Ronald Reagan
Traveled after his presidency; wrote a book called *An American Life* in 1990; was diagnosed with Alzheimer's; passed away

Oliver North
North said that to protect the lives of those with whom he was dealing in Iran and Central America, he was forced to lie to Congress and others in the administration whom he did not trust. He was tried on twelve criminal counts

and convicted on May 4, 1989 of three felony counts, including altering and destroying NSC documents, aiding and abetting the obstruction of a congressional inquiry, and illegally accepting a home security system as a gift. He was given a $15,000 fine, 1,200 hours of community service, a 3-year suspended sentence, and 2 years' probation (North 1991: 477–78). On July 20, 1990, a three-judge panel of the U.S. Court of Appeals reversed one of the three outstanding counts against him and vacated the other two. The special prosecutor asked the court to reverse its decision, but on November 27, 1990, the Court of Appeals again decided in his favor by upholding the panel's decision. It went to the Supreme Court; on May 1991, the Court reaffirmed the two earlier decisions by the Appeals Court and declined to hear the case. On September 15, 1991, Lawrence Walsh decided to drop the two remaining charges, saying that that his testimony in front of Congress (which was given with immunity) may have influenced his trial (Oliver 1991: 490–91). He receives a lieutenant colonels' pension. He wrote books and ran for Senate from Virginia in 1994. He is now on a cable TV talk show.

Fawn Hall
Hall admitted to helping North shred documents after disclosure. After the hearings, Hall moved to LA and attempted a career in television journalism. There she developed an addiction to crack cocaine. She overdosed while in LA and entered a four-month treatment program in Florida. She married Danny Sugerman, a former manager of The Doors.

John Poindexter
As the former national security advisor, Poindexter was convicted on five felony counts and sentenced to six months in prison. In November 1991, a federal appeals court overturned the convictions because his immunity testimony tainted their criminal trials. With a colleague, he started a software company.

George McFarlane
McFarlane attempted suicide in 1987 with an overdose of Valium. He pleaded guilty to four misdemeanor counts of lying to Congress and was sentenced to two years' probation and a $20,000 fine. He was pardoned by Bush. He went into business in Southeast Asia and makes utility and energy deals.

Caspar Weinberger
Weinberger was indicted on five felony counts of perjury and obstructing justice, he says because he refused to falsely implicate Reagan. He pleaded innocent to lying to Congress in November 1992, and was pardoned by Bush. He became a publisher of *Forbes Magazine* and has an estate in Maine called Windswept.

Edwin Meese
Meese accepted a job at the Hoover Institute on War, Resolution and Peace at Stanford University. He also works for the Heritage Foundation, a conservative research foundation. There he holds the R. Reagan chair in public policy. He wrote his memoirs called *With Reagan* in 1992.

George Bush

Bush ran for president and won, but lost his reelection bid. Since he was never indicted by Walsh, he was entitled to compensation for his legal expenses. He was awarded $272,352—somewhat less than the $461,346 he sought. As former president, he is "very, very happy" in retirement. He lives in Houston, gives speeches, and jumped out of an airplane to celebrate his birthday.

George Shultz

Shultz lectures, golfs, writes, and sits on corporate boards. The court ruled the government must pay his legal fees of $281,000.

Richard Secord

Secord pled guilty to one felony count of lying to Congress and received two years' probation.

Albert Hakim

Hakim pled guilty to one misdemeanor count of giving $13,000 to North, a government employee. His company pled guilty to theft of government funds (arms sales profits). He was allowed to keep $1.7 million profit. He was sentenced to two years' probation and $5,000 fine.

J. Why Was Reagan Not Impeached?

There are many reasons why Reagan was not impeached for his involvement in the Iran-Contra affair. These include:

1. Timing: When Iran-Contra unfolded, Reagan was in the third year of his second term. Impeachment proceedings could not have been completed before he was out of office. Moreover, many people remembered how Watergate had brought the government's work to a standstill for two years and were reluctant to let that happen again.[157] Many citizens were mindful that this country would have been paralyzed again, and people did not want to see that happen.[158] This was of particular concern because at the time, Reagan was in negotiations with the Soviet Union concerning nuclear weapons, and the public was anxious to see some conclusion there.

Moreover, by the time Walsh's report was released and the congressional Iran-Contra report was released, other things had happened to distract the American public. There was a Supreme Court nomination (Robert Bork), a stock market plunge, and a turn in U.S. relations with the Soviet Union.[159] Also, not only had Reagan left office, so had his successor, George Bush.[160] Bill Casey died May 6, 1987. Many of the primary actors were gone, and there were other issues to address.

2. Lack of Evidence: There was no "smoking gun," or documented proof of Reagan's involvement in Iran-Contra.[161] North and Hall had shredded a great deal of documentation,[162] and there was no definite evidence that Reagan ordered the events or even that he knew about them.[163] Because of that, it could never be definitively established that he was personally involved in the affair. Reagan had what Nixon did not: plausible deniability.[164] Most people seem to agree that he probably knew, but there was nothing to prove it. His knowledge remained unclear.[165] Some believe that most of the events were hidden from the president by McFarlane, Poindexter, and North.[166] They had a deliberate strategy to insulate Reagan from the potential consequences of the scandal.[167] Similarly, some of those involved in the affair, particularly Poindexter and North, refused to testify against Reagan. Many people around the president tried to protect the highest office and the man who occupied it.[168]

Reagan was willing to "play the fool" and appear as if he did not understand or did not know, or that he was confused, about the events, where Nixon was not. Reagan often appeared contrite in news conferences, apologizing to the American public. He also appeared to cooperate with Congress and the investigators.[169] Although there were some in the administration who said that he was informed every step of the way, there was also a lot to suggest Reagan either did not know, or did not want to know, the details.[170]

Reagan was a very popular president,[171] and remained that way throughout his two terms of office, even when his policies were not so popular.[172] More than likely, opponents would not have been able to gather enough votes to impeach him.[173] In the end, Reagan remained personally popular, although confidence in his leadership was severely weakened.[174]

The actions of those directly involved in Iran-Contra, even if carried out by unconstitutional or illegal means, were geared toward objectives that many Republicans and even some Democrats in Congress supported.[175] The safe release of the hostages was something everyone wanted.

The events of the scandal were in a hazy realm of foreign policy where the president is historically given more leeway. Presidential actions in the domestic realm are more constitutionally limited and watched, where presidential actions in foreign affairs are more arbitrarily exercised.[176]

Many Americans supported establishing new contacts between the United States and Iran, and Reagan was just showing his support for this.[177] Some argued that he believed the arms transfers would create a new beginning in U.S.-Iran relations.[178] In general, Reagan could be seen as meaning well and attempting to achieve some important foreign policy goals.[179] These particular actions were undertaken by a president who sought to promote policies he believed in. They were not domestic crimes and misdemeanors, as in Watergate or Abscam, or actions taken to meet his own needs, such as reelection.[180]

Reagan's response to the revelations contrasted sharply with Nixon's. Reagan and his administration behaved very differently than Nixon's in the months after the scandal broke.[181] The press conference held before the public in which Reagan and Meese admitted that wrongdoing had occurred before it could be exposed by others was critical. The next day, Reagan appointed an investigatory panel, which demonstrated that the White House was not engaging in a cover-up, as Nixon did. Soon after, Reagan called for the appointment of an independent counsel to pursue the matter further.[182] These all showed that they were not attempting to cover up their actions.[183]

The public just did not understand the seriousness of the Iran-Contra affair. It was a complicated scandal that involved many countries, personalities, and events. Most did not have the time to learn about it, nor the desire. The general public did not have the patience to grasp the serious constitutional violations involved.

K. Conclusion

The Reagan administration was certainly not immune from scandal. Like Nixon, Reagan spent a good portion of his last few years in office trying to deal with the investigation and aftermath of publicity surrounding some possibly illegal behavior. The revelations surrounding Iran-Contra prevented the president from being effective in his final year, as he and his advisers were preoccupied with investigations and allegations. Much of the investigation surrounded attempts to decipher who was responsible for the choices made: the president or his associates. Some would argue that the "prime mover" in the initiative was Reagan,[184] and that he knew what was happening from the start. But even today, it is unclear what he knew. To many, it showed that Reagan was not the strong and effective leader that his aides portrayed him to be. Nearly every report about Iran-Contra produced new evidence that he could be easily manipulated by his aides, that he asked few questions, and that he did not always understand the full implications of the decisions he was asked to make.

For some, the Iran-Contra scandal was more frightening than Watergate because it revealed that the entire U.S. national security apparatus could made by lower-level employees, possibly without the president's input or knowledge. In this case, North, an NSC aide, was allowed to step in and control national foreign policy.[185] It seems apparent that North and a handful of men tried to use the U.S. government to achieve their personal missions, especially because the regular process was too slow and too uncertain.[186]

It could be argued that the arms-for-hostages policy was a failure. During this time, three hostages were released and three others were kidnapped.[187]

The U.S. relations with Iran worsened. Private arms merchants working on behalf of the administration made profits of millions of dollars. Reagan's public approval never fully recovered after the scandal,[188] despite his popularity.

George H.W. Bush

There were few scandals in the Bush administration, which lasted only four years. Many of the scandals involved other personnel in the administration or people with ties to Bush.

A. Iran-Contra Pardons

In December 1992, George Bush issued full pardons to six people involved in the Iran-Contra scandal, including former Defense Secretary Caspar Weinberger and five others. He believed that Reagan's policies toward Iran and the Contras were important foreign policy decisions. Critics said he did it to protect himself from being more deeply implicated in the scandal.[189]

B. Affair

During the 1992 campaign, Bush was plagued by rumors that he had a sexual relationship with Jennifer Fitzgerald, his aide at the Republican National Committee and when he was in China. Bush strongly denied all of the rumors, and no improper relationship was ever proven.[190]

C. Jeb Bush

Bush's son Jeb defaulted on a $4.56 million loan from a Florida thrift, leaving taxpayers to cover more than $4 million in costs. Another one of Bush's sons, Neil, became the director of the Silverado Savings and Loan in Denver in 1985. In that job, he approved more than $150 million in questionable loans for some business associates. To make matters worse, one of the associates used part of the loan to buy Bush's failing oil business, JNB Exploration. When Silverado Savings and Loan collapsed in 1988, it cost taxpayers more than $1 billion.[191]

D. John Sununu

In December 1991, Chief of Staff John Sununu was forced to resign after the *Washington Post* revealed that he had flown on various personal trips at great expense to the taxpayers.[192] It was alleged that he used government military aircraft for his own use. He took military jets to fundraisers, ski trips, golf vacations, and a dentist appointment in Boston. Because of this, the scandal was termed Air Sununu. Because of the publicity, he repaid the government about $47,000, an amount much less than the actual cost of the trips.

E. Vice President Dan Quayle

As a young man, Dan Quayle joined the National Guard in his home state of Indiana. However, at the time he joined, Indiana had a waiting list of about 1,000 people. Quayle got right in, so there were allegations that he used his family connections to help him. He said he did not agree with the United States' involvement with the Vietnam War, but he nonetheless supported the president.[193]

There were also charges of adultery made against Quayle. The allegations involved a lobbyist, Paula Parkinson, who had a condo in Florida.[194] Groups of senators would go there for golfing weekends.[195] There were allegations that votes were being traded for sex.

There were also drug allegations against Quayle. During college, his fraternity had psychedelic parties, and people there claimed he took part in them. One person in particular, a convicted felon, said he knew Quayle from parties and even supplied him with marijuana about once a month. He claimed to have given him hash and marijuana as a wedding present. The supplier was supposed to have a press conference, but it was canceled and he was put in the hole as punishment. As vice president, Quayle spoke against the use of illicit drugs.

In school, Quayle had a 2.4 GPA, but still got into law school, one where his family had donated money. He got in through a program for minorities and disadvantaged.

Conclusion

During the presidencies of Ford, Carter, Reagan, and Bush, political scandals continued. There were fewer in the Ford, Carter, and Bush administrations, but the Iran-Contra affair in the Reagan administration was a serious scandal with many long-term impacts. Many argued that Iran-Contra was worse than Watergate, as it involved foreign policy and our relations with other countries. It also demonstrated the ease with which a private individual could impact foreign policy to such an extent. The Iran-Contra affair did not have the same impact on Reagan as Watergate had on Nixon for many reasons. However, it was still an important national political scandal.

Review Questions

1. What was the scandal referred to as "Billygate?"
2. Describe the events of the Iran-Contra affair.
3. What laws were broken in the Iran-Contra scandal?
4. Describe some short-term and long-term impacts of Iran-Contra.
5. What was the Tower Commission and why was it important?
6. Why was Reagan not impeached?

Special Terms

Billygate
Iran-Contra
Boland Amendments
Tower Commission

Discussion Questions

1. Were the actions Billy Carter took regarding Libya appropriate?
2. Are the actions of presidential family members a reflection on the president? What about his cabinet or other appointed officials?
3. Is it possible for a candidate to promise a scandal-free and honest administration?
4. Which was worse: Iran-Contra or Watergate?
5. Should private individuals be able to get involved in U.S. foreign policy?
6. What role should covert actions play in foreign policy?
7. Was it appropriate for Bush to pardon people intimately involved in the Iran-Contra affair?
8. Should Reagan have been impeached for his role in Iran-Contra?

Chapter 6

Clinton Scandals

Introduction

The 1970s were slack years for presidential sex scandals, with presidents Nixon, Ford, and Carter seemingly faithful spouses.[1] This changed when President Bill Clinton entered office. Clinton was a popular president, elected twice by voters. But during his administration, there were numerous allegations of wrongdoing and sexual misconduct, some of which led to his impeachment. These are all described in this chapter.

Clinton Scandals

A. Draft

As a young man, Clinton managed to avoid the Vietnam War, possibly with the help of special treatment from the Hot Springs, Ark., draft board. He originally registered for the draft, as all young men were required to do, in 1964. He went to Georgetown University and received a student deferment so he was able to avoid the draft for that period of time. When he left Georgetown, Clinton was again eligible for the draft. He was accepted to Oxford University and got another deferment so he could attend school there, allegedly partly due to assistance from Arkansas Senator William Fulbright and Governor Winthrop Rockefeller. Midway through his Rhodes scholarship at Oxford, he pledged that if his deferment was extended, he would enter the Reserve Officers Training Corps (ROTC) program once he finished at Oxford. On returning to Arkansas, he enrolled in the ROTC program at the University of Arkansas Law School.[2] But he never enrolled in law school in Arkansas, choosing instead to go back to Oxford.[3] At that time, Congress changed the draft to a lottery system, and Clinton drew a high enough number to avoid the draft, then withdrew his ROTC pledge. Meanwhile, he participated in anti-Vietnam War demonstrations in England.[4] Clinton's actions regarding the draft raised questions not just about his patriotism and willingness to serve in the armed forces but his honesty and integrity.[5]

B. Drug Use

While running for governor of Arkansas in 1986, Clinton denied allegations that he used illicit drugs as a young man. Then in 1989 he expanded that statement to indicate that he never used drugs as an adult. In 1991, he specifically claimed that he never tried marijuana in college. But in 1992 his story changed again. That year, Clinton claimed that while he was in England attending Oxford University, he experimented with marijuana once or twice, but denied inhaling, and then never tried it again.[6]

C. Pardongate

On his final day in office, January 20, 2001, President Clinton pardoned numerous felons, including Marc Rich, a financier who fled the country and was hiding in Europe on charges of illegal commodities trading. It was also alleged that Rich traded with enemies of the United States as well as a drug dealer who was serving a long sentence in prison for importing drugs into the United States. After Clinton left office, it was discovered that Rich's wife had given a large amounts of cash to the Democratic Party and to the Clinton Presidential Library in Arkansas. There were additional allegations that involved Hillary Clinton's brother, Hugh Rodham, and Bill Clinton's brother, Roger Clinton, for taking kickbacks in exchange for presidential pardons.[7]

D. Cabinet Members/Other Personnel

Many of Clinton's Cabinet were involved in scandal, which may be a reflection on Clinton himself. The large number of unethical administrators may reflect the overall unethical environment in the administration. On the other hand, it may simply point to the increased media coverage that was established after Watergate. Nonetheless, the following are some of the administrators involved in scandal during the Clinton years.

1. Bruce Babbitt

In May 1998, Clinton's secretary of the Interior, Bruce E. Babbitt, was investigated by special prosecutor Carol Elder Bruce surrounding allegations that he made false statements during congressional testimony in 1997 concerning an Interior Department decision to deny an application by three Native American tribes to operate a casino in Hudson, Wisconsin. The investigation also focused on accusations that political contributions to the Democratic Party influenced the department's decision. Independent Counsel Bruce announced on October 13, 1999, that there was not enough evidence to support the allegations against Babbitt or anyone else in the agency, and there was no evidence of an agreement between any opponent of the casino application and any government official involved in the Hudson decision to perform an official act in exchange for a political contribution. As a result, there were no criminal indictments brought against Babbitt.[8]

2. Web Hubbell

Web Hubbell was an attorney who worked in the Rose Law Firm in Arkansas. In addition to his legal duties, he was elected to the Little Rock City Board in 1978 and was named Little Rock's mayor the following year, serving a two-year term. When Clinton became president, he named Hubbell to the Arkansas Supreme Court, and he served there for six months.[9] Clinton then appointed Hubbell to serve as deputy attorney general for the U.S. Department of Justice in Washington.

After serving only a short time in that position, Hubbell was forced to resign from office,[10] pleading guilty on December 6, 1994, to income tax evasion and mail fraud, both felonies.[11] Specifically, he admitted that he defrauded the Rose Law Firm and its clients of $390,000 to cover his personal credit card purchases. He agreed to cooperate fully with independent counsel Kenneth Starr.[12]

He was sentenced to twenty-one months in a federal facility, ordered to pay restitution to the Rose Law Firm, and given three years of supervised release after the prison term. After fifteen months, he was then required to speak in prisons once a month for a year, traveling to Arkansas at his own expense to talk about the necessity of accepting responsibility.[13] Hubbell publicly apologized, saying that he only intended to "borrow" the money, and did intend to steal it.[14]

3. Dick Morris

Dick Morris was one of Clinton's chief political consultants during his 1996 reelection bid and was credited by many for the success in that campaign. Morris, a native of New York City, got along well with the president. He was originally contacted by Clinton when he was attorney general of Arkansas and only considering a run to be governor of Arkansas. After Clinton won that election, he felt that he no longer needed Morris and let him go. In the 1980 campaign, Hillary Clinton placed an emergency call to Morris late in the campaign, but it was too late and Clinton was defeated. Morris and Clinton then worked again in 1982, 1986, and 1990. In 1990 Morris and Clinton had an argument about Morris working for Republican clients. Morris, who was bipartisan, claimed he could work for both.

For Clinton, the first two years of his administration were a disaster. In 1994, when the Republicans got the majority in the House and Senate, Clinton had to deal with Newt Gingrich and Bob Dole. Clinton found himself struggling, so he brought Morris back to help. Morris agreed to do nothing but work to get Clinton reelected in 1996, and then leave town. He had no interest in a permanent job in the Clinton administration.

With Morris's help, Clinton's approval ratings started to go up. But the day that Clinton was to give his acceptance speech at the Democratic convention, there was a report in a tabloid newspaper that Morris was having an affair with a prostitute,[15] and he immediately resigned. The prostitute's name was Sherry Rowlands,[16] who charged $200 per hour. The report said that Morris whispered campaign secrets to the woman and privately referred to Clinton as "the Monster." He admitted to the affair but said that he did not allow Rowlands to hear plans and conversations, but she had tapes of their conversations and was able to prove her allegations.

The scandal broke in the middle of the Democratic National Convention in Chicago in August 1996. The story received a lot of attention in the media. It had been an uneventful convention, and many media personnel had even left, but returned when the story broke. Clinton almost immediately tried to distance himself from Morris, afraid that campaign secrets would be revealed, but that did not happen.

4. Ron Brown

Ron Brown was Commerce Secretary under President Clinton. Before becoming secretary, he was a lawyer-lobbyist earning nearly $1 million a year. As Commerce Secretary, he earned only $148,400 a year.

After a preliminary investigation, Attorney General Janet Reno said that there was evidence that Brown received nearly $500,000 from First International while serving as Commerce secretary. Brown said that he and his business partner, Nolanda Hill, formed First International in 1990 as a "merchant bank," with the aim of matching potential investors with promising international projects. They each owned 50 percent of the stock, even though Brown invested no money in the company. Brown then sold his interest back to the company in December 1993 and received payment in multiple installments. One was a payment of $135,000, in part a forgiveness of a $72,000 debt he owed to a company owned by Hill. Another payment paid off $300,000 of his personal debts.

On his 1993 annual disclosure report, Brown reported that he had sold his interest in First International for somewhere between $250,000 and $500,000, but on other sections of the form, he did not record the $135,000 payment or the company's obligation to pay off $300,000 in loans for him. Reno also said that Brown failed to disclose that he held his interest in the Boston Bank of Commerce through a partnership and that he misidentified the location of property held by Potomac Housing Fund Limited, a real estate partnership in which he was a limited partner.

In May 1995, Reno asked for an independent counsel to determine whether Brown violated federal laws in his business dealings and financial reports. On July 6, 1995, a three-judge panel of the U.S. Appeals Court named Daniel Pearson as independent counsel to determine whether Brown broke the law by accepting money from Hill and whether he falsified disclosure forms and a mortgage application. The investigation ended after Brown was killed in a plane crash in Croatia.[17]

5. Alexis Herman

Alexis Herman, Clinton's secretary of Labor, was charged with taking cash bribes and illegal campaign donations while an aide to Clinton from 1994 to 1996. There were accusations from Laurent Yee, a businessman from Cameroon, that Herman took cash kickbacks from a client of his seeking a federal license for a satellite telephone system. There were also allegations that Herman used her position as White House director of public liaison in Clinton's first term to illegally solicit campaign contributions from clients of the consulting firm she ran before joining the administration in 1993. On May 26, 1998, Ralph I. Lancaster was appointed to serve as an independent counsel to review the allegations.[18] Lancaster found no evidence demonstrating wrongdoing on Herman's part. She was eventually cleared of the charges.[19]

6. Vince Foster Jr.

Vince Foster Jr. was a close associate of Hillary Clinton and her former partner at the Rose Law Firm who had come to the White House from Arkansas to serve as the White House deputy counsel. He had been Hillary's legal representative on many matters at the White House, and in doing so, had been involved in several controversies. He was involved in the decision to fire seven employees of the White House travel office[20] and was also working on the Whitewater investigation.[21] As a result, the *Wall Street Journal* had written several editorials that were critical of him.[22]

Foster was described as a steadying influence, a person others turned to for support and reassurance,[23] but he was unaccustomed to the Washington po-

litical environment. Even though many of his friends and relatives denied that
he had been depressed,[24] it was later confirmed that he was confronting unaccustomed pressure and suffering from clinical depression.[25]

This all came to a head on July 20, 1993. Foster left the White House and
drove his car to Fort Marcy Park in northern Virginia. Using an antique 0.38-
caliber Colt revolver, he put the gun in his mouth and shot. The bullet perfo-
rated his brain and came out the back of his skull, killing him instantly.[26] A little
bit later, a man found the body, went to a nearby maintenance station for the
National Park Service, and told them to call the police. Two rescue teams and
a single Park Police officer arrived at the scene.[27]

Foster's office was not sealed until the day after he died,[28] meaning that anyone who wanted to could simply walk in.[29] It was alleged that White House
officials removed sensitive files and records of business deals between President Clinton, his wife, and Whitewater Development Corporation.[30] They also
removed files concerning Whitewater's income tax returns for 1990–92, although Clinton denied knowing that Foster had worked on the tax return.[31] The
removal of documents suggested to many that the White House was attempting to coverup something.[32] Eventually, the office was sealed and formally
searched by Clinton associates with law enforcement present.[33] This included
Justice Department lawyers, FBI agents, and Park Police officers.[34] They found
a torn-up suicide note in Foster's briefcase about thirty hours after the body
was first found.[35]

A White House intern testified at the Senate hearings that he took a box of
documents from Foster's office to the Clintons' residence. He was told that the
First Lady would review the documents. But Hillary's chief of staff said that it
was not true, and that the box of papers was always in Foster's office. A Secret
Service officer testified that he saw Hillary's chief of staff remove documents
from Foster's office and took two polygraph tests to support it.

There are many questions involving Foster's role in Clinton's investments that
were suspicious.[36] These questions resulted in many suspicions about the events
of Foster's death. Some of the unanswered questions are listed in Table 6.1.

The underlying reason why Foster killed himself was questioned. There were
allegations that he was murdered,[37] but there was little evidence of that. There
was some speculation that he had somehow managed to learn—on the day of
his death—that a federal judge signed a search warrant for the Little Rock offices of David Hale.[38] Back in April 1986, Hale's company had loaned $300,000
to Susan McDougal and allegedly, a portion of this loan ended up in the bank
account of the Whitewater Development Corporation.[39]

An independent counsel, Robert Fiske, was assigned to determine the cause
of Foster's death. On Thursday, June 30, Fiske released a fifty-eight-page re-

port on the events surrounding Foster's demise. The report concluded that he committed suicide.[40] In an odd twist, Fiske was later replaced by Starr, who was again given the responsibility to reinvestigate the death of Foster.[41] On Tuesday, July 15, Starr announced, once again, that his office concluded that Foster committed suicide.[42] Additionally, the Park Police, the Department of Justice, and the FBI each concluded that he committed suicide.[43]

Table 6.1: Inconsistencies in the Vince Foster Suicide

a. No one could account for Foster's whereabouts for the five-hour period from the time he left the White House until his body was found.

b. No fingerprints were found on the gun in Foster's right hand.

c. The bullet that killed Foster could not be located.

d. A blood transfer stain on Foster's right cheek could not be fully explained; the investigators found his head straight up, not resting on his right shoulder where blood had accumulated.

e. A roll of 35 mm film that the police had used to take pictures of the crime scene was underexposed and worthless.

f. Two back-up Polaroid photographs taken at the scene were missing.

g. None of the investigators at the crime scene were present at the autopsy.

h. Foster's clothes were stacked in a pile by a coroner's assistant, causing possible cross-contamination.

i. No gunpowder was found on Foster's tongue.

j. The mystery man in the white van who discovered Foster's body could not be identified or located.

k. Other visitors to the park reported seeing several unidentified men behaving suspiciously.

l. No one from Foster's family could positively identify the gun as being his.

m. Two rescue workers at the crime scene had seen little or no blood and no exit wound in Foster's head.

n. Skull fragments and brain matter were not recovered at the crime scene.

o. The ambulance driver who had picked up Foster's body had coded the death as a homicide.

p. The Park Police did not have Foster's gun tested by firearms examiners until after the case had been publicly closed.

q. The former director of the FBI, who had been fired by the president the day before Foster's death, claimed that the investigation had been politicized.

r.   There were no pools of blood.

s.   There was no record that Foster ever left the White House on the day he died.

t.   There were irregularities about the gun; at the scene they said it was a black gun, but later they said it was silver; the serial number was taken off the gun.

Source: Moldea 1998: 3–4, 8; Stewart 1996: 393

7. Hillary Clinton: Commodities Trading

On March 30, 1994, it was disclosed that Hillary Clinton invested $1,000 in commodities trading and came out with $100,000.[44] This profit was unusual because commodities trading is a very risky business whereby traders bet that the future value of a commodity, such as cattle or pork, will rise or fall. Some investors have long been drawn to the commodities markets, often losing a lot of money.[45]

Hillary's first investment was probably the short sale of ten live cattle contracts with a value of $220,000 on October 11, 1978. In less than two weeks, she was able to recoup five times this original investment. In Hillary's next six trades, half were losers, including a loss of over $17,000 on a short sale of live cattle. Overall, she ended the year with net profits of over $26,000, bringing her total gains to just under $100,000.[46]

Some said that her top performance was virtually impossible without some special treatment or information. She had expressed interest to a friend in investing some money, but admitted to knowing little about commodities markets. She counted on some friends to help her, including Jim Blair and Robert L. "Red" Bone. Bone handled the actual trading, but Hillary retained all the decision-making authority.[47] There are no insider trading laws in the commodities field,[48] so having help is not necessarily illegal. Nonetheless, the excessive profit in such a short time seemed unusual to many Americans.

8. Nannygate

Two of Clinton's nominees for attorney general had issues with their child care providers, thus the term "nannygate." The first controversy, over nominee Zoe Baird, came to light before Clinton even took the oath of office.[49] Baird was a corporate lawyer and a moderate, and her nomination seemed uncontroversial.[50] Unfortunately, it was soon discovered that she and her husband had hired two illegal immigrants to help with child care and to act as a chauffeur[51] and that the couple did not pay Social Security taxes on the immigrants.[52] Baird's nomination was voluntarily withdrawn.[53]

Clinton's second nomination for attorney general, Kimba Wood, had also hired an illegal alien as a nanny, but she had paid Social Security taxes and begun the steps for her nanny to obtain legal residency status. However, under much publicity, she also withdrew from consideration.[54]

9. Lani Guinier

Lani Guinier was Clinton's choice to be the assistant attorney general for the Civil Rights Division of the Justice Department in late 1993. The media made public her controversial views on proportional representation in local elections. She also supported racial quotas as opposed to affirmative action. It was rumored that her interviews with senators prior to the nomination hearings did not go well, and some urged Clinton to withdraw the nomination, which he chose to do.[55]

10. Henry Cisneros

Henry Cisneros served as Housing and Urban Development Secretary from 1993 to 1996. He was educated at Harvard and began his political career as a city councilman. He won a campaign for mayor of San Antonio, Texas, in 1981, serving as mayor for four terms, then declined to run for a fifth term. He was chosen to serve as HUD secretary because Clinton wanted a multicultural cabinet and Cisneros was a well-respected person in the Hispanic community.

Cisneros was investigated for lying to federal investigators about how much money he had paid his former mistress.[56] During the background check for approval of his nomination, he was questioned about payments he made to Linda Medlar. Cisneros admitted to having an affair with her from 1987–90 while he was still mayor and sending her money. When asked how much, he told them more than $10,000 a year between 1990 and 1993. But court documents said that he paid her between $42,000 and $60,000 a year.

Because there was controversy over the amount of money Cisneros paid Medlar, the FBI turned the matter over to the Justice Department and Reno, who appointed an independent counsel in December 1997. His name was David M. Barrett, and he was given the power to look into charges that Cisneros lied to FBI investigators during background checks. The investigation found that Cisneros had vastly underestimated the amount of his payments to Medlar and lied about their duration. Cisneros told investigators he never gave Medlar more than $10,000 a year and that the payments had stopped. In fact, the independent counsel said Cisneros was still paying his mistress and gave her more than $250,000 by the time those payments stopped in January 1994. He said he gave her $10,000 a year for three years, but the FBI said it was $60,000 per year. Medlar agreed with the higher amounts. She said that out of moral obligation, Cisneros agreed in early 1990 to pay her $4,000 a month until 1999, when her daughter would be out of college. Cisneros acknowledged telling the FBI agent in January 1993 that he had paid Jones about $2,500 a month, when he knew that the amount was considerably higher.

Cisneros was indicted December 1997 on eight felony counts of conspiracy, obstructing justice, and making false statements to the FBI about his payments to Medlar. He pleaded not guilty to all counts, but resigned before the investigation was over, pleading guilty to a misdemeanor charge of misleading the FBI and fined $10,000.[57] He then went into private business, taking a job at Univision network television where he was president and chief operating officer. In all, Independent Counsel Barrett spent more than two years and $9 million pursuing the Cisneros investigation.

11. Mike Espy

Mike Espy was Clinton's Secretary of Agriculture. On September 9, 1994, Donald C. Smaltz was appointed as an independent counsel to investigate charges that Espy received $33,000 in gifts and entertainment from companies his department regulated.[58] It was alleged that Espy received sporting event tickets and free air travel from the nation's largest chicken producer, Tyson Foods.[59] Smaltz also found that Espy had delayed and suspended department regulations on poultry makers. Espy was indicted in 1997 on thirty-five counts of criminal activity and resigned from office.[60]

In the end, Smaltz was able to obtain eight guilty pleas and one "no contest" plea from individuals and companies. There were two settlements of civil suits, resulting in fines. Smaltz also won six jury convictions against other parties. Despite these successes, Smaltz was not able to convict Espy, who was acquitted on all counts in 1999.[61]

E. Filegate

The scandal called Filegate (1996) involved charges that Clinton's White House aides deliberately obtained sensitive FBI files of some prominent Republicans[62] for unknown reasons. Approximately 700 FBI files were allegedly improperly ordered by the Clinton administration during his first year in office. College-age interns between the ages of eighteen and twenty who helped manage paperwork in the office and other volunteers who did not have appropriate security clearances had open access to the files.[63]

Republicans publicly raised the possibility that the FBI background files were misused and denounced any possible criminal activity related to the misuse of the files. They questioned if the White House was keeping an enemies' list. This was made all the more curious when new reports indicated that the

White House was compiling a list of about 200,000 lawmakers, news media, and campaign contributors that included personal data about their political loyalties, military records, college degrees, and family relationships. Some claimed the list could be used as a way to keep track of their enemies. The White House said the list was comprised of names of people to invite to functions, social events, and as a Christmas card list.

In January 1998, independent counsel Starr questioned Hillary Clinton under oath about the possibly improper acquisition of the confidential files. Janet Reno also directed the FBI to launch an investigation to determine whether there was any criminal liability in the case. There were congressional hearings in two committees: the House Government Reform and Oversight Committee and the Senate Judiciary Committee. Each was trying to determine how and why the reports ended up at the White House.

In the end, there were no charges brought, but the White House said there would be an internal reorganization to tighten procedures for handling such files.

F. Travelgate

In the first few months of the Clinton administration, Hillary Clinton was accused of illegally firing seven members of the White House Travel Office to replace them with friends from Arkansas.[64] They were fired for "gross mismanagement."[65] In response, Representative Bob Barr of Georgia filed an impeachment resolution on November 5, 1997, but it went nowhere.[66]

G. Women: Paula Jones, Monica Lewinsky, and Others

Before and during Clinton's term in office, there was a plethora of women alleged to have had sexual affairs with Bill Clinton.[67] There is not much doubt that he had several indiscreet relationships after marrying his wife,[68] one of which led to his impeachment. The Flowers, Jones, and Lewinsky cases, in a broader context, demonstrated a pattern of abusive conduct toward women, sexual harassment, and the abuse of presidential power by ordering state employees (state police troopers) to procure women, by promising jobs to buy silence, and by spending government money to facilitate trysts.[69]

The first allegation made regarding Clinton's sex life was made in 1991, in an article in *Penthouse* magazine. The author recounted the memoirs of a rock groupie named Connie Hamzy.[70] Hamzy claimed that in 1984, while hanging around a pool in Little Rock, she was approached by an Arkansas state trooper who asked if she would like to meet the governor.[71] Another female who was allegedly abused by Clinton was Sally Perdue, a former Miss Arkansas. She claimed she had been intimidated to keep silent about an affair she had with him.[72] Yet another woman, Elizabeth Ward Gracen, claimed similar events. She described how, when she was twenty-one and serving as Miss America, she was offered a ride in Clinton's state limousine. Gracen had been doing a public service announcement in Hot Springs when, according to her, Clinton flirted with her, and then invited her to the apartment of one of his friends, where they had sex.[73] Clinton allegedly also had relations with Lencola Sullivan, another Miss Arkansas.[74]

Juanita Broaddrick, also known as Jane Doe #5, reported that Clinton forced her to have sex with him in 1978, when he was making a first run for governor. Broaddrick was working as a campaign volunteer and, during a campaign stop, Clinton invited her to his office. When she was in town again, she contacted him. He suggested they meet in a hotel coffee shop, but later suggested they have coffee in her room instead because there were too many reporters. She agreed. After a few minutes, he began to kiss her and forced her to have sex with him.[75]

The three most well-known liaisons of Clinton's were Gennifer Flowers, Paula Jones, and Monica Lewinsky. The Jones case began with an encounter in a hotel room and ultimately resulted in an extensive investigation by a special prosecutor, multiple lower federal court cases, and a major U.S. Supreme Court decision concerning executive immunity from civil law suits and the impeachment of a popular president.[76]

1. Flowers

Gennifer Flowers was a former Arkansas state employee who claimed that she and Clinton had a twelve-year affair.[77] She was a nightclub performer in Little Rock and a television news reporter when they first met in 1977.[78] She acknowledged that during their affair, Clinton often smoked marijuana.[79] After their affair ended, she asked him to get her a government job, which he did.[80] Flowers also admitted that she lied in an earlier hearing after Clinton told her to.[81]

The affair remained secret until the 1992 election when the tabloid magazine *Star* printed a story that Flowers had a long-term relationship with Clinton.[82] Even though she had audio recordings to prove the affair,[83] the Clinton campaign denied it. To emphasize the denial, the Clintons appeared on the news show *60 Minutes* after the Superbowl. In the interview, Clinton acted like a caring, honest husband and flatly denied having an affair with Flowers, although he did admit to "causing pain in my marriage."[84] After the appearance, his popularity shot up in the polls.[85]

2. Jones

In 1993, a new scandal named "Troopergate" was made public when four Arkansas state troopers told stories about soliciting women and facilitating extramarital trysts for Clinton while he was governor.[86] They claimed he offered federal jobs in exchange for the troopers' silence,[87] an obvious misuse of state employees by the governor. The story of one trooper in particular, Danny Ferguson, was the beginning of many problems for Clinton.

On May 8, 1991, Ferguson approached Paula Corbin Jones while she was working at a conference and told her that the governor wanted to see her. At the time, Jones was a twenty-three-year-old state employee who thought Clinton wanted to offer her a job, so she went willingly. Ferguson took her to the governor's suite at the Excelsior Hotel.[88] As soon as she and Clinton were alone, he took her by the hand and made an unwanted sexual advance.[89] He pulled out his penis and asked her to kiss it.[90] She declined.

When a magazine called the *American Spectator* reported that Clinton had had an affair with someone named "Paula," and inferred that she had sexual relations with him, she wanted to clear her name.[91] On February 11, 1994, Jones held a press conference where she told her version of what happened.[92] At the press conference, she said she wanted an acknowledgment of misconduct and an apology from Clinton. He refused, claiming that he did not recall meeting her,[93] that he was never alone in a hotel room with her, and he did not make any sexual advances toward her.[94] Instead, the White House said that Jones was making these claims to cash in with the tabloids.[95] Jones replied by claiming there were distinguishing characteristics in Clinton's genital area that she could identify.[96]

Three months later, on May 6, 1994, since there was no action from the president, Jones filed a $700,000 civil suit for sexual harassment in the federal district court in Little Rock.[97] She was able to because she was a state employee at the time, making Clinton her boss.[98] She claimed that Clinton caused her "severe emotional distress."[99] She alleged four counts against him: deprivation of civil rights, conspiracy to deprive her of her civil rights, intentional infliction of emotional distress, and defamation. It was the first such lawsuit against a sitting president.[100]

In August, Clinton's lawyers offered to give Jones full payment plus a general statement, acknowledging no sexual misconduct but regretting that her character and reputation had been harmed. By this time, her lawyers upped the amount they demanded to $1.2 million. Jones's lawyers turned down the offer because it did not have a full public apology.[101]

Attorneys for the president filed a dismissal motion in an attempt to delay the legal proceedings, arguing that a chief executive, while in office, should be immune from civil as well as criminal suits even if they involve matters that preceded his presidency.[102] The attorneys contended that Jones needed to wait until Clinton left office before a court could hear the complaint. The judge in the federal court in Little Rock to which the case was assigned was Susan Webber Wright. She ruled on December 28, 1994, that the Constitution clearly specified that the overriding interest of the nation required that an incumbent president should not be diverted from carrying out his public duties, and that allowing suits to be brought against him might result in harassment of the president. Therefore, the trial of any civil suit should be postponed until the defendant was no longer president.[103] Even though the president did not enjoy absolute immunity from the legal process, he was entitled to a temporary postponement of the trial.[104]

Jones appealed that decision to the Eighth Circuit Court of Appeals in St. Louis, and Webber Wright delayed the rest of the proceedings pending the outcome of the appeal.[105] In January 1996, the appeals court overturned Webber Wright's ruling in a two to one decision.[106] They held that a suit arising out of activities prior to becoming president and not related to official duties should proceed,[107] thus paving the way for the trial.[108] Clinton could not postpone the civil lawsuit until after he left office.[109]

This time it was Clinton's turn to appeal. On May 15, 1996, his lawyers took the case to the U.S. Supreme Court, asking the justices to delay the trial until he left office. In June, the Court agreed to review the lower court's decision, thus delaying trial again, at least until after the November elections.[110]

In the meantime, in August 1996, Webber Wright set May 27, 1998, as the date for the Jones trial to begin. At the time, she threw out two of the four claims she made against Clinton, finding that there was no basis for the claims that he had deprived her of her constitutional rights, nor had he defamed her.[111]

The Supreme Court case, now called *Clinton v. Jones* (520 U.S. 681), was heard by the justices in January 1997, one week before Clinton's second inauguration. On May 27, 1997, the Court unanimously affirmed the judgment of the appellate court by ruling that this case did not represent a diversion of presidential time and energy. In fact, the Jones suit would not absorb much of the president's time and would only minimally divert him from other activities.[112] The case would not seriously disrupt the functioning of the presidential office.[113] Further, there was no serious risk of exposing the presidency to "politically motivated harassing and frivolous litigation."[114] They said that Clinton could be sued for acts unrelated to his presidential office. Thus, according to the Supreme Court, the Paula Jones case against the president could proceed.[115]

Jones accused Clinton of conspiring to deprive her of her constitutional rights when he was governor of Arkansas. To gather evidence for the trial, her lawyers sought out other women who had sexual affairs with the president to show a pattern of sexual harassment on the part of the president. If they could find other women, it would show a pattern of importuning employees. The lawyers found five women who were reported to have had sexual contact with Clinton, but they all denied the rumors in pretrial depositions.

One woman who was asked about her sexual relationship with the president was Kathleen Willey, whom the lawyers heard was offered a job in exchange for sex with Clinton.[116] Willey was a former flight attendant and campaign volunteer. She claimed that in November 1993, Clinton propositioned her in the Oval Office. He made an "unwelcomed sexual advance" by wrapping his arms around her and putting her hands on his groin. This took place the day before Willey's husband, an attorney accused of embezzling $275,000 from a client, committed suicide.[117] After the suicide, she went back to see Clinton a second time on December 10, 1993 to ask for a better job, and they just talked. However, Willey served as the only nonexpert member of the U.S. delegations to Copenhagen and Jakarta. Although she was unsalaried, she was comfortably accommodated. Her son, Patrick, was accepted as a White House intern.[118]

Another woman identified as a potential witness was Monica Lewinsky.[119] Lewinsky was a 1995 graduate of Lewis and Clark College in psychology who served as an unpaid intern in the White House in 1995, working for Leon Panetta, then Clinton's chief of staff. Some say she was obsessed with the president. Because she seemed to be spending too much time around the Oval Office, she was transferred to a staff position at the White House Office of Legislative Affairs in fall 1995. She then moved to the Pentagon in April 1996.[120]

Lewinsky was accused of having an affair with Clinton in the executive mansion for eighteen months, from November 1995 to May 1997,[121] when the affair began, she was twenty-one, only a few years older than Clinton's daughter.[122] Lewinsky visited the Oval Office often after she transferred to the Pentagon. She usually checked in to see Clinton and his private secretary, Betty Currie. She would arrange through Currie for visits to the study outside the Oval Office, where she would perform oral sex on Clinton.[123] He allegedly asked Lewinsky to lie about their relationship, and promised her a job to keep her quiet.[124]

Lewinsky gave her deposition in the Jones case on January 7, 1998, to discuss her relationship with the president. In the deposition, when asked if she had sexual relations with Clinton, she denied it. She testified that after she left the White House, she only saw the president at formal functions, official receptions, or events related to the Department of Defense.

Clinton gave a videotaped deposition on the Jones sexual harassment law-suit on Saturday, January 17, 1998 at the White House.[125] Jones was in atten-dance. Clinton testified under oath in a six-hour closed door hearing that he could not remember meeting her. He also denied having a sexual relationship with Lewinsky[126] and answered questions about his relationships with several other women, finally admitting an affair with Flowers.[127] He then repeated that denial about his relationship with Lewinsky to the national public.[128] He pointed his finger at the TV camera for emphasis he told the public that he "did not have sexual relations with that woman, Miss Lewinsky."[129]

About that same time, a close friend of Lewinsky's, Linda Tripp, knew that Lewinsky and Clinton had both lied in their depositions. Lewinsky had met Tripp while working at the Pentagon. Tripp had worked in the White House during the Bush administration and into Clinton's, but was not a fan of Clinton.[130] Lewin-sky told Tripp how she met the president in the Oval Office and had given him oral sex and that they had phone sex in the early hours of the morning.

Tripp, claiming she feared for her job, contacted Lucienne Goldberg, a New York literary agent, about writing a book about Clinton and the affair. Gold-berg realized they needed proof of the affair and suggested Tripp tape conver-sations with Lewinsky to back up her statements.[131] So Tripp began taping Lewinsky's phone calls.[132] She made tapes of twenty-one conversations be-tween herself and Lewinsky. The tapes showed that Clinton bought her gifts, including a dress, and a volume of Walt Whitman's *Leaves of Grass*. Lewinsky also bought Clinton gifts, including cigars, ties, and a statue of a frog. She de-scribed the love letters and a sexually explicit tape she sent Clinton and the messages he left on her answering machine. Lewinsky was also recorded on tape saying she was going to lie under oath to help Clinton. Moreover, she gave Tripp a three-page memo with hints for how to handle a deposition.[133] It was titled "Talking Points" and provided details that were very legal and tech-nical, pointing to the possibility that the memo was not written by Lewinsky. In any event, the memo suggested that Tripp should recant her earlier story and to tell Jones's lawyers that she never saw the president acting inappropri-ately with anyone.

Tripp took the tapes to Ken Starr and convinced him that Lewinsky and Clinton had lied under oath in their depositions. On January 16, 1998, Starr met with the Justice Department to obtain permission to expand his original mandate to investigate Clinton's alleged relationship with Lewinsky.[134] Starr had originally been appointed to look into the Whitewater land deal in Arkansas, but later investigated the firing of staff from the White House travel office, and then investigated charges relating to the misuse of FBI files.[135] But when he was presented with information about the president's sexual behavior that may have been related to another ongoing legal matter, he decided to pursue it. To do that, he first needed to consult with the panel of three senior federal judges who oversee the operations of all independent counsels.[136] He wanted to expand his inquiry to include possible obstruction of justice in the Jones and Lewinsky matters. Reno and the three-judge panel granted Starr's request.[137] Now he could investigate the rumors about Clinton's affair with Lewinsky. If they were true, it meant that the president had lied in a legal deposition, thus committing perjury.[138]

On January 16, 1998, the independent counsel's staff swooped down on Lewinsky. Starr questioned her for twelve hours and eventually persuaded her to cooperate with them.[139] They told her that she could be charged with numerous federal crimes, including perjury, subordination of perjury, obstruction of justice, and witness tampering, which were all felonies, and she could go to jail for twenty-seven years.[140]

Starr subpoenaed billing records of her purchases, excavated her computer files, interviewed her friends, and questioned her mother. He looked at her telephone records, e-mail correspondence, and logs of entry and exit to the White House. These logs showed that Lewinsky visited the Oval Office thirty-seven times after leaving to work at the Pentagon. Starr even subpoenaed records from her purchases at book store, *Kramerbooks and Afterwords,* to verify a book purchase she made as a gift for Clinton.[141] He subpoenaed advertising billing records from the *Washington Post* that show that Lewinsky purchased a personal ad for Valentine's Day. It was addressed to Handsome and signed "M." He subpoenaed courier service records that show Lewinsky sent parcels from her Pentagon office to Betty Currie. He also subpoenaed her credit card receipts to learn about gifts from her to Clinton. He also verified that Clinton's close associate, Vernon Jordan, helped get Lewinsky a job to keep her quiet about the affair.[142]

Lewinsky provided Starr with fingerprints, samples of hair, and a recording of her voice. She also turned over several taped phone messages from Clinton, and the infamous blue dress that was stained with the president's semen. The dress was analyzed by the FBI for traces of Clinton's DNA.[143]

In late July 1998, Lewinsky agreed to testify in return for immunity from prosecution.[144] Starr made a deal with her that if she testified in detail, he would give her immunity from prosecution testimony.[145] If she chose not to, then he would charge her with perjury over her testimony in the Jones case. At her trial, Clinton would be called as a witness. She agreed to the deal.

Because he lied in the January 17 deposition, Starr realized Clinton had lied under oath, obstructed justice, and suborned perjury, all criminal offenses. So Starr decided to subpoena the president for the grand jury. On August 17, 1998, Clinton appeared before the grand jury via closed-circuit television from the White House.[146] He was the first sitting president to be summoned to a grand jury in an investigation of his own conduct. He was able to have his lawyers present, something that ordinary citizens cannot have.

In the grand jury testimony, Clinton changed his story from his earlier testimony. He admitted to having an inappropriate relationship with Lewinsky,[147] but claimed that he had not committed perjury in the earlier deposition because he did not interpret their activities as sexual.[148] He claimed that as the judge in the Jones case defined "sexual relations," there was no sex act committed between himself and Lewinsky. The definition given by the previous judge was that a person engages in sexual relations when that person "knowingly engages in or causes contact with the genitalia, anus, groin, breast, inner thigh or buttocks of any person with an intent to arouse or gratify the sexual desire of any person," and Clinton claimed that he did not touch those parts of her body. The definition did not cover oral sex performed by one party. He claimed he never engaged in "sexual relations" with Lewinsky, which he defined narrowly as intercourse.[149] He also did not consider oral sex to be a "sexual relationship" or adultery.[150] But Lewinsky testified that he touched her breasts and touched her genitals.

That evening, after testifying in front of the grand jury, Clinton again appeared before the American people, this time admitting to an inappropriate relationship with Lewinsky.[151] He apologized to the nation for misleading them and denying the affair.[152] He said he misled his wife, but that it was a private matter between them. He denied that he asked anyone to lie, hide or destroy evidence, or take any other unlawful action.

On August 6, 1998, Lewinsky testified before the grand jury and said that she and Clinton had a sexual affair within the White House. It happened in a small, private study down a short hallway from the Oval Office. She said that they always talked about ways to conceal the relationship, but that Clinton never told her to lie under oath. On August 21, 1998, she gave another grand jury testimony to give more specific details concerning any contradictions between her testimony and Clinton's.

Tripp also testified in front of the grand jury in late June 1998 and early July. She gave six hours of testimony and finished on July 29, 1998.

In the middle of this, on April 1, 1998, Webber Wright dismissed Jones's entire sexual harassment lawsuit against Clinton, four years after it was filed. The judge said that Jones could not prove that she had been harmed. Even if the encounter had happened as Jones said, Webber Wright said that it was not enough to justify a legal remedy. The episode was brief, isolated, and did not harm her physically or in her job. Moreover, Webber Wright explained that there was insufficient evidence to conclude that Jones's claims constituted a violation of her civil rights.

Jones appealed, but before the appeals process fully began, the two parties settled their case on November 13, 1998. Her lawyers wanted $1 million, and Clinton agreed to pay $850,000.[153] Even though Clinton settled, he did not admit any wrongdoing.[154] As expected, his lawyers said that the allegations were baseless but wanted to get the dispute behind him. Some of the money was to come from Chubb Group Insurance, and the balance from Clinton's Legal Expense Trust. He also drew $375,000 from his and his wife's personal funds. It was estimated that Jones will receive about $200,000 from the settlement, and the rest would go to the attorneys.

On June 2, 1998, Starr for the first time brought up the possibility of an impeachment referral against Clinton. He decided to inform Congress that he had found evidence of an impeachable offense. In August 1998, some people brought up the idea of censure for the president. With a censure, the president would basically be scolded as a symbolic punishment. Some said this was not constitutional, as it was not outlined in the Constitution.

3. Starr Report

Starr delivered his 445-page report to the House on September 9, 1998.[155] It was made public two days later. In it, he chronicled the intimate details of the president's affair according to Lewinsky's descriptions of her sexual encounters with him.[156] The report contained many details that some thought should not have been included, such as that of a sex act performed while Clinton was talking on the phone to a member of Congress. Starr said the details were necessary because they were evidence of wrongdoing.[157] Although it may have appeared as if Starr was interested in the president's private sex life, in reality he was more interested in the steps taken to cover up these indiscretions.[158]

In all, the report showed evidence that Clinton committed perjury, suborned perjury, obstructed justice, tampered with witnesses, and abused the power of his office.[159] It showed that he lied multiple times during his civil deposition in the Jones sexual misconduct lawsuit and during his grand jury testimony. The president lied about his sexual relationship with Lewinsky repeatedly. He also lied in his televised press conference to Americans and to his Cabinet and White House aides.[160] He also was guilty of encouraging others to lie under oath on his behalf and of promising jobs to keep people quiet.

The report described eleven counts of possible impeachment offenses against Clinton, including five counts of lying under oath, four counts of obstruction of justice, one count of witness tampering, and one count of abuse of constitutional authority. It also contained allegations of crimes for which the president could face criminal prosecution if he left office through resignation or impeachment.

Some people, particularly Democrats, were angry about the level of sexual detail in the report. The report was based largely on grand jury testimony, elicited by one side only and not subject to cross-examination by the other side. Some of the testimony came from immunized witnesses or witnesses who feared prosecution. Many of the witnesses were "prepared" by prosecutors before they were questioned in front of the grand jury.[161]

The White House responded to the Starr Report with a seventy-eight-page rebuttal, alleging that it was a politically motivated attempt to humiliate the president. The administration argued there was personal but not impeachable misconduct described in the report and that Starr was only trying to have the president removed from office for a sexual indiscretion. They denied that Clinton committed perjury, obstructed justice, tampered with witnesses, or abused the power of his office.

4. House Judiciary Committee

On September 11, 1998, the House voted 363–63 to set forth a review by the Judiciary Committee and the possibility of impeachment.[162] At the time, the House Judiciary Committee was comprised of twenty-one Republicans and sixteen Democrats, and was led by Representative Henry Hyde (R-IL). On September 30, 1998, the committee prepared a draft of a resolution to formally open an impeachment inquiry against Clinton. On October 5, 1998, the committee voted to recommend that the House open a formal impeachment investigation into Clinton's behavior. They sent the House a resolution authorizing the committee to investigate whether sufficient grounds existed for the House to impeach Clinton. The Democrats tried for a limited inquiry, but their proposal failed. The committee members said they had evidence of fifteen impeachable offenses. They dropped two of Starr's accusations, and added several new including "conspiracy to obstruct justice."[163] On October 8, the committee voted to authorize an impeachment inquiry on a strict party-line vote.[164] They voted to launch a full-scale, open-ended inquiry into possible grounds for impeachment by a vote of 258–176.

Starr testified in front of the House Judiciary on November 19, 1998. He testified that Clinton misused the machinery of government and "thwarted the search for truth." He acknowledged that he found no evidence to accuse the president of criminal conduct in other areas, such as Whitewater or the White House travel office firings, or the possible misuse of FBI files. He defended his four-year, $40 million investigation, saying that it was possible to criminally indict Clinton when he left office, but he was unsure if it would happen.

5. Impeachment

Much of the debate in the Judiciary Committee centered on the meaning of "high crime" and the definition of an impeachable offense.[165] Although the Constitution says that the president can be removed for treason, bribery, "or other high crimes and misdemeanors," there are no specific guidelines as to what that means. Is an impeachable offense an indictable crime or a crime against the state? Does it have to involve the president's official duties, or personal life as well? Were Clinton's misdeeds official acts? His offenses did not involve the powers of his office or directly affect the operation of government, and there was no existing precedent for considering impeachment of a president for remotely similar offenses.[166]

Did Clinton commit a "high crime" or misdemeanor? Technically, adultery is a misdemeanor in D.C., but he maintained that he did not commit adultery, or have sexual relations, as defined by the judge. But Starr argued that Clinton lied under oath in his deposition and therefore was guilty of perjury. Further, if he put pressure on Lewinsky to lie about their relationship in her deposition, then he was guilty of suborning a witness. Additionally, if he had some gifts removed from her apartment, he was guilty of obstructing the course of justice. Since Clinton, as president, was the chief law enforcement officer of the United States, these were serious, or impeachable, offenses. On the other hand, some argued that trying to conceal an improper sexual relationship is not what the Founding Fathers had in mind when they specified the offenses for which a president could be removed from office.[167]

On December 9, the House Judiciary Committee formally called for the president's removal from office in four draft articles of impeachment, including two counts of perjury, one count of obstruction of justice, and one count of abuse of power. These are presented in Table 6.2. Three days later, the Judiciary Committee began two days of voting on the four articles of impeachment against Clinton. A week after that, by a near party-line vote, the House narrowly voted two articles of impeachment of the president. The first article, passed by a vote of 228 to 206, charged that the president had given "perjuries, false and misleading testimony to a federal grand jury." The second article, passed by a vote of 221 to 212, charged that he had committed obstruction of justice in the sexual harassment lawsuit filed against him by Jones.[168] With that, Clinton became only the second president in the nation's history to be impeached by Congress and the first elected president to suffer that fate.[169]

The Senate trial started on January 14, 1999.[170] Whereas articles of impeachment pass by simple majority vote,[171] the Constitution requires that at least two-thirds of the Senate vote to convict for removal to occur. This means that if there was a two-thirds majority vote in the Senate on either article of impeachment, Clinton would be forced to leave the presidency and turn the position over to the vice president. It is not easy to get such a high degree of consensus among senators, particularly when the stakes are so high.[172] Accordingly, on February 12, 1999, the Senate voted not to remove Clinton from office, as neither of the two articles commanded enough votes.[173] On the issue of perjury, forty-five senators voted "guilty" and fifty-five voted "not guilty." The vote on obstruction of justice was only fifty to fifty, far short of the two-thirds needed for removal.[174]

On April 12, 1999, Judge Webber Wright found the president in civil contempt of court for giving what she called intentionally false testimony about his relationship with Lewinsky.[175] She said he lied under oath about his relationship with Lewinsky in the sexual misconduct suit filed by Jones. Further, the president "responded to plaintiffs' questions by giving false, misleading and evasive answers that were designed to obstruct the judicial process." She ordered him to pay a $90,000 fine to cover "reasonable expenses," including the legal fees incurred by Jones as a result of his false testimony. She also ordered him to pay her court $1,202, the cost of her travel to Washington in January 1998 to preside over the deposition in the Jones suit. The case was referred to the Professional Conduct Committee of the Arkansas Supreme Court to determine if any further disciplinary action was appropriate. In 2001, Clinton agreed to a five-year suspension of his Arkansas law license in return for the suspension of the independent counsel investigation. Because of the suspension, he was automatically suspended from the U.S. Supreme Court bar. He later chose to resign from that voluntarily.

Table 6.2: Impeachment Charges against Clinton

Articles of Impeachment

RESOLVED that William Jefferson Clinton, President of the United States, is impeached for high crimes and misdemeanors, and that the following articles of impeachment be exhibited to the United States Senate:

ARTICLES OF IMPEACHMENT EXHIBITED BY THE HOUSE OF REPRE-SENTATIVES OF THE UNITED STATES OF AMERICA IN THE NAME OF IT-SELF AND OF THE PEOPLE OF THE UNITED STATES OF AMERICA, AGAINST WILLIAM JEFFERSON CLINTON, PRESIDENT OF THE UNITED STATES OF AMERICA, IN MAINTENANCE AND SUPPORT OF ITS IM-PEACHMENT AGAINST HIM FOR HIGH CRIMES AND MISDEMEANORS.

Article 1: Perjury before Independent Counsel Ken Starr's grand jury.

In his conduct while President of the United States, William Jefferson Clinton, in violation of his constitutional oath faithfully to execute the office of President of the United States and, to the best of his ability, preserve, protect, and defend the Constitution of the United States, and in violation of his constitutional duty to take care that the laws be faithfully executed, has willfully corrupted and manipulated the judicial process of the United States for his personal gain and exoneration, impeding the administration of justice, in that:

On August 17, 1998, William Jefferson Clinton swore to tell the truth, the whole truth, and nothing but the truth before a Federal grand jury of the United States. Contrary to that oath, William Jefferson Clinton willfully provided perjuries, false and misleading testimony to the grand jury concerning one or more of the following:

(1) the nature and details of his relationship with a subordinate Government employee;

(2) prior perjuries, false and misleading testimony he gave in a Federal civil rights action brought against him;

(3) prior false and misleading statements he allowed his attorney to make to a Federal judge in that civil rights action; and

4) his corrupt efforts to influence the testimony of witnesses and to impede the discovery of evidence in that civil rights action.

In doing this, William Jefferson Clinton has undermined the integrity of his office, has brought disrepute on the Presidency, has betrayed his trust as President, and has acted in a manner subversive of the rule of law and justice, to the manifest injury of the people of the United States.

Wherefore, William Jefferson Clinton, by such conduct, warrants impeachment and trial, and removal from office and disqualification to hold and enjoy any office of honor, trust or profit under the United States.

(Approved 21–16 by the House Judiciary Committee on Friday, December 11, 1998)

(Passed 228–206 in the House of Representatives on Saturday, December 19, 1998)

Article 2: Perjury in the Paula Jones civil case.

In his conduct while President of the United States, William Jefferson Clinton, in violation of his constitutional oath faithfully to execute the office of President of the United States and, to the best of his ability, preserve, protect, and defend the Constitution of the United States, and in violation of his constitutional duty to take care that the laws be faithfully executed, has willfully corrupted and manipulated the judicial process of the United States for his personal gain and exoneration, impeding the administration of justice, in that:

(1) On December 23, 1997, William Jefferson Clinton, in sworn answers to written questions asked as part of a Federal civil rights action brought against him, willfully provided perjurious, false and misleading testimony in response to questions deemed relevant by a Federal judge concerning conduct and proposed conduct with subordinate employees.

(2) On January 17, 1998, William Jefferson Clinton swore under oath to tell the truth, the whole truth, and nothing but the truth in a deposition given as part

of a Federal civil rights action brought against him. Contrary to that oath, William Jefferson Clinton willfully provided perjurious, false and misleading testimony in response to questions deemed relevant by a Federal judge concerning the nature and details of his relationship with a subordinate Government employee, his knowledge of that employee's involvement and participation in the civil rights action brought against him, and his corrupt efforts to influence the testimony of that employee.

In all of this, William Jefferson Clinton has undermined the integrity of his office, has brought disrepute on the Presidency, has betrayed his trust as President, and has acted in a manner subversive of the rule of law and justice, to the manifest injury of the people of the United States.

Wherefore, William Jefferson Clinton, by such conduct, warrants impeachment and trial, and removal from office and disqualification to hold and enjoy any office of honor, trust or profit under the United States.

(Approved 20–17 by the House Judiciary Committee on Friday, December 11, 1998)

(Failed 229–205 in the House of Representatives on Saturday, December 19, 1998)

Article 3: Obstruction of Justice related to the Jones case.

In his conduct while President of the United States, William Jefferson Clinton, in violation of his constitutional oath faithfully to execute the office of President of the United States and, to the best of his ability, preserve, protect, and defend the Constitution of the United States, and in violation of his constitutional duty to take care that the laws be faithfully executed, has prevented, obstructed, and impeded the administration of justice, and has to that end engaged personally, and through his subordinates and agents, in a course of conduct or scheme designed to delay, impede, cover up, and conceal the existence of evidence and testimony related to a Federal civil rights action brought against him in a duly instituted judicial proceeding.

The means used to implement this course of conduct or scheme included one or more of the following acts:

(1) On or about December 17, 1997, William Jefferson Clinton corruptly encouraged a witness in a Federal civil rights action brought against him to execute a sworn affidavit in that proceeding that he knew to be perjurious, false and misleading.

(2) On or about December 17, 1997, William Jefferson Clinton corruptly encouraged a witness in a Federal civil rights action brought against him to give perjurious, false and misleading testimony if and when called to testify personally in that proceeding.

(3) On or about December 28, 1997, William Jefferson Clinton corruptly engaged in, encouraged, or supported a scheme to conceal evidence that had been subpoenaed in a Federal civil rights action brought against him.

(4) Beginning on or about December 7, 1997, and continuing through and including January 14, 1998, William Jefferson Clinton intensified and succeeded in an effort to secure job assistance to a witness in a Federal civil rights action brought against him in order to corruptly prevent the truthful testimony of that witness in that proceeding at a time when the truthful testimony of that witness would have been harmful to him.

(5) On January 17, 1998, at his deposition in a Federal civil rights action brought against him, William Jefferson Clinton corruptly allowed his attorney to make false and misleading statements to a Federal judge characterizing an affidavit, in order to prevent questioning deemed relevant by the judge. Such false and misleading statements were subsequently acknowledged by his attorney in a communication to that judge.

(6) On or about January 18 and January 20–21, 1998, William Jefferson Clinton related a false and misleading account of events relevant to a Federal civil rights action brought against him to a potential witness in that proceeding, in order to corruptly influence the testimony of that witness.

(7) On or about January 21, 23 and 26, 1998, William Jefferson Clinton made false and misleading statements to potential witnesses in a Federal grand jury proceeding in order to corruptly influence the testimony of those witnesses. The false and misleading statements made by William Jefferson Clinton were repeated by the witnesses to the grand jury, causing the grand jury to receive false and misleading information.

In all of this, William Jefferson Clinton has undermined the integrity of his office, has brought disrepute on the Presidency, has betrayed his trust as President, and has acted in a manner subversive of the rule of law and justice, to the manifest injury of the people of the United States.

Wherefore, William Jefferson Clinton, by such conduct, warrants impeachment and trial, and removal from office and disqualification to hold and enjoy any office of honor, trust or profit under the United States.

(Approved 21–16 by the House Judiciary Committee on Friday, December 11, 1998)

(Passed 221–212 in the House of Representatives on Saturday, December 19, 1998)

Article 4: Abuse of Power by making perjurious statements to Congress in his answers to the 81 questions posed by the Judiciary Committee.

Using the powers and influence of the office of President of the United States, William Jefferson Clinton, in violation of his constitutional oath faithfully to execute the office of President of the United States and, to the best of his ability, preserve, protect, and defend the Constitution of the United States, and in disregard of his constitutional duty to take care that the laws be faithfully executed, has engaged in conduct that resulted in misuse and abuse of his high office, impaired the due and proper administration of justice and the conduct of lawful inquiries, and contravened the authority of the legislative branch and the truth-seeking purpose of a coordinate investigative proceeding in that, as Pres-

ident, William Jefferson Clinton, refused and failed to respond to certain written requests for admission and willfully made perjuries, false and misleading
sworn statements in response to certain written requests for admission pro-
pounded to him as part of the impeachment inquiry authorized by the House
of Representatives of the Congress of the United States.

William Jefferson Clinton, in refusing and failing to respond, and in making
perjurious, false and misleading statements, assumed to himself functions and
judgments necessary to the exercise of the sole power of impeachment vested by
the Constitution in the House of Representatives and exhibited contempt for the
inquiry.

In doing this, William Jefferson Clinton has undermined the integrity of his office, has brought disrepute on the Presidency, has betrayed his trust as President, and has acted in a manner subversive of the rule of law and justice, to the
manifest injury of the people of the United States.

Wherefore, William Jefferson Clinton, by such conduct, warrants impeachment
and trial, and removal from office and disqualification to hold and enjoy any
office of honor, trust or profit under the United States.

(Approved 21–16 by the House Judiciary Committee on Saturday, December 12, 1998)

(Failed 285–148 in the House of Representatives on Saturday, December 19, 1998)

6. Public Opinion

The public's opinion toward Clinton and his impeachment were often contradictory. They showed support for the president, but not his behavior. They
wanted him reprimanded, but not punished, and certainly not removed from
office.[176]

He was already a popular president, and the allegations of scandal only
seemed to drive the president's approval ratings higher. Prior to the news of the
Lewinsky affair, Clinton's approval rating stood at about 60 percent in several
polls.[177] Immediately after the charges were made public, respondents briefly
disapproved of the president but then quickly bounced back.[178] Initially, Clinton's job approval rating dropped to 51 percent in one ABC News/*Washington
Post* poll.[179] A week after the scandal broke, his approval rating reached 67 percent and remained there throughout the trial.[180] After Clinton's speech to the
American public on January 21, 1998, his approval rating soared to 73 percent.[181] Further, a Gallup survey showed 43 percent of the public was very con-
fident in Clinton's abilities to carry out his duties as president.[182]

However, only 33 percent of the nation said that the phrase "honest and
trustworthy" applied to Clinton.[183] The majority of people believed he was

lying about his relationship with Lewinsky. When he initially denied the rumors, the results of an ABC News poll showed that 62 percent of the public believed that he had had a sexual relationship with her. Further, over half of the poll respondents (51 percent) thought that he had asked her to lie in a legal document.[184] Over 70 percent believed Clinton was guilty of the charges in the first article of impeachment.[185] Many respondents to a *Washington Post* poll (63 percent) believed that he should resign if it was discovered that he lied under oath or encouraged Lewinsky to lie (64 percent in an ABC News poll).[186]

Most people seemed to differentiate between the president's private conduct and his official duties. One poll found 76 percent of respondents believed the case against him involved purely private misconduct that should not be the basis for his impeachment. Another found that about two-thirds of the public regarded his behavior as a private matter and not an impeachable offense.[187] All in all, most of the public did not believe the charges constituted appropriate grounds for his removal, and they opposed removing him from office.[188] Most did not want to see the president impeached. A poll taken in October 1998 showed that 65 percent of Americans opposed impeachment.[189] Many also saw it as a partisan battle[190] and developed a strong distaste for Starr's investigation and the media coverage of the scandal.[191] As one might expect, most Republican voters favored impeachment, many of them strongly, and very few Democrats favored it.[192] Instead, a majority of the public favored censure.[193] In a national poll taken in September 1998, 54 percent of respondents indicated that they disapproved of the way the House Judiciary Committee handled the investigation.[194]

For the most part, people just did not seem to care. A Pew Research Center Poll found that only 30 percent of the public was even following the story closely.[195] Only 28 percent thought the scandal was "very important" for the country.[196] In the end, virtually every poll indicated that the majority of Americans were tired of the trial by the time it was over and they simply wanted to end the investigation.[197]

7. Why Was Clinton Not Removed?

One reason Clinton was able to survive the impeachment process was because of the positive image he projected throughout the crisis and the popularity of his policies.[198] Unlike Richard Nixon, Clinton had an ability to connect with the American public and maintained a favorable image among the American people,[199] thereby having great public support. The public focused on his achievements in office, especially the economic prosperity of the several preceding years.[200] As a result, his job performance evaluations remained high, even when the scandal dominated the news.[201] At the same time, many of his enemies were unpopular with the public.[202]

In comparison, the Watergate scandal occurred in a time where there was a faltering domestic economy and Nixon's public support plummeted.[203] There was a broad coalition who supported the Watergate investigation so that it was almost impossible for Nixon to argue that the attacks against him were partisan.[204] Moreover, the charges against him were based on his official duties while in office, but for Clinton, the charges were personal. Clinton also eventually admitted his wrongdoing and accepted his punishment for his actions. Nixon lost support because he never came to grips with the seriousness of his actions, always putting the blame on others.

8. Long-Term Effects of the Scandal: Political and Social Ramifications

The Jones/Lewinsky scandal affected not only President Clinton but his family, friends, the administration, and the institution of the presidency. There were both short- and long-term ramifications on the political process from the events.[205]

One had to do with the media. For many years, the press did not report on presidential sexual misconduct. After Watergate, there was more reporting about the private lives of public people. That coverage expanded even more after Clinton. Prior to the Lewinsky scandal, most news organizations would never have considered publishing the kind of material that was in the Starr Report.[206] Serious journalists did not ask questions pertaining to sexual misconduct or report on it in any detail.[207] After the Jones/Lewinsky matter, there were no rules on where to draw the line concerning what to report.[208] Now, reports of sexual misdeeds are common.

Another impact was on Clinton himself. The affair and investigation tainted his legacy. He was only the second president—and the first elected—to be impeached.[209] His respect within the Democratic Party and in the public diminished, and many other Democrats tried to separate themselves from him. In the long run, the scandal caused him to limit his campaigning and fundraising for other Democrats who were running for office.

The Jones/Lewinsky scandal may scare potential political candidates from running for office.[210] Many qualified candidates may be afraid of the intense scrutiny of their private lives. Those who run for office, or those who win an election, may find their private lives probed and scrutinized. That might even extend to their family members. Public attention will be focused on personal and trivial facts and events.[211] The recent trend toward press invasion of a candidate or officeholder's privacy is leading to the erasure of the line between a person's private life and public work. This makes the price of holding office enormously high.[212]

The allegations of sexual misconduct distracted Clinton from fully addressing his agenda.[213] He had planned to address serious issues such as education, child care, and Medicare, but the charges prevented him from doing so. In terms of time, the scandal consumed about a year of his administration.[214] Second, the charges eroded his credibility. Traditionally, in a president's second term of office, he is looking toward establishing a legacy and achieving policy or constitutional objectives of lasting significance.[215] In Clinton's case, he was more concerned with protecting himself and staying in office.

Congress was also prevented from doing its work, as it was spending time investigating the charges and going through the impeachment process instead of passing needed legislation. Even the judiciary was pulled into the scandal, especially when Chief Justice William Rehnquist presided over the hearings.[216] Toward the end of the scandal, many people simply wanted the whole thing to end and the government to return to necessary business.[217]

The Jones/Lewinsky scandal may have influenced the morals of the country, which are constantly evolving. The intense media attention on a married man's sexual behavior may have forced others to consider their personal beliefs. The scandal also affected the way the nation talks about sexual practices and mores. It is now talked about more openly in the media and within relationships.

The Jones/Lewinsky scandal had an impact on the political scene in 1998. It was originally predicted that there might be a backlash against the Republicans for their treatment of Clinton. On the flip side, there was concern that there may be a backlash against the Democrats because of Clinton's behavior. During the November 1998 elections, the Republicans lost badly.[218] They lost five seats in the House and broke even in the Senate. For the first time in sixty-four years, the party out of the White House lost seats in a midterm congressional election.[219] Additionally, Speaker of the House Newt Gingrich (R-GA) chose to resign his seat in Congress.[220] This may be related to the public's negative reaction to the Judiciary Committee's impeachment hearings.

As a result of the scandal, it is clear now that presidents can be sued for private conduct while still in office.[221] Clinton asked for "temporary immunity" until he left office, because a president should not have to drop national affairs every time someone decides to sue. The court decisions in the Jones case allowed civil suits to proceed during a presidency.[222] This has the potential for more lawsuits against presidents in office.

There was also a weakened traditional presidential power with respect to executive privilege. The notion that executive privilege protects a president's conversation with his advisers has been restricted.

In a related decision, in May 1998, U.S. District Judge Norma Holloway Johnson affirmed the right of the president to assert claims of executive privilege concerning conversations with senior officials, but then said that those claims were outweighed by the independent counsel's request to have access to such information for its criminal investigation. Judge Johnson also concluded that the First Lady was a senior adviser and therefore could be covered by an executive privilege claim.[223]

The investigation of Clinton and his impeachment exposed several fatal flaws in the Independent Counsel statute.[224] The impeachment demonstrated that the law did not provide adequate safeguards against overly aggressive efforts of an independent counsel to influence the course of the impeachment proceedings.[225] As a result, Congress chose not to reauthorize the Independent Counsel Law for the time being.

Finally, the Jones/Lewinsky scandal had an effect on the impeachment process. At first, Congress was hesitant to use impeachment against Clinton, but the effort against him made impeachment an attractive tool for winning future policy debates between the president and Congress. Since then, the impeachment process has been seen as a tool to oppose a president's policies. In the future, the decision to bring impeachment charges against a president will be decided, to some extent, on the strength of parties rather than on the innocence or guilt of the people involved. Some say that future Congresses may be tempted to pursue impeachment to remove a president with whom they have a policy difference.[226]

9. Jones/Lewinsky Conclusion

The Jones/Lewinsky scandal began as a relationship with a White House intern[227] and resulted in the impeachment of a popular president. There is little doubt that Clinton intended to deceive, withhold information from, and mislead, the Jones lawyers, his own lawyers, advisers, friends, family, and the nation.[228] The Jones/Lewinsky affair demonstrated a pattern of extensive lying and cover-up by the president. There were also examples of careless use of taxpayer money and resources, particularly for state troopers who were asked to procure women. There was a pattern of arrogance shown by Clinton in an apparent belief that the normal rules of social and political conduct do not apply to him. He was willing to use the powers of his office for personal gain. It also shows sexism by Clinton, especially because he seemed to view women as objects of sexual desire and among the perks of high office.[229]

These issues are disturbing to some people because we teach our children that this behavior is morally and ethically wrong. We teach them that these behaviors sometimes have serious consequences. Most people learn that if you tell one lie, there will probably be more. At some point, when you have told so many, no one will believe you. At the presidential level, this is called credibility. A leader who is not believed is not likely to be effective because they do not have the trust of the people.[230]

The affair said a lot about Clinton's honesty, judgment, self-control, and character. In the end, it was shown that he lied under oath, lied to his wife and family, his Cabinet, and his advises. Does this indicate that he would be willing to deceive people under any circumstances? Some argue that he only lied about a private matter, adultery. But William Bennett, author of *Book of Virtues,* Reagan's Education secretary, and Bush's Drug Czar, said that presidential adultery is not a private matter. Although adultery by itself does not automatically disqualify a president, it may reveal something important about a person's character and judgment. He wrote that Clinton revealed a chronic lack of discipline, compulsion, exploitation, and the easy betrayal of vows, which may suggest something wrong at a deeper level. Further, Bennett said not all politicians act this way. He said that most presidents do not behave illegally, lie under oath, or thumb their noses at the law. But in his opinion, a president who shows reckless personal conduct, relies on deceit, abuses his power, and has contempt for the rule of law cannot be a good president. Clinton's behavior during the Jones case raised serious doubts about his character for many voters, and that can eventually suggest something about suitability to serve the public.[231]

In a broader sense, Clinton's serial indiscretions really did matter. They demonstrated a willingness to deceive others, and they mattered because he may have been far more psychologically disturbed than the public ever imagined. They mattered because private misbehavior on this scale required routine and repetitive lies to conceal it.[232]

The case brought up many constitutional questions. One is whether a president, while in office, can be indicted and criminally prosecuted for a crime. The Paula Jones case had to do with Clinton's behavior before coming into office. But the Lewinsky case dealt with behavior while in office. Second, how should such criminal behavior be handled? Possibly the only proper route for dealing with presidential wrongdoing is impeachment. This question was left unanswered.

H. Whitewater

The Whitewater scandal began before Clinton was elected to the White House and even before he became governor of Arkansas.[233] The scandal itself involved allegations of financial misconduct in a twenty-year-old failed land deal. The case resulted in no actionable charges against Clinton,[234] but did distract people from the real issues at hand and further tarnished the reputation of the president. By the end, it had come to signify more broad-ranging questions about the character of the president. Table 6.3 presents a list of some of the major participants in the Whitewater affair.

Table 6.3: Selected Actors in the Whitewater Affair

Bill Clinton: President of the United States; investor in Whitewater Development Corp., friend of McDougals; accused of showing favoritism to McDougal as Madison was failing

Hillary Rodham Clinton: Partner in the Rose Law Firm in Little Rock, which represented Madison S&L (McDougal) and later represented the Federal Deposit Insurance Corp.

Robert Fiske: First special prosecutor investigating the Clintons' Whitewater land deal; appointed by Janet Reno with Clinton's support

Vincent Foster Jr: Deputy White House Counsel and close personal friend of Hillary Clinton; managed the Clintons' legal problems related to Whitewater; committed suicide in July 1994

James B. McDougal: Clinton's partner in Whitewater and former head of Madison Guaranty Savings and Loan; accused of improperly diverting money from Madison to benefit Whitewater or benefit the Clintons

Kenneth Starr: Replaced Fiske as special prosecutor in August 1994

Rose Law Firm: Where Hillary Clinton worked; represented both the S&L and the government

RTC: Resolution Trust Corporation, a government agency charged with cleaning up the financial mess caused by failures of hundreds of S&Ls

---

1. Whitewater Created

In the late 1970s, when Bill Clinton was Arkansas attorney general, the Clintons and their friends, James and Susan McDougal, created the Whitewater Development Corporation.[235] James McDougal served as an aide to the governor and was a major contributor to Clinton's political campaigns.[236] As they set up the company, the McDougals were corporate officers and the Clintons were shareholders. The Clintons were entitled to an equal split on any profits,[237] even though they put little money into the corporation at the start.[238] The company bought 200 acres of land in the Ozark Mountains with $200,000 they borrowed from banks.[239] The loan was financed at a below-market interest rate, and the bank sought no security for the loan.[240] The plan was to subdi-

vide the land into forty-four lots to be sold individually for vacation and retirement homes. The sale of the lots would enable them to pay off the loan.[241]

By the end of summer 1979, more than a year after the land was purchased,
not a single lot had been sold.[242] Part of the problem was that the Whitewater
property had never been surveyed, and without a survey, the new individual lots
could not be sold.[243] Reportedly, even by 1983, no new lots had been purchased.
Even though no money was coming in, McDougal still had to make interest payments on the loans.[244] The company lost nearly $51,000, much of which was paid
by borrowing more money.[245] One lot was sold in 1984, but Whitewater continued to lose money, over $20,000, all of which was covered by McDougal. With
more payments due, 1985 was even worse for the Whitewater Development Corporation. Only one lot was sold, and the company lost over $75,000.[246] At one point,
the company traded its remaining land for an airplane, and McDougal sold the
plane to a partner of Mrs. Clinton's in the Rose Law Firm.[247] McDougal seemed
to keep the Clintons in the dark about much of what was going on.[248]

Because he needed money to make the payments for Whitewater, and as a
new business venture, the McDougals decided to buy a bank,[249] which they
named the Madison Bank and Trust Company of Kingston. They advertised higher
rates on deposits made in the bank, and assets in the bank swelled to $3.6 mil-
lion in the first five months.[250] However, McDougal then offered low-interest
loans to businesses that were willing to renovate and restore their buildings. This
was devastating to profits.[251]

Meanwhile, the Whitewater Development Corporation required one stop-
gap measure after another to keep it out of default. Since the Madison Bank
and Trust was not permitted by law to invest directly in real estate, and McDougal
was not permitted to establish branches in more populated centers to raise
funds,[252] he decided, in 1983, to purchase a savings and loan in Augusta,
Arkansas.[253] He called it the Madison Guaranty Savings and Loan. To purchase
the S&L, he had to borrow over $200,000.[254]

To help the sale of the Whitewater lots, the Clintons and McDougals decided to build a model home on one of the lots. To fund it, Hillary took out a
loan of $30,000 from Madison Bank and Trust with the idea that the loan would
be repaid using proceeds from the sale of the house.[255] In September 1982,
after Clinton returned to the governor's mansion, federal and state banking
authorities launched an investigation of Madison Bank and Trust for a series
of questionable practices, specifically citing the Whitewater loan as "unsound."[256]

In 1984, federal regulators began another special review of Madison S&L.
This time, they found that McDougal shifted five bad loans from his bank to
his S&L on the eve of an audit. It was also discovered that the Whitewater Corporation was permitted overdrafts on its checking account that was held at the

Madison S&L. Further, Whitewater made payments on a $20,000 loan that Bill Clinton had taken at another Arkansas bank.

In addition, there were some allegations that Whitewater accounts were used to funnel money to Clinton's campaign funds. In 1985, McDougal hosted a fundraiser for Clinton and raised $35,000, but it is believed that some of the money came from Madison S&L.[257] Federal prosecutors wanted to know if money from McDougal's thrift was illegally diverted to the campaign of Governor Clinton.[258] It was further discovered that the Clintons had improperly deducted interest payments related to Whitewater on their tax returns.[259]

By March 1985, after Clinton had won his third term as governor, Madison Guaranty had grown rapidly but ran into trouble and faced closure by the state.[260] About a year later, Madison was again under review from federal regulators. This time, investigators were looking into claims that McDougal and Clinton went to a former judge, David Hale, and asked for money to "clean up" Madison's books. Hale, a municipal court judge who was appointed to office by Clinton, also had a lending operation called Capital Management Services, which was licensed by the Small Business Administration to invest in disadvantaged small businesses. He loaned $300,000 to Susan McDougal so she could finally fix up the Whitewater land and sell the lots.[261] Later, Hale reported that he had been pressured by Clinton to make a loan to McDougal.[262] Hale was also under investigation for fraudulently misrepresenting the kinds of loans he was making to the SBA to get the matching funds. Instead of legitimate small businesses, many of the loans had actually gone to as his Democratic "political family" in Arkansas.

Throughout these many investigations, McDougal retained Hillary Clinton and the Rose Law Firm at $2,000 a month to help with his legal needs and stop foreclosure on his bank.[263] McDougal later claimed that he did so at the behest of Governor Clinton.[264] As his attorney, Hillary was responsible for preparing a plan for state regulators to keep the S&L open. However, the S&L was regulated by the state and overseen by a new state securities commissioner who had been appointed by her husband, the governor.[265] The state agency delayed the closing of Madison Guaranty S&L, thereby giving McDougal the ruling he wanted.[266] Some said Clinton may have used his power as governor to influence the decision in return for McDougal's hiring of the Rose Law Firm or in exchange for campaign contributions.[267]

Additionally, many questions arose as to whether a governor should be involved in a business deal with the owner of a business that is regulated by the state and whether, having done so, the governor's wife, through her law firm, should be receiving legal fees for work done for the business.[268] A conflict exists when a spouse of a high public official practices law in front of judges, administrators, and others whose careers may be influenced by that official.[269]

Oddly enough, federal regulators also hired the Rose Law Firm to represent them. In 1985, the Federal Savings and Loan Insurance Corporation (FSLIC) approached the Rose Law Firm about representing the agency in litigation involving one of Arkansas's S&Ls it had seized (not owned by the McDougals). If that worked out, then the regulators declared that they might be interested in using the Rose Law Firm in future cases.[270] The Rose Law Firm's representation of the FSLIC in its claims against Madison after it previously was the lawyer for Madison appears to constitute a classic conflict of interest.[271]

After more investigations and charges by federal banking authorities, Mc-Dougal was removed from the board of Madison Guaranty in August 1986, and federal regulators ordered Madison Guaranty shut down.

2. Election 1992: Publicity

After Clinton declared his candidacy for the presidency, the *New York Times* published an article detailing some of the activities of Whitewater.[272] The Clinton campaign denied any wrongdoing. To prove their point, they requested that attorney James Lyons prepare a report on their investment. Lyons concluded that the Clintons had lost approximately $69,000 in Whitewater. After the report was made public, the story disappeared for the rest of the campaign.[273]

By December 1992, the Clintons wanted out of Whitewater, so McDougal bought out their interest in the company for $1,000. The lawyer representing the Clintons was Vincent Foster Jr., another partner in the Rose Law Firm. He also oversaw the preparation of Whitewater's delinquent tax return. On July 20, 1993, Foster was found dead after committing suicide. Allegations immediately arose that he did so because of his involvement with Whitewater, but this seemed to be untrue.

But the Whitewater issue reemerged in fall 1993 when the *Washington Post* reported on October 31 that the Resolution Trust Corporation (RTC, the federal agency charged with disposing of the assets of failed savings institution) had asked the Justice Department to probe James McDougal for possible misuse of depositor funds from his S&L to help retire Clinton's campaign debt.[274] That, along with Foster's death, created a new interest in Whitewater.[275]

3. Special Prosecutor

In the midterm elections in November, the Republicans gained control of both houses of Congress. In the fall of 1993, Republicans and a few Democrats began calling for the appointment of an independent counsel to investigate the Clinton's possible wrongdoing in connection with their Whitewater investments.[276] At first, Clinton said he would not ask for a special prosecutor, saying that there was no need for an investigation. But in early 1994, in an attempt to ward off a congressional inquiry, Clinton asked Attorney General Janet Reno to appoint a special counsel to investigate Whitewater.[277]

At first, Reno pointed out that an independent counsel was not possible because the Ethics in Government Act, which created the Office of Independent Counsel, had lapsed. She also argued that the Justice Department was already investigating Madison and Whitewater. If the Justice Department appointed another investigator, it would lead to too much overlap.[278] Nonetheless, Reno reluctantly complied with Clinton's request.

Reno appointed Robert Fiske to serve as independent counsel on January 20.[279] He was a respected Republican former New York attorney and former federal prosecutor.[280] Fiske was to investigate allegations that McDougal improperly diverted funds from Madison Guaranty S&L to Whitewater and to the Clinton campaigns. The Foster suicide was also on the agenda. A third agenda item was to decide if the Rose Law Firm had any conflicts of interest in representing both regulators and McDougal in the savings and loan cases.

Fiske promptly set up an office in Little Rock. After five months, he issued two preliminary reports. The first determined that Foster had been a suicide victim of untreated clinical depression, and no further investigation of his death was warranted. The second found insufficient evidence to establish that there had been any White House effort to influence the probes of Whitewater or Madison Guaranty. No indictments were justified, Fiske concluded.[281] However, he was still investigating whether administration officials removed papers and documents from Foster's office immediately after his death, and if that action was obstruction of justice.[282]

The same day that Fiske issued his report, the 1978 Independent Counsel Law was renewed and signed by Clinton. This meant that a panel of three federal judges now had control over the decision of who should serve as independent counsel. The panel, instead of simply confirming Reno's appointment of Fiske and allowing him to wrap up his work, selected a new independent counsel who they said would be more independent.[283] On August 6, 1994, Fiske was replaced by Kenneth Starr,[284] a former Bush administration solicitor general turned private attorney.[285] Starr had no experience whatsoever in conducting a prosecution.[286] When he stepped in for Fiske, he decided to start the investigation at the beginning.[287]

When Starr was appointed, his central mission was to investigate potential financial improprieties by President Clinton and the First Lady involving the failed Arkansas Whitewater real estate deal that occurred in the late 1970s.[288] His mission included:

- a $300,000 loan to Susan McDougal, some of which went to fund the Whitewater Development Corporation;
- the disappearance and reappearance of Hillary Clinton's Rose Law Firm billing records to determine how much time she spent on the land deal;
- the dismissal of seven members of the White House travel office, who were replaced by Clinton friends;
- the 1993 suicide of Vincent Foster, White House lawyer and longtime friend of the First Lady;
- the collection of hundreds of FBI files of prominent Republicans by low-level White House aides;
- the $700,000-plus paid to former Associate U.S. Attorney General Webster Hubbell by prominent Democrats just as he came under Starr's scrutiny.[289]

4. Senate Hearing

In addition to an independent counsel, there were also calls for congressional hearings being made by the Republicans. They wanted to know whether the Clintons filed inaccurate income tax returns showing losses in the Whitewater real estate development, if relevant documents in the case were destroyed at the Rose Law Firm, and whether a cover-up existed.

Even though Fiske asked that Congress wait until he was done with his investigation before they began theirs, the House and Senate called for hearings into Whitewater on March 23, 1995. In May 1995, the Senate passed a resolution to create a special Whitewater Committee to look at the handling of Whitewater-related documents by White House officials after Foster's suicide, the Justice Department's handling of criminal investigations prepared by the RTC, whether McDougal improperly or illegally diverted funds to the Whitewater venture, and if the financing of Clinton's 1990 gubernatorial campaign was legal. They wanted to know if money from Madison was used illegally to support the Clinton's real estate deal, if the failure of Whitewater contributed to the collapse of Madison, and if the money from Madison was funneled to Clinton's 1984 campaign. The Senate Select Committee was chaired by Senator Alphonse D'Amato of New York.[290]

On June 14, 1994, President Clinton and Hillary Clinton were put under oath by federal investigators and questioned in separate interviews about Whitewater and the suicide of Foster.

The Senate committee and Starr both asked for subpoenas to examine specific documents, but President Clinton, at first, invoked presidential privilege and refused to provide them. However, the White House eventually agreed to hand over the documents. It was then discovered that many of the records concerning Whitewater were lost or missing. In 1987, McDougal said that Mrs.

Clinton requested all records on Whitewater and he delivered them to the governor's mansion. On more investigation, it was discovered that one particular file relating to Whitewater was missing that had been in the office of Associate White House Counsel Foster when he committed suicide. It was later reported that the file had been secretly removed during a search of Foster's office after his death.[291] It was also reported that the Rose Law Firm shredded documents relating to Whitewater,[292] but the firm denied the report.

The Clintons denied that they were trying to hide something. Delays in disclosure of the documents only raised further suspicions about what they were trying to hide.[293]

Some of Hillary's legal records for her work on behalf of Madison Guaranty were found in a storage closet in her third-floor residence. They turned out to be her billing charges on legal work she performed.[294] They contained no incriminating or embarrassing information.[295] Investigators also found some of her billing records in Foster's attic. His wife, Lisa, found the records in a briefcase that Foster used right before his suicide.

The House and Senate hearings ended on August 10, 1995, then submitted its report in June 1996 after thirteen months of investigation. The overall report was deeply divided based on party lines, comprised of two contradictory and incompatible reports.[296] The majority report was critical of the way White House officials handled Whitewater by concealment and removal of documents from Foster's office. It suggested that there was a pattern by the Clintons of concealing their involvement with Whitewater and McDougal's savings and loan. It said that Foster's office had damaging evidence about Whitewater and Travelgate, and that a number of White House officials were engaged in improper conduct in the removal and handling of documents from Foster's office. Finally, the report said that many White House staff members gave incomplete and inaccurate statements and testimony to the committee.[297]

The Democratic minority report denied the charges and refuted the allegations made in the majority report. It reported that the White House staff was motivated by good intentions, shock, and grief. It said there was no intervention in the investigations, with no improper meetings. Overall it found that the Clintons corrected past errors in their tax returns and that they were passive investors in Whitewater.[298]

5. Grand Jury

On January 26, 1996, Hillary Clinton testified in front of a grand jury investigating how long-missing billing records from the Rose Law Firm suddenly turned up in the White House. It was the first time that a sitting First Lady testified in front of a grand jury. The records were supposedly found by White House aide Carolyn Huber folded but in plain sight on a table in the book room, a room behind Hillary's personal office. Hillary testified for four-and-a-half hours, claiming that she did not know how the documents got into the book room. On April 25, 1998, she was questioned again by Whitewater prosecutors on tape for five hours about her work as a private attorney for the failed S&L. Her testimony was shown to the grand jury on April 30, 1998, and the public on March 16, 1999. It revealed that Hillary declined to answer two questions on the grounds of marital privilege. She also testified that she "never spent any significant time at all" monitoring records of the Whitewater land deal she and President Clinton shared with the McDougals. She said that she was unaware of the loans for Whitewater that had been taken out in her husband's name a decade before he became president. Even when prosecutors showed her the check, she said she did not know anything about it.

In February 1996, the federal judge issued a subpoena for President Clinton. The judge wanted him to testify in the criminal trial of Susan and James McDougal, who were on trial for arranging loans illegally through the S&L. On April 29, 1996, Clinton was questioned on videotape for three and a half hours in the fraud trial of the McDougals. On May 28, 1996, the jurors in federal court convicted the McDougals and Jim "Guy" Tucker of federal charges of fraud and conspiracy. They found Tucker guilty of two of seven charges against him, one each of fraud and conspiracy. He was facing a maximum prison term of ten years and maximum fine of $500,000. James McDougal was found guilty of eighteen of nineteen counts, including conspiracy, mail fraud, and falsifying records. His maximum prison term was eighty-four years and maximum fine $4.5 million. Susan McDougal was found guilty of four counts, including mail fraud, misapplication of funds, and falsifying records. Her maximum prison term was seventeen years, and the maximum fine was $1 million.

6. Outcomes

There were many short- and long-term outcomes to the Whitewater scandal. One is that James and Susan McDougal, the Clintons' former business partners in the Whitewater investment, were convicted on fraud and conspiracy charges.[299] On August 20, 1996, Susan McDougal was sentenced to two years in prison, three years' probation, a $5,000 fine, and $300,000 in restitution plus interest. She was also ordered to perform 300 hours of community service.

On September 5, 1996, federal prosecutors subpoenaed her to testify before the Whitewater grand jury and asked her if the president lied at her trial, and she refused to answer. The prosecution warned McDougal that if she did not answer the questions, she would go to jail and be held in contempt of court. She refused to answer, later explaining that her failure to cooperate with Starr was because prosecutors wanted her to implicate the Clintons falsely. So on September 10, 1996, was taken to jail for contempt.[300]

On April 23, 1998, McDougal again refused to answer questions before the Whitewater grand jury, even after being told that it may mean more time behind bars. On May 5, 1998, McDougal was indicted on three felonies for refusing to tell a grand jury what she knew. She served eighteen months for civil contempt for refusing to testify to Starr's Whitewater grand jury. That term ended in March, and she began serving a two-year term for fraud in the Whitewater real estate case. On June 25, 1998, a federal judge reduced her sentence to time served and ordered her to ninety days' home detention because she needed treatment for a health issue.

James McDougal was removed from the S&L in 1986. He was indicted in 1989 on eleven felony counts, including bank fraud and misapplication of bank funds, submitting false statements, and conspiracy.[301] He was sentenced to more than eighty-four years, but got a reduced sentence by agreeing to cooperate with prosecutors.[302] McDougal went to prison and died of cardiac arrest on March 8, 1998.

Governor Jim "Guy" Tucker resigned as governor of Arkansas. He was indicted on fraud and conspiracy charges.[303] On August 19, 1996, Tucker was sentenced to four years' probation and $150,000 in restitution, $120,000 in interest dating from the mid-1980s, and a $25,000 fine. He was also ordered to talk to junior and senior high assemblies across the state on values, respect for authority, and other topics.

Judge Hale was indicted on conspiracy and three counts of making false statements to the SBA on September 23.[304] He agreed to plead guilty to two felonies and to cooperate with the Fiske investigation.[305]

7. Whitewater: Conclusion

The Whitewater scandal, like scandals in other administrations, forced Clinton to spend great amounts of time answering charges and ignoring domestic and international issues. At the same time, he repeatedly deceived the public.[306] The special investigator in the case came under criticism for his investigation of the affair. Three years afterward, neither Mr. nor Mrs. Clinton were shown to have done anything wrong. Instead, one charge after another evaporated.[307]

I. Campaign Finance

During the 1996 campaign, President Clinton and Vice President Al Gore were accused of unethical and potentially illegal conduct in campaign fundraising activities. They allegedly took advantage of the perks of office to solicit cash and improper donations by foreign operatives, in exchange for political favors and access to the White House.[308] Often, the donations were from Asians or Asians living in the United States who were not legal citizens, which is illegal.[309] Large donors were rewarded with social gatherings with the president or could bring their business associates to meet the president. Some foreign companies without U.S. operations wrote campaign checks, which is clearly illegal, or laundered the money through employees and relatives, also illegal. There was even a sliding scale. Those raising $10,000 to $25,000 were invited to large dinners with the president, and those who gave between $50,000 to $100,000 were rewarded with more intimate dinners or even coffee with Clinton in the Map Room. Those who contributed over $500,000 were given the chance to ride on Air Force One, play a round of golf with Clinton, or sleep overnight at the White House.[310]

The primary foreign money raisers for Clinton/Gore and the DNC were James Raidy (and the Lippo Group), Roger Tamraz, John Huang, Yah Lin "Charlie" Trie, and Pauline Kanchanalak.

James Raidy/Lippo Group: Clinton often took money from overseas sources such as the Lippo Group, headed by friends of his, Mochtar Raidy and his young son James, Indonesian businessmen with close ties to China.[311] The money was donated in exchange for the coffees at the White House or for overnight stays in the Lincoln Bedroom.[312] It was alleged that the Chinese government tried to funnel donations through Lippo subsidiaries to influence U.S. elections. Raidy is reported to have visited the White House twenty-five times. There were also reports that the DNC got $425,000 from an Indonesian couple with ties to Raidy's Lippo Group.[313]

Roger Tamraz: International financier Roger Tamraz was given access to the White House in exchange for $200,000 in donations to the Democratic Party. A Lebanese American, he was seeking Clinton's support to build an oil pipeline from the Caspian Sea to the Mediterranean. At the same time, he was wanted by law enforcement in Lebanon on charges that he embezzled $20 million. Tamraz had a coffee with Clinton in April 1996 and dinner and a movie with him in June 1996.

John Huang: Another Clinton friend, John Huang, was found to have solicited money from the communist government in Beijing. When a subpoena was issued for his arrest, he fled the country.[314] Huang was an executive in the Lippo Group, served as a mid-level official at the Commerce Department, then served as vice chairman of the Democratic National Committee's (DNC'S) fundraising arm during Clinton's 1996 reelection bid. As such, he arranged Gore's visit to a Buddhist temple. White House records show that Huang was admitted to the White House seventy-eight times in fifteen months.[315] Together with Yah Lin Trie, a former Chinese restaurant owner from Little Rock, Huang collected hundreds of thousands of dollars from donors, some of whom were legally unable to contribute, while at the same time creating influence with and extracting favors from the DNC and White House.

Yah Lin "Charlie" Trie: One of the people who actively sought donations for Clinton/Gore was Charlie Trie, a Taiwan-born businessman and Chinese restaurant owner from Little Rock. Clinton got to know him while frequenting his restaurant.[316] Trie often pretended to have a lavish lifestyle and appeared to others as if he had connections in the White House, which many overseas businesses wanted. Foreign individuals and companies pumped $1.4 million into his bank account. His lavish lifestyle was largely paid for by Ng Lap Seng, a Hong Kong business associate of Trie's. Trie used some of Ng's money to make donations to the DNC. Investigators also say that Trie raised money in a suspicious way for the presidential Legal Expense Trust, a private fund set up to help the Clintons pay for their legal bills. Trie attempted to give money to the trust ($789,000), but the White House returned the money when it was discovered that it came from members of a Taiwan-based Buddhist sect. Many of the checks were suspected to have come from foreigners, people who seemed unable to afford the $1,000 donation, and some bearing similar handwriting.[317] Later, Trie attempted to donate again, this time around $1 million, but it was rejected. Trie tried a third time with $150,000, but it was turned away once again.

Pauline Kanchanalak: Pauline Kanchanalak was a businesswoman from Thailand who donated $253,000 to the DNC but had the money returned because of suspicions that she was not the true source of it. The DNC was concerned that she may have been the front for illegal donors. Kanchanalak often took foreign business and government official on White House visits. After one visit on June 18, 1996, during which U.S. policy toward China was discussed, Kanchanalak donated $85,000 to the DNC.

On July 13, 1998, Kanchanalak and her sister-in-law (Duangnet "Georgie" Kronenberg) were charged with funneling at least $679,000 in foreign and corporate contributions through straw donors to the DNC, state parties, and federal and state candidates. There was a twenty-four-count indictment against them. The indictment alleged that they wanted to gain access to Clinton and members of his administration to impress clients and help their business ventures. It was shown that in June and July 1996, they gave $457,000 to the DNC and state parties. They used funds from foreign corporations and individuals to make prohibited campaign contributions of at least $679,000 to the DNC, which got more than $333,000.

Johnny Chung: Johnny Chung was a California businessman who raised about $366,000 for the Democratic Party. Chung said he approached an aide to Hillary in March 1995 to get a group of Chinese businessmen invited to the

White House. He said he gave a $50,000 check to Hillary's chief of staff to defray the cost of White House Christmas parties in exchange for a lunch and photo session at the White House. The White House denied it, as it would be against federal law that forbids accepting contributions on federal property and soliciting funds on federal property.

In December 1994, Chung escorted the executive of a Chinese beer company through the West Wing, carrying two six-packs and taking pictures as they went. Then it was reported that Chung gave the DNC $50,000 in exchange for him and six business friends from China to watch Clinton's Saturday radio speech from the Oval Office on March 11, 1995. They paid $7,000 a head to watch it. Afterward, the businessmen had their pictures taken with the president. Under federal law, foreigners are strictly forbidden to give money to political parties.

On June 20, 1998, Chung told the Justice Department that top DNC officials knowingly solicited and accepted improper donations from him. Chung said that Richard Sullivan, then DNC finance director, personally asked him for a $125,000 donation in April 1995, and then took the money. Sullivan denies it. Chung later testified that campaign finance laws encouraged businessmen to use contributions to political parties to gain access to high-level U.S. government officials. He reportedly used money given to him by a Chinese intelligence official to gain entrance to the White House fifty times, where he had intimate political meetings with Clinton.

1. Gore's Fundraising Activities

Vice President Al Gore also collected questionable campaign donations while he was visiting a Buddhist temple in Los Angeles to collect funds and by making calls from his office.[318] He went to the His Lai Buddhist Temple in April 1996, where members contributed $50,000 to the DNC. At the temple, the penniless monks donated over $5,000 apiece. But they had taken a vow of poverty.[319] They were reimbursed by the temple, in violation of federal law.[320] Gore later explained he did not know that he was attending a fundraiser when he visited the Buddhist temple, but DNC documentation indicated that he did.

Gore also made phone calls from his office in the West Wing of the White House in the fall of 1995 to get donations, which is illegal. He allegedly made about ten phone calls and collected $50,000 in donations. There was an old and rarely enforced federal statute that barred solicitation of campaign contributions on federal property. Whether the statute, which was enacted before the widespread use of telephones, applied to phone solicitations was a matter of debate.[321]

The Hatch Act makes it illegal to raise money on federal property. In 1979, Congress tightened the definition of "contribution" from money donated for "any political purpose" to the much narrower one of money donated "for the purpose of influencing any election for federal office." This made it a crime only to raise on federal property the small amounts of "hard money" that go straight to the candidate and exempted the huge amounts of "soft" money funneled to the parties.[322] The administration argued that the Hatch Act's limits on fund raising did not apply to presidents and vice presidents.

Additionally, Gore was potentially misusing his office because many of the businessmen he called had careers and companies that depended in part on decisions made by the White House. Moreover, it is illegal to solicit funds from any federal building. Despite this, the White House said it was not illegal because there was no "controlling legal authority" that barred Gore from making fundraising calls in the White House.

Gore gave a news conference on March 3, 1997, to explain what he did to the American public. He said that he thought that everything he did was legal and that he did not break any laws. In any event, he promised that he would not do it again.

2. Investigations

There were some serious concerns raised over the campaign contributions. First, making a political contribution in the name of another person is against federal law, and it appeared as if this was done frequently. Second, donations from foreign sources are against federal law. In this case, foreign money was possibly funneled into the Democratic Party from Asia. Third, federal law forbids accepting contributions on federal property and soliciting funds on federal property. It was found that Gore made phone calls from his office to solicit contributions. Last, was China attempting to influence the elections or public policy with their donations and frequent access to the White House and President Clinton? It appeared that the Chinese government, acting through businesses under its control or their representatives, tried to use illegal campaign contributions to influence the outcome of the 1996 federal elections.

The Senate voted to authorize the Senate Governmental Affairs Committee to conduct an investigation into the campaign finance allegations.[323] The hearings were chaired by Fred Thompson (R-TN) and began on July 7, 1997. The committee was given the authority to investigate improper as well as illegal activity, giving them broad discretion and a significant amount of power. They sent out many subpoenas, but people did not heed them, saying they were too broad. On September 23, 1997, Thompson abruptly altered the course of the hearings by shifting away from an examination of the potential abuses to a focus on what was wrong with the current system and how to fix it. He pulled the plug on the hearings on October 31, because the hearings failed to capture the public's attention and the partisan feuding on the committee never ceased. He said the hearings showed the need for legislation to overhaul the campaign finance system. As a result, the Senate proposed legislation (S 25) to do that. Their proposal would ban "soft money," or the large and largely unregulated contributions to political party committees from wealthy individuals, corporations, and unions. The proposal put limits on the amount of money wealthy candidates could give to their own campaigns.

Another investigation was begun by the House Government Reform and Oversight Committee, chaired by Dan Burton (R-IN). The committee intended to begin hearings on September 17, 1997, but they were postponed because the first round of witnesses unexpectedly refused to testify without immunity from criminal prosecution.

3. Clinton's Response

Clinton said that there was no big conspiracy to break the laws and collect campaign funds; instead, it was simply a case of sloppiness and bad judgment. The administration gave an interview with the *New York Times* in which Clinton admitted that policy was discussed at these meetings. He admitted that he had personally approved a Democratic Party plan to "energize" donors by rewarding them with overnight stays, coffees, golf outings, and morning jogs with the President.

4. Independent Counsel

For many months, Janet Reno refused demands to appoint a special prosecutor to look into possible irregularities with campaign donations. In a memo written in November 1997, FBI director Louis Freeh warned Attorney General Reno that she was misreading the law by not seeking an independent counsel to investigate campaign fund raising by the Clinton administration. She was also told this by the departing chief of the Justice Department's campaign finance unit. In August 1998, the House Government Reform and Oversight Committee voted to cite Reno for contempt of Congress for resisting a subpoena to turn over reports recommending that she seek an independent counsel. On August 27, 1998, Reno gave in and ordered a ninety-day preliminary inquiry into whether Gore lied to investigators when he was initially interviewed about his telephone solicitations to donors from the White House. If she determined at the end of the three-month period that there was evidence that Gore misled investigators, she would be obligated under the law to refer the case to an outside prosecutor.

Reno expanded the Justice Department investigation in October 1998 to look into the fundraising calls made by Clinton and Gore. At issue was whether federal law prohibited the president and vice president from making fund-raising calls from the White House. The law says that "it shall be unlawful for any person to solicit or receive any contribution" in any federal government room. The law was written 114 years ago to protect federal employees from being coerced to contribute in their offices by their bosses. However, there was no suggestion that Clinton and Gore solicited money from federal employees. Gore repeatedly said that he did not remember whether he made calls or not.

In late November 1998, Reno said there were no "reasonable grounds" to appoint an independent counsel to investigate Gore's fundraising activities. She said the evidence was "clear and convincing" that he did not lie to FBI agents investigating the legality of fundraising telephone calls he made from his office at the White House during the campaign.

In August 1998, a memo written by the White House was released that seemed to contradict Gore's account of his fundraising phone calls. The handwritten notations on the sides of the document indicate that at a meeting on November 21, 1995, Gore and several campaign officials discussed how some of the contributions raised by the vice president that could be used only for general party purposes could actually be diverted to "hard money" accounts to directly finance the Clinton-Gore reelection. Reno said that telephone solicitations for hard money by the president or vice president were subject to federal campaign finance laws and could be illegal.

J. Chinagate

During the Clinton administration, there were revelations of a direct connection between a state-owned Chinese aerospace company and an American aerospace company and the disclosure of sensitive weapons technology to the Chinese in exchange for campaign contributions. This was one of the most, if not the most, potentially serious scandals in the Clinton administration.

It began in 1989 when Senator Al Gore (D-TN) helped pass legislation that banned U.S.-made satellites from being launched on Chinese booster rockets unless the president agreed that the launch was in the interest of the United States. The legislation was part of a sanctions package designed to punish Beijing for the massacre of students in Tiananmen Square who had wanted democratic reforms in their country. President George Bush issued nine waivers for satellites between 1989 and 1992. One of the American companies that lobbied Bush for such waivers was Loral Space and Communications, a New York City-based former defense contractor with a specialty in manufacturing electronic warfare equipment. Loral had sold off its defense operations two years prior and was concentrating solely on its commercial satellite business, utilizing much of the same technology as used in military applications. Companies such as Loral, which provided the technology to make satellite guidance systems perform accurately, were able to save money be having other countries, such as China, launch U.S. satellites on their booster rockets.

The CEO of Loral was Bernard Schwartz, a longtime supporter of the DNC and one of the first executives of a major company to support Clinton's bid for the presidency in 1992. Schwartz contributed over $1 million to Clinton and the DNC, making him the single largest individual contributor.[324] Despite that, Schwartz said he never talked to the president about his business. However, he did ask the president to be included as a member of a trade mission coordinated by then secretary of Commerce Ron Brown.[325] Brown favored ending sanctions and loosening regulations concerning satellite technology, whereas many others, especially in the Department of State, wanted tighter control over transfers of American satellite technology. In March 1996, Clinton approved transferring control of satellite technology from the Department of State to the Department of Commerce.[326] Later, Schwartz went to China with Brown to sign an agreement that "helped open doors that were not open before."[327]

In February 1996, a Chinese rocket carrying a Loral satellite crashed twenty-two seconds after liftoff. It slammed into a village and killed six people, injured fifty-seven others, and destroyed about eighty homes.[328] After a brief investigation by Loral, it was discovered that the problem could only be fixed by using American technology that had never been approved for foreign use. In April, China Aerospace requested assistance from Loral officials to formally review the cause of the failed launch. The chairman of China Aerospace specifically requested that Wah Lim, a Chinese-born American citizen and vice president of Loral, be in charge of the review. China Aerospace brought Lim to China to assess the failed satellite launch. Loral used the technology, or the "patch," to solve the problem, even though it had not been approved for foreign use. China then used that patch for their intercontinental ballistic missiles to make them more reliable. Many of the missiles were aimed at the United States.[329]

Before he went to China, Lim was briefed as to what information he could give the Chinese and was forbidden from giving them information on how to improve launch accuracy. Without informing the State Department, the Loral team gave the results of its investigation to China Aerospace.[330] Loral documents acknowledged to the State Department in June 1996 that the company should have asked the department to review the activities of Lim and his review team and it was a "serious mistake" not to have done so. Additionally, Loral acknowledged that the issue of whether illegal assistance was given to the Chinese as a result of Lim's review is "more problematic."

On March 8, 1996, Chinese military forces carried out one of the largest military exercises in the communist regime's history. The exercise kicked off with test firings of M-9 short-range mobile missiles into "impact areas."[331] The show of military force by the Chinese People's Liberation Army nearly resulted in a direct military conflict with the United States.[332]

In July 1996, it was alleged that Democratic fundraiser Johnny Chung received $300,000 from China Aerospace, of which he passed at least $110,000 to Clinton and the DNC, although the exact amount of the contribution was disputed. Some reports indicate that the source of the money was Lieutenant Colonel Lin Chaoying, an official in China Aerospace and the daughter of the highest ranking officer in the Chinese People's Liberation Army, who oversaw all of China Aerospace rocket contracts. Lin Chaoying issued a statement on May 19, 1998, and said that the campaign contribution was made by her acting as an individual using her own funds and not those of China Aerospace.[333] Federal election laws prohibit accepting campaign funds from foreign nationals. In March 1998, Chung pled guilty for violating campaign laws and for illegal campaign contributions. Some have raised the possibility that Chung cooperated with investigators to secure protection from the U.S. government from China Aerospace officials, who wanted to know how the balance of the $300,000 given to him was spent.

Some have charged that Clinton and the DNC knew or should have known the source of the funds to be unreliable. Given the close ties that the leaders of China Aerospace have with the Chinese Communist Party, concerns were raised about why Clinton and the DNC would accept campaign contributions from Chung. He was well known at the White House because of his many meetings with Hillary Clinton to discuss the United States and China's "bridge building" missions.

In February 1997, Clinton signed an order making the transfer of technology that Loral had done completely legal.[334] This came just before a classified Pentagon report concluded that the review conducted by Loral's review team and Lim for China Aerospace over its failed launch had harmed national security by providing technological assistance to the company, which in turn was used to improve the internal guidance systems and accuracy of Chinese rockets. These are the same intercontinental ballistic missile rockets that the Chinese army would use to launch nuclear weapons. The report concluded that Loral's review of China's satellite program was wrong. Based on this report, the Justice Department began a criminal investigation into the actions of Loral and the assistance they provided to the Chinese.

A year later, President Clinton overruled the objections of the State Department, the Pentagon, and Department of Justice and authorized another waiver for Loral, giving them permission to work with China to set off another rocket.[335] This launch was part of a contract Loral had with China Aerospace for a project that had a value of $65 million. Clinton signed the waiver request, calling it unfair to penalize Loral before they had been charged with a crime, categorizing his actions as "routine."

On May 22, 1998, Trent Lott asked Intelligence Committee Chairman Richard Shelby to begin the Senate's inquiry into possible technology transfers to China and possible breaches of national security. They were investigating allegations that Clinton had been too lenient in approving U.S. technology exports to China and that those approvals may have been linked to Democratic campaign contributions. Then in June 1998, Congress established the bipartisan Select Committee on U.S. National Security and Military/Commercial Concerns with the People's Republic of China to investigate the claims of missile technology transfers to China by Loral. Every witness they called claimed their Fifth Amendment rights, and no firm evidence could be found linking the donations with waivers.[336] They determined that serious damage had resulted as a consequence, but the report was kept secret.[337]

At that same time, Liu Chaoying, a Chinese aerospace executive was accused of contributing nearly $100,000 to the Democratic Party through a middle man in 1996, but denied doing so. She said she never gave any money, directly or indirectly, to any U.S. political organization. Liu said that the money originally came from the Chinese army, where she served as a lieutenant colonel. She also had multiple, if indirect, ties to the satellite business.

In July 1998, Republicans on the committee reported that their preliminary investigation found that the Clinton administration violated U.S. policy by providing China with sensitive satellite technology that included military benefits. Some of the data was believed to have been taken from Los Alamos.

On May 14, 1999, intelligence officials in the U.S. reported that China was close to deploying a nuclear missile with a warhead whose design was based on Unites States secrets. A few days later, the head of a House investigating committee reported that China's nuclear weapons program benefited directly from the theft of U.S. secrets and that they obtained sensitive information about seven major weapons in the U.S. nuclear arsenal. Investigators at the Pentagon concluded that U.S. national security had been harmed by the technology transfer to China.[338] Moreover, the Air Force's National Air Intelligence Center said that "U.S. national security has been harmed" by the assistance that engineers from Loral and Hughes provided to the Chinese after the 1996 launch failure.[339]

Questions were building in Congress as to whether China funneled U.S.-based technology from Loral to Pakistan. On May 18, 1998, Clinton said he "welcomed" an investigation into the matter. A few days later (5/20/98), the House voted (417 to 4) to block future satellite exports to China and declared that Clinton's approval of such an export earlier in the year "was not in the national interest." They also decided to begin an investigation. The Republican who led the House investigation was Christopher Cox (R-CA). As chairman, he wanted two questions answered. First, how did American technology get to China, and second, had the Chinese military, through China Aerospace, tried to influence the U.S. presidential elections? They began by looking for possible impeachable offenses in the Clinton administration's policy of encouraging commercial exports to China.

The Cox Report came out on May 26, 1999. The 700-page report said that there was a theft of nuclear weapons technology and as a result, China now has more accurate nuclear weapons. They concluded that China had been systematically stealing information on American nuclear warheads and missiles from the 1970s. Cox found out that there was relentless espionage and open exchanges with American scientists that had saved China incalculable time and money in building a modern nuclear arsenal.

Implications

In April 1992, the United States discovered that the Chinese were secretly selling missiles to Pakistan. Then from May 11–13, 1998, India conducted a series of five underground nuclear tests, citing that they were responding to the military threat from Pakistan, which received missile technology from China. Shortly thereafter, on May 28, 1998, Pakistan conducted its own nuclear tests in response. At that time, Pakistan was the first developing nation in two decades to test a nuclear weapon and, in so doing, to become a nuclear power.[340] There was little doubt that China played a pivotal role in Pakistan's nuclear program.[341] Moreover, these tests only served to escalate an unstable region with a new threat of a nuclear arms build-up. The testing caused international concerns and calls to halt any future tests and eliminate any attempt to stockpile nuclear weapons. The emerging nuclear arms race on the Indian sub-continent is a direct result of the technology transfer that occurred during the Clinton administration.[342] So in the long run, it may affect the power structure in Asia.

When President Clinton loosened export controls on several high-technology sectors, including U.S. high-speed computer manufacturers, software makers, and communications satellite makers who wanted to sell such information China, he circumvented U.S. laws.[343] Both Loral Space and Communications, and Hughes Electronics were able to pass militarily useful rocket technology to Beijing without licenses.[344] There is clear evidence that American technology was transferred to China by some of our best aerospace engineers that allowed China to upgrade their weapons systems.[345] Clinton continued to ignore and cover up dangerous developments that affected vital U.S. interests.[346] His decisions concerning satellite technology left the United States weaker militarily as its enemies were able to grow stronger.[347] There were then allegations made that he tried to cover up the seriousness of his mistakes and either brushed them off as trivial or lied outright about them.[348]

Conclusion

During the Clinton administration, there were many political scandals. Some had to do with the president and his behavior, whereas others dealt more directly with other people in his administration. Of course, Clinton was impeached for his actions regarding Paula Jones and Monica Lewinsky, but not removed from office. Some have suggested that the nation could never understand the complexities of Whitewater and the other financial transactions that were Starr's original mandate. But we can all understand forbidden sex and the efforts by those who engage in it to keep it private.[349]

The question, of course, becomes if Clinton was more unethical than other presidents, or if independent counsel Kenneth Starr had the opportunity to "look for" illegal behavior, and if the new media blew up the allegations into something more than they were. It may also have been an attack by the Republicans against a Democratic presidential administration.

Review Questions

1. Describe some of the minor scandals to that affected the Clinton administration: his evasion of the draft, his prior drug use, Pardongate, and Filegate.
2. Who were some of Clinton's Cabinet that found themselves under investigation for illegal or unethical behavior?
3. What were the impeachment charges against Clinton?
4. Describe the public's opinion about the Jones/Lewinsky matter.
5. Why was Clinton not removed from office by the Senate?
6. What were some short-term and long-term impacts of the Jones/Lewinsky matter and Whitewater?
7. Describe the events of Whitewater.
8. What was the campaign finance scandal in the Clinton administration?
9. What was Chinagate?

Special Terms

Pardongate   *Clinton v. Jones*
Travelgate   Chinagate
Nannygate   Hatch Act
Filegate   Whitewater Scandal

Discussion Questions

1. Should Clinton have been impeached? Removed from office?
2. Was Starr's investigation a "fishing expedition" that allowed him to discover any criminal acts and bring down the Clinton administration?
3. Is it fair to bring charges against a sitting president for actions he may have committed before becoming president?

Chapter 7

Congressional Scandals

Introduction

It is not only presidents but also members of Congress who sometimes find themselves embroiled in scandal. At times, congressional scandals arise because legislators continue to behave in accordance with a code or practice that has become outdated, and the individual member fails to change his or her behavior to new expectations and standards of conduct.[1] For example, accepting gifts and money from lobbyists used to be quite common in the time before Watergate and did not attract much public attention, let alone disapproval or punishment.[2] However, over time, attitudes and standards evolved. What was once normal behavior is now regarded as scandalous.[3] An example is Dan Rostenkowski, who went to prison for embezzling public funds and mail fraud. He insists he did nothing wrong, except he did not notice when the old rules for getting things done changed.

The punishment for members of Congress who participate in inappropriate behavior is left to their own chambers. The Constitution is clear that judges and presidents can be removed from office by the Senate after being impeached by the House, but the Constitution gives both the House and the Senate ultimate responsibility for disciplining their own members. Thus, the Senate can expel a member without the prerequisite of a House impeachment, as can the House. Over time, the ultimate punishment of expulsion has been used sparingly by Congress. A lesser punishment is censure, where a member is formally reprimanded by the entire House or Senate, although this sanction has rarely been used.[4] Today, the House and Senate Ethics Committees evaluate the misconduct of their colleagues as the need arises. The Ethics Committees are evenly balanced between Democrats and Republicans, so that any action requires bipartisan consensus. Typically only intense public pressure can spur these committees into action, and only after a lawmaker has publicly embarrassed the institution.[5]

The Senate established its first ethics committee, called the Select Committee on Standards and Conduct, in 1964. It was bipartisan and created only after the resolution of the Robert Baker scandal. The House established its first ethics committee in 1967, after a high-profile scandal involving Representative Adam Clayton Powell. However, the political fallout from the Baker and Powell cases, along with a scandal involving Senator Thomas Dodd, prompted both the House and the Senate to adopt their first formal codes of conduct in 1968. After Watergate, both chambers adopted even more stringent conduct codes as a condition of a salary increase. These new codes imposed restrictions that legislators regarded as unthinkable a few years earlier. They limited the outside earned income of members, abolished office accounts, and required full disclosure of income, financial holdings, debts, and gifts.[6]

Abscam

One of the major scandals to hit Congress was Abscam, where many members were convicted of accepting bribes in exchange for promising legislative action. It occurred during the Carter administration, not long after Watergate. In the end, several congressmen and one United States senator were forced to resign from office.[7] The primary actors involved in the scandal are noted in Table 7.1. The Abscam investigation brought down more members of Congress than any other scandal.[8] All of those arrested were Democrats except for one, but none were among the most prominent congressional members. The scandal was known as Abscam because it was an "Arab scam," involving Arab characters, and a scam being a confidence trick. It is alleged, however, that President Jimmy Carter took exception with this explanation on racial grounds and subsequent official accounts suggest that Abscam actually stood for "Abdul scam,"[9] or even Abdul Enterprises, Inc-scam.[10]

Table 7.1: Actors in the Abscam Scandal

Tony Amoroso: FBI agent who posed as Sheik Yassir Habib

James Earl Carter: President of United States

Angelo Errichetti: Mayor of Camden, N.J., and New Jersey State senator

Melvin Weinberg: Con man, hustler, FBI informant

The scam began in 1978 and lasted about two years.[11] It began with an investigation into allegations that organized crime figures were selling stolen securities and art objects.[12] It was a sort of sting operation designed to trap public officials who were suspected of corruption. The investigation grew when FBI agents, disguised as an Arab sheikhs and their entourage, offered bribes to numerous congressmen and senators in exchange for a promise of help with immigration and business problems.[13] During Abscam, over 100 federal agents were engaged in the undercover investigation of legislative corruption.[14]

One person directly involved in the affair was Melvin Weinberg, a fifty-five-year-old con man, swindler, and hustler with a thirty-five-year career in white-collar crime. He was hired by the government to be part of Abscam[15] after pleading guilty to federal offenses in Pittsburgh. His name came to the attention of the FBI as a potential informant as he knew how to con people and was believable. The FBI paired Weinberg with FBI agent Tony Amoroso. Weinberg posed as an American representative of two imaginary Arab sheikhs, Kambir Abdul Rahman and Yassir Habib, who wanted to invest billions of dollars of their money in the United States and eventually get permanent asylum in the country.

1. Initial Scam

The basic version of the scam had Weinberg acting as the American agent of millionaire Arab businessman Kambir Abdul Rahman. Abdul's money could not be loaned out at interest because of Islamic laws against usury. As a result, people were told, he needed an unlimited supply of bogus certificates of deposit from offshore banks or forged certificates from legitimate banks. These certificates would be given by him to his Moslem banks and he would then be able to withdraw cash equal to the face amount of the certificates and quietly invest the cash at interest elsewhere. Some were told that Abdul wanted to invest as much of his millions in the United States as possible because he felt it was only a matter of time before he would have to flee the wrath of his ripped-off citizenry. Weinberg began to say his friend was in the ruling class (an emir). Others were told that Abdul was a lavish patron of the arts and was not averse to purchasing paintings, jewelry, and other items that were stolen. It was only natural that Abdul would have a corporation to handle all of these activities. It was called Abdul Enterprises, Ltd. The FBI had a man at Chase Manhattan bank who agreed to tell anyone who might call that Kambir Abdul Rahman had millions on deposit with the bank.

The FBI discovered that the mayor of Camden, New Jersey, and New Jersey State Representative Angelo Errichetti had beaten an indictment for fraud and perjury several years before when he was Camden city purchasing director. There were also unconfirmed reports that organized crime was moving in on Atlantic City, and that Errichetti might be involved. The FBI decided to approach Errichetti and present the scam to him.[16] The story they gave him was that Abdul wanted to invest in casinos in Camden and Atlantic City, but there was nothing to be gained from financing hotels unless he could be guaranteed a gambling license. Of course, the sheik could not use his own money since it was tied up in Moslem banks in his home country. To free up his money, he would need certificates of deposit, gold certificates, or anything that could be sent to the Arab banks in exchange for cash. The money would be transferred to Chase Manhattan Bank. It was implied (but never spoken) that they could be fake.

It was at this point that the FBI decided to begin videotaping sessions.[17] On December 1, 1978, Mayor Errichetti arrived at Abdul's office. Errichetti said that he could promise a gambling license if he cashed in on favors by others. When he left, his assistants described what the mayor meant. It would cost between $350,000 and $400,000 in bribes passed through the mayor for an Atlantic City casino license. Over the next year, Errichetti offered or gave Abscam agents stolen diamonds, guns and munitions, forged CDs, counterfeit money, stolen paintings, leasing contracts, municipal garbage contracts, unregistered boats for drug running, the use of Port Camden as a narcotics depot, Atlantic City zoning changes, and a list of thirteen bribable state and city officials, including the vice chairman of the State Casino Control commission, the chairman of the New Jersey State Democratic Committee, and, directly or indirectly, five U.S. congressman and a senator.

Weinberg and Errichetti then had a meeting with Kenneth MacDonald, the vice chairman of the Casino Control Commission. He wanted $100,000 as a bribe in exchange for a gambling license. Errichetti gave Weinberg $435 million in counterfeit certificates, and the FBI gave a $100,000 bribe to MacDonald. Errichetti then told the FBI agents he would need $400,000 total for the license. He also arranged to meet a friend in New Jersey, lawyer Alexander Feinberg, who was in a partnership in a titanium mine operation with Henry Williams, Senator Harrison Williams, and a New Jersey garbage contractor named George Katz. The partners could make millions if Abdul would loan them the money to clear the mine of mortgages and pick up a small processing plant nearby.

On January 29, 1979, Errichetti was paid $25,000 in cash to start the action on Abdul's gambling license. He was the first politician to accept a bribe in the Abscam investigation. It was also the most important because he felt the whole thing was real, and he felt safe to get more involved.

The FBI began using a yacht that had been seized by the government because of drugs to host lavish parties. Senator Williams was in attendance at the yacht parties, as were mayor Errichetti, an FBI agent posing as Yassir, and many others involved in Abscam. The party was supposedly given in honor of Mayor Errichetti. For a gift, Weinberg remembered a knife he had bought years before at a flea market for $2.75, and presented it to Errichetti as a ceremonial knife of friendship. At that party, Senator Williams would be committing a federal crime if he agreed to use his position as a senator to help the mining venture in return for a share in it. There was an implicit understanding that Senator Williams would use his influence with the government to help the new corporation in any way possible, including government contracts for the titanium, but Williams had not verbalized this yet, which the FBI needed.

On January 15, 1980, at another meeting, Sheik Yassir said he planned to come and reside in the United States in the near future. He asked Senator Williams to arrange legislation to give him permanent status or citizenship. Williams said that it could be done and that he would do it. It is illegal for a senator to make promises about legislation in this way.

Eventually, Mayor Errichetti offered to bring two other congressmen into the scam: Michael (Ozzie) Myers and Raymond Lederer, both of Philadelphia, Pennsylvania. The FBI needed the congressmen to pledge the use of their offices to help Abdul and Yassir stay in the United States and acknowledge they were getting the money to do just that. The price for each congressman, said Errichetti, would be $100,000 in cash. Errichetti also said he could arrange meetings with U.S. Senator Herman Talmadge of Georgia and two other congressmen from Georgia, Elliott H. Levitas and Donald Fowler.

On August 22, Ozzie Myers took a bribe for arranging permanent residency in the United States for the sheik. It took place in a suite in the Travel Lodge Hotel near the Kennedy Airport. FBI agent Amoroso gave him the $50,000 bribe.[18] Myers complained later that he thought it contained $100,000. It was also discovered later that Myers only got $15,000; the rest of it went to the middlemen, including Errichetti and others. This pattern was followed with the others nabbed in Abscam. Weinberg handled the preliminary contacts with the middlemen. Amoroso would dominate the actual payoff meetings, asking the essential questions necessary to establish a federal crime and handling the bribe money. Weinberg helped, serving food and drinks.

When it was his turn, Representative Raymond Lederer (D-PA) behaved the same way as Myers. It took place in a hotel suite at Kennedy Airport again. Lederer promised to push a bill through Congress to give Yassir asylum, and took the $50,000 bribe.[19]

After that, the FBI moved its operations to a four-bedroom townhouse in Georgetown, near the Capitol building. The apartment had already been used by the FBI in another sting operation, so it had previously been wired and set with video cameras. Two of the first congressmen to be invited to the townhouse, Talmadge and Fowler, canceled. Talmadge had recently been censured in the Senate and did not think the timing was right. Fowler claimed a death in the family. Both later denied knowledge of the proposed meetings.

On October 9, 1979, two congressmen had appointments to come to the townhouse. They were Frank Thompson of New Jersey, chairman of the House Administration Committee, and Jim Mattox of Texas. When asked if he would introduce a bill to grant the Arabs refuge in the United States., Mattox told them that he was not looking for any money and could not guarantee anything, so they did not give him the money. However, Thompson accepted the money.

The next congressman was John Jenrette Jr. of South Carolina, a member of the House Appropriations Committee. At that time, he was under investigation by the Justice Department in connection with a South Carolina real estate deal and subsequent tampering with a federal grand jury. At the townhouse, he said he would take the money if the government dropped its investigation of him. He sent someone else the next day to pick up the bribe, and acknowledged over the phone that he had received it. Jenrette also wanted a loan from the Arabs to save the failing real estate venture in which he was involved.

John Murtha of Johnstown, Pennsylvania, was next. He promised to help Abdul and Yassir stay in the United States, but would not take the money. Then Florida congressman Richard Kelly came to the townhouse on January 8, 1980, and the FBI gave him $25,000.

On February 2, 1980, details of the Abscam investigation were first revealed in the Long Island newspaper *Newsday* and the *New York Times*.[20] That same day, all seven legislators were indicted on charges of bribery. Other officials, including Mayor Errichetti and George Katz, a businessman and Democratic Party fundraiser, were also indicted.[21]

In the trials, the FBI showed videotapes that featured politicians receiving tens of thousand of dollars in return for offers of service. The defendants claimed entrapment. They claimed Weinberg had gone too far in enticing them. Additionally, the chief government witness against them was a known swindler and liar. Myers, Jenrette, and Thompson all said they were drunk when the bribes were passed, and Kelly said he had taken the money as part of his secret investigation of organized crime. Kelley was seen on a videotape stuffing money in his pockets and asking if the money made visible bulges in his clothing.[22] They were all convicted anyway.

Senator Williams was convicted on bribery and conspiracy to use his office to aid in a business venture. He was sentenced to three years in prison. Because of the conviction, the Senate voted to censure him and started proceedings to expel him for bringing dishonor on the House. Before the vote could be taken, he resigned. He served two years of his sentence in a federal penitentiary. He applied for a pardon from President Bill Clinton, but was denied.

Myers was convicted on all charges and was expelled from the House on October 2, 1980. He was the first sitting member to be expelled since the Civil War. Jenrette and Thompson both lost their reelection attempts. Thompson resigned his seat several days after his defeat. He was convicted on bribery and conspiracy charges, and sentenced to three years in prison. Kelly was not renominated by the Republicans in 1980; was convicted of taking a bribe and served thirteen months in prison. Lederer resigned his seat on April 29, 1981. After being threatened with expulsion, Senator Williams resigned on March 11, 1982.[23] The outcomes of Abscam are presented in Table 7.2.

Table 7.2: Those Convicted in Abscam

Senator Harrison A. Williams (D-NJ)

Rep. John Jenrette (D-SC)

Rep. Richard Kelly (R-FL)

Rep. Raymond Lederer (D-PA)

Rep. Michael "Ozzie" Myers (D-PA)

Rep. Frank Thompson (D-NJ)

Angelo Errichetti, mayor of Camden, N.J., and New Jersey State senator

---

Abscam was the most extensive investigation and prosecution of legislative corruption in the nation's history.[24] In no previous federal investigation had so many elected officials at the federal, state, and local levels been found guilty of such behavior. It was a very innovative investigation, but at the same time very controversial.[25] The government taped everything almost from the beginning. They used video cameras with special lenses, taking a very active role in the investigation, spending around $500,000. Because of their active role, the end results were contentious.

It could be argued that Abscam was not as significant as Watergate or later scandals that involved the president, because the president is the center of national politics and media attention and therefore attracts a lot of attention. Congress, on the other hand, has many people. Plus, the individual legislators only influence events rather than determine them. Nonetheless, there were some long-term impacts of Abscam. First, the political careers of those directly involved in the scandal were ruined, as were the careers of others indirectly involved. For example, Harry Jannotti, a Philadelphia councilman, also went to jail for accepting a $10,000 bribe during Abscam. He had been a city council majority leader, chairman of the Finance Committee, and vice chairman of the Rules and Appropriations Committee. He was videotaped taking the money from an FBI agent (a phony sheik) and promising to use his influence to win approval for a luxury hotel that the sheik wanted to build. He served four-and-a-half years in federal prison.

Second, the Abscam affair, which occurred not too long after Watergate, was making many citizens think that the government was totally corrupt, including the president, Congress, Republicans, and Democrats. It also showed that Carter was unable to have an honest government, which he had promised during his campaign.

Other Congressional Scandals

Besides Abscam, there have been many other political scandals to appear in Congress. They have involved both Republicans and Democrats, present and prior members. Some minor Congressional scandals are presented in Table 7.3, and others are described below.

Table 7.3: Congressional Scandals

Hugh Joseph Addonizio: U.S. Representative from N.J. 1949–1962 and mayor of Newark 1962–79: convicted of charges of taking kickbacks from organized crime figures who were allowed to control the city. Addonizio was convicted and sentenced to ten years in prison and fined $25,000.

Bob Barr: U.S. Representative from Georgia 1995–2003: photographed at a fundraising event licking whipped cream off the chest of a woman, supposedly raising money for leukemia research.

Mario Biagi: U.S. Representative from New York 1969–88: implicated in financial and kickback scandal but resigned before he could be expelled.

Walter Brehm: U.S. Representative from Ohio 1943–53: convicted of unlawfully accepting a campaign contribution of $1,000 from one of his clerks.

William A. Clark: U.S. Senator 1899–1900 and 1901–07 from Montana: resigned from the Senate when accused of electoral misconduct and bribery, but was re-elected the following year to the same seat.

Charles C. Diggs Jr: U.S. Representative from Michigan 1955–80: became the first congressman censured by the House since 1921 because of a court conviction involving charges of mail fraud and falsifying payroll form.

Thomas Dodd: U.S. Representative 1953–57 and senator 1959–71 from Connecticut: censured by the Senate in 1967 for misuse of campaign and office funds for personal use.

William Augustus Gilbert: U.S. Representative from New York 1855–57: accused of corruption and censured by the House.

Allan T. Howe: U.S. Representative from Utah 1975–77; arrested for soliciting a sex act for hire from two policewomen decoy prostitutes in Salt Lake City.[26]

Carroll Hubbard Jr.: U.S. Representative from Kentucky 1975–93; pled guilty in 1994 to conspiracy to defraud the FEC by illegally spending campaign funds for personal use and to the theft of government property.

Jay C. Kim: U.S. Representative from California 1993–99: pled guilty in 1997 to raising more than $230,000 in illegal campaign contributions.

Nicholas Mavroules: U.S. Representative from Massachusetts 1979–93: pled guilty in 1993 to charges of tax fraud and accepting gratuities while in office. Mavroules was sentenced to fifteen months in prison.

James Patterson: U.S. Representative 1863–67 and U.S. Senator 1867–73 from New Hampshire; implicated in the Credit Mobilier scandal and threatened with expulsion from the Senate.

Carl Perkins: U.S. Representative from Kentucky 1984–93: pled guilty to conspiring to defraud the Federal Elections Commission by writing bad checks and filing false personal finance disclosure statements.

Melvin Reynolds: U.S. Representative 1993–94 from Illinois: convicted in 1997 of fifteen counts of bank fraud, wire fraud, and lying to the Federal Election Commission.

Bud Schuster: U.S. Representative from Pennsylvania 1973–2001; rebuked by the House Ethics Committee for allegedly accepting improper gifts and favoring a lobbyist.

John Thomas: U.S. Representative from N.J. 1937–50: convicted of fraud and sent to prison for nine months.

James Traficant Jr.: U.S. Representative from Ohio 1985–2002: convicted in April 2002 of bribery, racketeering, and fraud and expelled from the House of Representatives.

Bill Janklow: U.S. Representative from South Dakota 2003–04: convicted of second-degree manslaughter, reckless driving, speeding, and running a stop sign; killed a fifty-five-year old motorcyclist; was sentenced to 100 days and forced to resign.

A. William Blount (1797)

The scandal surrounding William Blount was the first serious impeachment case in Congress.[27] Blount represented North Carolina at the 1787 Constitutional Convention before moving west, and then became the first and only governor of the Southwest Territory. He was then a U.S. senator from Tennessee. He took part in a complicated and possibly treasonous conspiracy to maneuver Great Britain into an invasion of Spanish-held Louisiana, thereby leaving Spanish territory there and in Florida vulnerable to takeover by a small private army organized by Blount and fellow land speculators. In January 1798, the House adopted five articles of impeachment against Blount and voted to impeach him, as well as disqualify him from holding future office. The Senate voted to expel him in 1797.[28] They began impeachment proceedings, but dropped the charges on the grounds that no further action could be taken against someone who was no longer a member of the House.

B. Daniel Sickles (1859)

Sickles was a Democrat from New York who was a friend of Captain Phillip Barton Key, U.S. attorney for the District of Columbia and son of Francis Scott Key, the author of the *Star-Spangled Banner*. Key had had an affair with Sickles's wife, Teresa. He would sometimes appear outside their home and wave a white handkerchief to get Mrs. Sickles's attention. In 1859, Representative Sickles discovered Key waving his handkerchief, and forced his wife to sign a confession about her affair with him. The next day when Key appeared at the window, Sickles shot him to death.[29] He went to trial and his attorney argued that Sickles was innocent since he had been driven insane by his wife's affair with Key. He was the first American to successfully claim temporary insanity and was acquitted of the charges related to the murder.[30]

C. William Sharon (1883)

Senator William Sharon (R-Nevada) was involved in one of the juiciest scandals of the time. In 1883 a woman named Sarah Althea Hill claimed that Senator Sharon had "married" her with an official ceremony. He sued to have the alleged marriage annulled, which resulted in two lawsuits that went on for many years. She won the first case in 1884, but the second case, which was decided in his favor, was decided after his death. During one of the trials, there was a knife fight in the courtroom. Later, Supreme Court Justice Stephen J. Field was attacked by his colleague, David S. Terry, Hill's lawyer. Terry was killed, and Field was briefly arrested in connection with Terry's death.[31]

D. William Breckinridge (1893)

William Breckenridge was a Kentucky Democratic Representative whose mistress sued him in 1893 for breach of promise. When he ran for reelection, crowds of women protested his immorality. He was defeated in the primary.[32]

E. Robert Baker (1963–66)

Robert Baker worked for Lyndon Johnson when Johnson, was a senator from Texas, as the secretary to the Senate Majority Leader. Charges were made against Baker in September 1963 that he used his position for personal and financial gain. He demanded payoffs of $5,000 from a vending machine representative have the man's vending machines put into government offices.[33]

Baker resigned his office on October 7, 1963.[34] A month later, John F. Kennedy was assassinated and Johnson became president. Baker was indicted in 1966 on charges of tax evasion and defrauding the government. He was then convicted in 1967 and after a series of appeals went to prison in January 1971, and was released in June 1972.[35]

Because there was no Ethics Committee at the time, the Senate Rules Committee had to investigate the charges against Baker. This scandal led to the establishment in 1964 of the bipartisan Senate Select Committee on Standards and Conduct. Three years later the House of Representatives also recognized the need for such a committee and created its own bipartisan ethics committee, called the Committee on Standards of Official Conduct. The House made its committee permanent and gave it both enforcement and investigative powers.[36]

F. Ted Kennedy: Chappaquiddick (1969)

During Robert Kennedy's campaign for president in 1968, there were a group of young females, nicknamed the "boiler-room girls" for the tough campaign work they performed. As a reunion for the women, a party was planned for the weekend of July 18 and 19 at Martha's Vineyard by Kennedy supporters.

The party was held at Chappaquiddick, a small island off the coast of Martha's Vineyard. To get to it, visitors had to take a ferry that operated from 7:30 A.M. until midnight each day. The Kennedy's rented a small cottage for the weekend to host the party. The party consisted of twelve people, the six young single women and six married men. Lots of noise was reported by outsiders.

Kennedy later reported that he had four rum and Cokes at the party, a total of six for the day. Some of the girls reportedly were drunk by 10 P.M. According to Kennedy, around 11:15 or 11:30 p.m., he announced that he was tired and was going to catch one of the last ferries to town and return to his motel. He said that one of the women, Mary Jo Kopechne, asked for a ride. He left with Kopechne along the one paved road on the island.

Less than a mile from the ferry crossing, the road bears sharply to the left. Kennedy accidentally took a right turn instead. The road led to a small bridge crossing Poucha Pond to a secluded beach area. Kennedy's car plunged off the bridge into the pond, drowning Kopechne.[37] Kennedy later said that he blacked out for a few seconds then awoke as Mary Jo was flailing about, perhaps kicking and punching him. He said there was complete darkness, water was rushing in from everywhere, and he was aware of the fact that he was upside down. Kennedy was able to free himself and get to shore.

Kennedy reportedly attempted to return to the vehicle "seven or eight times" but was pushed away by the strong current. He walked back to the cottage, taking about fifteen to twenty minutes. Along the way, he saw no cars or people. He later returned to the accident scene with two men from the party. Two of the men dove into the water in an effort to reach Mary Jo, but could not reach her. Kennedy then swam across the channel to Martha's Vineyard and walked to his motel room, arriving at 2 A.M.

He appeared in the hotel lobby at 2:30 A.M. in dry clothes and complained to the innkeeper about the noise from a party, then went to his room. The innkeeper noticed nothing unusual, except that those complaining about noise usually telephoned instead of dressing and walking down to the front desk. At 7 a.m., Kennedy was shaven and appeared normal while dressed in "yachting clothes" when he borrowed a dime from the innkeeper to use the payphone. He made seventeen undocumented calls over the next few hours before reporting the accident to the police. There was a ten-hour delay in reporting the accident.[38]

After making his way into the local police station the following day, Kennedy asked to use the phone there. The local dispatcher invited him to use the phone in the absent sheriff's office so he could speak in private. After making the calls, Kennedy told the police about the accident the night before. The sheriff said he had already been to the scene to see the car and the corpse of the young woman. After calling Mary Jo's parents and his own mother, Kennedy left the police station to tell the news to his sick father.

When Kennedy appeared at Kopechne's funeral, he was in a neck brace. By then, he had appeared live on television from the family compound to get his version of events out as quickly as possible. Although he would not comment on specifics, he asserted that he and Mary Jo were not drunk, that the incident was a tragic accident, and no improper behavior had taken place or was planned between the married senator and the young single woman.

An inquest was held on the matter to determine if there was any basis for criminal charges. After a four-month, closed-door inquest, a 763-page transcript was released. District Court Justice James Boyle concluded that negligent driving appeared to have contributed to Kopechne's death. Justice Boyle wrote that Kennedy's "turn onto Dike Road was intentional." The judge could have ordered Kennedy's arrest on manslaughter charges, but he chose not to do so. Instead he retired from the bench the following day.

Absent from the inquest was any testimony on the actual cause of Kopechne's death. The day following the accident, when divers worked to retrieve the body and the car from the pond, Kopechne's body was found arched against a small air pocket inside the rear section of the car. Divers concluded that she freed herself from her seat and moved toward the air pocket to breathe the little bit of trapped oxygen inside the car. There was a consensus that she did not drown, but more than likely lived for three to five hours before finally suffocating. Local authorities estimated to reporters that Kopechne could have been removed from the car alive in about twenty minutes.

Kennedy pled guilty to leaving the scene of a crime, possibly to stop the investigation. Days after the accident, he appeared on TV and asked voters if he should resign. His aides reported that there was an overwhelming response of telephone calls, telegrams, and letters, most urging him to remain in office. He was reelected to the Senate.

Immediately after Robert Kennedy was assassinated, many urged Ted Kennedy to seek the Democratic nomination for president. There were also calls for him to run for president in 1972 and in 1976, but he declined them all. He made only one serious attempt in 1980 against Carter. The country was facing high inflation and high unemployment, with no economic recovery in sight. American hostages had been held in Iran for more than a year, and it appeared as though the Democrats would lose the office. While running for the nomination, Kennedy was asked direct questions about drinking, drug use, womanizing, and the events at Chappaquiddick. He stammered through the questions, gave vague responses to allegations of moral impropriety, and did not seem to be able to crystallize his ideas. Kennedy was unable to convince voters of his ability to run the country, and he did not get the nomination. Chappaquiddick is widely believed to have kept him out of the White House.[39]

G. Carl Albert (1972)

In 1972, Carl Albert was the Democratic Speaker of the House from Oklahoma. As such, he was a well-respected and powerful member of Congress. One evening around midnight, he was driving his car in D.C. and struck two other cars. Several witnesses said he was obviously drunk. When a policeman came, he identified himself as Carl Albert, and continued to yell, "You can't touch me!" A few days later, he denied his actions at a press conference. He denied that he had been drunk, but admitted that he "took something" that evening at a cocktail party.[40]

H. Thomas Eagleton (1972)

Thomas Eagleton was the Democratic nominee chosen to run with George McGovern for president in 1972. But it quickly became known that the Missouri senator had been hospitalized on three separate occasions for depression and had undergone electroshock therapy. It was then falsely reported that he had been arrested for drunk driving and other criminal offenses. These rumors along with the mental issues forced him to withdraw from the ticket.[41]

I. Wayne Hayes (1974)

Wayne Hayes, a Democrat from Ohio, was a U.S. representative from 1949 to 1976. At the time of his scandal, Hayes was the powerful chairman of the House Administration Committee, which had control over the money spent in the House, and served on the Democratic National Congressional Committee (DNCC).[42] In 1974, he hired his thirty-three-year-old mistress, Elizabeth Ray, as a typist on his staff. She earned $14,000 a year, even though she could not type, file, or answer the phone and claimed she never performed those jobs.[43] In the meantime, he got a divorce from his wife and was planning to marry another woman. Ray then decided to call a reporter at the *Washington Post* and expose her story in a front-page article.[44] At first, Hayes denied it, and most people believed him.[45] After a while, Hayes finally admitted that he had a personal relationship with Ray.[46] The House Ethics Committee investigated and brought charges against him that he used public funds to pay her off.[47] On June 3, he voluntarily stepped down as chairman of the DNCC. About two weeks later he stepped down as chairman of the Committee on House Administration,[48] and eventually resigned from the House.[49] He ran for reelection and got the Democratic Party nomination but withdrew before the general election so that another candidate could take his place.[50] He was never charged with a crime. After leaving Washington, Hayes served as a member of the Ohio State House of Representatives for a short time.[51]

J. Wilbur Mills (1974)

Wilbur Mills, a Democrat from Arkansas from 1939–77, was involved with the first sex scandal after Watergate, sometimes referred to as the "Tidal Basin Incident."[52] As a young man, Mills attended Harvard Law School but quit in his final semester. Nonetheless, he passed the Arkansas bar in 1934 and became judge. He served four years as judge, and was then elected to the House as the second youngest member. In 1939, he was appointed to the House Banking Committee. He eventually was appointed to the House Ways and Means Committee, becoming chairman in 1957, making him one of the most well respected and powerful politicians in Washington, responsible for formulating tax policy.[53] At one point, Mills was mentioned as a possible presidential candidate. However, it was discovered that he hired a prostitute in his House office, which ended that proposal.

The scandal revolving around Mills occurred on October 7, 1974, when park police stopped a Lincoln for driving erratically and without headlights at 2 A.M. As they were giving him a ticket, they noticed that Mills was drunk and bleeding from multiple cuts on his face. A woman got out of the car and jumped into the Tidal Basin in an attempt to get away. She turned out to be a thirty-eight-year-old Argentine stripper Annabelle Battistella, also known as Fanne Foxe.[54] Mills, who was sixty-five at the time, denied any wrongdoing for three days. Three days later, he finally decided to explain. Mills said they were neighbors and he had gone out with her for a going away party. The car lights were off simply because the driver did not know how to turn them on. He then explained that he did not come out from the beginning because his wife felt responsible for the scandal and he did not want her to feel bad.

Eventually it was revealed that Mills and Battistella had a sexual relationship. He had gone to the strip bar where she worked several times, and they had returned home together. Some nights he would spend $1700 on tips. The two fought quite frequently, so no one really took the whole thing seriously. The media knew but did not report it.

Mills was facing reelection in November. His secrets began to emerge and it became obvious that he had a drinking problem. Soon the House took away some power of the Ways and Means Committee chair.[55] He said he was an alcoholic since 1963 and had a drug problem since 1972. He checked in to a treatment center and stopped drinking.

Mills returned to House but decided to retire in 1976 after forty years in Congress. He later said that during half of his time in Congress he was drunk and often did not remember White House meetings. After retirement, he became a tax consultant. Mills died in 1992.

K. Koreagate (1977)

Allegations persisted that the government of South Korea bribed members of Congress to exert influence concerning policy toward their country. The president of South Korea, Park Chung Hee, put Park Tong Sun in charge of the lobbying effort. While in Washington, Park Tong Sun went by the name Tongsun Park. Tongsun Park was involved in the rice trade with the United States, but he also had links with the South Korean intelligence agencies. His role was to cultivate as many friends as possible in Congress.

Although it was alleged that over 100 congressmen accepted bribes,[56] Park gave evidence to the House Ethics Committee that he had given gifts and made campaign contributions to thirty current or former congressmen. Park was indicted in 1977 on charges of conspiring to bribe public officials, but he was never prosecuted in exchange for agreeing to give testimony about whom he had paid, how much, and in what form.[57]

Representative Richard Hanna was the only person implicated in the Koreagate scandal and spent time in prison for his actions. He pled guilty to charges that he accepted a $200,000 bribe from Park and Korean religious figure Sun Myung Moon to help influence members of Congress.[58]

L. Pages (1982)

Pages are teenagers who work in Congress for up to a year as gofers. In 1982 there were allegations that pages were participating in organized homosexual activity and that a cocaine ring was operating on Capitol Hill. Two lawmakers, Representatives Dan Crane and Gerry Studds, were accused of having sexual relations with teenage pages, Crane with a woman and Studds with a young man.[59] Studds apparently took them to bars.[60] Later, one page said he made up part of the story and exaggerated others.[61]

M. John Mack (1983)

John Mack was the manager of a furniture store in 1973 when Pamela Small came in to buy some new furniture. He took her to a back room, beat her with a hammer, stabbed her, and stuffed her body into the car and went to the movies.[62] Small was able to get away and drive herself to the hospital. Mack was caught the next day and confessed. He was given a suspended sentence and served twenty-seven months in jail.

A little while later, Mack's brother married Representative Jim Wright's daughter. Mack needed a job, and he started working for Wright as a file clerk. Over time he was promoted and moved up in his status as Wright moved up in Congress. The story of Mack's "mistake" was published in 1983 in a newspaper in Wright's home town and eventually in the *Washington Post*. When the story broke, Mack was thirty-five years old and a very powerful staff member, working for the Speaker of the House.[63] Wright apologized publicly, admitting that he had made a mistake in hiring Mack and promoting him to such a powerful position. He denied knowing the facts of the case and what Mack had done before working in Congress. Mack argued that he had served his time and that people should allow him to do his job. However, some members of Congress wanted to get rid of him, believing that he should not have such a powerful position in Congress. Most women agreed, and he was fired.

N. Joe Biden (1987)

Joe Biden was a senator representing Delaware who was first elected to office in 1972 at the age of twenty-nine. He eventually became the ranking Democratic member on the Senate Judiciary Committee. As a student, Biden plagiarized speeches from Robert Kennedy and other political leaders.[64] While a first-year law student, he stole five pages from a law review article and presented them to his professor for a grade as his own paper. He was almost expelled for this.

Another scandal hit Biden in 1987, when he was the front-runner for the Democratic presidential nomination for the 1988 campaign after Gary Hart dropped out of the race. While campaigning in New Hampshire, he lashed out at a member of the audience after a man in the audience asked him what law school he attended and what grades he got. Biden shot back, "I think I have a much higher IQ than you do. I went to law school on a full academic scholarship and ended up in the top half of my class. I won the international moot court competition. I was the outstanding student in the Political Science Department of my college. I graduated with three degrees from college. And I'd be delighted to sit back and compare my IQ to yours if you'd like." During the outburst, Biden appeared nervous and insecure. To make matters worse, what he said was not true. He did not attend law school on a full academic scholarship, but on a partial scholarship that was based on financial need, not on academic achievement. Nor did he finish in the top half of his law class. He was ranked as seventh-sixth in a class of eighty-five. He graduated with only one degree, not three, and he did not win any awards given to the outstanding political science student.[65] A videotape of the event was sent to C-SPAN where it was broadcast nationally. After the outburst, Biden was widely censured by the media and his opponents, and was forced out of the race in ten days. But he continued to serve as Senate Judiciary Committee chair and a member of Congress and was elected to serve as vice president in the 2008 election.

O. Buz Lukens (1985, 1988)

Buz Lukens, a Republican Representative from Ohio, was accused of having sexual relations with an underage teenager in 1985 when she was thirteen, and then again in 1988. The girl's mother called Lukens, and they met at a fast-food restaurant to talk about the situation. All the while, the mother was wired and taped the entire conversation, while television reporters video taped it. During the meeting, Lukens offered the mother a government job if she would keep quiet. Using the tapes as evidence, Lukens went to trial and was convicted. He served nine days of a thirty day sentence.[66]

P. Gary Hart (1988)

Gary Hart from Colorado was the Democratic presidential front-runner in the 1988 campaign, and it was expected that he would win the nomination. Before the campaign, in 1984, it was discovered that Hart shortened his name from Hartpence, shaved a year off his age, and changed his signature. When questioned, he offered vague and misleading explanations.[67] During the 1988 campaign, Hart was questioned about his relationship with his wife. He denied that he was having extramarital affairs and challenged the press to prove him wrong. Two reporters from the *Miami Herald* staked out his townhouse and caught him escorting a woman inside.[68] The lady was Donna Rice, known to be a party girl. She met Hart in Colorado in 1987 and then again at a fundraiser in Miami. At the party, Hart asked for her phone number and called her the next day. They went on a yacht called *Monkey Business* and ended up in the Bahamas.[69] He could not leave his wife because of his presidential bid, but he kept calling Rice nonetheless. Hart withdrew from the race a week later.[70] To some, his dalliance exposed strong defects of judgment and possible issues about his morality, and he had to drop out of the presidential race.[71]

Q. Barney Frank (1989)

Barney Frank was the Representative from the fourth District of Massachusetts and ranking Democrat on the House Judiciary Committee who was first elected to Congress in 1980. He was a graduate of Harvard, a lawyer, and once taught at the Harvard University Kennedy School of Government and its Institute of Politics. He was considered to be one of the most intellectual and political leaders of the Democratic Party in the House.[72]

In August 1989, the conservative *Washington Times* and the liberal *Boston Globe* printed a series of news stories that revealed that Frank had paid for sex with a notorious Washington male prostitute named Steve Gobie, whom he later employed as a housekeeper and chauffeur for $20,000 per year.[73] Frank had first met Gobie after answering an ad in a newspaper in which Gobie solicited sex from paying gay customers. Frank had allowed Gobie to use his Capitol Hill house as a brothel for gay male prostitution.[74] Frank then admitted to failing to report his employment of Gobie to the government, and said that he had not even reported his employee-lover's salary to the IRS, nor withheld Social Security taxes.[75] At that time, the maximum penalty for solicitation of a prostitute at that time in the District of Columbia was ninety days in jail and a hefty fine.

The House Ethics Committee investigated Frank's behavior, and in the end recommended a reprimand, rather than a censure, on two minor charges. The full House voted 287–141 against censure, and 408–18 for reprimand. Frank was easily reelected to Congress.[76] He was one of the few who was able to survive a public scandal concerning his employment of a former lover.[77]

R. Jim Wright (1989)

In 1989, Jim Wright became the first Speaker of the House to resign from office because of scandal after a thirty-four-year-long career, two of which were as Speaker. Wright was described as an autocratic and abrasive leader who had no time and little consideration for minority Republicans in the House. He was even aggressive and assertive with members of his own party, which caused great tension. A year-long House Ethics Committee investigation of his finances found that Wright might have violated House rules in sixty-nine instances. The charges centered around $145,000 in gifts he and his wife received from a Fort Worth developer, and the profits from speeches that were sold in bulk in lieu of speaking fees, which were limited by House rules.[78] It was also alleged that Wright received income from a book deal that violated House rules on honorariums and outside income. He may have used bulk sales of his book in an attempt to disguise large corporate contributions to his personal income.[79] It was said he received gifts from a constituent who had a direct interest in legislation pending before Congress, and profited improperly from an oil-well deal.[80] Then more allegations emerged in early May 1989 that he used his influence to ensure that his son-in-law's brother (John Mack) received a lenient sentence for a horrific crime of violence. Over time, Mack had become Wright's top aide in Congress.[81] Wright resigned from office in 1989.[82]

S. Keating Five (1990)

In 1984, Charles Keating Jr. bought the Lincoln Savings and Loan based in California. Keating was the owner of a construction company based in Arizona and, like many other similar entrepreneurs, he shifted Lincoln's assets from home loans to more speculative investments and construction projects.[83] By 1987, Keating was in deep financial trouble with Lincoln Savings and Loan, and the federal government seemed ready to take it over. However, over the years, Keating had given tens of thousands of dollars to politicians from both parties and now wanted the help of the U.S. senators to whom he had donated money and whom he thought could help him avoid federal regulation.[84] He gave most donations to five men, nicknamed the "Keating Five" in the Senate, who went to bat for him in dealing with the regulators.[85] They were Alan Cranston (D-CA), Dennis DeConcini (D-AZ), John Glenn (D-OH), John McCain (R-AZ), and Donald Riegle (D-MI). The Keating Five senators received a total of $1.3 million in campaign contributions.[86] Keating approached these senators in an effort to get their help in preventing federal banking investigators from looking into the financial affairs of his institutions.[87]

In November 1990, the Senate Ethics Committee began hearings on the senators associated with Keating. The senators were formally rebuked for accepting large campaign contributions from the owner of a savings and loan, while also intervening on his behalf with regulators.[88] The committee found that DeConcini, Cranston, and Riegle had interfered with the investigation, but that McCain and Glenn had not been intimately involved.[89] They found that of the five senators involved, Cranston was the most culpable, citing four different occasions when he worked to assist Keating after Keating delivered campaign donations. Cranston received the harshest punishment of the five,[90] and he left the Senate on January 3, 1993.[91] Keating was imprisoned on fraud and racketeering charges and served a total of five years in prison.[92]

T. House Banking Scandal (1991)

The House Banking Scandal arose in mid-1991 after a report from the General Accounting Office detailed the practice in the House of Representatives Bank that allowed its members to write check overdrafts without penalty.[93] The GAO found many instances where the bank was cashing checks written by congressmen for more money than they had in their bank accounts.[94] The report indicated that members had written more than 8,000 bad checks in twelve months.[95] The bank allowed them to write these overdrafts if they promised to return the money at a future time.[96] The practice had been going on since the early 1950s, but it was not widely known to the public.

Although taxpayer funds were never in jeopardy, it angered people,[97] especially when the press reported that some of the congressmen who wrote overdrawn checks loaned money to their campaigns, whereas others made profitable investments during periods when they were overdrawn.[98]

Slowly, those Congressmen who had written bad checks began to admit their wrongdoing publicly. The House voted to have the Ethics Committee investigate and decided to release the names of the offenders.[99] It was discovered that one member, Mary Rose Oakar of Ohio, used the bank to funnel money from campaign donors.[100] Ohio voters were not pleased, and she lost her reelection bid. Another member of Congress, Thomas Downey of New York, lost his reelection bid because of the scandal as well.[101] In the end, the scandal did not just affect those two members but brought the entire Congress into disrepute.[102]

U. Chuck Robb (1991)

In 1991, Democratic Senator Chuck Robb, from Virginia, admitted to spending time alone in a hotel room with former Miss Virginia Tai Collins in the late 1980s when he was governor of Virginia, but denied having an affair with her. He claims the two shared a bottle of champagne and he received a nude massage from Collins, but that was it. Later, in an interview with *Playboy* magazine, Collins admitted that they were having an affair that began in 1983. There were also rumors that, as governor, Robb attended parties where cocaine was used. He denied using the drug, even denying knowing what it looked like.

V. Dan Rostenkowski (1994–96)

Dan Rostenkowski was a U.S. representative from Illinois from 1959–95. Early in his career he was the youngest member of the state legislature, then the youngest in the state senate. As a member of the House, he was a powerful chairman of the Committee on Ways and Means, but was investigated by a federal grand jury probing the House post office scandal.[103] The charges included allegations that he kept ghost employees on the payroll, traded in officially purchased stamps for cash at the House post office, and used congressional funds to buy chairs and other gifts for friends.

At first, Rostenkowski said the charges were "false and baseless," but the investigation found that about a third of the $358,331 in operating expenditures reported by his campaign and his PAC in 1990 and 1991 went to enhance his lifestyle or income, including travel, chauffeurs, car insurance, cable TV bills, dinner out, and golf caddy and rental payments for himself and his family. His taxpayer-financed House office account also helped cover his auto expenses. Interest groups regularly flew him to the nation's best golf courses for charity tournaments. He billed his campaign and PAC for more than $33,000 worth of dinners during those two years, an average of $300 per week.

On May 31, 1994, a District of Columbia grand jury returned indictments against Rostenkowski on seventeen counts, alleging that he and others had devised a scheme to defraud the United States of its money. This included a "payroll scheme," a "House Stationery Store scheme," and other counts, including that he stole nearly $700,000 from the government, used public funds for personal gain, lavished gifts on friends, and had ghost employees kick back paychecks to his office. The specific charges included:

- Mail fraud: including receiving thousands of dollars from the House post office in exchange for stamp vouchers that lawmakers submit for postage spent on official mailings;
- Obstruction of justice: by asking a congressional employee not to tell a grand jury about engraving fifty glass crystal sculptures of the U.S. Capitol he gave to friends as gifts;
- Embezzling public funds: including $500,000 for payroll abuses—among them paying a future son-in-law for doing no work and a photographer who took pictures at family parties and weddings;
- Fraudulent car-lease agreements: by submitting car-lease agreements to the House to cover the purchase of seven cars from a suburban Chicago dealership; and
- Concealing a material fact: withholding information from prosecutors and the Federal Election Commission.

In November 1994, Rostenkowski lost his reelection effort. On April 9, 1996, he pled guilty to reduced charges of two counts of mail fraud in exchange for dropping a complaint that he ran multiple petty scams out of his office. He was sentenced to seventeen months in prison and fined $100,000.[104] He served 451 days in prison.[105]

While in prison, he shared a room with two other men, rose early each day and reported to his job, recording the pressure readings on boiler room gauges every two hours. He accepted no visitors other than his lawyer and his biographer, but did keep tabs on national government. He took four-mile walks in the facility's exercise yard and lost sixty pounds.

After his prison stay, Rostenkowski built a legislative consulting firm he called Danross Associates and has appeared on Chris Matthews's *Hardball* on MSNBC for some political analysis. He has also been on Fox News to discuss events.

W. Bob Packwood (1992–95)

Bob Packwood was a Republican senator from Oregon who represented the state for about twenty-five years. He became chairman of the Finance Committee, one of the most powerful positions in the Senate.[106] He was a strong supporter of women's causes such as abortion rights, family leave, and equal opportunity in the workplace.[107] He was considered a progressive leader within the Republican Party.[108]

At the same time, many women with whom he worked said he grabbed, kissed, or propositioned them without warning and without encouragement on their part. [109] In late October 1992, two reporters from the *Washington Post* presented Packwood with allegations of unwelcome sexual advances by ten women, most of whom had worked with him.[110] The *Post* reported that the women had charged him with sexual harassment going back to 1989. Packwood replied that he was sorry for causing any discomfort or embarrassment.[111] A few days later, his situation escalated when he checked into an alcoholism diagnostic and treatment program.[112] All along, he denied the allegations and provided statements to discredit the women, basically stalling publicizing the allegations until after his reelection in November.[113] In January 1994, Packwood finally acknowledged that he made sexual advances toward a campaign worker, but he claimed it was part of a "warm relationship."

The Senate Ethics Committee began an investigation into the allegations. The committee was comprised of three Republicans and three Democrats. On October 6, 1993, while giving a deposition to the Ethics Committee, he referred to his personal diaries. Investigators demanded to see what was in the diaries as evidence of these and other possible offenses. Packwood made a plea for his privacy and resisted the Senate's demands to turn over the more than 8,000-page document. There was a lengthy fight over access to them. After the committee voted unanimously to seek the diaries, the full Senate voted ninety-four to six to allow the Ethics Committee to enforce a subpoena requiring Packwood to submit the diaries.[114] Then, on December 16, 1993, U.S. District Judge Thomas Penfield Jackson ordered Packwood to give all of his diaries and other material to the Ethics Committee so that it could pursue its investigation. They decided the diaries were "unquestionably relevant" to the Senate Ethics Committee and must be provided to them. Packwood appealed the decision, but the Supreme Court upheld the federal court decision, and he had to provide his diaries to the Ethics Committee. Before the diaries were turned over, a court-appointed special master would exclude entries that were purely personal or contained private medical information or confidential communications between Packwood and his lawyers. The special master was Kenneth Starr.

Lawyers for the Senate Committee accused Packwood of altering his diaries while he was being investigated, which is obstruction of justice. They asked a federal court to seize the material immediately. The contents of the diaries were quite embarrassing to Packwood, as his private thoughts and actions became public.[115] He had written about his affairs and fantasies with other women in quite some detail.[116]

Packwood may have broken lobbying, conflict-of-interest, or other laws in addition to the initial allegations of sexual misconduct. He may have tried to limit alimony payments by getting his wife a high-salary job with lobbyists, former aides or other political acquaintances, including a lobbyist for the Japanese government and corporate interests. He was also facing perjury charges if his diary contradicted the information he provided in his testimony.

In May 1995, the Senate committee concluded that there was "substantial credible evidence" that Packwood engaged in sexual misconduct, tampered with evidence, and solicited favors from people with businesses. The exact charges against him are noted in Table 7.4. In a five-page resolution, the equivalent of a bill of indictment, the committee also said there was "substantial evidence" of other misconduct, including the possible solicitation of lobbyists with business before his committees to provide employment for his wife, and possible alteration of audio tapes and other diary material that might have revealed details of some of his misbehavior.

Table 7.4: Charges against Packwood

Sexual Misconduct

1990: In his Washington Senate office, Packwood kissed a staff member on the lips.

1985: In Bend, Ore., he "fondled a campaign worker as they danced." Later, in Eugene, Ore., he grabbed the same worker's face and "with his hands, pulled her toward him and kissed her on the mouth, forcing his tongue into her mouth."

1981 or 1982: In his Washington Senate office, he kissed a lobbyist on the mouth.

1981: In a room in the Capitol basement, he grabbed a former staff assistant and kissed her, forcing his tongue into her mouth. While the same woman was on Packwood's staff in 1975, he grabbed her, pinned her against a wall or desk, fondled her, and kissed her, forcing his tongue into her mouth.

1980 or 1981: In a Portland, Ore., hotel, Packwood kissed a desk clerk on two separate occasions.

1979: In Washington, he kissed a Senate staff member on the lips.

1977: In a Capitol elevator, he pushed the operator up against the wall, kissed her on the lips, and later "came to this person's home, kissed her and asked her to make love with him."

1977: In an Oregon motel room, Packwood "grabbed a prospective employee by her shoulders, pulled her to him and kissed her."

1975: In his Washington Senate office, he kissed a staff assistant on the mouth.

Early 1970s: In his Portland Senate office, Packwood "chased a staff assistant around a desk."

1970: In a Portland restaurant, Packwood "ran his hand up the leg of a dining room hostess and touched her crotch area."

1970: In his Washington Senate office, Packwood kissed a staff member on the mouth.

1969: In his Washington Senate office, he "made suggestive comments to a prospective employee."

1969: At his home, Packwood "grabbed an employee of another senator who was babysitting for him, rubbed her shoulders and back, and kissed her on the mouth, forcing his tongue into her mouth." He also reached under her skirt and grabbed at her undergarments.

Evidence Tampering
The committee also found "substantial credible evidence" that Packwood altered his diary entries after "he knew or should have known" that the ethics panel would want to see them. The committee also suggested Packwood may have violated federal law in this case.

Abuse of Office
The committee found "substantial credible evidence" that Packwood may have abused his Senate office by linking personal financial gain to his official position in that he solicited offers of financial assistance from people who had a particular interest in legislation or issues that he could influence.

On September 7, 1995, the Senate Ethics Committee voted unanimously to recommend that Senator Packwood be expelled for sexual and official misconduct. It was an extraordinary punishment, simply because it is used so infrequently. The Republicans lost a very powerful member. On September 8, 1995, Packwood announced his resignation as he fought back tears.

X. Ken Calvert (1993)

In 1993, Ken Calvert, a Republican House member from California, was found partially dressed in his car with a prostitute who was performing oral sex.[117] He was arrested for soliciting a prostitute. Calvert was named one of the twenty most corrupt members of Congress by the Citizens for Responsibility and Ethics in Washington.

Y. Jay Kim (1992–96)

Kim was a Republican from Southern California who won a seat in the House of Representatives in 1992. He was the first Korean American elected to serve in Congress. He and his wife, June, pled guilty to federal charges that they accepted illegal campaign contributions of $250,000. He was sentenced to two months of house arrest. Although he kept his seat, he lost the primary election in 1998.

Z. Carol Moseley Braun (1993)

In 1992, Carol Moseley Braun, from Chicago, became the first African American woman ever elected to the Senate. After attending law school, she became a federal prosecutor. In 1978 she was elected to the Illinois legislature, then the Cook County Recorder of Deeds.[118] In 1993, she allegedly violated campaign contribution laws by using campaign funds for personal use. The Federal Elections Commission investigated why she had over $249,000 in unaccounted campaign funds. They found small violations but took no action against her. After columnist George Will wrote an article reviewing the violations, she retorted, "I think because he couldn't say nigger, he said corrupt." She then compared Will to a Ku Klux Klansman, later apologizing.[119] Her fiancé was accused of sexually harassing several female campaign workers.[120] Then in 1997, her fiancé, Ksogie Matthews, a registered foreign agent and lobbyist for the government of Nigeria, disappeared after failing to pay for over $250,000 in travel expenses. To date, he has not been found.[121]

AA. Newt Gingrich (1994–97)

Newt Gingrich was the first Republican Speaker of the House in forty years. As such, he was a very powerful person in Congress. He held master's and Ph.D. degrees in history from Tulane University. In Congress, he was behind the ethics charges that brought down Democratic speaker Jim Wright. Gingrich was accused of improperly using his congressional payroll for political purposes, which involved his relations with GOPAC, his improper use of staff, his video-taped university course, his links with cable television stations, tax violations, and a questionable book deal with publisher Harper Collins.[122] Gingrich raised money for a supposedly nonpolitical educational foundation that he actually used in violation of the federal tax code to promote Republican causes and his own political agenda.[123]

Gingrich's scandals began early on. His first marriage was to his high school math teacher. A former campaign worker told *Vanity Fair* in 1995 that she had a torrid affair with Gingrich while he was married to his first wife. His first marriage is said to have ended bitterly when he visited his wife's hospital room after her surgery for uterine cancer to discuss the terms of their divorce. He then married Marianne Ginther, whom he has since divorced.

There were some initial charges brought against Gingrich surrounding two early scandals, both of which were dismissed by the Ethics Committee. First, while he was Minority Leader in 1990, he intervened with the EPA administrator William Reilly for a donor who had complained that asbestos regulation was hurting his business. Second, it was alleged that Gingrich intervened with the Commerce Department in 1989 on behalf of a Houston-based cement company that donated to GOPAC and asked for government help in stopping the influx of cheap Mexican cement into the American market.

Another scandal surrounding Gingrich revolved around a deal he had with Harper Collins to write two books.[124] One book title was *To Renew America*, which became a bestseller on the *New York Times* list for nonfiction. The original deal said that Gingrich would receive $4.5 million advance, but after this caused a commotion, he turned down the advance. It was alleged that he was improperly helping Rupert Murdoch, who owns Harper Collins and does frequent business with Congress. It was argued that Murdoch's company could benefit from legislation then pending before Congress and subject to Gingrich's influence.[125]

At that time, members were allowed to earn an amount equal to 15 percent of their salaries outside of their House salaries, but book royalties did not count. As a result, the committee said it would recommend a new rule to put book incomes within the overall ceiling on members' outside income.

Yet another scandal revolved around something called GOPAC, which was a political action committee dedicated to achieving Republican control of the U.S. House of Representatives.[126] Their method for accomplishing their goal was to develop and disseminate a political message that would appeal to voters. This would, in turn, increase their chances of winning more seats in all levels of office (local, state, national) and influencing policy. Gingrich was general chairman of GOPAC from September 1986 to May 1995. As such, he wanted to implement conservative values and create a better America.

In 1990, GOPAC developed and carried out a project called American Opportunities Workshop (AOW). They produced and broadcast a television program centered on a citizen's movement to reform government. AOW was described as nonpartisan, but mailings sent to supporters described AOW as having partisan, political goals. AOW consumed a large portion of GOPAC's financial resources that year.

There was also the Abraham Lincoln Opportunity Foundation (ALOF). This agency had tax-exempt status and operated out of GOPAC offices. People listed as working for ALOF were GOPAC employees or consultants. ALOF raised and expended tax-deductible charitable contributions to carry out different projects. One was called American Citizen's Television.

In 1992 and 1993, GOPAC's limited financial resources were not sufficient to enable it to carry out all of the political programs at its usual level. So Gingrich decided to teach a course called "Renewing American Civilization" at Kennesaw State College in Georgia in the fall of 1993, and at Reinhardt College in Georgia in December 1994 and 1995. It lasted ten weeks, of which he taught five, and another professor taught five. Since Gingrich holds a Ph.D. in European history, he was qualified to do it. The lectures were at the colleges, but a satellite hookup beamed them to Gingrich supporters nationwide. The lectures were also distributed via videotape and audiotape. The main message of the course was renewing American civilization by replacing the welfare state with an opportunity society. Although Gingrich described the courses as educational, not political, and completely nonpartisan, they were found to be otherwise. In a number of instances, he applied the ideas of the course to partisan, political purposes.

GOPAC had a number of roles in regard to the course. Employees or consultants for GOPAC were involved in developing the course. The executive director and two assistants even resigned to manage the operations of the course, but they maintained a consulting contract so that GOPAC paid one-half of their salaries. Additionally, GOPAC charter members took part in a planning session for the course, employees took part in fundraising for the course, and GOPAC was involved in the promotion of the course. GOPAC even prepared and sent a letter to college Republicans asking them to enroll in the course. The letters described a political role for the course.

The universities where this was taught were tax-exempt organizations. Legally, an organization that is exempt from taxation is also prohibited from any participation in a political campaign or from providing any support to a political action committee. Gingrich did not seek specific legal advice concerning the application of the IRS Code in regard to the facts described about AOW, ALOF, and GOPAC (etc.). He also did not take actions to ensure that such legal advice was obtained by others from an appropriate source. A tax counsel said if he had been consulted, he would have advised that the class not be conducted.

A complaint was filed against Gingrich on September 7, 1994, by Ben Jones, a former Democratic representative who was defeated by Gingrich. Jones brought the charges as a private citizen. He argued that the course was part of a political operation and should not have qualified as a tax-exempt activity. The complaint alleged that Gingrich used his congressional staff to work on the course, and that he misused organizations that were exempt from taxation. Specifically, he misused the college foundations and a Gingrich-affiliated think-tank (the Progress and Freedom Foundation) to raise tax-deductible contributions for a partisan-oriented activity. Further, Jones argued that he violated tax laws by raising tax-exempt money for Kennesaw State College and used it to teach a politics course. Tax-deductible donations were solicited to finance the course and satellite hookups that beamed the lectures across the country.

Jones also alleged that Gingrich made personal use of GOPAC resources, including $250,000 a year in support and having the committee pay the annual fee for his American Express card, that he rewarded some GOPAC donors by championing their causes with federal agencies, and that he violated House rules by letting a Wisconsin businessman with an interest in telecommunications legislation work as a volunteer in his office.

The House Ethics Committee agreed to investigate the charges. The committee was made up of five Democrats and five Republicans. The committee voted unanimously to hire a special counsel to look into charges against Gingrich. The special counsel would be a lawyer who would help examine whether Gingrich did anything wrong. They hired James Cole in December 1995, and he was asked to submit a report first to a four-member investigative subcommittee, which would decide if formal charges should be filed or if the case should be dismissed. In December 1996, Cole gave his report to the Ethics Committee.[127]

The subcommittee consulted with a tax law expert, who said that Gingrich's activities violated ALOF's tax-exempt status because the activities were intended to confer more than insubstantial benefits on GOPAC and Republican entities and candidates. Further the activities violated tax-exempt status because they provided support to GOPAC. Internal revenue tax codes prohibit tax-exempt organizations, such as college foundations and the Progress and Freedom Foundation, from engaging in partisan political activities. The subcommittee found that the cost of transmitting the course via satellite was mostly absorbed by donors to the colleges or the Progress and Freedom Foundation.

The subcommittee also found that GOPAC improperly aided Gingrich's 1990 House campaign in Georgia. GOPAC was registered only to be involved in state and local races, not federal ones. It was charged that Gingrich encouraged GOPAC contributors to donate $124,503 to his personal campaign committee in 1990, where he won reelection by fewer than 1,000 votes.

Moreover, the subcommittee found that Gingrich improperly used the House floor to advertise how to buy tapes of his college course, that he improperly used the House floor to promote a political meeting sponsored by GOPAC, that he violated House rules when he had a political aide conduct official business, and that he gave conflicting information to the committee. Additionally, the Subcommittee members decided that Gingrich's GOPAC activities violated a House rule requiring a member to "conduct himself at all times in a manner which shall reflect credibility" of the House. The members said Gingrich failed to seek and follow the legal advice. When the investigation was over, the committee reported only minor improprieties.

Gingrich eventually admitted to the charges made against him. He admitted that he had misled the House Ethics Committee over his handling of a tax-exempt college course, and also admitted giving misleading information to the committee. He accepted responsibility, saying he deeply regretted his actions. The admission spared him from a trial-like proceeding. Gingrich was formally reprimanded by the House and fined $300,000 for violating House rules.[128] He became the first sitting Speaker to be formally reprimanded by the House.

The scandal had enormous implications for Gingrich. He was running for reelection for Speaker. Many Republicans did not want to vote for him unless his problems were resolved or clarified. Other Republicans wanted to sever any association with him, but they also wanted to support him. Nonetheless, Gingrich was narrowly elected on January 7, 1997.

After the scandal died down, the House passed new rules that prohibited citizens from bringing ethics charges. Under the old rule, any person could bring charges if three members of Congress refused to do so. This is what happened in Gingrich's case. Under new legislation in the House, citizen complaints are banned. Instead, a citizen must find a member to file a complaint for them. This makes it easier for lawmakers to dismiss complaints.

BB. Helen Chenoweth (1995)

Helen Chenoweth, from Idaho, was a lobbyist for timber and mining companies, and then worked on statewide political campaigns before serving in Congress. Her first race for the House of Representatives was in 1992 but she lost. She ran again and won in 1994. It was alleged that her quick rise to power was made possible by $70,000 of illegal campaign money from Hong Kong.[129]

In 1995, Chenoweth admitted that she had not reported an unsecured $40,000 loan.[130] In September 1988, she conceded that she had a six-year affair with a married man who was once her business partner.[131]

CC. Dan Burton (1997, 1998)

For many years, Dan Burton (R-IN) served in the Indiana legislature before being elected to serve in Washington. While in the House, he was chairman of the Government Reform and Oversight Committee and was head of the House committee that investigated President Bill Clinton for taking improper campaign contributions in the 1996 campaign.[132]

In April 1997, Burton was caught accepting illegal campaign contributions from Sikh temples, which are barred from financing elected officials' campaigns. Burton also supported legislation in the House favorable to the Sikh donors. When he was caught, he returned the contributions, saying that he really did not need the money.[133]

About the time the Starr Report came out, *Vanity Fair* uncovered that Burton had an illegitimate son and threatened to print the story in the next issue. On Monday, September 1, 1998, expecting the disclosure, Burton went public and explained that he and his wife had separated on many occasions. Three days later, the *Indianapolis Star* reported that he had had an extramarital affair in the early 1980s and had fathered a child.[134] The affair took place when Burton served in the Indiana Senate and the woman worked for a state agency. Burton explained that his wife was fully aware of the affair, and that he paid child support, but he never fully acknowledged the child as his son.[135] The boy's birth certificate does not list a father.[136]

DD. Henry Hyde (1998)

Henry Hyde was the Republican representative from Illinois and House Judiciary Committee chairman. As such, he was one of the most senior and powerful Republicans in Congress. He was regarded as a man of integrity and intellectual honesty and promoted himself as a paragon of family values and integrity.[137] He acted as the chief prosecutor of Clinton during the impeachment proceedings.

In 1965, when he was forty-one and a lawyer running for office for the first time, he had been married eighteen years and had four sons. But at that time he began an extended affair with a young woman, twenty-nine-year-old Cherie Snodgrass, a married mother of three children.[138] Hyde set his mistress up in a fashionable, well-furnished apartment, unknown to his wife and Mrs. Snodgrass's husband. They continued their affair for five years while he served as an elected official in the Illinois State House of Representatives.[139]

In 1969, the woman's husband, Fred Snodgrass, found out, and told Hyde's wife. The Snodgrass marriage broke up and they divorced, but Hyde walked away from the affair with his own marriage intact and he went on to higher office in Congress. He never took responsibility for the Snodgrass divorce.[140]

The affair was made public on the Internet on September 17, 1998. At first, Hyde dismissed it, saying "the statute of limitations has long since passed away on my youthful indiscretions. Suffice it to say, Cherie Snodgrass and I were good friends."[141]

Conclusion

Congressional scandals have played a part in politics for many years. Scandals have happened to people in all political parties, and for a wide range of behaviors, including sex scandals, financial scandals, and illicit drug use. Almost everyone involved in a scandal had their reputation damaged to some extent. Very few are able to get out unscathed. Many times, ethics investigations are more political than factual, but can have just as much impact.

Review Questions

1. Describe some congressional scandals.
2. Describe Abscam. Why was it significant?
3. What are the impacts of congressional scandals?

Special Terms

Abscam

Discussion Questions

1. Are congressional or presidential scandals worse?
2. Did the FBI go too far in the Abscam investigation?
3. Why do some elected officials emerge from scandals relatively unscathed whereas others seem to lose all?

Chapter 8

Judicial Scandals

Introduction

After the Watergate scandal, more attention was paid to the standards of judicial conduct and the policing thereof. In fact, the Judicial Conduct and Disability Act was passed in 1974 for this reason. Under the act, written complaints from any source about possible judicial misconduct or mental or physical disability of any federal judge would be referred to the chief judge of the circuit. The chief judge would decide to dismiss or pursue each complaint on an individual basis. The judge's decision could be appealed by either the party that lodged the complaint or the judge about whom the complaint was made. The chief judge would then appoint an investigating committee of judges within the circuit to make a recommendation to the judicial council about the most appropriate action short of removal from office. These decisions could be appealed to the Judicial Conference for another investigation and possible disciplinary measures. If necessary, the confidentiality surrounding the entire proceeding to this point could be waived and the case referred to the House for possible impeachment action.[1]

Throughout our history, judges have been the most frequent targets of impeachment.[2] Over time, three judges have been impeached by the House, tried by the Senate, convicted, and removed from the bench. Three others, including one Supreme Court justice, resigned while their impeachment was under consideration but had yet to be formally initiated. Only two of the eight judges, both Supreme Court justices, escaped relatively unscathed.[3]

Below is a brief discussion of some judicial impeachments that have occurred in the United States and their ramifications.

Peter Oliver (1774)

The chief justice in Massachusetts, Peter Oliver, was appointed in 1774 by Governor Thomas Hutchinson. Oliver and Hutchinson were related by marriage. There was some thought that the governor appointed Oliver in an attempt to keep the judiciary under "royal control." Hutchinson had proposed that judicial salaries should be paid out of royal accounts rather than through legislative appropriations. The legislature was opposed to this idea, fearing that those judges who were paid by the royal group would then make decisions that favored the British rather than being sensitive to local interests. The legislature therefore approved its own judicial salaries and at the same time prohibited judges from accepting royal salaries. Justice Oliver refused to decline the royal salary, and officials thus refused to place him on the bench. Since the legislature thought the judicial system might be in jeopardy, it decided it was best to impeach the chief justice and request a trial by the governor and council. The Massachusetts General Assembly charged that Oliver had allowed himself to be bought by a salary that was unconstitutionally levied and in so doing committed "high crimes and misdemeanors." Governor Hutchinson was caught between orders coming from the British government and the legislature's probable conviction of Oliver. He responded by ending the session of the General Court. Despite having been dismissed by the governor, the legislature and council had won an important victory. The final outcome reinforced the opinion that the king's authority could not be part of our representative government.[4]

John Pickering (1803)

Pickering was a district judge for New Hampshire from 1795–1804. He had served as a state assemblyman, attorney general, and chief justice of New Hampshire before receiving his appointment to the federal bench.[5] He had a long history of mental difficulty, including a fear of traveling over water that had kept him from attending the Continental Congress as a delegate. Over time, he became increasingly senile and reportedly was intoxicated while holding court. Despite his health concerns, Pickering refused to retire from the bench. When the House of Representatives was informed of his behavior, they took little time to decide to impeach him. They voted on March 2, 1803, to impeach by a vote of 48–8. Judge Pickering was unable to attend his trial and present a defense because of his mental state.[6] The Senate recognized that although Pickering did not commit a high crime or misdemeanor, he was mentally incompetent. Senators recognized that the Constitution made no provision for removing a judge because of a mental disability,[7] so the Senate convicted Pickering and removed him from office in March 1804 on the basis that he could no longer function effectively as a federal judge. They recognized that there was no other alternative for dealing with a federal judge who had become completely dysfunctional.[8] Pickering was the first federal official removed from office.[9] Once the Senate impeached him successfully, they recognized that the impeachment power could easily be used against others on the bench, even as a political attack.[10]

Samuel Chase (1804)

Samuel Chase was a signer of the Declaration of Independence as a delegate from Maryland to the Continental Congress, and then became a judge on Maryland's highest court in 1791. He was named to the Supreme Court in 1796 by George Washington, and served as a justice until he died in 1811.

As a justice, Chase was accused of a variety of offenses, all driven by the fact that he was a staunch Federalist. On the bench he had become a determined supporter of the Alien and Sedition Acts of 1798. He then angered more Republicans by openly campaigning for John Adams in 1800. In cases before the court, he repeatedly made decisions that Republicans found offensive.[11] Chase's judicial behavior outraged them so much, it made him the target of a campaign to remove him from office. He faced eight articles of impeachment in the House in 1804. The articles focused on procedural errors he made during different cases as a trial judge in a lower circuit court. He was impeached by the House and remains the only U.S. Supreme Court justice to have been impeached.

The Republicans in the Senate continued their attack on Justice Chase for judicial misbehavior. Chase defended himself by saying that although he might have made mistakes, he was certainly not guilty of any of the impeachable offenses of "treason, bribery, or other high crimes or misdemeanors."[12] He was able to persuade enough members of the Republican majority that his conduct, although highly partisan, was not criminal and was therefore not impeachable. As a result, though a Senate majority voted to convict him, the vote was not even close to the necessary two-thirds margin for removal. In other words, enough Republicans in the Senate balked at making partisanship a standard for impeachment rather than the evidence. Chase returned to his position on the Court. The failure to remove him brought an end to the use of impeachment as a partisan tool, for a short time.[13]

James H. Peck (1830)

District Judge James Peck was nominated for office by President James Monroe to a new seat established by Congress, the U.S. District Court of Missouri.

He was nominated on March 29, 1822, and confirmed by the Senate on April 5, 1822.[14] This made him the first federal district judge in Missouri. Luke Lawless, a fellow lawyer, was upset with Peck over a decision concerning Spanish land claims as part of the Missouri Compromise. Lawless wrote an article in the local newspaper that criticized Peck. Peck had Lawless brought into court for contempt and sentenced him to twenty-four hours in jail and barred him from practicing law for eighteen months.[15] Lawless, being politically well connected, convinced a member of the House Judiciary Committee that his contempt charge was a "high misdemeanor" and therefore justified impeachment. In December 1829, the House Judiciary Committee began investigating Peck and in 1830 recommended impeachment. The case against him was the only federal impeachment case ever brought based on a single complaint by a single individual. Since there was not any evidence of impeachable conduct or improper ruling, the Senate votes divided evenly and Peck was not removed from office. The vote, however, reaffirmed high standards for judicial impeachment.[16] The Senate chose not impeach Peck simply because another lawyer disagreed with him. That was not enough evidence to warrant removal from office.

Levi Hubbell (1853)

Justice Hubbell ran in the first judicial election after Wisconsin became a state in 1848, and won office to be a circuit judge for the Second Judicial Circuit. He served as an associate justice from 1848–1851 when he became chief justice of the Wisconsin Supreme Court. In 1853, he returned to his position as a circuit judge. That year, his opponents began an impeachment for accepting bribes, using court funds for his personal use, and overseeing cases in which he had a financial interest. Hubbell was acquitted of his charges, and resigned because the salary was too low.[17]

In 1863, Hubbell served one year as a state assemblyman, and then was again appointed to serve as judge, this time for the Eastern District of Wisconsin. Once again, he faced accusations of misconduct and was forced to resign.[18]

West H. Humphreys (1862)

District Judge West H. Humphreys, a federal district judge in Tennessee beginning in1853, was removed from office during the Civil War when he failed to resign after joining the Confederacy. During the Civil War, when many

Southern states seceded from the Union, many members of government also resigned their jobs if they were loyal to the South. Judge Humphreys did not resign, even after accepting appointment as the Confederate district judge for Tennessee.[19] When he was appointed to the Confederate bench, he stopped holding court for the United States.[20]

The House impeached Humphreys for malfeasance for not holding court, gross misconduct that violated the "good behavior" clause, and high treason for having advocated and supported secession. In June 1862, the Senate held a three-hour trial to debate the charges. Humphreys did not appear at the trial and gave no defense. The Senate quickly found him guilty on all seven articles of impeachment. The senators took the additional step of unanimously disqualifying Humphreys from holding any federal office in the future.[21]

Mark H. Delahay (1873)

District Judge Mark H. Delahay was a federal district judge for Kansas who was appointed by President Abraham Lincoln in 1863. He was often intoxicated when he was serving on the bench and when he was off the bench as well.[22] Delahay was impeached by the House because his "personal habits unfitted him for the judicial office." Because he resigned after the impeachment, no trial was held in the Senate.[23]

Stephen J. Field (1889)

Justice Field served on the Supreme Court from 1863–1897, one of the longest-serving justices. In 1889, one of Field's former colleagues, David S. Terry, assaulted him in a California train depot. Terry was shot and killed by Field's bodyguard, David Neagle, a deputy U.S. marshal. Officials attempted to prosecute Neagle for the death of Terry. The case resulted in *In Re Neagle*, decided by the Supreme Court without Justice Field, in which the other justices held that a federal officer is immune from prosecution if the act committed was necessary and reasonable and committed in the performance of his official duties.[24]

Charles Swayne (1905)

Swayne was a federal district judge for northern Florida from 1890–1907. He was a Republican, appointed by Benjamin Harrison. Swayne was impeached in 1905 at the request of the Florida legislature and by a House vote of 198 to 61. He was charged with expense-account padding (filing false travel vouchers), improper use of a private railcar owned by a bankrupt railroad under his jurisdiction, failure to live in his judicial district as required by Congress, and improper citation of three individuals for contempt of court. The judge was acquitted by the Senate, whose members did not feel that his offenses amounted to high crimes and misdemeanors. The vote did not come anywhere close to the two-thirds vote required for any of the impeachment charges.[25]

Robert W. Archbald (1912)

Robert W. Archbald was named as the presiding judge of the Forty-fifth Judicial District of Pennsylvania in 1888, where he served until 1901. He was appointed to be a U.S. district judge of the Forty-fifth Judicial District of Pennsylvania by President William McKinley in 1901. President William Taft appointed Archbald to be a judgeship in the Third Circuit Court of Appeals in 1910 and on February 1, 1911, to the U.S. Commerce Court, where he heard appeals from Interstate Commerce Commission rulings.[26] The Commerce Court was widely perceived as favoring the railroads that were its principal litigants. As such, the Commerce Court quickly became very unpopular.[27] In fact, the court was abolished by Congress within two months of Archbald's removal.[28]

Archbald was accused of using his position as a federal judge to enter into profitable business arrangements with potential litigants who appeared before his court.[29] This was a clear abuse of his office, but not an offense that would result in criminal prosecution if committed by a businessman. For example, Archbald wrote letters on Commerce Court stationery encouraging property owners to sell or lease property on favorable terms to third parties who, in turn, rewarded him. In another instance, he secretly corresponded with an appellant's attorney in a railroad case before his court, and asked the lawyer his opinion on the case. He then supported the successful appeal. This all violated judicial ethics. In another instance, Archbald "induced" the Erie Railroad Company to sell him properties owned by a subsidiary corporation at a cheap price, despite the fact that the railroad had cases pending before his court.[30] It was further alleged that he influenced a litigant to lease him land with large coal deposits on it. Evidence also showed that Archbald purchased stock in a gold mining concern from a litigant who had business before his court, after which he ruled in the litigant's favor.

The House voted on thirteen articles of impeachment.[31] Archbald was convicted and removed from the U.S. Commerce Court. After investigation by the Justice Department and the House, Archbald was impeached in July 1912 by a bipartisan vote of 223 to 1. He was convicted of four of six articles involving his appellate court behavior. The senators failed to convict Archbald on six articles relating to his activities while on the district court. Some senators did not feel the evidence supported the charges, whereas others did not believe that the judge could be impeached for a position he no longer held. The Senate then voted to disqualify Archbald from holding future U.S. office. [32]

George Washington English (1925)

George English was a federal district judge for the U.S. District Court for the Eastern District of Illinois. He was accused of disbarring attorneys who had appeared before him without any notice or hearing and of using his judicial power to summon state and local officials to him so he could harass and threaten them by using a loud voice and profane language.[33] On one occasion, he had federal marshals round up all sheriffs and state's attorneys in the district to appear in his court for what turned out to be an imaginary case. Once there, the judge then subjected them to a loud, angry, and profane rant in which he threatened to remove all of them from office. English was also charged with threatening attorneys and reporters who covered his courtroom and with colluding with bankruptcy referees to place funds in banks in which he had an interest.[34] Other critics accused him of showing favoritism in connection with bankruptcy cases after he appointed a friend as a referee for cases that appeared before his court. English was supposed to have received an illegal gratuity of $1,435. Moreover, he was supposed to have deposited and transferred bankruptcy funds to himself. Finally, he reportedly treated members of the bar in a coarse, indecent, and arbitrary manner.[35] Because of these charges, English was impeached by the House of Representatives on April 1, 1925. However, he resigned less than a week before a Senate trial could take place, so the Senate dismissed the charges.[36]

Harold Louderback (1933)

Judge Louderback was appointed to serve as a district judge for the Northern District of California by President Calvin Coolidge and confirmed by the Senate on April 17, 1928.[37] He served from 1928–1941, during which time he was accused of favoritism in the appointment of bankruptcy officers who appeared in his court.[38]

The House held an investigation into the allegations. The Judiciary Committee found that Louderback used bad judgment, but his behavior did not rise to the level of an impeachable offense and as such, they recommended censure rather than impeachment.[39] Despite that recommendation, a minority was able to push through five articles of impeachment against Louderback that charged the judge with using his influence to appoint bankruptcy receivers.[40] Louderback was impeached on February 24, 1933. A few weeks later, on March 3, 1933, the House sent all five articles of impeachment to the Senate, where Louderback was found not guilty.[41] He returned to serving on the bench.[42]

Halsted L. Ritter (1936)

Ritter was a successful Denver attorney who had moved to Florida in 1925 for his wife's health and who, four years later, was appointed by President Coolidge to be a federal judge for the state's southern district and served from 1929–36. There were charges that he failed to dismiss a foreclosure suit so that he could appoint a colleague of his former law partner as a receiver. In doing so, Ritter received a kickback from his former law partner. In addition, he practiced law in violation of the prohibition on judges practicing law. He also failed to report his fees from practicing law on his income tax returns.[43]

Ritter was convicted and removed from office in 1936 for taking a kickback in a resort hotel bankruptcy case, evading income taxes, and continuing to practice law after going on the bench. All of the alleged misconduct dated from the first year of his judgeship. A three-year investigation by the House Judiciary Subcommittee produced a recommendation for impeachment. The Judiciary Committee voted 10–8 to impeach him and the entire House voted 181–146 for impeachment.[44] The Senate agreed, and he was convicted in the Senate for accepting fees regarding cases he was adjudicating[45] by a vote of 56–28. They described that Ritter brought his court into "scandal and disrepute, to the prejudice of said court and public confidence in the administration of justice." With that vote, Ritter was removed from the federal bench.[46] In protest, he brought a suit to the Court of Claims to recover his unpaid salary. This was the first judicial challenge ever to an impeachment verdict.[47]

Martin T. Manton (1939)

President Woodrow Wilson named Martin Manton to the U.S. District Court for the Southern District of New York, and two years later, elevated him to the

U.S. Court of Appeals for the Second Circuit. It was alleged that Manton was involved in massive and unethical corruption, and that he received more than $400,000 from individuals interested in matters handled by his court. In April 1939, Manton was indicted on charges of bribery and conspiracy to commit bribery but convicted only of conspiracy to obstruct justice. He was sent to prison for two years. He served one year and seven months of his sentence. He was one of the few sitting federal judges in American history to be convicted of a crime and imprisoned.[48] He resigned on January 20, 1939 upon publication of the charges against him.

Abe Fortas (1968)

Abe Fortas was appointed to the U.S. Supreme Court in 1965 by President Lyndon Johnson and was, as expected, a liberal justice. In 1968 when Chief Justice Earl Warren had plans to retire, Johnson wanted Fortas to fill that position. Congress did not like the fact that Fortas seemed to have too many meetings with the president. Fortas acknowledged that he had conferred with Johnson about Vietnam and urban rioting, but he insisted they never discussed any specific issues that might come before the court.[49] Nonetheless, members of Congress feared a Supreme Court chief justice who catered to a president.

At one point, Fortas told President Johnson about an illegal wiretap of a Washington lobbyist that had been authorized by Robert Kennedy. Fortas learned the information through a private discussion among the justices. The sharing of such information is a violation of judicial ethics. At the same time, Fortas was teaching a class at American University Law School. He was paid $15,000 for a nine-week seminar that was supported by his former clients[50] and others who might have an interest in business coming before the court.[51]

The Judiciary Committee voted eleven to six to recommend Fortas's confirmation to the Senate,[52] but in the long run, his nomination for chief justice failed. It turned out that Justice Warren had not really resigned, and President Johnson had not properly accepted a resignation from him.[53] After the controversy over the Fortas nomination, Justice Warren asked Johnson to withdraw Fortas's name from nomination, and he did.[54]

After the nomination failed, Fortas remained a target for attack. It became even worse after Richard Nixon took office. Within four months, the justice's questionable but not illegal conduct became the basis of a highly publicized scandal. The new attacks on Fortas centered on his relationship with Louis Wolfson, a financier and philanthropist. Wolfson was a client of Fortas's law firm in the mid-1960s. He had made millions in construction and shipbuilding and had diverse investments. After his appointment to the Supreme Court, Fortas agreed to serve as a consultant to the Wolfson Family Foundation, which had been established to work on issues of civil rights, juvenile delinquency, and social welfare. Under their agreement, Fortas would advise the foundation on its charitable efforts in areas where he had expertise for a fee of $20,000 per year for life. If his wife were to outlive him, she would continue to receive the same money from the foundation.[55]

Within a few months, Wolfson and a business associate were investigated by the Securities and Exchange Commission for failing to register a planned sale of his company's stock. In June 1966, well before the case came to trial, Justice Fortas announced that it would be inappropriate for him to continue his involvement with the Wolfson Family Foundation, so he ended the arrangement and returned the $20,000 he had received. Wolfson was eventually indicted and convicted in 1967 and sent to prison after the Supreme Court declined to review his case.

Neither during nor after his involvement with the foundation was there any evidence that Fortas ever engaged in legal work for Wolfson or interceded with the government on his behalf.[56] Neither his activity in the American University seminar or his Wolfson Family Foundation involvement presented a prima facie case of unethical conduct. Fortas routinely recused himself from cases before the Court involving clients of his former law firm, thus all the donors to the seminar as well as Wolfson. He could not be charged with any actual misdeeds.[57]

Despite this, then Assistant Attorney General William Rehnquist devised a plan to prosecute Fortas for having intervened in the government's case concerning Wolfson's stock market activities. Even though there was no strong evidence to support such an allegation, Attorney General John Mitchell nevertheless threatened Fortas with the case unless he resigned from the court.[58] Mitchell knew that there was not enough evidence that Fortas committed any crime, or he would have pursued an indictment against him. He probably also knew he did not have enough evidence of an impeachable offense, or he would have taken it to the House. More than likely, the attorney general only had information that would embarrass Fortas and the Warren Court.[59]

Fortas responded that he had done nothing improper, but he acknowledged the damaging effect of the investigation on the reputation of the Court.[60] Members of the House began discussing impeachment, and a few members even prepared impeachment resolutions.[61] On May 14, Fortas sent a letter of resignation to the president.[62] In the end, the resignation grew out of purely partisan motives to hold open the position of chief justice so that it could be filled by a different president.[63]

The Fortas resignation permanently changed the process by which justices are confirmed to the Supreme Court. Prior to 1968, most confirmations were finished quickly and were perfunctory ratifications of presidential nominations. Fortas's own 1965 confirmation as an associate justice involved a three-hour Senate Judiciary Committee hearing less than two weeks after his nomination and full Senate approval by voice vote shortly thereafter. The Fortas inquiry did not end with investigation of his actions, but extended to information regarding his friend, Wolfson.[64] The extended hearings and debate of the 1968 nomination of Fortas to be chief justice changed the way Congress approved judicial nominations. After the events of the Fortas case, Congress began to examine a nominee's credentials more than they had previously.

Clement F. Haynsworth Jr. (1969)

Clement Haynsworth was nominated and confirmed to serve on the U.S. Court of Appeals for the Fourth Circuit in 1957. When Fortas resigned from the Supreme Court in 1969, President Nixon nominated Haynsworth to a position on the Court. He was opposed by Democrats and some liberal Republicans, especially after charges were made that he had not recused himself from cases before his court in which he appeared to have a financial interest.[65] Many also did not like his past record in support of segregation. There was a negative 45–45 roll call vote in the Senate on his nomination. Since the Democrats controlled the Senate by a margin of fifty-eight to forty-two, some critics argued that the vote was a partisan act of revenge for the ousting of Fortas.[66]

Harrold Carswell (1970)

Harrold Carswell was from Florida and had been on the federal District Court for twelve years. He was elevated to the U.S. Court of Appeals for the Fifth Circuit through a nomination by President Nixon after Haynsworth was declined. At the time, Carswell was known to be both a homosexual and a segregationist.[67] While he had been a federal district judge, more than 40 percent of his appealed rulings had been overturned, a reversal rate higher than almost every other judge in his circuit. Revelations of his racial attitudes were more disturbing to many people. He advocated white supremacy and racial segregation when he was a political candidate for public office in a 1948 campaign in Georgia. While serving as a U.S. attorney in Tallahassee, Florida, in 1956, he had drawn up documents to convert a local public golf course partially constructed with federal funds into a whites-only private country club. The club's ninety-nine-year dollar-a-year lease from the city, which Carswell helped draw up while serving as the federal government's chief law enforcement officer in the area, appeared to be an effort to circumvent a six-month-old Supreme Court desegregation order for municipally owned recreational facilities.[68] Because of these controversial policy positions, Judge Carswell's nomination was rejected by a vote of 51–45 on April 8, 1970.[69]

William O. Douglas (1970)

Justice William O. Douglas was nominated for a seat on the Supreme Court by Franklin Roosevelt in 1939. At age forty, he became one of the youngest men ever elevated to the Court. He had built a reputation as an unwavering liberal over three decades on the bench.[70] With liberal decisions, Douglas outraged conservatives with his strong support for civil rights for racial minorities, criminal suspects, makers and distributors of books and films they thought obscene, or others he considered victims of an abusive government. He also angered conservatives when he divorced his third wife in the summer of 1966. She was a college student when they met four years earlier. Three weeks later he married an even younger woman, a twenty-three-year-old college student who was forty-five years younger than he was. This reinforced the image of the "dirty old man."[71]

There were also concerns about Douglas's involvement with the Parvin Foundation.[72] The foundation was founded in 1960 to support graduate fellowships for students from underdeveloped African, Asian, Middle Eastern, and Latin American nations to attend Princeton University and UCLA. The story quickly faded.[73]

In early 1970, Douglas published a small book titled *Points of Rebellion*. It described many situations surrounding freedom of expression, poverty, and environmental degradation in which he believed American policy was falling short of what the Constitution required.[74] The book contained a caricature of Richard Nixon as King George III of England. The book infuriated conservatives across the country even more.[75]

The conservatives fought back. Five days after Nixon was sworn into office, his administration initiated an investigation of Justice Douglas.[76] The White House directed the IRS to audit Douglas's tax returns.[77] In April 1970, Gerald Ford introduced a controversial resolution to authorize an impeachment inquiry against Douglas. Ford laid out his charges in a lengthy address to the House of

Representatives.[78] The charges were based on his controversial decisions and lifestyle while serving on the Supreme Court.[79] At the time, Douglas was the second most senior member of the Court.[80]

In discussing the definition of an impeachable offense, Ford said, "The only honest answer is that an impeachable offense is whatever a majority of House of Representatives considers [it] to be at a given moment in history; conviction results from whatever offense or offenses two-thirds of the other body considers to be sufficiently serious to require removal of the accused from office. Again, the historical contest and political climax are important; there are few fixed principles among the handful of precedents."[81] Ford suggested that Douglas had the same type of conflict of interest that had led Fortas to resign previously. He explained that Douglas had dissented from rulings against publisher Ralph Ginzburg, in 1966 and 1970, while at the same time, publishing essays in other magazines owned by Ginzburg.[82] Ford also discussed Douglas's ties to the Parvin Foundation, focusing on Parvin's connections with Las Vegas gambling figures, implying that Douglas might be associated with organized crime.[83]

Douglas would not resign from the Supreme Court because he knew it would appear to be a confession of guilt.[84] There were many supporters who argued that the charges against him were partisan and did not merit impeachment.[85] They said that Douglas did not authorize excerpts from his book to be reprinted in Ginzburg's magazine. The article happened to be placed next to an erotic photograph that was not part of the original article. They argued that the placement of Douglas's articles was not his choice.[86]

A special subcommittee looking into the matter voted three to one that there were no grounds for impeaching Douglas.[87] This meant that the matter died in committee.[88] The impeachment process for Douglas again altered the standards and the practices for evaluating members of the Court. The case reinforced the practice of completing in-depth examinations of judicial nominees.[89]

Otto Kerner (1973)

Otto Kerner was the former governor of Illinois and the chair of a presidential commission on civil disorders during the 1960s. He became the judge of the U.S. Court of Appeals for the Seventh Circuit, but was convicted in February 1973 of accepting a bribe, evading income tax, and committing perjury in a case involving an Illinois horse-racing track. Kerner resigned from the judiciary only two weeks before Nixon stepped down.[90]

Alcee Hastings (1981–83)

Alcee Hastings had been appointed as a state Circuit Court judge in 1977, and then President Jimmy Carter raised him to the federal bench as part of an effort to expand the ranks of minorities in the federal courts. In 1979, the president named Hastings to the U.S. District Court for the Southern District of Florida, and the Senate easily confirmed him.[91] He gained national attention by barring the federal government from deporting Haitian "boat people" who were seeking political asylum. He was the first black lawyer ever to be appointed as a federal judge in that state.[92] As such, he could only be removed from office through impeachment by the House and conviction by Senate.[93]

On December 29, 1981, Hastings was indicted by a grand jury in Miami for conspiring to accept a $150,000 bribe. The charges were made by William Dredge, a Miami antiques dealer who approached FBI officials with the story. Dredge was facing drug charges and wanted them dropped in exchange for the information. He claimed to have paid off Hastings through William Borders, a politically well-connected Washington attorney.[94] Prosecutors charged that Hastings, using Borders as a middleman, offered to reduce the prison sentence of two racketeers whose cases had come before him in exchange for the bribe. Even though Hastings said he was never in on the deal, there was a satchel full of $100 bills. Borders was convicted, but Hastings was acquitted and returned to the bench.[95]

Even though Hastings was not formally convicted, his actions provoked calls for his impeachment.[96] Two U.S. district judges filed a complaint with the U.S. Court of Appeals for the Eleventh Circuit because they believed Hastings was really guilty. The chief judge of the circuit reviewed the complaint and referred it to a special committee to investigate the charges. The committee later returned a report that concluded that Hastings had lied at his trial.[97] The Judicial Council of the Eleventh Circuit accepted the report and in September 1986 reported to the U.S. Judicial Conference that Hastings had engaged in conduct that could be grounds for impeachment and removal from office. The Judicial Conference agreed and in spring 1988, Chief Justice of the Supreme Court William Rehnquist wrote to the U.S. House of Representatives that Hastings had engaged in conduct that might constitute grounds for impeachment.[98]

The House subcommittee that was investigating Hastings decided to recommend seventeen articles of impeachment against him. The first alleged a conspiracy with Borders to obtain a bribe. The next fourteen articles alleged that he provided false statements during his 1983 trial. Article sixteen charged that, in 1985, Hastings disclosed confidential information about an FBI wiretap to Miami's mayor, warning him that he was under surveillance. The full House voted to impeach Hastings on August 3, 1989, on charges of perjury, bribery, and corruption by a vote of 426–3.[99] The Senate voted in October, and they chose to remove him from office by a vote of 69–26.

Since Hastings was acquitted in criminal court, he argued that it was unfair that Congress take up the same matter because of limits of double jeopardy. He said the charges were racially motivated.[100]

Even though the Senate voted to remove Hastings as a judge, they did not vote to disqualify him from future office holding. So three years after Congress impeached him, Hastings ran in the Democratic primary for governor of Florida in 1990, but his campaign floundered and he chose to run for Congress. He easily prevailed in the general election to represent Florida in Congress[101] and was sworn in as a member of the House of Representatives from the twenty-third district of Florida.[102] By 2006 he was the ranking minority member on the Subcommittee on Terrorism and Homeland Security of the Permanent Select Committee as well as a congressional delegate to the Organization for Security and Cooperation in Europe. He was also selected as a member of the House Rules Committee.[103]

Operation Greylord (1983)

In 1983, it was announced that for three years, the FBI and the IRS had been running a joint undercover investigation of corruption in the Cook County (Chicago), Illinois, court system. There were allegations that judges fixed all kinds of cases, from drunk-driving cases to those that involved felony charges. When the investigation ended, almost 100 people were indicted, including seventeen judges, eight policemen, ten deputy sheriffs, eight court officials, and one state legislator.[104]

Harry Claiborne (1986)

Harry Claiborne was a district judge from Las Vegas, Nevada, who was nominated by President Carter to a federal district bench. The nomination was approved by the Senate[105] after a background check by the FBI.

The allegations against Claiborne revolved around his hiring a private investigator to conduct illegal wiretaps while he was an attorney. The charges were brought to a grand jury, which declined to indict him. Prosecutors then brought new charges that Claiborne took bribes from two other grand juries. They also presented a case that he evaded income taxes. A fourth grand jury heard the charges against him and indicted him for taking bribes, obstruction of justice, and tax evasion.[106]

Claiborne filed a motion in the U.S. Court of Appeals for the Seventh Circuit in January 1984, claiming that as a sitting judge, he could only be impeached and not criminally indicted. The trial court denied his motion as frivolous. Claiborne appealed the court's decision, so a three-judge panel of the U.S. Court of Appeals for the Ninth Circuit agreed to hear the appeal. The panel concluded that the Constitution did not preclude prosecution for judges in calling on the executive branch to enforce the laws. On review by the Supreme Court, the justices refused to grant a further appeal, allowing Claiborne's trial to move forward.[107]

The judge assigned to hear the case was Walter E. Hoffman, a senior federal district judge.[108] In April 1984, after the jury declared that it was deadlocked in the case, Hoffman declared a mistrial.[109] The prosecutors decided to drop all of the charges except two counts of making false statements on his 1979 and 1980 income tax returns. They considered these charges to be the strongest ones. The court heard testimony that during and after his transition from private practice to the bench, the judge failed to report $108,000 of income in attorney fees, had repeatedly cashed large checks at casinos making the funds untraceable, had switched from the accountant who had handled his affairs for thirty years to an unlicensed tax preparer, and could not produce documents to substantiate his explanations for his behavior. His 1979 and 1980 tax returns appeared to have underreported income and had questionable capital gain claims regarding the sale of his law practice and a home.[110]

On August 10, 1984, a jury found him guilty on both tax evasion counts.[111] He was sentenced to a $10,000 fine and two years in prison. Claiborne told the court of his remorse at having been sloppy in his personal affairs and embarrassing the judiciary. He pointed out, however, that he had not been given the chance for an IRS audit and the opportunity to correct his mistakes like "normal" taxpayers. He denied that he was guilty of any crime and then alleged a pattern of government harassment. He appealed his conviction to the Ninth Circuit, but his case was rejected.[112]

Claiborne entered the federal minimum security prison at Maxwell Air Force Base in Alabama on May 16, 1986. He was the first sitting federal judge ever incarcerated. To top it off, he refused to resign his position and continued to draw his $78,700 salary,[113] claiming that he would be eligible to return to the bench following his release from prison and would then be eligible to retire at full pay.[114]

Claiborne's refusal to resign on imprisonment angered James Sensenbrenner, a prominent member of the House. There was a central concern that the judge had become disabled from functioning as a federal judge because of his criminal conduct.[115] Sensenbrenner threatened to begin impeachment proceedings unless Claiborne resigned. Claiborne wanted an impeachment hearing to take place. This would give him the chance to have a proper hearing that he had been denied. It would be a chance to tell his side of the story.[116]

When Claiborne did not resign, another prominent member, Peter Rodino, introduced an impeachment charge against him. The House Judiciary Subcommittee treated his criminal conviction as proof of improper behavior and refused to reconsider his case.[117] The subcommittee drafted four articles of impeachment, two dealing with filing false income tax returns, the third declaring that the failure to resign following conviction and exhaustion of appeals itself represented misconduct, and the fourth asserting that Claiborne had violated his oath of office and thus brought disrepute on the federal courts.[118] On July 22, the House voted 406–0 to send all four articles to the Senate. The Senate hearings began on September 15, 1986.[119] Claiborne himself took the stand, testifying in his own defense for most of the final two and half days of the hearing.[120]

On Article I, alleging high crimes and misdemeanors by willfully falsifying his 1979 federal income tax return, the Senate voted 87–10 to find Claiborne guilty. On Article II, the same charge applied to his 1980 return, the Senate again voted to find him guilty ninety to seven.[121] On Article III, seventeen senators voted not guilty and thirty-five declined to cast a ballot, but acknowledged that they were present when the roll was called. This meant that fifty-two senators failed to support the article, so he was not found guilty on that charge.[122] Finally, on the final article, charging betrayal of the public trust in the judiciary by falsifying his taxes, the senate voted 89–8 for conviction.[123]

Claiborne retuned to prison in Alabama for another year before being put on parole. He then returned to Nevada to try to rebuild his life. In May 1988, the Nevada Supreme Court readmitted him to practice in the state courts, and a year and a half later, he was readmitted to practice in the federal courts.[124]

As part of this case, the Supreme Court ruled on whether a sitting federal judge can be criminally prosecuted before being removed from office by impeachment by the Senate.[125] In *Claiborne v. United States* (465 U.S. 1305 (1984)), the justices held that a sitting federal judge could be impeached and removed for taking bribes.[126]

Robert Bork (1987)

Judge Robert Bork was nominated to a seat on the U.S. Supreme Court by President Ronald Reagan on July 1, 1987, to replace retiring Justice Lewis Powell. Bork had spent five years as a judge on the U.S. Circuit Court of Appeals for the District of Columbia and also as the U.S. solicitor general from 1972–77. He was best known for his role in the Saturday Night Massacre during the Watergate affair, when he carried out Nixon's order to fire special prosecutor Archibald Cox in 1973. The Senate rejected his nomination 58–42 on October 23.[127] The Senate, along with women's and civil rights groups, attacked him for being an extreme conservative. During the nomination hearings, Bork's video rental history was released, and although there were no surprises, it led to a new law called the Video Privacy Protection Act, passed in Congress in 1988.[128]

Douglas Ginsburg (1987)

When Bork's nomination failed, President Reagan then nominated Judge Douglas Ginsburg for a seat on the Supreme Court. Ginsburg had been a professor at Harvard Law School and had been in the Reagan administration in the Office of Information and Regulatory Affairs, the Office of Management and Budget, and as deputy assistant attorney general in the Justice Department. During his nomination hearings, Ginsburg admitted that he had smoked marijuana in the 1960s and 1970s as a college student and while he was a law professor at Harvard.[129] The admission of drug use (especially as a professor) was disappointing to many members of the public and Congress, and he was forced to withdraw as the nominee for the position.[130]

Robert Aguilar (1989, 1996)

Robert Aguilar was from California and was appointed by President Carter. In 1989, Judge Aguilar was indicted on allegations of corruption and racketeering arising from his possible involvement with a Teamsters Union official who was convicted of embezzlement. The judge was accused of unlawfully giving information about a wiretap and obstructing justice. The charges against him were based on evidence collected during eighteen months of wiretaps on his phone.[131]

In March 1990, Aguilar was tried on eight felony charges. A jury acquitted him on one count and deadlocked on the others. Prosecutors retried him in August, and this time Aguilar was convicted on the wiretap disclosure and obstruction of justice charges. The U.S. Court of Appeals for the Ninth Circuit eventually overturned the convictions. The government appealed the decision, and in 1995 the Supreme Court reinstated the verdict, sending the case back to the Ninth Circuit for further proceedings. The Justice Department continued to pursue Aguilar until June 1996, when the two sides finally struck a bargain. The Justice Department allowed Aguilar to retire immediately from the federal bench with a full pension. In return, the judge acknowledged that in 1987 he had improperly divulged the existence of a wiretap.[132]

Walter Nixon (1989)

Walter Nixon was a district judge who was appointed to fill a newly created third federal judgeship for the Biloxi district. Justice Nixon was nominated by President Johnson in May 1968 to fill the new seat. He was confirmed by the Senate nine days later. He was only thirty-nine, young for a federal judge at that time.[133]

Nixon found himself in financial trouble soon after being seated on the bench. He started looking for some new investment opportunities. A man named Wiley Fairchild offered to sell him leases on three oil properties that had not yet begun to produce. He was also willing to loan the judge, at 10 percent interest, the $9,500 he sought for the properties. Because of these arrangements Nixon would be able to pay for his investment from revenues it generated and make a profit (eventually about $51,000) at virtually no cost.[134] Fairchild did not have contracts drawn up until 1982, but had them backdated to February 1980.[135]

In 1980, Fairchild's son Drew was managing an airport when three men were arrested for smuggling more than a ton of marijuana into the country. Drew was implicated in the crime. Although his lawyer negotiated a plea bargain with federal prosecutors, Fairchild failed to pay his legal fee, so the lawyer encouraged a state prosecution against Drew.[136]

In July 1984, Nixon was called before a grand jury looking into whether he tried to thwart Drew's prosecution as the result of a bribe from Fairchild.[137] In 1985, Holmes and Nixon were both indicted, Holmes on five counts of perjury and Nixon for accepting an illegal gift and three counts of perjury. Nixon was tried in 1986 based on his improper intervention in the Drew Fairchild case.[138]

The jury acquitted Nixon of receiving an illegal gratuity and one count of perjury, but convicted him on two other perjury counts involving the Drew Fairchild case. On March 31, 1986, Nixon was sentenced to two concurrent five-year terms in the federal prison camp at Eglin Air Force Base. When he was imprisoned, he refused to resign his judgeship.[139]

Nixon appealed to the U.S. Court of Appeals for the Fifth Circuit. His appeals were rejected on April 30, 1987, and the Supreme Court denied his petition for certiorari on January 19, 1988. The Judicial Conference of the United States recommended to the House that Nixon be impeached. The judiciary subcommittee voted unanimously on July 12 to recommend his impeachment,[140] and on May 10, 1989, the House voted 417–0 for three articles of impeachment, one for each of Judge Nixon's two perjury convictions and a third for having made a series of fourteen other false statements that raised substantial doubts as to his judicial integrity.[141] The Senate voted ninety to eight to convict Nixon on Article I involving lying to a grand jury when he said he had not discussed the Drew Fairchild case with District Attorney Holmes. On Article II, regarding perjury in denying saying or doing anything to influence the Fairchild case, the Senate voted 78–19 to convict.[142] On Article III, fifty-seven Senators voted to convict Nixon on its list of charges, whereas forty disagreed. Thus, this article fell well short of the two-thirds necessary for adoption.[143]

Clarence Thomas (1991)

Clarence Thomas was nominated to the U.S. Supreme Court in 1991 by President George H.W. Bush to replace retiring justice Thurgood Marshall. When nominated, Bush called him the best qualified jurist in America.[144] He had a compelling story of rising from poverty in Georgia.[145] At the same time, some of Bush's aides thought Thomas lacked enough judicial experience, since he had never litigated a case in front of a jury or issued a substantive constitutional opinion,[146] which explains why he was not nominated earlier.[147] The Senate Judiciary Committee voted thirteen to one to send Thomas's nomination to the Senate floor.[148] They expected an easy confirmation to the Court. He was a preeminent African American neoconservative in the Reagan administration and had been investigated previously by the FBI and confirmed by the Senate four times.[149]

But when the nomination got to the Senate, a female law professor from Oklahoma, Anita Hill, accused Thomas of sexual harassment and inappropriate sexual conduct when they worked together in the Equal Employment Opportunity Commission and the Department of Education from 1991 to 1992.[150] Hill described how Thomas repeatedly asked her out and when she refused, he tormented her by talking obscenely about sex.[151] She provided a detailed statement about how he discussed his obsessive interest in pornographic movies and described his boasting to female co-workers of his sexual prowess.[152] Thomas had used crude sexual comments to her repeatedly and used suggestive language,[153] even describing a pubic hair on a Coke can.[154]

Hill's descriptions of Thomas's behavior were graphic and shocked Americans. The fourteen male senators on the Judiciary Committee were forced to reopen its televised hearings to discuss the allegations.[155] They found some inconsistencies in her testimony that was contradicted by other witnesses.[156] Questions also arose surrounding the fact that Hill left the Department of Education to go with Thomas to the EEOC, an unusual step for someone who was sexually harassed in such a manner.[157]

Of course, Thomas denied the allegations. Republicans said she concocted the story.[158] Thomas was confirmed by a vote of fifty-two to forty-eight.[159] The attention given to Hill's allegations, and the seriousness with which they were taken by the press and the public, made it clear that sexual harassment was an important political issue.[160]

Robert F. Collins (1991)

Robert Collins of Louisiana was a black judge put on the federal bench in the late 1970s by President Carter.[161] A drug smuggler, Gary Young, who was facing a long prison term and large fine for drug smuggling, claimed that he had been approached by Judge Collins's friend, John Ross, who said that for $100,000 the judge would reduce his sentence from eight years to three and a half. Young agreed to cooperate with the FBI and deliver the money to the judge. The case was then found in Collins's chambers. Collins was indicted and accused of taking a bribe to give favorable sentencing treatment to a man convicted of smuggling 2500 pounds of marijuana into Louisiana from Belize. The defense was that the money found was really a down payment on property he was buying from the judge.[162]

Nonetheless, a jury convicted both Collins and Ross on all counts. Collins was sentenced to prison in 1991, but did not immediately resign his judgeship and continued to receive his salary. In July 1993 the Judicial Conference of the U.S. recommended that the House undertake impeachment proceedings against Collins, but in August 1993 he decided to give up his seat rather than go through the hearing.[163]

Conclusion

As this discussion shows, judges are not immune to scandal. Over the years, many have been involved in scandals. They have been involved in financial scandals, scandals that relate to appropriate behavior required for justices, and even sex scandals. They have happened across all time periods and to members of all political parties. Like congressional and presidential scandals, those scandals that involve judges have both long-term and short-term impacts. In almost every situation, a judge's reputation is damaged, which is all the worse for judges because their reputation (or lack thereof) can have a major impact on their ability to perform their job duties. When a judge loses the respect of the public, the public is far less likely to respect their decisions. In some cases, although few, there are laws passed (such as the Video Privacy Protection Act) after a judicial scandal. Another long-term impact is the effect on the judicial system when good judges are lost because of scandals. Conversely, scandals serve as a method to rid the system of bad judges. Nonetheless, bringing charges against judges can also be a means of attacking members of the opposing party and the policies they support, which has become more common in recent years.

Review Questions

1. Describe some judicial scandals to be made public.
2. What was the Video Privacy Protection Act?
3. Describe the Judicial Conduct and Disability Act. Why is it significant?

Special Terms

Video Privacy Protection Act
Judicial Conduct and Disability Act

Discussion Questions

1. Are scandals involving judges worse than those affecting presidents or Congress simply because they are supposed to uphold the law?
2. Are scandals used as political weapons against judges?

Chapter 9

Conclusion

Introduction

Like other presidential administrations, the most recent administration of George W. Bush has seen its share of political scandal. There have been many allegations made against Bush, but there have been few independent counsels appointed to investigate those allegations. Many of the charges are ongoing, so it is difficult to determine the full extent of the scandals and the impacts they may have on government and society. There will undoubtedly be both long- and short-range impacts, but many of those are yet to be discovered. Below is a brief introduction to some emerging scandals in the Bush administration and some concluding statements.

George W. Bush

George Bush was elected to serve as president in 2000 in a controversial election. Although he received the majority of Electoral College votes, he did not receive more popular votes than his opponent. Because of this, many Bush opponents have argued from the start that he should never have been inaugurated—a scandal in and of itself. But the Supreme Court declared Bush the winner, and he became president for eight years. During his two terms in office, many other potential scandals became apparent.

A. Drug/Alcohol Use

When running for governor of Texas in 1994, Bush acknowledged that as a young man, he had been an irresponsible youth and had, on occasion, overindulged in alcohol. In 1999, he denied being a "clinical alcoholic." During the 2000 campaign when he was asked about drug use, Bush refused to talk about what he did as a child, but said he had learned from the mistakes he made when he was younger.[1] He continued to repeat the story that he stopped drinking alcohol on his fortieth birthday.

On November 2, 2000, five days before the presidential election, a television channel in Maine reported that in 1976, Bush had been arrested for drunken driving. He was thirty years old at the time. He admitted to the officer that he had been drinking and was arrested. He paid a find of $150 and had his driving privileges revoked in Maine. Bush acknowledged the report was accurate, but he did not reveal the arrest to the public because he did not want to set a poor example for his daughters.[2]

B. Valerie Plame

George Bush's administration was accused of leaking the name of a CIA operative, Valerie Plame, to the public, a potential felony offense. Plame was a CIA operative from 2002 onward, serving in at least two positions in Athens and Brussels. As such, she posed in different professional roles to gather information. She pretended to be a junior consular officer and as an energy analyst for a private company. When her identity was exposed, Plame was working in Iran, ensuring that the country did not acquire nuclear weapons. When her identity was made public, the cover of at least one CIA front company where she worked was blown by the leak.

It began on July 14, 2003, when a journalist named Robert Novak identified Plame by name in his column in the *Washington Post*.[3] Novak reported that he learned her identity from two senior administration officials.[4] The leak was allegedly revenge for articles written by her husband, retired ambassador Joe Wilson, that were critical of the White House.[5] In the articles, which were published on July 6, Wilson contradicted Bush's claims that Niger provided uranium to Iraq. The articles were titled "What I Did Not Find in Africa."[6]

Since identifying a CIA operative is a crime under the Intelligence Identities Protection Act of 1982,[7] the CIA investigated the leak, as did the Justice Department. After a long delay, Attorney General John Ashcroft turned the inquiry over to a nonpartisan career federal prosecutor, Patrick Fitzgerald of Chicago.[8] Fitzgerald convened a grand jury, which did not result in the indictment or conviction of anyone for any crime in connection with the leak itself.

The investigation led to the indictment of Vice President Dick Cheney's chief of staff, Lewis "Scooter" Libby.[9] Libby was found guilty in March 2007 of perjury and obstruction of justice for lying under oath regarding conversations with reporters about Plame.[10] He was sentenced to a $250,000 fine, thirty months in prison, and two years of probation. In July 2007, Bush commuted

Libby's sentence shortly before he was to begin the jail term,[11] saying that the punishment was excessive.

A civil lawsuit was filed by Plame and her husband, *Plame v. Cheney*, against presidential adviser Karl Rove, Libby, Cheney, and others for their role in the disclosure of her identity. The case was dismissed in July 2007.[12] After working for the CIA for twenty years, Plame was forced to resign, basically ending her career.[13]

C. Firing of U.S. Attorneys

President Bush's Justice Department dismissed seven U.S. attorneys midterm on December 7, 2006. They were dismissed without explanation and replaced with interim attorneys. The attorneys had all been appointed by President Bush and confirmed by the Senate more than four years prior. It was alleged that the seven who were dismissed were involved with investigations against prominent Republican politicians, or that they refused to investigate charges that would damage Democratic politicians. This meant that the Justice Department and the White House were using the U.S. attorney positions for their own political advantage.

President Bush and the Justice Department had the power to dismiss the attorneys as a result of the reauthorization of the USA PATRIOT Act in 2006. The new law eliminated the 120-day limit on interim appointments that were made to fill temporary vacancies. Any attorneys placed by the attorney general did not require Senate approval, whereas those appointed by the president did.

Traditionally, U.S. attorneys are replaced when a new president is inaugurated. U.S. attorneys serve at the "pleasure of the president." At the beginning of a new term, it is typical for all U.S. attorneys to submit a letter of resignation. The president can choose which attorneys to keep or to replace. In most cases, if a new president is of a different political party, the attorneys are replaced with new appointees who are members of the president's political party.

The Senate committee responsible for oversight of the U.S. attorneys, the Judiciary Committee, was concerned that the confirmation process had been bypassed. Members introduced legislation to repeal that part of the new USA PATRIOT Act. They also decided to investigate if there was any wrongdoing by the Bush administration, as did the House Committee on the Judiciary. The Senate committee chairman, Patrick Leahy, subpoenaed officials from the Justice Department and the White House, including Karl Rove and former White House counsel Harriet Miers, to testify in front of the committee. President Bush declared that his aides would not testify, claiming presidential privilege. Despite his claims, both the House and Senate investigating committees subpoenaed the officials. When some refused to testify, the House voted 223–32 to pass contempt resolutions against White House Chief of Staff Joshua Bolten and counsel Miers.

In April 2007, the House Judiciary Committee issued a subpoena for documents related to the dismissals from the attorney general, Alberto Gonzales. The White House claimed that many of the documents, particularly e-mails, had been lost because they were conducted on Republican Party accounts and not stored properly.[14]

After the firings and during the investigation, Gonzales came under great pressure to resign from office. Even Republican Senator John Sununu, from New Hampshire, called for his resignation.[15] He eventually did, as did many other members of the Bush staff.

D. Prisoner Abuse

During the Bush administration, there were accusations of American mistreatment of Afghan and Iraqi prisoners of war, as well as of other suspected enemies, in the American military detention center in Guantanamo Bay and at the Abu Ghraib prison in Baghdad.[16] Abuse was also alleged to be happening at various other secret foreign locations to which suspects were transferred.[17]

In 2002, a CIA analyst visited Guantanamo Bay, a U.S. naval base in Cuba. He found there were approximately 600 prisoners being held there, many having been captured in Afghanistan. Some were being subjected to cruel, inhumane, and degrading treatment.[18] They were held in wire mesh cages in the hot sun. They were held without access to lawyers and could be held there indefinitely.[19] The prisoners could be treated this way because they were considered to be "enemy combatants" rather than prisoners of war.[20] The deplorable conditions have led to many suicide attempts.[21] It was alleged that the officers supervising Guantanamo Bay were violating both the Geneva Conventions and the federal antitorture statute.[22]

While at Guantanamo, the CIA and military interrogators worked to get information out of the detainees. They were held in "stress and duress" positions that included stripping detainees, depriving them of sleep, subjecting them to bright lights and blaring noises, hooding them, exposing them to extreme heat or cold, and binding them in stressful positions.[23] But the interrogations were not going well for the American soldiers, and they were getting very little information from the detainees. There was debate among the White House about how to get more information, and what tactics could be used.[24]

Similar events were occurring at Abu Ghraib in Baghdad. There were an estimated 50,000 men and women in the prison at one time.[25] Early on, the facility was being run by Janis Karpinsky, an Army Reserve brigadier general with no experience in running a prison system.[26] Under her administration, there were "sadistic, blatant, and wanton criminal abuses."[27] In other cases of alleged abuse, a soldier was accused of drowning an Iraqi after forcing him into the Tigris River. Yet another was charged with dragging an Iraqi prisoner out of his holding cell by the neck, where he was stripped naked and left outside for seven hours.[28]

In January 2005, Army Spec. Charles A. Graner Jr. was convicted of abusing Iraqi detainees at Abu Ghraib. He was the first soldier who was tried on charges of abusing prisoners. Seven other soldiers were charged with similar offenses, four of whom have pled guilty. The charges stemmed from incidents where prisoners were photographed in sexually humiliating positions.[29]

In 2005, it was learned that an adviser to secretary of Defense Donald Rumsfeld learned of allegations that the military in Iraq was beating detainees there. It was further alleged that the Defense Department personnel confiscated evidence of the abuse and intimidated those who were making the complaints.[30]

At first, President Bush promised a "full accounting" of the abuse of prisoners by U.S. soldiers, but repeated his claim that Rumsfeld was doing a "superb job." Later, in 2004, Bush apologized for the abuse, but refused to fire Rumsfeld. Rumsfeld offered President Bush his resignation more than once during the scandal.[31] Congress held hearings about the abuse charges. Rumsfeld testified for six hours in front of Congress, during which time he apologized and claimed responsibility for the abuses.

The U.S. Supreme Court ruled in June 2008 that the prisoners had the right to have their detention reviewed in civilian courts rather than in military courts.[32] In military court, judicial rules and procedures that are routine in U.S. courts do not apply. Trials are held in secret, and no information is made public. Sentences can range up to life imprisonment or execution, and the accused has no recourse to appeal.[33] When the Supreme Court made that decision, the Bush administration wanted to opportunity to rewrite the official evidence against the detainees at Guantanamo Bay to shore up its cases before being scrutinized by civilian judges, thereby putting off the reviews.[34] The Bush administration fought for years to prevent civilian judges from reviewing evidence in these cases.[35] However, a federal judge in July 2008 ordered the Justice Department to move forward on cases concerning lawsuits from detainees at Guantanamo Bay.

E. Domestic Surveillance

Under the PATRIOT Act, the FBI can search citizens' homes, offices, or records, or conduct electronic surveillance of telephone and Internet use, without probable cause. Additionally, the legal standards for obtaining search warrants were much lower than typical criminal investigations.[36] In the end of 2005, the *New York Times* published a story that described how the National Security Agency (NSA) had been wiretapping American citizens without first obtaining a warrant, which is required under the Foreign Intelligence Surveillance Act of 1978. Violation of this law is a felony.[37]

F. War in Iraq

Bush had been under pressure for military confrontation with Iraq prior to the September 11, 2001, attacks on the United States.[38] His father had driven Saddam Hussein out of Kuwait during the Persian Gulf War in 1991, but did not go into Baghdad. Many conservatives did not believe that George H.W. Bush had finished the job. Additionally, there were reports that Saddam Hussein tried to have Bush Sr. assassinated.[39]

It was alleged that the Bush administration persuaded Congress and the public to undertake the war in Iraq partly on the basis of claims that Iraq possessed weapons of mass destruction (WMDs). Bush and his supporters believed that the "terror states" and organizations that formed an "axis of evil" against the United States were planning additional attacks. Three states made up the axis: North Korea, Iran, and Iraq.[40] The United States would probably be attacked again by one, if not all, of these countries. According to Bush, the United States had to strike first to protect itself and other countries from the threat they imposed.[41] Iraq posed the biggest threat to the United States because it had vast stores of potentially lethal WMDs.[42] It turns out that the country did not have them.[43]

Another way Bush justified the war in Iraq was to show a link between Hussein and Al Qaeda, a terrorist group that was responsible for the 9/11 attacks on New York and Washington, and who threatened us with future attacks with weapons of mass murder.[44] Bush argued that Hussein possessed usable weapons of mass destruction, and he could get them to Al Qaeda at any time.[45] No one could ever produce any credible evidence of this connection.[46] Critics allege that President Bush exaggerated the extent of the WMD capability of Iraq and used it to invent a link between Iraq and Al Qaeda.[47]

Bush also stated that the war was about liberating Iraq from the brutal Saddam Hussein and bringing democracy to the Iraqi people.[48] If the United States invaded Iraq solely because of its human rights abuses, there would be numerous other countries that would also qualify for invasion.[49]

Bush convinced the United Nations Security Council to pass Resolution 1441 to allow for an enhanced inspection schedule for Iraq's disarmament.[50]

When inspectors went to Iraq, they were denied access. A report from the International Atomic Energy Agency (IAEA), claimed that Iraq was only six months away from developing a nuclear weapon.[51]

Most people agreed that in the past, Hussein had possessed WMDs. He used them against the Kurds and Iran in the 1980s. He tried to hide a WMD program from U.N. inspectors in the 1990s. There were also WMD materials and possibly some weapons that were missing when the U.N. inspections ended. But this was in the past, and Bush needed to show that Iraq had them now. He cited U.N. inspectors to prove Iraq had stockpiles of WMDs. But the inspectors had not concluded that such stockpiles existed. Instead, they only concluded that Iraq could have produced more weapons, not that they did.[52] Based on that report, Bush gave Hussein forty-eight hours to leave Iraq or have his country invaded.[53] Since he did not leave, the U.S. military invaded.

In the months after the war began, soldiers failed to locate the weapons that Bush described as the cause of the invasion.[54] Neither the British nor the American troops found any WMDs.[55] To liberals, it was becoming clear that Bush had been dishonest with the public before the war.[56] They argued that he gave the impression that there was strong intelligence that Iraq had WMDs, but it was actually based on circumstantial evidence rather than hard facts.[57] Much of the evidence was ambiguous, and the CIA did not have proof of operational ties between Al Qaeda and Hussein.[58] Some liberals have implied that Bush conjured up a stockpile of weapons and a link to terrorists simply to fit his agenda of war with Iraq.[59]

G. Hurricane Katrina

Scandals arose out of the Bush administration's insufficient response to the September 2005 devastation of New Orleans, Louisiana, by Hurricane Katrina.[60] There was a delayed evacuation of the citizens and a failure of the administration to act on early reports of levee failures.[61] White House documents showed that Bush was informed of possible events in a briefing the day before the hurricane hit, and that he had been apprised of the imminent danger in the New Orleans area.[62] Bush declared a national emergency on Saturday, August 27, and according to the Stafford Act of October 2000, the federal government is then in charge.[63] Soon after the hurricane hit, Bush, speaking in a press conference from Texas, vowed that the federal government would do everything to help the people of New Orleans.[64] However, help was not quick in coming. In December 2005, FEMA officials said they had been overwhelmed, and that local and state officials had failed to do their jobs with evacuations and shelters.[65] To date, the city of New Orleans has still not been fully rebuilt from the damage left by Hurricane Katrina.

H. Alphonso Jackson

The secretary of Housing and Urban Development in the Bush administration, Alphonso Jackson, was accused of showing political favoritism in awarding federal contracts. The allegations were made by the Philadelphia Metropolitan Housing Authority, which accused Jackson of threatening to withdraw federal aid because it did not hire one of his friends as a contractor. Jackson denied the allegations, but nonetheless decided to resign, only ten months before the end of the Bush tenure as president.[66]

I. Impeachment

Because of these scandals, there were multiple calls, from inside and outside of government, for Bush's impeachment. The reasoning included that Bush misled Congress and the American public about the war in Iraq, that he condoned the torture and abuse of prisoners, that he authorized illegal electronic surveillance on members of the American public under the guise of stopping terrorism, and that he refused to comply with subpoenas from congressional committees investigating these charges. Representative Dennis Kucinich introduced a thirty-five-count indictment against Bush, as outlined in Table 9.1. These were not addressed by the House.

**Table 9.1: Articles of Impeachment for President Bush,
by Rep. Dennis Kucinich**

Introduced in Congress June 9, 2008.

Resolved, that President George W. Bush be impeached for high crimes and misdemeanors, and that the following articles of impeachment be exhibited to the United States Senate:

Articles of impeachment exhibited by the House of Representatives of the United States of America in the name of itself and of the people of the United States of America, in maintenance and support of its impeachment against President George W. Bush for high crimes and misdemeanors.

In his conduct while President of the United States, George W. Bush, in violation of his constitutional oath to faithfully execute the office of President of the United States and, to the best of his ability, preserve, protect, and defend the Constitution of the United States, and in violation of his constitutional duty to take care that the laws be faithfully executed, has committed the following abuses of power.

1. **Article I**—Creating a Secret Propaganda Campaign to Manufacture a False Case for War Against Iraq.

2. **Article II**—Falsely, Systematically, and with Criminal Intent Conflating the Attacks of September 11, 2001, With Misrepresentation of Iraq as a Security Threat as Part of Fraudulent Justification for a War of Aggression.

3. **Article III**—Misleading the American People and Members of Congress to Believe Iraq Possessed Weapons of Mass Destruction, to Manufacture a False Case for War.

4. **Article IV**—Misleading the American People and Members of Congress to Believe Iraq Posed an Imminent Threat to the United States.

5. **Article V**—Illegally Misspending Funds to Secretly Begin a War of Aggression.

6. **Article VI**—Invading Iraq in Violation of the Requirements of HJRes114.

7. **Article VII**—Invading Iraq Absent a Declaration of War.

8. **Article VIII**—Invading Iraq, A Sovereign Nation, in Violation of the UN Charter.

9. **Article IX**—Failing to Provide Troops With Body Armor and Vehicle Armor

10. **Article X**—Falsifying Accounts of US Troop Deaths and Injuries for Political Purposes

11. **Article XI**—Establishment of Permanent U.S. Military Bases in Iraq

12. **Article XII**—Initiating a War Against Iraq for Control of That Nation's Natural Resources

13. **Article XIII**—Creating a Secret Task Force to Develop Energy and Military Policies With Respect to Iraq and Other Countries

14. **Article XIV**—Misprision of a Felony, Misuse and Exposure of Classified Information And Obstruction of Justice in the Matter of Valerie Plame Wilson, Clandestine Agent of the Central Intelligence Agency

15. **Article XV**—Providing Immunity from Prosecution for Criminal Contractors in Iraq

16. **Article XVI**—Reckless Misspending and Waste of U.S. Tax Dollars in Connection With Iraq and US Contractors

17. **Article XVII**—Illegal Detention: Detaining Indefinitely And Without Charge Persons Both U.S. Citizens and Foreign Captives

18. **Article XXVIII**—Torture: Secretly Authorizing, and Encouraging the Use of Torture Against Captives in Afghanistan, Iraq, and Other Places, as a Matter of Official Policy

19. **Article XIX**—Rendition: Kidnapping People and Taking Them Against Their Will to 'Black Sites' Located in Other Nations, Including Nations Known to Practice Torture

20. **Article XX**—Imprisoning Children

21. **Article XXI**—Misleading Congress and the American People About Threats from Iran, and Supporting Terrorist Organizations Within Iran, With the Goal of Overthrowing the Iranian Government

22. **Article XXII**—Creating Secret Laws

23. **Article XXIII**—Violation of the Posse Comitatus Act

24. **Article XXIV**—Spying on American Citizens, Without a Court-Ordered Warrant, in Violation of the Law and the Fourth Amendment

25. **Article XXV**—Directing Telecommunications Companies to Create an Illegal and Unconstitutional Database of the Private Telephone Numbers and Emails of American Citizens

26. **Article XXVI**—Announcing the Intent to Violate Laws with Signing Statements

27. **Article XXVII**—Failing to Comply with Congressional Subpoenas and Instructing Former Employees Not to Comply

28. **Article XVIII**—Tampering with Free and Fair Elections, Corruption of the Administration of Justice

29. **Article XXIX**—Conspiracy to Violate the Voting Rights Act of 1965

30. **Article XXX**—Misleading Congress and the American People in an Attempt to Destroy Medicare

31. **Article XXXI**—Katrina: Failure to Plan for the Predicted Disaster of Hurricane Katrina, Failure to Respond to a Civil Emergency

32. **Article XXXII**—Misleading Congress and the American People, Systematically Undermining Efforts to Address Global Climate Change

33. **Article XXIII**—Repeatedly Ignored and Failed to Respond to High Level Intelligence Warnings of Planned Terrorist Attacks in the US, Prior to 911.

34. **Article XXXIV**—Obstruction of the Investigation into the Attacks of September 11, 2001

35. **Article XXXV**—Endangering the Health of 911 First Responders

ARTICLES OF IMPEACHMENT FOR PRESIDENT GEORGE W. BUSH

Resolved, that President George W. Bush be impeached for high crimes and misdemeanors, and that the following articles of impeachment be exhibited to the United States Senate:

Articles of impeachment exhibited by the House of Representatives of the United States of America in the name of itself and of the people of the United States of America, in maintenance and support of its impeachment against President George W. Bush for high crimes and misdemeanors.

In his conduct while President of the United States, George W. Bush, in violation of his constitutional oath to faithfully execute the office of President of the United States and, to the best of his ability, preserve, protect, and defend the Constitution of the United States, and in violation of his constitutional duty to take care that the laws be faithfully executed, has committed the following abuses of power.

Source: http://www.impeachbush.org; accessed 7/21/2008

J. Bush: Conclusion

Many of the scandals noted here are currently being investigated, so it is difficult to predict what might happen. Some of the events have tarnished the reputations of those working in the administration and that of President Bush. Many staff members resigned in the wake of scandal. It is hard to say why the scandals in the Bush administration have not led to as many investigations as in the Clinton administration. John Dean, counsel to Richard Nixon during Watergate, provides one reason. He argues that the Bush White House created a secret government whereby the president and his staff members are obsessed with secrecy because it enables them to hide the president's weaknesses.[67] In any event, in time, we will have a better understanding of the Bush scandals and what they mean.

Political Scandals: Conclusion

Scandals are part of our political system and have been for many years, but their nature and consequences have changed.[68] Those politicians who find themselves embroiled in a scandal each have had to endure the public discovery of their unethical or immoral behavior, and intense and extended scrutiny by the media and the public of that behavior.[69] Once uncovered, those officials involved in the scandal have faced repercussions, either personal or criminal, or both. Beyond that, each of the scandals had both short- and long-term implications for society as a whole and for government. In the end, political scandals affect not only those involved, but our entire political system and social mores.

Although scandals are not unique to the American political system, they are possibly more relevant in the United States than in other countries. This is because in most parts of the world, political leaders do not run for office on the basis of their personal lives. In the United States, the personal lives of our candidates are a large part of their campaign. Our presidential candidates rarely run simply on their records, the issues, or party platforms. Instead, they place their family values, religious values, and their sexual values at the forefront. They also run on their character, charm, charisma, photogenic quality, and even their spouse's popularity or the behavior of their family members.[70] When this is tarnished, a politician's entire basis may be ruined alongside it.

A distinction can obviously be made between a sex scandal, such as Wilbur Mills or Barney Frank, and scandals related to abuse of power, such as Watergate or Abscam. One has to do with the private life of the politician, and the other the politician's professional life. As such, a politician can build up two types of reputations. One is skill-specific reputation, which refers to a person's ability to perform his or her job. This usually requires acquiring certain skills to enable that person to be efficient and effective in executing his or her responsibilities. The second type of reputation is character reputation, which refers to being a reliable and trustworthy person. If a person's reputation is seriously depleted through a scandal, it may be difficult to restore. A reputation that has taken years to build may be quickly and permanently destroyed. A scandal can easily harm or destroy a reputation, sometimes quickly, and sometimes permanently, but not always. A good reputation is more important in some fields than in others, but in politics, a good reputation is important because it is a vital source of symbolic power. Scandals can expose dishonesty or deceit, which can only damage the character or reputation of a leader.

The importance of reputation and trust can be reinforced as a result of political scandal. In a representative democracy such as ours, trust between the voters and the elected officials is essential. We have to trust our representatives to "do the right thing." When a politician errs, he or she loses that personal trust with the public. He or she may thus become ineffective in performing his or her job and in representing the voters. Scandals make people distrust politicians and government agencies and make them ineffective in performing their job tasks. Trust can be depleted in the aftermath of a scandal. Trust is an important part of social relations and interaction, but scandals can create suspicion and distrust.

Obviously the public should be made aware of wrongdoing related to a person's professional life, but the question becomes: is there a difference between a politician's personal and professional life? Can an office holder draw a line between a personal and professional career? Or are they one in the same?

To some, political scandals relating to the private sexual behavior of presidents should not be a public concern, since it does not have to do with the performance of official duties or public policy.[71] However, the opposing view is that a candidate's private life should be made public if he or she lies, no matter the circumstance.[72] Most personal scandals inherently involve lies, whether they be to family members, staff, or the public. Some raise the question: if a President cannot be trusted to be faithful to his spouse, then how can we have confidence that he will tell the truth to the American people?[73] Sexual infidelity to a spouse can be viewed as a breach of trust, a key element for elected officials. Knowing about a politician's personal life is a convenient way to assess a politician's character.[74]

Of course, simply because one is faithful to his or her spouse does not necessarily indicate that they will be a competent president. A person's sexual indiscretion is not always associated with poor presidential performance.[75] Sexual fidelity and truthfulness in an individual are not guarantees that he or she would make a good president.[76] Just like average citizens, presidents can act wisely in some areas and show very poor judgment in others.[77] It can be argued that those who succumb were simply tantalized by the temptations of power.[78] However, if one supposes that one purpose of government, and the presidency in particular, is to elevate, educate, and enlighten the people, then those entrusted with public office should represent the finest moral examples.[79] Presidents can serve as inspirations and provide good examples,[80] but they can also do the opposite.

But scandals now are being used in a different way. Now, a person's ethics and morals (or lack thereof) are used as a political weapon.[81] The country is criminalizing political differences by using multiple investigations and threats of impeachment.[82] Impeachment may be more of a political, rather than a legal, proceeding.[83] It has become easy for members of Congress to bring charges against a president simply as a way to ruin his reputation, whether there has been criminal wrongdoing or not. In fact, Nixon often said that the modern political scandal really was less about the scandalous behavior itself than about the political agenda of the opponents who were launching the allegations. He believed that Watergate was about his stands against Alger Hiss and the Vietnam War. Secord believed that the Iran-Contra investigation was an attack by congressional Democrats who finally had the opportunity they had been seeking since Watergate to return the White House to Democratic control.[84] The Whitewater investigation was about Democrats who condemned the greed of the 1980s and then indulged in it themselves and tried to conceal it. Each scandal was a pretext, designed to remove enemies.[85] If this is true, as long as the system remains dominated by ideological opposites, the temptation to bring the other side down through professional or personal scandal will be unavoidable.[86]

Scandal Consequences

As the previous chapters show, there are consequences to every scandal. Some of the impacts are as follows:

New laws are created: New rules, laws, and procedures are often the result of scandals. The new legislation is an attempt to prevent future scandal in some way. There have been new laws and regulations that require more records, more agency openness, and more investigators. These have each made it more likely than before that the violators will get caught.[87]

Removal from office: Political scandals often lead to ruined political careers and removal from office, either through impeachment, resignation, or a failure to win reelection. Many times, a politician's public life is over, and they must find an alternative career.

Punishment: Often, but not always, a politician involved in a scandal will face punishment. There are a wide variety of punishments that have been used. Sometimes a reprimand is used, or a censure. For more serious offenses, impeachment or even imprisonment are used.

Loss of public morale and growing public cynicism: Our views of politicians and government have changed because of scandals. Many citizens have lost faith in public institutions because they are run by corrupt or incompetent people who are in office for the perks rather than to do a job. In short, scandals tend to deepen public cynicism about politics.[88]

Permanent investigative agencies: Scandals have resulted in the development of permanent investigative agencies to look into allegations of illegal or unethical behavior. Because of tighter ethics rules, independent counsels to investigate the executive branch have been created, as have permanent investigative units in most major media outlets.

Changes in elections and campaigns: Political scandals and allegations of such have become important elements in campaigns. Such charges have been incorporated into the campaign strategies of both parties. Further, when one party attacks, the other promises or seeks revenge.

Changes in the media: There has been a change in the way the press deals with politicians as a result of scandals. The media now ask questions of politicians and demand answers.[89] The public wants to know if their elected officials are being honest and truthful. The media's efforts to report more about the candidates and officeholders means that the news media are more likely to print rumors and innuendos that in years past would not have been considered newsworthy. The media, especially the new media, are likely to use scandal as entertainment news. Today's journalists have increased incentives to investigate the private as well as public conduct of public figures in far greater depth and detail than previously.[90] This has inspired journalists to seek out scandals.[91] Some journalists pounce on any scandal no matter how trivial and blow it up to Watergate proportions to advance their careers.[92]

Loss of attention to significant national issues: An administration may have a difficult time functioning during and after a scandal. It might have to spend a lot of time trying to deal with the charges and investigation, rather than enacting their legislative agenda. A full-fledged scandal, or even charges of one, can divert energy from other activities such as a critical analysis or debate of the real and serious problems facing the country. The public's preoccupation with scandal may undermine public discourse about important policies.[93] In many cases, the public would rather hear about lurid stories concerning an officeholder's personal indiscretions than substantive problems facing the nation. While this is happening, the public is not learning about the issues facing the country. At the same time, members of Congress may become involved with hearings and investigations, rather than debating needed legislation. At the same time, legislators are not passing needed laws.[94]

Good people may be prevented from getting involved in public life: Some dedicated people may choose to stay out of politics completely because of a fear of intense and unwanted scrutiny by the media and the toll it may take on them and their families.[95] The private lives of national public figures are now featured prominently in the news.[96] Some people may be discouraged from seeking public office because of the scrutiny under which they and their families and friends must live.[97] In this sense, the media has replaced the political parties as the screening committee for candidates and officeholders. Conversely, more intense scrutiny by the press and opponents can drive away unqualified politicians, or those who seek personal rewards from public office.[98] It can increase public accountability or even foster more realistic attitudes about the human fallibility of elected leaders.

Effects on politicians: Scandals affect politicians in many ways. As mentioned, they must deal with the media scrutiny of their private lives, which might affect their marriage and family. Of course, if a scandal erupts, it can have a bigger impact on a politician's marriage and family. Scandals affect politicians in another way, too. Not only are officeholders much more afraid of the media, those inside government are afraid to make an honest written record of their actions for fear that some enemy will get hold of it and use it to damage them and their reputation.[99] This means that there are few written records of events for historical purposes.

Effects on voters: Some voters are concerned that the media is screening candidates rather than allowing the normal process that allows the voters to choose who is a viable or acceptable candidate. Additionally, there is concern that the media provides a great amount of information on a candidate's personal life rather than focusing on his or her policy stances. This means that voters may be less informed when they walk into their polling places. In the long run, there is a greater chance that unqualified candidates will be elected.

Every political scandal has some consequences. They impact those directly involved in the events. Some involved in scandal may face only temporary inconveniences. For most others, however, there can be long-term, even fatal consequences. The reputations and careers of those investigated are often badly damaged or ruined.[100] The person involved will probably lose his or her job and may find the prospects for getting another one severely reduced.[101] Legal bills can be staggering to those directly involved, and they may face severe financial problems.[102] Some may face criminal fines, probation, or even prison.

The impact of political scandals does not stop there. They influence others, such as staff members who may lose their jobs if an officeholder is impeached, for example. Other family members are impacted. On a broad level, government is impacted through new laws or because of a lack of trust.

The ultimate impact of a scandal depends on the political context and social climate in which they occur. Many factors can influence the form, speed, and tone of the public's reaction.[103] Whether revelations about a politician's private life will cost a person his or her office depends on a number of variables. Factors that can influence the impact of scandal include the timing in the electoral cycle, the partisan balance in Congress and the party of the president, the president's approval ratings or public support, the politician's response, the quality of his or her opponent, and the press coverage.[104] Obviously, the facts of the scandal are critical. In Watergate, the misbehavior was serious and the evidence of Nixon's involvement was overwhelming. On the other hand, in the Iran-Contra scandal, the responsibility was blurred and certain outcomes could be positively valued. In Whitewater, the facts of the case were ambiguous.[105]

In the end, it is difficult to maintain that scandals have had no significant and determinate impact.[106] Instead, they have changed many things, sometimes significantly. They have impacted those involved, the media, policy debates, and laws. They have had an influence on candidates, voters, and the political system. They have impacted society and the norms and mores by which we all live.

Conclusion

Scandals are part of government and have long-term impacts. They impact not only those involved but others as well, including the country. Even though new laws have been passed to decrease the opportunities for scandal,[107] they continue to occur.

Is it possible to reduce the number of scandals that occur? One proposal to reduce scandal and corruption is to increase the risk of getting caught.[108] This would mean even more media scrutiny and oversight than currently exists. Beyond that, a free press that reported to the people about events and people's actions and made them aware of any abuses of power is essential.[109] Preventing scandal may also involve more investigations by special prosecutors, or some similar body, appointed to investigate and prevent wrongdoing. This type of system, used in America for the past 200 years, has worked to bring immoral behavior to light and punish those who were guilty.[110]

All in all, it appears as if the flood of scandal shows no sign of abating any time soon.[111] The attraction of ordinary citizens to the drama and suspense that surrounds political scandal, the readiness of the media to cater to this attraction, and the potential rewards for a media outlet or reporter to expose and publicize possible wrongdoing will continue to come together and result in scandal. In the next few years, there will undoubtedly be public officials accused of serious offenses and subjected to investigation.[112] Political scandals seem to be an inescapable part of American politics. They are here to stay and it is essential that we understand their nature and significance.[113]

Notes

Chapter 1

1. Alan Feuer, "Four Charged with Running Online Prostitution Ring," *New York Times*, March 7, 2008; Stephanie Gaskell and Bill Hutchinson, "Jersey Girl Is Revealed as Kristen," *New York Daily News*, March 13, 2008.

2. Marcus Franklin, "Law Tied to Spitzer Scandal was Used Vs. Famous Men," *The (Canton, Ohio) Repository* (Associated Press), March 17, 2008, A-2; Amy Westfeldt and and Michael Gormley, "Unraveling Spitzer's Bank Accounts," *The (Canton, Ohio) Repository* (Associated Press), March 16, 2008, A-1.

3. Ellen Wulfhorst, "Sex Scandal Passes but Spitzer May Face Legal Woes," March 13, 2008, http://www.reuters.com; retrieved 7/16/2008.

4. Danny Hakim and Ian Urbina, "Spitzer Charged Campaign for Hotel Bills, Raising Questions on His Use of Funds," *New York Times*, July 16, 2008, http://www.nytimes.com, accessed 7/16/2008.

5. Danny Hakim, "Eliot Spitzer," *New York Times*, July 16, 2008, http://wwwtopics. nytimes.com; accessed 7/16/2008.

6. Ellen Wulfhorst, "Sex Scandal Passes but Spitzer May Face Legal Woes," March 13, 2008, Reuters; http://www.reuters.com; retrieved 7/16/2008.

7. Amy Westfeldt,"N.Y. Governor Linked by Feds to Prostitution," *Akron (Ohio) Beacon Journal* March 11, 2008, A-1.

8. Lynn Sweet, "Blagojevich's Conduct Audacious, Raises Questions About Filling Seat" *Chicago Sun Times* December 9, 2008, (http://www.suntimes.com/news/sweet/ 1321678,blagojevich-sweet-120908.article; accessed 3/7/2009; "Charges Claim Illinois Governor Blagojevich Sought to Sell Obama's Senate Seat" *Chicago Sun Times* December 9, 2008, http://www. suntimes.com/news/metro/blagojevich/1321363,Blagojevich-Obama-Senate; accessed 3/7/2009.

9. Natasha Korecki and Abdon M. Pallasch, "Illinois Governor Rod Blagojevich Taken Into Federal Custody" *Chicago Sun Times* December 9, 2008; http://www.suntimes.com/news/ metro/blagojevich/1321300,rod-blagojevich-illinois-governor; accessed 3/7/2009.

10. "Blagojevich Returns to Work a Day After Arrest" *Chicago Sun Times* December 10, 2008; http://www.suntimes.com/news/metro/blagojevich/1323576,blagojevich-corrupt-governor; accessed 3/7/2009.

11. Dave McKinney, "Obama Calls for Illinois Governor Rod Blagojevich to Resign" *Chicago Sun Times* December 11, 2008; http://www.suntimes.com/news/politics/obama/ 1323708,obama-blagojevich-resign-governor; accessed 3/7/2009.

12. Dave McKinney, "House Committee Begins Blagojevich Impeachment Exploration" *Chicago Sun Times* December 16, 2008; http://www.suntimes.com/news/metro/blagojevich/1333956,house-panel-blagojevich; accessed 3/7/2009.

13. Dave McKinney and Jordan Wilson, "Illinois House Votes to Impeach Gov. Blagojevich" *Chicago Sun Times* January 9, 2009; http://www.suntimes.com/news/metro/blagojevich/1369667,blagojevich-impeach-vote; accessed 3/7/2009.

14. Dave McKinney, Chris Fusco and Carol Marin, "Senate Votes 59–0 to Impeach Blagojevich" *Chicago Sun Times* January 30, 2009; http://www.suntimes.com/news/metro/blagojevich/1403925,blagojevich-arrives-senate; accessed 3/7/2009.

15. Suzanne Garment, *Scandal: The Culture of Mistrust in American Politics* (New York: Anchor Books, 1991): 2.

16. *Ibid.*

17. Mark Grossman, *Political Corruption in America* (Santa Barbara, CA: ABC Clio, 2003): x.

18. Garment, *Scandal*: 109; Robert Williams, *Political Scandals in the USA* (Chicago: Fitzroy Dearborn, 1998): 4.

19. Paul J. Quirk, "Scandal Time: The Clinton Impeachment and the Distraction of American Politics," in Mark J. Rozell and Clyde Wilcox, eds; *The Clinton Scandal* (Washington, DC: Georgetown University Press, 2000, 119–141): 130.

20. John B. Thompson, *Political Scandal: Power and Visibility in the Media Age* (Malden, MA: Polity, 2000): 114.

21. Quirk, *Scandal Time*: 120.

22. James B. Stewart, *Bold Sport: The President and His Adversaries* (New York: Simon and Schuster, 1996): 39.

23. Myra MacPherson, *The Power Lovers* (New York: Ballantine Books, 1976): 255.

24. Garment, *Scandal*: 2.

25. Williams, *Political Scandals*: 1.

26. Quirk, *Scandal Time*: 119.

27. Williams, *Political Scandals*: 1–2.

28. Susan J. Tolchin and Martin Tolchin, *Glass Houses: Congressional Ethics and the Politics of Venom* (Cambridge, MA: Westview Press, 2001): 9.

29. Quirk, *Scandal Time*: 120.

30. *Ibid.*: 119.

31. Ibid: 130, citing Garment, *Scandal*; Williams, *Political Scandals*: 5.

32. Jeffrey D. Schultz, *Presidential Scandals* (Washington, DC: CQ Press, 2000): xviii; Mark Grossman, *Political Corruption in America* (Santa Barbara, CA: ABC Clio, 2003): x.

33. Garment, *Scandal*: 14.

34. Thompson, *Political Scandal*: 15.

35. Schultz, *Presidential Scandals*.

36. *Ibid.*

37. *Ibid.*

38. Sam Dillon, "Lurid Memoir Reminds Mexicans of Salinas Days," *New York Times*, July 24, 2000, A3.

39. Stephanie Strom, "Top Adviser to Japan's Premier at Center of a Political Scandal," *New York Times*, August 3, 2000, A11.

40. "Cheng Kejie Executed for Corruption" People's Daily Online, September 15, 2000; http://english.peopledaily.com.cn/english/200009/14/eng20000914_50513.html; accessed 3/2/2009.

41. Craig S. Smith, "Senior Chinese Official Sentenced to Death in Corruption Case," *New York Times,* August 1, 2000, A4.

42. "Videotape Seems to Show Aide to Fujimori Bribing Opposition," *New York Times,* September 16, 2000, A7.

43. Thompson, *Political Scandal*: 17, 131–137.

44. Williams, *Political Scandals*: 3.

45. Thompson, *Political Scandal*: 16.

46. Williams, *Political Scandals*: 3.

47. Russ Witcher, "The Media," in Harry P. Jeffrey and Thomas Maxwell-Long, eds., *Watergate and the Resignation of Richard Nixon: Impact of a Constitutional Crisis* (Washington, DC: CQ Press, 2004, 113–124): 122.

48. Quirk, *Scandal Time*: 130.

49. MacPherson, *Power Lovers*: 256.

50. *Ibid.*: 264.

51. *Ibid.*: 262.

52. *Ibid.*: 207.

53. Larry J. Sabato, *Feeding Frenzy* (New York: Free Press, 1991): 16.

54. Joe Mandak, "Pa. Senator Cleared in Suicide," *Centre Daily (Pennsylvania) Times,* July 12, 2008, A4.

55. Sabato, *Feeding Frenzy*: 17.

56. Grossman, *Political Corruption*: 54–55.

57. Thompson, *Political Scandal*: 91.

58. *Ibid.*: 13.

59. *Ibid.*: 14; Grossman, *Political Corruption*: ix.

60. Grossman, *Political Corruption*: ix.

61. Schultz, *Presidential Scandals*: xv.

62. Williams, *Political Scandals:* 6.

63. Thompson, *Political Scandal*: 22.

64. Williams, *Political Scandals*: 6.

65. *Ibid.*

66. *Ibid.*

67. *Ibid.*: 7.

68. *Ibid.*: 6.

69. Grossman, *Political Corruption*: x.

70. Williams, *Political Scandals:* 7.

71. Grossman, *Political Corruption*: x.

72. Williams, *Political Scandals*: 8.

73. Thompson, *Political Scandal*: 91.

74. Williams, *Political Scandal*: 8.

75. Thompson, *Political Scandal*: 18.

76. Williams, *Political Scandal*: 8.

77. *Ibid.*: 12.

78. Thompson, *Political Scandal*: 17.

79. *Ibid.*: 19.
80. *Ibid.*: 20.
81. *Ibid.*: 28.
82. Schultz, *Presidential Scandals*: xv.
83. Thompson, *Political Scandal*: 25.
84. Sabato, *Feeding Frenzy*: 8–9.
85. *Ibid.*: 10.
86. *Ibid.*
87. *Ibid.*: 12.
88. Frank Rich, "Journal: Closet Clout," *New York Times*, 1995.
89. Thompson, *Political Scandal*: 5.
90. *Ibid.*: 5.
91. Williams, *Political Scandals*: 5.
92. Thompson, *Political Scandal*: 7.
93. Michael Schudson, "Notes on Scandal and the Watergate Legacy," *American Behavioral Scientist*, 47 (2004), 1231–1238: 1236.
94. Quirk, *Scandal Time*: 130.
95. Stanley G. Hilton and Anne-Renee Testa, *Glass Houses* (New York: St. Martin's, 1998): 14.
96. MacPherson, *Power Lovers*: 8–9.
97. *Ibid.*: 9.
98. Benjamin Ginsberg and Martin Shefter, *Politics by Other Means* (New York: Norton, 1999); David E. Kyvig, *The Age of Impeachment* (Lawrence: University Press of Kansas, 2008): 388.
99. Ginsberg and Shefter, *Politics*.
100. Garment, *Scandal*: 10; Harry P. Jeffrey and Thomas Maxwell-Long, *Watergate and the Resignation of Richard Nixon: Impact of a Constitutional Crisis* (Washington, DC: CQ Press, 2004): xi; Williams, *Political Scandals*: 10.
101. Ginsberg and Shefter, *Politics*: 29.
102. *Ibid.*: 26–28.
103. *Ibid.*
104. Quirk, *Scandal Time*: 130, citing Ginsberg and Shefter, *Politics*.
105. Quirk, *Scandal Time*: 131.
106. *Ibid.*: 132; Michael Schudson, *Watergate in American Memory* (New York: Basic Books, 1992): 163; Stephen Early Bennett, "Another Lesson about Public Opinion during the Clinton-Lewinsky Scandal," *Presidential Studies Quarterly*, 32 (2002) 276–292: 285.
107. Garment, *Scandal*: 7.
108. Williams, *Political Scandals*: 4.
109. Thompson, *Political Scandal*: 106.
110. Garment, *Scandal*: 169.
111. Thompson, *Political Scandal*: 107.
112. Garment, *Scandal*: 109.
113. Thompson, *Political Scandal*: 147.
114. *Ibid.*: 148.
115. Garment, *Scandal*: 5.
116. *Ibid.*: *Scandal*: 2.
117. Williams, *Political Scandals*: 4.

118. Thompson, *Political Scandal*: 109.

119. Larry Sabato, Mark Stencel, and S. Robert Lichter, *Peepshow: Media and Politics in an Age of Scandal* (Lanham, MD: Rowman and Littlefield, 2000).

120. John Anthony Maltese, "The Media: The New Media and the Lure of the Clinton Scandal," in Mark J. Rozell and Clyde Wilcox, eds., *The Clinton Scandal* (Washington, DC: Georgetown University Press, 2000), 195–210: 208.

121. Schultz, *Presidential Scandals*: xvi.

122. Diana Owen, "Popular Politics and the Clinton/Lewinsky Affair: The Implications for Leadership," *Political Psychology*, 21 (2000) 161–177: 162.

123. *Ibid.*: 162.

124. *Ibid.*: 162.

125. Maltese, "The Media": 198.

126. Owen, "Popular Politics": 162.

127. *Ibid.*: 163.

128. *Ibid.*: 164, 174.

129. Sabato, *Feeding Frenzy*: 136.

130. *Ibid.*: 5.

131. *Ibid.*: 55.

132. *Ibid.*: 139.

133. *Ibid.*: 3.

134. Thompson, *Political Scandal*: ix.

135. Owen, "Popular Politics": 167.

136. Sabato, *Feeding Frenzy*: 55–56.

137. Thompson, *Political Scandal*: 32.

138. Garment, *Scandal*: 10.

139. Sabato, *Feeding Frenzy*: 57.

140. *Ibid.*: 25.

141. Williams, *Political Scandal*: 128.

142. Sabato, *Feeding Frenzy*: 26.

143. *Ibid.*

144. *Ibid.*

145. *Ibid.*: 59.

146. *Ibid.*: 61.

147. *Ibid.*: 46.

148. *Ibid.*: 69.

149. Thompson, *Political Scandal*: 147.

150. Gene Lyons, *Fools for Scandal* (New York: Franklin Square Press, 1996): 6.

151. Marion Just and Ann Crigler, "Leadership Image-Building: After Clinton and Watergate," *Political Psychology*, 21 (2000): 179–198.

152. *Ibid.*: 180.

153. Robert J. Spitzer, "The Presidency: The Clinton Crisis and Its Consequences," in Mark J. Rozell and Clyde Wilcox, eds., *The Clinton Scandal* (Washington, DC: Georgetown University Press, 2000, 1–17): 12.

154. David E. Kyvig, *The Age of Impeachment* (Lawrence: University Press of Kansas, 2008): 319.

155. Garment, *Scandal*: 173.

156. Thompson, *Political Scandal*: x.

157. John W. Dean, *Warren G. Harding* (New York: Times Books, 2004): 99.

158. Sabato, *Feeding Frenzy*: 30.

159. Howard Kurtz, *Spin Cycle: Inside the Clinton Propaganda Machine* (New York: Free Press, 1998): xx.

160. Sabato, *Feeding Frenzy*: 31.

161. *Ibid.*: 34.

162. Kurtz, *Spin Cycle*: xx.

163. *Ibid.*

164. Sabato, *Feeding Frenzy*: 43.

165. Hilton and Testa, *Glass Houses*: 16.

166. Kurtz, *Spin Cycle*: xx.

167. *Ibid.*: xxi.

168. Elizabeth Drew, *Richard M. Nixon* (New York: Times Books, 2007): 37.

169. Kyvig, *Age of Impeachment*: 120.

170. Monica Crowley, *Nixon off the Record* (New York: Random House, 1996): 65.

171. Kurtz, *Spin Cycle*: xviii.

172. *Ibid.*: 69–77.

173. *Ibid.*: xvi.

174. MacPherson, *Power Lovers:* xii.

175. Larry Sabato and S. Robert Lichter, *When Should the Watchdogs Bark?: Media Coverage of the Clinton Scandals* (Washington, DC: Center for Media and Public Affairs, 1994): 6.

176. MacPherson, *Power Lovers*: xii.

177. Michael Isikoff, *Uncovering Clinton: A Reporter's Story* (New York: Crown, 1999): 353.

178. Sabato and Lichter, *Watchdogs*.

179. *Ibid.*: 62–3; Sabato, Stencel, and Lichter, *Peep Show*; Sabato, *Feeding Frenzy*.

180. Michael J. Gerhardt, "The Impeachment and Acquittal of President William Jefferson Clinton," in Mark J. Rozell and Clyde Wilcox, eds., *The Clinton Scandal* (Washington, DC: Georgetown University Press, 2000, 142–170): 147.

Chapter 2

1. Suzanne Garment, *Scandal: The Culture of Mistrust in American Politics* (New York: Anchor Books, 1991): 84.

2. Katy J. Harriger, "Special Prosecutors and Independent Counsels," in Harry P. Jeffrey and Thomas Maxwell-Long, eds., *Watergate and the Resignation of Richard Nixon: Impact of a Constitutional Crisis* (Washington, DC: CQ Press, 2004, 47–61): 52.

3. Michael Schudson, *Watergate in American Memory* (New York: Basic Books, 1992): 89.

4. *Ibid.*

5. Harriger, "Special Prosecutors": 51.

6. Garment, *Scandal*: 85; Harriger, "Special Prosecutors": 47.

7. Thomas A. Kazee, "The Congress: the Politics of Impeachment," in Mark J. Rozell and Clyde Wilcox, eds., *The Clinton Scandal* (Washington, DC: Georgetown University Press, 2000, 18–39): 21.

8. Schudson, *Watergate*: 88; Mark Grossman, *Political Corruption in America* (Santa Barbara, CA: ABC Clio, 2003): 117.

9. Schudson, *Watergate*: 94.

10. Garment, *Scandal*: 99.

11. Harriger, "Special Prosecutors": 54.

12. "Congress Extends Special-Prosecutor Law" *Congressional Quarterly Almanac* (Washington, DC: CQ Press, 1987, 363–366).

13. Louis Fisher, "The Independent Counsel Statute," in Mark J. Rozell and Clyde Wilcox, eds., *The Clinton Scandal* (Washington, DC: Georgetown University Press, 2000, 60–80): 64; Garment, *Scandal*: 99–100; Schudson, *Watergate*: 94–95; Grossman, *Political Corruption*: 117.

14. Garment, *Scandal*: 105.

15. *Ibid.*: 100.

16. *Ibid.*: 105.

17. Fisher, "Independent Counsel": 64.

18. Garment, *Scandal*: 106.

19. Leon Friedman, "Separation of Powers," in Harry P. Jeffrey and Thomas Maxwell-Long, eds., *Watergate and the Resignation of Richard Nixon: Impact of a Constitutional Crisis* (Washington, DC: CQ Press, 2004, 31–46): 44.

20. David E. Kyvig, *The Age of Impeachment* (Lawrence: University Press of Kansas, 2008): 320; Grossman, *Political Corruption:* 234.

21. Paul J. Quirk, "Scandal Time: The Clinton Impeachment and the Distraction of American Politics," in Mark J. Rozell and Clyde Wilcox, eds., *The Clinton Scandal* (Washington, DC: Georgetown University Press, 2000, 119–141): 134.

22. "Independent Counsel Law Expires" *Congressional Quarterly Almanac* (Washington, DC: CQ Press, 1992, 315–317).

23. Fisher, "Independent Counsel": 64.

24. Grossman, *Political Corruption*: 117; The Oyez Project, *United States v. National Treasury Employees Union,* 513 U.S. 454 (1995), available at http://www.oyez.org/cases, accessed 7/16/2008.

25. Harriger, "Special Prosecutors": 47, 59.

26. *Ibid.*

27. *Ibid.*: 48.

28. *Ibid.*: 47.

29. *Ibid.*: 59.

30. *Ibid.*

31. Oliver L. North, *Under Fire: An American Story* (New York: Harper Collins, 1991): 454.

32. *Ibid.*

33. Harriger, "Special Prosecutors": 59.

34. Garment, *Scandal*: 90.

35. James B. Stewart, *Bold Sport: The President and his Adversaries* (New York: Simon and Schuster, 1996): 370.

36. Harriger, "Special Prosecutors": 54.

37. *Ibid.*: 54; Schudson, *Watergate*: 93.

38. Schudson, *Watergate*: 93.

39. Harriger, "Special Prosecutors": 54; Garment, *Scandal*: 91–93.

40. Garment, *Scandal*: 87.

41. *Ibid.*

42. *Ibid.*: 88.

43. Harriger, "Special Prosecutors": 57.

44. Fisher, "Independent Counsel": 60.

45. *Ibid.*: 64.

46. Alan M. Dershowitz, *Sexual McCarthyism* (New York: Basic Books, 1998): 11–12; Karen O'Connor and John R. Hermann, "The Courts: The Perils of Paula," in Mark J. Rozell and Clyde Wilcox, eds., *The Clinton Scandal* (Washington, DC: Georgetown University Press, 2000, 40–59): 51; Fisher, "Independent Counsel": 66.

47. Dershowitz, *Sexual McCarthyism*: 70.

48. Ibid,: 10.

49. *Ibid.*

50. *Ibid.*: 40.

51. *Ibid.*: 76.

52. Schudson, *Watergate*: 92.

53. Dershowitz, *Sexual McCarthyism*: 76.

54. *Ibid.*: 9.

55. *Ibid.*: 41.

56. *Ibid.*: 31.

57. Kyvig, *Age of Impeachment*: 114.

58. Michael J. Gerhardt, "The Impeachment and Acquittal of President William Jefferson Clinton," in Mark J. Rozell and Clyde Wilcox, eds., *The Clinton Scandal* (Washington, DC: Georgetown University Press, 2000, 142–170): 154.

59. Dershowitz, *Sexual McCarthyism*: 31.

60. *Ibid.*: 186.

61. *Ibid.*: 186–87.

62. Kyvig, *Age of Impeachment*: 6.

63. *Ibid.*: 1.

64. *Ibid.*: 2.

65. *Ibid.*: 5.

66. *Ibid.*: 9–10.

67. *Ibid.*: 9.

68. *Ibid.*: 10.

69. *Ibid.*

Chapter 3

1. Robert Williams, *Political Scandals in the USA* (Chicago: Fitzroy Dearborn, 1998): 1.

2. Jeffrey Schultz, *Presidential Scandals* (Washington, DC: CQ Press, 2000): 3.

3. Wesley O. Hagood, *Presidential Sex: From the Founding Fathers to Bill Clinton* (Secaucus, NJ: Citadel Press, 1998): 10.

4. *Ibid.*: 10.

5. Schultz, *Presidential Scandals*: 3.

6. Nigel Cawthorne, *Sex Lives of the Presidents* (New York: St. Martin's Press, 1996): vii.

7. *Ibid.*: vii.

8. Myra MacPherson, *The Power Lovers* (New York: Ballantine Books, 1976): 203; Cawthorne, *Sex Lives*: vii; Hagood, *Presidential Sex*: 8.

9. James MacGregor Burns and Susan Dunn, *George Washington* (New York: Times Books, 2004): 134; Kenneth T. Walsh, "Sex, Lies, and Major Headlines," *U.S. News and World Report*, January 28–February 4, 2008, 36–37.

10. Schultz, *Presidential Scandals*: 3.

11. *Ibid.*: 4.

12. *Ibid.*: 3.

13. John B. Thompson, *Political Scandal: Power and Visibility in the Media Age* (Malden, MA: Polity Press, 2000): 143.

14. Suzanne Garment, *Scandal: The Culture of Mistrust in American Politics* (New York: Anchor Books, 1991): 17.

15. Schultz, *Presidential Scandals*: 7.

16. *Ibid.*: 5.

17. *Ibid.*: 8.

18. Alf J. Mapp Jr., *Thomas Jefferson: Passionate Pilgrim* (New York: Madison Books, 1991): 364.

19. Schultz, *Presidential Scandals*: 23; Hagood, *Presidential Sex*: 12.

20. Schultz, *Presidential Scandals*: 23.

21. Fawn M. Brodie, *Thomas Jefferson: An Intimate History* (New York: Norton, 1974): 221–227.

22. Schultz, *Presidential Scandals*: 23.

23. Shannon Lanier and Jane Feldman, *Jefferson's Children* (New York: Random House, 2000).

24. Schultz, *Presidential Scandals*: 24; Mapp, *Thomas Jefferson*: 35.

25. Lanier and Feldman, *Jefferson's Children*.

26. Brodie, *Thomas Jefferson*: 228–245.

27. Mapp, *Thomas Jefferson*: 34.

28. Lanier and Feldman, *Jefferson's Children*.

29. *Ibid.*

30. Schultz, *Presidential Scandals*: 24.

31. Mapp, *Thomas Jefferson*: 35; Brodie, *Thomas Jefferson*: 357, 315–323, 348–349; Lanier and Feldman, *Jefferson's Children*; Joshua Rothman, "James Callender and Social Knowledge of Interracial Sex in Antebellum Virginia," in Jan Ellen Lewis and Peter S. Onuf, eds., *Sally Hemings and Thomas Jefferson* (Charlottesville: University Press of Virginia, 1999): 87–113.

32. Thompson, *Political Scandal*: 144.

33. Hagood, *Presidential Sex*: 19; Brodie, *Thomas Jefferson*: 367, 374.

34. Schultz, *Presidential Scandals*: 43; C. Vann Woodward, *Responses of the Presidents to Charges of Misconduct* (New York: Delacorte Press, 1974): 47.

35. Schultz, *Presidential Scandals*: 54; Woodward, *Responses*: 55–57.

36. Schultz, *Presidential Scandals*: 55; Cawthorne, *Sex Lives*: 55.

37. Robert V. Remini, *Andrew Jackson* (Baltimore: Johns Hopkins University Press, 1998): 91.

38. *Ibid.*: 37–38.

39. *Ibid.*: 143.

40. Schultz, *Presidential Scandals*: 59.

41. Garment, *Scandal*: 18.

42. Remini, *Andrew Jackson*: 57–69.

43. Cawthorne, *Sex Lives*: 67; Hagood, *Presidential Sex*: 27.

44. Sean Wilentz, *Andrew Jackson* (New York: Times Books, 2005): 21.

45. *Ibid.*: 24.

46. *Ibid.*: 25.

47. *Ibid.*: 40.

48. Schultz, *Presidential Scandals*: 63–64; Arthur M. Schlesinger Jr., *The Age of Jackson* (New York: Mentor Books, 1945); Woodward, *Responses*: 62–65.

49. Schultz, *Presidential Scandals*: 69.

50. John Niven, *Martin Van Buren* (New York: Oxford University Press, 1983). Joel H. Silbey, *Martin Van Buren and the Emergence of American Popular Politics* (New York: Rowman and Littlefield, 2002).

51. Schultz, *Presidential Scandals*: 72.

52. Cawthorne, *Sex Lives*: 74.

53. Woodward, *Responses*: 71–77.

54. Cawthorne, *Sex Lives*: viii.

55. Schultz, *Presidential Scandals*: 97; Cawthorne, *Sex Lives*: 90.

56. Hagood, *Presidential Sex*: 34–39.

57. Cawthorne, *Sex Lives*: 92.

58. *Ibid.*: viii; Hagood, *Presidential Sex*: 41.

59. Woodward, *Responses*: 98.

60. *Ibid.*: 97.

61. *Ibid.*: 99–100.

62. Cawthorne, *Sex Lives*: 103.

63. Schultz, *Presidential Scandals*: 113; Woodward, *Responses*: 119.

64. Schultz, *Presidential Scandals*: 114.

65. Woodward, *Responses*: 113–114; Nathan Miller, *Stealing from America* (New York: ParagonHouse, 1992): 148.

66. Cawthorne, *Sex Lives*: 109.

67. Schultz, *Presidential Scandals*: 124.

68. Emily Van Tassel and Paul Finkelman, *Impeachable Offenses* (Washington, DC: Congressional Quarterly, 1999): 223.

69. David E. Kyvig, *The Age of Impeachment* (Lawrence: University Press of Kansas, 2008): 26–27.

70. Van Tassel and Finkelman, *Impeachable Offenses*: 221; Alan M. Dershowitz, *Sexual McCarthyism* (New York: Basic Books, 1998): 33.

71. Kyvig, *Age of Impeachment*: 26.

72. Van Tassel and Finkelman, *Impeachable Offenses*: 222.

73. Kyvig, *Age of Impeachment*: 26.

74. *Ibid.*

75. Dershowitz, *Sexual McCarthyism*: 33.

76. Kyvig, *Age of Impeachment*: 27.

77. Van Tassel and Finkelman, *Impeachable Offenses*: 221.

78. *Ibid.*: 222.

79. William S. McFeely, *Ulysses S. Grant* (New York: Norton, 2004): 42.

80. Schultz, *Presidential Scandals*: 154.

81. Woodward, *Responses*: 134–137; Miller, *Stealing*: 164–182.

82. Van Tassel and Finkelman, *Impeachable Offenses*: 192.

83. Garment, *Scandal*: 3.

84. Van Tassel and Finkelman, *Impeachable Offenses:* 193; Woodward, *Responses*: 151; Mark Grossman, *Political Corruption in America* (Santa Barbara, CA: ABC Clio, 2003): 23–25.

85. Woodward, *Responses*: 151.

86. Van Tassel and Finkelman, *Impeachable Offenses*: 193.

87. Kyvig, *Age of Impeachment*: 30.

88. Grossman, *Political Corruption*: 83.

89. Woodard, *Responses*: 146.

90. Grossman, *Political Corruption*: 83; Woodward, *Responses*: 146.

91. Grossman, *Political Corruption*: 84.

92. *Ibid.*

93. Woodward, *Responses*: 146.

94. Grossman, *Political Corruption*: 85.

95. Woodward, *Responses*: 146.

96. Grossman, *Political Corruption*: 84–85.

97. Schultz, *Presidential Scandals*: 158.

98. *Ibid.*: 156; Woodward, *Responses*: 163–5.

99. Woodward, *Responses*: 164.

100. Schultz, *Presidential Scandals*: 169; Cawthorne, *Sex Lives*: 120; Hagood, *Presidential Sex*: 46–52.

101. Cawthorne, *Sex Lives*: viii; Hagood, *Presidential Sex*: 54.

102. Schultz, *Presidential Scandals*: 169; Hagood, *Presidential Sex*: 53–54.

103. Grossman, *Political Corruption*: 139.

104. Cawthorne, *Sex Lives*: 125.

105. Henry F. Graff, *Grover Cleveland* (New York: Times Books, 2002): 38.

106. *Ibid.*: 36.

107. MacPherson, *Power Lovers*: 203; Cawthorne, *Sex Lives*: viii.

108. Graff, *Grover Cleveland*: 60.

109. *Ibid.*

110. *Ibid.*: 61.

111. *Ibid.*

112. *Ibid.*: 61; Schultz, *Presidential Scandals*: 181; Hagood, *Presidential Sex:* 60; Thompson, *Political Scandal*: 144.

113. Graff, *Grover Cleveland*: 61.

114. Walsh, "Sex, Lies, and Major Headlines."

115. Hagood, *Presidential Sex*: 63; MacPherson, *Power Lovers*: 203.

116. Hagood, *Presidential Sex*: 64.

117. Kevin Phillips, *William McKinley* (New York: Times Books, 2003): 18.

118. *Ibid.*: 25.

119. *Ibid.*: 26.

120. *Ibid.*: 27.

121. Cawthorne, *Sex Lives*: 135.

122. Woodward, *Responses*: 209–215.

123. Schultz, *Presidential Scandals*: 232; Hagood, *Presidential Sex*: 78–81.

124. MacPherson, *Power Lovers*: 203; Cawthorne, *Sex Lives*: vii; Hagood, *Presidential Sex*: 76.

125. John W. Dean, *Warren G. Harding* (New York: Times Books, 2004): 1.

126. James P. Pfiffner, "Presidential Character: Multidimensional or Seamless?" in Mark J. Rozell and Clyde Wilcox, eds., *The Clinton Scandal* (Washington, DC: Georgetown University Press, 2000, 225–255): 227.

127. Schultz, *Presidential Scandals*: 255.

128. Dean, *Warren G. Harding*: 1.

129. Laton McCartney, *The Teapot Dome Scandal* (New York: Random House, 2008): 39.

130. Schultz, *Presidential Scandals*: 252; McCartney, *Teapot Dome*: 19; Hagood, *Presidential Sex*: 88–91; Thompson, *Political Scandal*: 145.

131. McCartney, *Teapot Dome*: 39.

132. Cawthorne, *Sex Lives*: ix; Hagood, *Presidential Sex*: 91–104; Thompson, *Political Scandal*: 109.

133. Stephen E. Ambrose, *Eisenhower: Soldier and President* (New York: Simon and Schuster, 1990): 125.

134. McCartney, *Teapot Dome*: 26.

135. Thompson, *Political Scandal*: 181.

136. McCartney, *Teapot Dome*: 86; Dean, *Warren G. Harding*: 156.

137. Schultz, *Presidential Scandals*: 254.

138. McCartney, *Teapot Dome*: 89.

139. *Ibid.*: 29.

140. Dean, *Warren G. Harding*: 155.

141. *Ibid.*: 156.

142. McCartney, *Teapot Dome*: 27.

143. *Ibid.*: 29.

144. Dean, *Warren G. Harding*: 156.

145. Schultz, *Presidential Scandals*: 255.

146. McCartney, *Teapot Dome*: 29.

147. *Ibid.*: 19.

148. *Ibid.*: 42.

149. *Ibid.*: 4.

150. *Ibid.*: 19.

151. *Ibid.*: 53.

152. *Ibid.*: 31; Grossman, *Political Corruption*: 125.

153. McCartney, *Teapot Dome*: 34.

154. *Ibid.*: 66.

155. *Ibid.*: 29.

156. *Ibid.*: 67; Grossman, *Political Corruption*: 94.

157. McCartney, *Teapot Dome*: 84.

158. *Ibid.*: 85; Grossman, *Political Corruption*: 125.

159. McCartney, *Teapot Dome*: 86; Dean, *Warren G. Harding*: 156.

160. Ambrose, *Eisenhower*: 125.

161. McCartney, *Teapot Dome*: 96; Miller, *Stealing*: 277.

162. Ambrose, *Eisenhower*: 125.

163. *Ibid.*

164. McCartney, *Teapot Dome*: 103.

165. *Ibid.*: 120.

166. *Ibid.*: 121.

167. *Ibid.*: 48.

168. *Ibid.*: 19.

169. *Ibid.*: 115.

170. Dean, *Warren G. Harding*: 138; Grossman, *Political Corruption*: 125.

171. McCartney, *Teapot Dome*: 140.

172. *Ibid.*: 169.

173. *Ibid.*: 225.

174. *Ibid.*: 211.

175. Joseph E. Persico, *Franklin and Lucy* (New York: Random House, 2008): 189–194.

176. McCartney, *Teapot Dome*: 210.

177. *Ibid.*: 248; Grossman, *Political Corruption*: 125.

178. McCartney, *Teapot Dome*: 255.

179. *Ibid.*: 147.

180. Woodward, *Responses*: 290.

181. Hagood, *Presidential Sex*: 111–115; Thompson, *Political Scandal*: 145; Persico, *Franklin and Lucy.*

182. Roy Jenkins, *Franklin Delano Roosevelt* (New York: Times Books, 2003): 35.

183. Cawthorne, *Sex Lives*: ix; Pfiffner, "Presidential Character": 227.

184. Schultz, *Presidential Scandals*: 301.

185. *Ibid.*: 301; Persico, *Franklin and Lucy*: 43.

186. Jenkins, *Franklin Delano Roosevelt.*

187. Hagood, *Presidential Sex*: 115–116.

188. Schultz, *Presidential Scandals*: 301; Hagood, *Presidential Sex*: 116; Pfiffner, "Presidential Character": 227.

189. Schultz, *Presidential Scandals*: 314.

190. Cawthorne, *Sex Lives*: x; Hagood, *Presidential Sex*: 117–118; Persico, *Franklin and Lucy*: 200–214.

191. Persico, *Franklin and Lucy*: 175.

192. *Ibid.*: 189–194.

193. Schultz, *Presidential Scandals*: 314.

194. McCartney, *Teapot Dome*: 86; Dean, *Warren G. Harding*: 156.

195. Grossman, *Political Corruption*: 73.

196. *Ibid.*: 74.

197. Cawthorne, *Sex Lives*: x; Michael Korda, *Ike: An American Hero* (New York: Harper-Collins, 2007): 270.

198. Korda, *Ike*: 270.

199. Ambrose, *Eisenhower*: 102.

200. Pfiffner, "Presidential Character": 227; Hagood, *Presidential Sex*: 119–134; Thompson, *Political Scandal*: 145; Ambrose, *Eisenhower*: 125.

201. Ambrose, *Eisenhower*: 102.

202. *Ibid*: 125.

203. Korda, *Ike*: 562.

204. Carlo D'Este, *Eisenhower: A Soldier's Story* (New York: Henry Holt, 2002): 420.

205. Ambrose, *Eisenhower*: 125.

206. D'Este, *Eisenhower*: 419.

207. Ambrose, *Eisenhower*: 125.

208. New York: Prentice Hall, 1948.

209. New York: Simon and Schuster, 1975.

210. D'Este, *Eisenhower*: 388.

211. Ambrose, *Eisenhower*: 125.

212. D'Este, *Eisenhower*: 388.

213. *Ibid*: 388.

214. *Ibid*.: 420.

215. Thompson, *Political Scandal*: 146; Richard D. Mahoney, *Sons and Brothers* (New York: Arcade Publishing, 1999).

216. Hagood, *Presidential Sex*: 150.

217. *Ibid*.: 144–146.

218. *Ibid*.: 151–160; Pfiffner, "Presidential Character": 228.

219. Hagood, *Presidential Sex*: 160–162.

220. *Ibid*.: 163–164.

221. *Ibid*.: 164–165.

222. Schultz, *Presidential Scandals*: 345–348; Hagood, *Presidential Sex*: 165–171.

223. Robert Dallek, *An Unfinished Life* (New York: Back Bay Books, 2003): 375.

224. Pfiffner, "Presidential Character:" 228; Cawthorne, *Sex Lives*:10.

225. Hagood, *Presidential Sex*: 188–190.

226. McCartney, *Teapot Dome*: 86; Dean, *Warren G. Harding*: 156.

227. Hagood, *Presidential Sex*: 194.

228. Schultz, *Presidential Scandals*: 364.

229. Dallek, *Unfinished Life*: 366.

230. *Ibid*.

231. Garment, *Scandal*: 10.

Chapter 4

1. Robert Williams, *Political Scandals in the USA* (Chicago: Fitzroy Dearborn, 1998): 25.

2. Robert L. Bartley, *Whitewater: A Journal Briefing* (New York: Dow Jones and Company, 1992): 199.

3. Jeffrey D. Schultz, *Presidential Scandals* (Washington, DC: CQ Press, 2000): 371; Nigel Cawthorne, *Sex Lives of the Presidents* (New York: St. Martin's Press, 1996): xi.

4. Schultz, *Presidential Scandals*: 371.

5. Mark Grossman, *Political Corruption in America* (Santa Barbara, CA: ABC Clio, 2003): 9.

6. *Ibid*.: 9; Richard Nixon, *The Memoirs of Richard M. Nixon* (New York: Touchstone Books, 1978): 913; David E. Kyvig, *The Age of Impeachment* (Lawrence: University Press of Kansas, 2008): 129–130; Fred Emery, *Watergate: The Corruption of American Politics and the Fall of Richard Nixon* (New York: Touchstone Books, 1994): 377.

7. Douglas Brinkley, *Gerald R. Ford* (New York: Times Books, 2007): 50.

8. Kyvig, *Age of Impeachment*: 115.

9. *Ibid*.: 117.

10. *Ibid*.: 116.

11. John Ehrlichman, *Witness to Power: The Nixon Years* (New York: Simon and Schuster, 1982), 143; Kyvig, *Age of Impeachment*: 130.

12. Emery, *Watergate*: 383.

13. Brinkley, *Ford*: 51; Kyvig, *Age of Impeachment*: 137; Emery, *Watergate*: 383.

14. Grossman, *Political Corruption*: 9; Michael Schudson, "Notes on Scandal and the Watergate Legacy," *American Behavioral Scientist*, 47 (2004): 1231–1238; Kyvig, *Age of Impeachment*: 138.

15. Harry P. Jeffrey, "The Life, Presidency and Resignation of Richard Nixon," in Harry P. Jeffrey and Thomas Maxwell-Long, eds., *Watergate and the Resignation of Richard Nixon: Impact of a Constitutional Crisis*, (Washington, D.C.: CQ Press, 2004), 1–16: 12.

16. Katy J. Harriger, (2004) "Special Prosecutors and Independent Counsels" in Harry P. Jeffrey and Thomas Maxwell-Long, eds., *Watergate and the Resignation of Richard Nixon: Impact of a Constitutional Crisis* (Washington, DC: CQ Press, 2004, 47–61): 49; Jeffrey, "The Life, Presidency": 12.

17. Michael J. Gerhardt, "Nixon and Impeachment," in Harry P. Jeffrey and Thomas Maxwell-Long, eds., *Watergate and the Resignation of Richard Nixon: Impact of a Constitutional Crisis* (Washington, DC: CQ Press, 2004), 77–94: 85, 88; Harry P. Jeffrey and Thomas Maxwell-Long, *Watergate and the Resignation of Richard Nixon: Impact of a Constitutional Crisis* (Washington, DC: CQ Press, 2004): xiii.

18. Joseph A. Palermo, "Politics, Public Opinion and Popular Culture," in Harry P. Jeffrey and Thomas Maxwell-Long, eds., *Watergate and the Resignation of Richard Nixon: Impact of a Constitutional Crisis* (Washington, DC: CQ Press, 2004, 17–29): 19.

19. Theodore H. White, *Breach of Faith: The Fall of Richard Nixon* (New York: Atheneum Publishers, 1975): 56; Elizabeth Drew, *Richard M. Nixon* (New York: Times Books, 2007): 10; David Halberstam, *The Fifties* (New York: Random House, 1993): 312.

20. Russ Witcher, "The Media," in Harry P. Jeffrey and Thomas Maxwell-Long, eds., *Watergate and the Resignation of Richard Nixon: Impact of a Constitutional Crisis* (Washington, DC: CQ Press, 2004, 113–124): 113; Nixon, *Memoirs*; Drew, *Richard M. Nixon*: 10; Halberstam, *The Fifties*: 312.

21. Jeffrey, "The Life, Presidency": 4; Monica Crowley, *Nixon off the Record* (New York: Random House, 1996): 147; Nixon, *Memoirs*.

22. Dan Rather, *The Palace Guard* (New York: Warner Paperback Library Edition, 1975): 139; Crowley, *Nixon off the Record*: 147; Nixon, *Memoirs*; Drew, *Richard M. Nixon*: 10; Halberstam, *The Fifties*: 314.

23. Halberstam, *The Fifties*: 327.

24. Palermo, "Politics": 17; Witcher, "The Media": 114; Larry J. Sabato, *Feeding Frenzy* (New York: Free Press, 1991): 8: Emery, *Watergate*: 8; Nixon, *Memoirs*: 92; White, *Breach of Faith*: 68; Drew, *Richard M. Nixon*: 14; Kyvig, *Age of Impeachment*: 188.

25. Jeffrey, "The Life, Presidency": 4; Palermo, "Politics": 17; Witcher, "The Media": 114; Nixon, *Memoirs*: 99; Drew, *Richard M. Nixon*: 15; Halberstam, *The Fifties*: 240; David LaGesse, "The Dog Carries the Day for Nixon," *U.S. News and World Report,* January 28–February 4, 2008, 42.

26. Jeffrey, "The Life, Presidency": 5.

27. Palermo, "Politics": 18; Crowley, *Nixon off the Record*: 147; Emery, *Watergate*: 8; Drew, *Richard M. Nixon*: 17.

28. Jeffrey, "The Life, Presidency": 6; Palermo, "Politics":18; Witcher, "The Media": 116; Nixon, *Memoirs*; White, *Breach of Faith*: 72; John W. Dean and Barry M. Goldwater Jr., *Pure Goldwater* (New York: Palgrave Macmillan, 2008).

29. Jeffrey, "The Life, Presidency": 7; Palermo, "Politics": 18; Drew, *Richard M. Nixon*: 20–22.

30. Jeffrey, "The Life, Presidency": 7; Palermo, "Politics": 18.

31. Jeffrey, "The Life, Presidency:"7.

32. Rather, *Palace Guard*: 35; Drew, *Richard M. Nixon*: 24–25.

33. Jeffrey, "The Life, Presidency": 7.

34. Emery, *Watergate*: 4, 9; Drew, *Richard M. Nixon*: 68–78; Jeffrey, "The Life, Presidency": 9; Palermo, "Politics": 19.

35. Leon Friedman, "Separation of Powers," in Harry P. Jeffrey and Thomas Maxwell-Long, eds., *Watergate and the Resignation of Richard Nixon: Impact of a Constitutional Crisis* (Washington, DC: CQ Press, 2004, 31–46): 37.

36. White, *Breach of Faith*: 123.

37. Friedman, "Separation": 37; White, *Breach of Faith*: 125; Emery, *Watergate*: 13.

38. Drew, *Richard M. Nixon*: 68.

39. John Dean, *Blind Ambition* (New York: Pocket Books, 1977): 27.

40. Rather, *Palace Guard*: 338; Emery, *Watergate*: 27; Nixon, *Memoirs*: 92, 869; White, *Breach of Faith*: 127; Drew, *Richard M. Nixon*: 102; Williams, *Political Scandals*: 14; Stanley Kutler, *The Wars of Watergate* (New York: Norton, 1990): 101–106; Victor Lasky, *It Didn't Start with Watergate* (New York: Dial Press, 1977): 330–332.

41. Emery, *Watergate*: 23.

42. Rather, *Palace Guard*: 338; Bob Woodward and Carl Bernstein, *The Final Days* (New York: Avon Books, 1976): 18; White, *Breach of Faith*: 135.

43. Drew, *Richard M. Nixon*: 99.

44. Rather, *Palace Guard*: 337; Emery, *Watergate*: 36.

45. Emery, *Watergate*: 109.

46. Garment, *Scandal*: 39.

47. Emery, *Watergate*: 108.

48. G. Gordon Liddy, *Will: The Autobiography of G. Gordon Liddy* (New York: St. Martin's Press, 1996): 221–222.

49. Emery, *Watergate*: 110.

50. John Ehrlichman, *Witness to Power: The Nixon Years* (New York: Simon and Schuster, 1982): 342.

51. Leon Jaworski, *The Right and the Power* (New York: Pocket Books, 1977): 138.

52. Emery, *Watergate*: 30; Drew, *Richard M. Nixon*: 101, 110; Nixon, *Memoirs*: 789, 793, 837.

53. Emery, *Watergate*: 109.

54. *Ibid.*: 110.

55. *Ibid.*: 196.

56. *Ibid.*: 42.

57. Neil Sheehan, *The Pentagon Papers: As Published by the New York Times* (New York: Bantam Books, 1971).

58. Drew, *Richard M. Nixon*: 75; Friedman, "Separation": 39; Witcher, "The Media": 117; Emery, *Watergate*: 38; Jaworski, *The Right and the Power*: 37; Liddy, *Autobiography*: 146; White, *Breach of Faith*: 146; Williams, *Political Scandals*: 15; Kutler, *Wars*: 109.

59. Kyvig, *Age of Impeachment*: 119.

60. Witcher, "The Media": 118; Williams, *Political Scandals*: 15.

61. Liddy, *Autobiography*: 146.

62. Dean, *Blind Ambition*: 17, 38; Rather, *Palace Guards*: 339; Witcher, "The Media": 118; Jaworski, *Right and the Power*: 36; Jim Hougan, *Secret Agenda* (New York: Random House,

1984): 32–36; Schudson, "Notes on Scandal": 18; Drew, *Richard M. Nixon*: 99; Kyvig, *Age of Impeachment*: 119; Williams, *Political Scandals*: 15; Kutler, *Wars*: 111–112; Lasky, *It Didn't Start*: 247; Jeffrey, "The Life, Presidency": 12.

63. Emery, *Watergate*: 73.

64. Friedman, "Separation": 39; Witcher, "The Media": 118; Jaworski, *Right and the Power*: 37; Hougan, *Secret Agenda*: 41–48; Ehrlichman, *Witness*; White, *Breach of Faith*: 148; Drew, *Richard M. Nixon*: 100; Kyvig, *Age of Impeachment*: 119; Williams, *Political Scandals*: 15.

65. Emery, *Watergate*: 59–60; Hougan, *Secret Agenda*: 47; Liddy, *Autobiography*: 168; Drew, *Richard M. Nixon*: 103, 107.

66. Nixon, *Memoirs*: 632.

67. Liddy, *Autobiography*: 219, 237; Jeffrey and Maxwell-Long, *Watergate*: xiii.

68. Emery, *Watergate*: 5; Hougan, *Secret Agenda*: 148; Liddy, *Autobiography*: 58.

69. Emery, *Watergate*: 5–6, 120–121; Hougan, *Secret Agenda*: 152, 162, 165; White, *Breach of Faith*: 159; Drew, *Richard M. Nixon*: 106.

70. Emery, *Watergate*: 131–132; Hougan, *Secret Agenda*: 189–190; Liddy, *Autobiography*: 242; White, *Breach of Faith*: 159; Kyvig, *Age of Impeachment*: 120; Williams, *Political Scandals*: 15.

71. Emery, *Watergate*: 138.

72. Jeffrey, "The Life, Presidency": 12; Witcher, "The Media": 113; John B. Thompson, *Political Scandal: Power and Visibility in the Media Age,* (Malden, MA: Polity Press, 2000): 200; Emily Van Tassel and Paul Finkelman, *Impeachable Offenses* (Washington, DC: Congressional Quarterly, 1999): 254; Jaworski, *Right and Power*: 131; Hougan, *Secret Agenda*: xv; Schudson, "Notes on Scandal": 16; Monica Crowley, *Nixon in Winter* (New York: Random House, 1998): 283; Nixon, *Memoirs*: 625; Kyvig, *Age of Impeachment*: 121; Williams, *Political Scandal*: 15.

73. Jeffrey, "The Life, Presidency": 11; Emery, *Watergate*: 122; Hougan, *Secret Agenda*.

74. Emery, *Watergate*: 112; Hougan, *Secret Agenda*: 9–10.

75. Crowley, *Nixon in Winter*: 290; Nixon, *Memoirs*: 628; Drew, *Richard M. Nixon*: 98, 106; Thompson, *Political Scandal*: 200.

76. Dean, *Blind Ambition*: 84.

77. Liddy, *Autobiography*.

78. Emery, *Watergate*: 148; Hougan, *Secret Agenda*: 3–5.

79. Emery, *Watergate*: 148; Hougan, *Secret Agenda*: xv; Carl Bernstein and Bob Woodward, All the President's Men (New York: Warner Books, 1974).

80. Van Tassel and Finkelman, *Impeachable Offenses*: 254.

81. Schudson, "Notes on Scandal": 36–39.

82. Dean, *Blind Ambition*: 102; Nixon, *Memoirs*: 635; Drew, *Richard M. Nixon*: 107; Kyvig, *Age of Impeachment*: 121; Williams, *Political Scandals*: 16; Emery, *Watergate*: 156; Friedman, "Separation": 40; Thompson, *Political Scandal*: 202.

83. Hougan, *Secret Agenda*: 224–225.

84. Bernstein and Woodward, All The President's Men.

85. Van Tassel and Finkelman, *Impeachable Offenses*: 254.

86. White, *Breach of Faith*: 11, 194.

87. *Ibid.*: 7, 165.

88. Nixon, *Memoirs*: 635–636.

89. Kyvig, *Age of Impeachment*: 125; Emery, *Watergate*: 184, 193.

90. Emery, *Watergate*: 196–197; Williams, *Political Scandals*: 16, 18; Jaworski, *Right to Power*: 75; Kutler, *Wars*: 270.

91. Nixon, *Memoirs*: 650.

92. Emery, *Watergate*: 206.

93. Jaworski, *Right and Power*: 16; Ehrlichman, *Witness*: 354, 360; Emery, *Watergate*: 215; Kyvig, *Age of Impeachment*: 122.

94. Kyvig, *Age of Impeachment*: 121.

95. Dean, *Blind Ambition*: 292; Witcher, "The Media": 113; Emery, *Watergate*: 151; Drew, *Richard M. Nixon*: 107; Palermo, "Politics": 22; Kyvig, *Age of Impeachment*: 121, 122; Schudson, "Notes on Scandal": 123, Williams, *Political Scandals*: 27; Bernstein and Woodward, *All the President's Men*.

96. Kyvig, *Age of Impeachment*: 121.

97. Nixon, *Memoirs*: 707; Garment, *Scandal*; Crowley, *Nixon in Winter*: 298; Thomas M. DeFrank, *Write It When I'm Gone* (New York: G.P. Putnam's Sons, 2007): 213; Lasky, *It Didn't Start*: 365.

98. Hougan, *Secret Agenda*: 280–301; Kyvig, *Age of Impeachment*: 3, 122; Bernstein and Woodward, *All the President's Men*.

99. Kyvig, *Age of Impeachment*: 4, 122.

100. Jeffrey, "The Life, Presidency": 12; White, *Breach of Faith*: 227; Bernstein and Woodward, *All the President's Men*.

101. Jeffrey, "The Life, Presidency": 12; Bernstein and Woodward, *All the President's Men*.

102. Emery, *Watergate*: 195; Bernstein and Woodward, *All the President's Men*.

103. *Ibid.* 165; Ehrlichman, *Witness*; Williams, *Political Scandals*: 16.

104. Emery, *Watergate*: 196.

105. Bernstein and Woodward, *All the President's Men*.

106. Dean, *Blind Ambition*: 141.

107. Nixon, *Memoirs*: 711.

108. Emery, *Watergate*: 95; Jaworski, *Right and Power*: 45–46; Nixon, *Memoirs*: 708; Kyvig, *Age of Impeachment*: 120; Kutler, *Wars*: 187–211; Lasky, *It Didn't Start*: 310.

109. Bernstein and Woodward, *All the President's Men*: 139–42.

110. Bernstein and Woodward, *All the President's Men:* 132.

111. Ehrlichman, *Witness*: 379.

112. Nixon, *Memoirs*: 708.

113. Emery, *Watergate*: 95; Drew, *Richard M. Nixon*: 105; Nixon, *Memoirs*: 775.

114. Jaworski, *Right and Power*: 46.

115. Kyvig, *Age of Impeachment*: 120.

116. Emery, *Watergate*: 7, 52, 106; Ehrlichman, *Witness*: 69; White, *Breach of Faith*: 121; Drew, *Richard M. Nixon*: 101–102.

117. Emery, *Watergate*: 96.

118. *Ibid.*

119. *Ibid.*

120. Drew, *Richard M. Nixon*: 105.

121. Nixon, *Memoirs*: 709.

122. *Ibid.*: 775.

123. Harriger, "Special Prosecutors": 49.

124. Emery, *Watergate*: 217; Liddy, *Autobiography*: 273; Drew, *Richard M. Nixon*: 109.

125. Jeffrey, "The Life, Presidency": 11; Emery, *Watergate*: 224; Schudson, "Notes on Scandal": 117.

126. Jaworski, *Right and Power*: 16; Schudson, "Notes on Scandal": 18; Van Tassel and Finkelman, *Impeachable Offenses*: 256.

127. Kyvig, *Age of Impeachment*: 124; Williams, *Political Scandals*: 18.

128. Garment, *Scandal*: 38; Emery, *Watergate*: 241; Ehrlichman, *Witness*: 367; Drew, *Richard M. Nixon*: 113.

129. Anthony Doyle, *Not Above the Law* (New York: William Morrow, 1977): 83.

130. Friedman, "Separation": 40.

131. Gerhardt, "Nixon and Impeachment": 85.

132. Dean, *Blind Ambition*: 180; Nixon, *Memoirs*: 802; Kyvig, *Age of Impeachment*: 122; Jeffrey, "The Life, Presidency": 12; White, *Breach of Faith*: 204.

133. Dean, *Blind Ambition*: 212; Thompson, *Political Scandal*: 202.

134. Emery, *Watergate*: 270; Jaworski, *Right and Power*: 141; Hougan, *Secret Agenda*: xvi; Liddy, *Autobiography*: 299; Schudson, "Notes on Scandal": 17; Ehrlichman, *Witness*: 372; Nixon, *Memoirs*: 803; White, *Breach of Faith*: 205; Kyvig, *Age of Impeachment*: 123; Williams, *Political Scandals*: 18; Harriger, "Special Prosecutors": 49.

135. Gerhardt, "Nixon and Impeachment": 85.

136. Emery, *Watergate*: 270; Kyvig, *Age of Impeachment*: 123.

137. Emery, *Watergate*: 238; Williams, *Political Scandals*: 17.

138. Emery, *Watergate*: 239.

139. Friedman, "Separation": 40; Thompson, *Political Scandal*: 202; Emery, *Watergate*: 238.

140. Nixon, *Memoirs*: 803.

141. Schudson, "Notes on Scandal": 17.

142. Van Tassel and Finkelman, *Impeachable Offenses*: 255; Emery, *Watergate*: 239; Liddy, *Autobiography*.

143. Nixon, *Memoirs*: 849.

144. Van Tassel and Finkelman, *Impeachable Offenses*: 256; Ehrlichman, *Witness*: 390; Drew, *Richard M. Nixon*: 111.

145. Doyle, *Not Above the Law*: 37.

146. Dean, *Blind Ambition*: 125.

147. White, *Breach of Faith*: 221; Drew, *Richard M. Nixon*: 111; Kyvig, *Age of Impeachment*: 125; Williams, *Political Scandals*: 19; Harriger, "Special Prosecutors": 49.

148. Nixon, *Memoirs*: 909–910; Schudson, "Notes on Scandal": 18; Kyvig, *Age of Impeachment*: 126; Williams, *Political Scandals*: 20; Lasky, *It Didn't Start*: 336; White, *Breach of Faith*: 250; Louis Fisher, "The Independent Counsel Statute," in Mark J. Rozell and Clyde Wilcox, eds,, *The Clinton Scandal* (Washington, DC: Georgetown University Press, 2000, 60–80): 61; Frank Mankiewicz, *U.S. v. Richard M. Nixon: The Final Crisis* (New York: Quadrangle, 1975).

149. Dean, *Blind Ambition*: 300; Woodward and Bernstein, *Final Days*: 50; Drew, *Richard M. Nixon*: 112.

150. Doyle, *Not Above the Law*.

151. Ehrlichman, *Witness*: 382.

152. Schudson, "Notes on Scandal": 17.

153. Nixon, *Memoirs*: 813.

154. White, *Breach of Faith*: 221, 235; Emery, *Watergate*: 359; Witcher, "The Media":113; Thompson, *Political Scandal*: 202; Schudson, "Notes on Scandal": 29.

155. Ehrlichman, *Witness*: 205.

156. Jeffrey, "The Life, Presidency": 12.

157. *Ibid.*

158. Jeffrey, "The Life, Presidency": 12; Rather, *The Palace Guard*: 355.

159. Emery, *Watergate*: 340, 359.

160. Dean, *Blind Ambition*: 310–331; Kyvig, *Age of Impeachment*: 124, 127; Schudson, "Notes on Scandal": 11, 1233; White, *Breach of Faith*: 235; Harriger, "Special Prosecutors": 49; Nixon, *Memoirs*: 890–891; Jaworski, *Right and Power*: 16; Van Tassel and Finkelman, *Impeachable Offenses*: 256; Bernstein and Woodward, *All the President's Men.*

161. Woodward and Bernstein, *Final Days*: 27, 41–42, 258.

162. Rather, *The Palace Guard*: 355.

163. Van Tassel and Finkelman, *Impeachable Offenses:* 256.

164. Gerhardt, "Nixon and Impeachment": 85; Jaworski, *Right and Power*: 55–56.

165. Jaworski, *Right and Power*: 55; Bernstein and Woodward, *All the President's Men.*

166. White, *Breach of Faith*: 236.

167. Jaworski, *Right and Power*: 16; Nixon, *Memoirs*: 900; White, *Breach of Faith*: 188, 246; Drew, *Richard M. Nixon*: xvi; Kyvig, *Age of Impeachment*: 128; Williams, *Political Scandals*: 21; Bernstein and Woodward, *All the President's Men.*

168. Dean, *Blind Ambition*: 335–338; Rather, *The Palace Guard*: 357; Woodward and Bernstein, *Final Days*: 46; Thompson: *Political Scandal*: 203; Van Tassel and Finkelman, *Impeachable Offenses*: 257; Harriger, "Special Prosecutors": 49; Gerhardt 2004: 85; Emery, *Watergate*: 367; Schudson, "Notes on Scandal": 18; White, *Breach of Faith*: 237.

169. Emery, *Watergate*: 35.

170. Drew, *Richard M. Nixon*: 116; Williams, *Political Scandals*: 21; Emery, *Watergate*; Nixon, *Memoirs*; White, *Breach of Faith*: 255; Thomas Maxwell-Long, "White House Crisis Management," in Harry P. Jeffrey and Thomas Maxwell-Long, eds., *Watergate and the Resignation of Richard Nixon: Impact of a Constitutional Crisis* (Washington, DC: CQ Press, 2004, 95–111): 105; Thompson, *Political Scandal*: 203.

171. Drew, *Richard M. Nixon*: 116; Williams, *Political Scandals*: 21; Emery, *Watergate*: 370; White, *Breach of Faith*: 238.

172. Schudson, "Notes on Scandal": 18.

173. Mark J. Rozell, "Politics, Public Opinion and Popular Culture," in Harry P. Jeffrey and Thomas Maxwell-Long, eds., *Watergate and the Resignation of Richard Nixon: Impact of a Constitutional Crisis* (Washington, DC: CQ Press, 2004), 63–75.

174. Drew, *Richard M. Nixon*: 116.

175. *Ibid.*: 117; Kyvig, *Age of Impeachment*: 150; Williams, *Political Scandals*: 22; White, *Breach of Faith*: 256, 263; Maxwell-Long, "White House Crisis": 105; Nixon, *Memoirs*: 918, 929.

176. Drew, *Richard M. Nixon*: 117.

177. Kyvig, *Age of Impeachment*: 150; Maxwell-Long, "White House Crisis": 105; Nixon, *Memoirs*: 931.

178. Emery, *Watergate*: 372.

179. *Ibid.*: 373.

180. White, *Breach of Faith*: 191.

181. Emery, *Watergate*: 380; Nixon, *Memoirs*: 909; Drew, *Richard M. Nixon*: 116; Woodward and Bernstein, *Final Days*: 154.

182. Kyvig, *Age of Impeachment*: 149–150.

183. Dean, *Blind Ambition*: 341; Kyvig, *Age of Impeachment*: 150; Williams, *Political Scandals*: 21; Drew, *Richard M. Nixon*: 116.

184. Nixon, *Memoirs*: 933.

185. Kyvig, *Age of Impeachment*: 150.

186. White, *Breach of Faith*: 265.

187. Drew, *Richard M. Nixon*: 117.

188. Kyvig, *Age of Impeachment*: 150; Drew, *Richard M. Nixon*: 119; Williams, *Political Scandals*: 22.

189. Dean, *Blind Ambition*: 341; Woodward and Bernstein, *Final Days*: 7, 60–61; Fisher, "Independent Counsel Statute": 61; Palermo, "Politics": 27; Gerhardt, "Nixon and Impeachment": 86; Van Tassel and Finkelman, *Impeachable Offenses*: 257; Emery, *Watergate*: 398; Jaworski, *Right and Power*: 2; Schudson, "Notes on Scandal": 11, 19; Nixon, *Memoirs*: 929.

190. Woodward and Bernstein, *Final Days*: 9.

191. Drew, *Richard M. Nixon*: 119; Kyvig, *Age of Impeachment*: 154; Schudson, "Notes on Scandal": 19; White, *Breach of Faith*: 5; Williams, *Political Scandals*: 23; Mankiewicz, *U.S. v. Richard M. Nixon: The Final Crisis*.

192. Harriger, "Special Prosecutors": 50; Emery, *Watergate*: 407; Nixon, *Memoirs*: 943.

193. Jaworski, *Right and Power*: 13.

194. Van Tassel and Finkelman, *Impeachable Offenses*: 258; Drew, *Richard M. Nixon*: 121.

195. Drew, *Richard M. Nixon*: 121.

196. Woodward and Bernstein, *Final Days*: 75, 83; Thompson, *Political Scandal*: 205; Emery, *Watergate*: 414; Schudson, "Notes on Scandal": 19; Nixon, *Memoirs*: 631; White, *Breach of Faith*: 163; Kyvig, *Age of Impeachment*: 159.

197. Nixon, *Memoirs*: 919, 948–953; Maxwell-Long, "White House Crisis": 105; Drew, *Richard M. Nixon*: 120.

198. Jaworski, *Right and Power*: 29.

199. Kyvig, *Age of Impeachment*: 159.

200. Van Tassel and Finkelman, *Impeachable Offenses*: 258.

201. Drew, *Richard M. Nixon*: 121; Williams, *Political Scandals*: 23; Jaworski, *Right and Power*: 128–129, 212; Bernstein and Woodward, *All the President's Men*.

202. Jaworski, *Right and Power*: 129.

203. Drew, *Richard M. Nixon*: 121; Alan M. Dershowitz, *Sexual McCarthyism* (New York: Basic Books, 1998): 33.

204. Jaworski, *Right and Power*: 117–118; Nixon, *Memoirs*: 999.

205. Nixon, *Memoirs*: 988.

206. Drew, *Richard M. Nixon*: 127; Woodward and Bernstein, *Final Days*: 284; Jaworski, *Right and Power*: 244–245; Schudson, "Notes on Scandal": 19; Nixon, *Memoirs*: 1051; Gerhardt, "Nixon and Impeachment": 87; Van Tassel and Finkelman, *Impeachable Offenses*: 258; Emery, *Watergate*: 446.

207. Thomas S. Langston, "The Nixon Resignation and the Ford Presidency," in Harry P. Jeffrey and Thomas Maxwell-Long, eds., *Watergate and the Resignation of Richard Nixon: Impact of a Constitutional Crisis* (DC: CQ Press, 2004, 125–138): 126; White, *Breach of Faith*: 8; Kyvig, *Age of Impeachment*: 163–166; Williams, *Political Scandals*: 24; Kutler, *Wars*: 513.

208. Witcher, "The Media": 119; Karen O'Connor and John R. Hermann, "The Courts: The Perils of Paula," in Mark J. Rozell and Clyde Wilcox, eds., *The Clinton Scandal* (Washington, DC: Georgetown University Press, 2000, 40–59): 43.

209. Gary Hartman, Roy A. Mersky, and Cindy L. Tate, *Landmark Supreme Court Cases* (New York: Checkmark Books, 2007): 234; Harriger, "Special Prosecutors": 2004: 51; O'-Connor and Hermann, "The Courts: The Perils of Paula": 40–59. 43.

210. Hartman, Mersky, and Tate, *Landmark Supreme Court Cases*: 234.

211. *Ibid.*: 233; Harriger, "Special Prosecutors": 51.

212. Hartman, Mersky, and Tate, *Landmark Supreme Court Cases*: 233.

213. Mark J. Rozell, "Politics, Public Opinion and Popular Culture," in Harry P. Jeffrey and Thomas Maxwell-Long, eds., *Watergate and the Resignation of Richard Nixon: Impact of a Constitutional Crisis*, (Washington, DC: CQ Press, 2004, 63–75), 63–4.

214. *Ibid.*: 72.

215. *Ibid.*: 63.

216. Harriger, "Special Prosecutors": 51.

217. Jeffrey and Maxwell-Long, *Watergate*: ix; Witcher, "The Media": 119; Langston, "Nixon Resignation": 126; Schudson, "Notes on Scandal": 20; Ehrlichman, *Witness*: 347; Kyvig, *Age of Impeachment*: 175–176; Bruce Oudes, *From: The President: Richard Nixon's Secret Files* (New York: Harper and Row, 1989): 502–509; Williams, *Political Scandals*: 24.

218. Jeffrey and Maxwell-Long, *Watergate*: ix.

219. Emery, *Watergate*: 189–190.

220. Jeffrey and Maxwell-Long, *Watergate*: ix.

221. *Ibid.*: x.

222. Palermo, "Politics": 20.

223. Emery, *Watergate*: 420.

224. Palermo, "Politics": 20.

225. Jaworski, *Right and Power*: 53.

226. Drew, *Richard M. Nixon*: 119.

227. Woodward and Bernstein, *Final Days*: 111.

228. Drew, *Richard M. Nixon*: 121.

229. *Ibid.*: 124.

230. Kyvig, *Age of Impeachment*: 160.

231. Van Tassel and Finkelman, *Impeachable Offenses*: 258; Emery, *Watergate*: 437.

232. Drew, *Richard M. Nixon*: 123.

233. Kyvig, *Age of Impeachment*: 161.

234. *Ibid.*: 168.

235. *Ibid.*: 162; Drew, *Richard M. Nixon*: 126.

236. Gerhardt, "Nixon and Impeachment": 86.

237. Drew, *Richard M. Nixon*: 127.

238. Kyvig, *Age of Impeachment*: 166.

239. Nixon, *Memoirs*: 1053; Drew, *Richard M. Nixon*: 128; Schudson, "Notes on Scandal": 20.

240. White, *Breach of Faith*: 320; Williams, *Political Scandals*: 24.

241. Nixon, *Memoirs*: 1055; Drew, *Richard M. Nixon*: 128; Schudson, "Notes on Scandal": 20.

242. Williams, *Political Scandals*: 24.

243. Schudson, "Notes on Scandal": 20.

244. Williams, *Political Scandals*: 24.

245. Nixon, *Memoirs*: 1055; Drew, *Richard M. Nixon*: 128; Gerhardt, "Nixon and Impeachment": 88; Van Tassel and Finkelman, *Impeachable Offenses*: 253, 258; Williams, *Political Scandals*: 24; Dershowitz, *Sexual McCarthyism*: 226.

246. Kyvig, *Age of Impeachment*: 175.

247. Jaworski, *Right and Power*: 259.

248. Woodward and Bernstein, *Final Days*: 388.

249. Drew, *Richard M. Nixon*: 135.

250. Harriger, "Special Prosecutors": 51.

251. Woodward and Bernstein, *Final Days:* 498; Van Tassel and Finkelman, *Impeachable Offenses*: 260; Emery, *Watergate*: 479; Liddy, *Autobiography*: 334; White, *Breach of Faith*: 32; Kyvig, *Age of Impeachment*: 3, 177; Williams, *Political Scandals*: 24; Kutler, *Wars*: 546.

252. Kyvig, *Age of Impeachment*: 183.

253. Thomas M. DeFrank, *Write It When I'm Gone* (NY: G.P Putnam's Sons, 2007): 105.

254. *Ibid.*: 106.

255. Schudson, "Notes on Scandal": 42; Palermo, "Politics": 22; Friedman, "Separation": 42; Harriger, "Special Prosecutors": 47; Van Tassel and Finkelman, *Impeachable Offenses*: 260; Emery, *Watergate*: 482; Brinkley, *Ford*: 68; Drew, *Richard M. Nixon*: 135; Williams, *Political Scandals*: 14, 25.

256. Schudson, "Notes on Scandal": 43.

257. Kyvig, *Age of Impeachment*: 184–185.

258. Richard Nixon, *In the Arena: A Memoir of Victory, Defeat and Renewal* (New York: Pocket Books, 1990), 15.

259. Jeffrey and Maxwell-Long, *Watergate*: x.

260. Schudson, "Notes on Scandal": 42.

261. Nixon, *In the Arena*: 39.

262. Kyvig, *Age of Impeachment*: 221.

263. Nixon, *In the Arena*: 30–42.

264. Jeffrey, "The Life, Presidency": 1.

265. *Ibid.*: 16; Drew, *Richard M. Nixon.*

266. Crowley, *Nixon in Winter*: 294; Drew, *Richard M. Nixon.*

267. Jeffrey, "The Life, Presidency": 16; Crowley, *Nixon in Winter*: 408.

268. Schudson, "Notes on Scandal": 11, citing CBS Morning News, 8 August 1975.

269. Jeffrey and Maxwell-Long, *Watergate*: x.

270. Harriger, "Special Prosecutors": 47.

271. Crowley, *Nixon in Winter*: 314.

272. Thompson, *Political Scandal*: 209.

273. Kyvig, *Age of Impeachment*: 202; Williams, *Political Scandals*: 9.

274. Palermo, "Politics": 26.

275. Schudson, "Notes on Scandal": 69.

276. Williams, *Political Scandals*: 32.

277. Schudson, "Notes on Scandal": 74.

278. Kyvig, *Age of Impeachment*: 202.

279. Schudson, "Notes on Scandal": 121.

280. Jeffrey and Maxwell-Long, *Watergate*: xii.

281. Williams, *Political Scandals:* 9.

282. Jeffrey and Maxwell-Long, *Watergate*: x.

283. Thompson, *Political Scandal*: 209.

284. Palermo, "Politics": 27.

285. Garment, *Scandal*: 39.

286. *Ibid.*

287. Kyvig, *Age of Impeachment*: 188.

288. *Ibid.*: 189.

289. Schudson, "Notes on Scandal": 99.

290. *Ibid.*

291. *Ibid.*: 100; Kyvig, *Age of Impeachment*: 190.

292. Friedman, "Separation": 42; Kutler, *Wars*: 563.

293. Kyvig, *Age of Impeachment*: 191.

294. *Ibid.*: 192.

295. *Ibid.*

296. Schudson, "Notes on Scandal": 83; Kyvig, *Age of Impeachment*: 187.

297. *Ibid.*

298. Schudson, "Notes on Scandal": 99.

299. *Ibid.*

300. Kyvig, *Age of Impeachment*: 187.

301. Harriger, "Special Prosecutors": 59.

302. Crowley, *Nixon in Winter*: 316.

303. Witcher, "The Media": 122.

304. Kyvig, *Age of Impeachment*: 5, 203.

305. Crowley, *Nixon in Winter*: 317.

306. Michael Isikoff, *Uncovering Clinton: A Reporter's Story* (New York: Crown, 1999): 8.

307. Palermo, "Politics": 21.

308. *Ibid.*

309. Sabato, *Feeding Frenzy*: 62.

310. Thompson, *Political Scandal*: 210.

311. Witcher, "The Media": 122.

312. *Ibid.*

313. Nixon, *In the Arena*: 229.

314. Sabato, *Feeding Frenzy*: 64.

315. Witcher, "The Media": 123.

316. Kyvig, *Age of Impeachment*: 206.

317. Williams, *Political Scandals*: 2; Schudson, "Notes on Scandal": 151; Kyvig, *Age of Impeachment*: 206.

318. Schudson, "Notes on Scandal": 123.

319. Woodward and Bernstein, *Final Days*: 7.

320. Drew, *Richard M. Nixon*: 121.

321. Woodward and Bernstein, *Final Days*: 136.

322. Kyvig, *Age of Impeachment*: 177.

323. Woodward and Bernstein, *Final Days*: 214.

324. Oudes, *From: The President*: xxiv.

325. Woodward and Bernstein, *Final Days*: 214.

326. Jeffrey and Maxwell-Long, *Watergate*: x.

327. Friedman, "Separation": 32; Jeffrey and Maxwell-Long, *Watergate*: xi.

328. Friedman, "Separation": 36.

329. *Ibid.*

330. Friedman, "Separation": 31.

331. Jeffrey and Maxwell-Long, *Watergate*: xi.

332. Schudson, "Notes on Scandal": 154; 14. Jeffrey and Maxwell-Long, *Watergate*: x.

333. Schudson, "Notes on Scandal": 163.

334. Palermo, "Politics": 24.

335. *Ibid.*

336. Gerhardt, "Nixon and Impeachment": 77; Kyvig, *Age of Impeachment*: 187.

Chapter 5

1. Elisabeth Goodridge, "What I Really Meant to Say Was ..." *U.S. News and World Report*, January 28–February 4, 2008, p. 31.

2. Douglas Brinkley, *Gerald R. Ford* (New York: Times Books, 2007), 142; Gerald Ford, *A Time to Heal* (New York: Harper and Row, 1979): 422.

3. Larry J. Sabato, *Feeding Frenzy* (New York: Free Press, 1991): 10.

4. Frederick M. Kaiser, "Executive Investigations of U.S. Legislators: A Comparison of Abscam and the Land Fraud Schemes," *Police Studies* 13 (1990): 14–25.

5. Suzanne Garment, *Scandal: The Culture of Mistrust in American Politics* (New York: Anchor Books, 1991): 56.

6. *Ibid.*: 10.

7. Sabato, *Feeding Frenzy*: 11; Garment, *Scandal*: 48–50.

8. Nadine Cohodas, "Law Enforcement/Judiciary" *Congressional Quarterly Almanac* (Washington, DC: CQ Press, 1980, 371–372): 372; "Billy Carter Probe" *Congressional Quarterly Almanac* (Washington, DC: CQ Press, 1980, 392.

9. Kaiser, "Executive Investigations."

10. Joseph A. Palermo, "Politics, Public Opinion and Popular Culture," in Harry P. Jeffrey and Thomas Maxwell-Long, eds., *Watergate and the Resignation of Richard Nixon: Impact of a Constitutional Crisis* (DC: CQ Press, 2004, 17–29): 25.

11. Garment, 43–47.

12. John B. Thompson, *Political Scandal: Power and Visibility in the Media Age* (Malden, MA: Polity, 2000): 187; Mark Grossman, *Political Corruption in America* (Santa Barbara, CA: ABC Clio, 2003): 209.

13. Michael Schudson, *Watergate in American Memory* (New York: Basic Books): 75–77; Bert Lance and Bill Gilbert, *The Truth of the Matter: My Life in and out of Politics* (New York: Summit Books, 1991).

14. Jeffrey D. Schultz, *Presidential Scandals* (Washington, DC: CQ Press, 2000): xvii.

15. Sabato, *Feeding Frenzy*: 11.

16. Schultz, *Presidential Scandals*: 404; Palermo, "Politics": 25.

17. Thompson, *Political Scandal*: 188.

18. Garment, *Scandal*: 2.

19. *Ibid.*: 58.

20. Thompson, *Political Scandal*: 188.

21. Louis Fisher, "The Independent Counsel Statute," in Mark J. Rozell and Clyde Wilcox, eds., *The Clinton Scandal* (Washington, DC: Georgetown University Press, 2000, 60–80): 65.

22. Richard Secord, *Honored and Betrayed* (New York: John Wiley and Sons, 1992): 203; Rodney P. Carlisle and Geoffrey Golson, *The Reagan Era from the Iran Crisis to Kosovo* (Santa Barbara, CA: ABC Clio, 2008): 125; Grossman, *Political Corruption*: 188; Garment, *Scandal*: 200; Oliver L. North, *Under Fire: An American Story* (New York: Harper Collins, 1991): 259; David E. Kyvig, *The Age of Impeachment* (Lawrence: University Press of Kansas, 2008): 237.

23. North, *Under Fire*: 262–264; Carlisle and Golson, *Reagan Era*: 127; Robert Williams, *Political Scandals in the USA* (Chicago: Fitzroy Dearborn, 1998): 38.

24. Kyvig, *Age of Impeachment*: 238.

25. Secord, *Honored*: 203, 205.

26. Kyvig, *Age of Impeachment*: 238.

27. North, *Under Fire*: 278.

28. Kyvig, *Age of Impeachment*: 239; Carlisle and Golson, *Reagan Era*: 127; Williams, *Political Scandals*: 41; John Patrick Diggins, *Ronald Reagan* (New York: Norton, 2007): 294.

29. Carlisle and Golson, *Reagan Era*: 128.

30. Kyvig, *Age of Impeachment*: 239; Carlisle and Golson, *Reagan Era*: 128; North, *Under Fire*: 279–280; Michael A. Ledeen, *Perilous Statecraft* (New York: Charles Scribner's Sons, 1988): 60–64; Williams, *Political Scandals*: 42; Diggins, *Ronald Reagan*: 294.

31. North, *Under Fire*: 279–280; Ledeen, *Perilous Statecraft*: 60–64; Williams, *Political Scandals*: 42; Diggins, *Ronald Reagan*: 294.

32. Kyvig, *Age of Impeachment*: 239; North, *Under Fire*: 278.

33. Garment, *Scandal*: 201; North, *Under Fire*: 205, 280–282; Secord, *Honored*: 203.

34. Williams, *Political Scandals*: 42; Carlisle and Golson, *Reagan Era*: 129.

35. Fisher, "Independent Counsels": 65; Thompson, *Political Scandal*: 211.

36. Kyvig, *Age of Impeachment*: 240.

37. Williams, *Political Scandals*: 42; Ledeen, *Perilous Statecraft*: 60–64.

38. Kyvig, *Age of Impeachment*: 240; Diggins, *Ronald Reagan*: 298; Carlisle and Golson, *Reagan Era*: 133; "Intelligence Authorization: Small Increase" *Congressional Quarterly Almanac* (Washington, DC: CQ Press, 1986, 383–384): 383.

39. Kyvig, *Age of Impeachment*: 240.

40. *Ibid.*: 239.

41. *Ibid.*: 240; Williams, *Political Scandals*: 42.

42. Garment, *Scandal*: 203.

43. North, *Under Fire*: 179.

44. Garment, *Scandal*: 204; North, *Under Fire*: 35.

45. Secord, *Honored*: 211.

46. North, *Under Fire*: 287; Williams, *Political Scandals*: 53; Diggins, *Ronald Reagan*: 294; Carlisle and Golson, *Reagan Era*: 128; Kyvig, *Age of Impeachment*: 240.

47. Secord, *Honored*: 211.

48. Carlisle and Golson, *Reagan Era*: 130.

49. Williams, *Political Scandals*: 53; Carlisle and Golson, *Reagan Era*: 130; Martin Anderson, *Revolution: The Reagan Legacy* (Stanford, CA: Hoover Institution Press, 1990): 415; Ledeen, *Perilous Statecraft*: 223–224.

50. North, *Under Fire*: 322; Ledeen, *Perilous Statecraft*: 224.

51. Secord, *Honored*: 147.

52. *Ibid.*

53. *Ibid.*

54. *Ibid.*

55. Kyvig, *Age of Impeachment*: 235.

56. *Ibid.*: 234, 236; Williams, *Political Scandals*: 38; Diggins, *Ronald Reagan*: 294; Donald T. Regan, *For the Record* (San Francisco: Harcourt Brace Jovanovich, 1988): 31.

57. North, *Under Fire*: 29; Secord, *Honored*: 218; Diggins, *Ronald Reagan*: 294.

58. North, *Under Fire*: 63; Secord, *Honored*: 279.

59. Williams, *Political Scandals*: 38.

60. Williams, *Political Scandals*: 39; Secord, *Honored*: 220; North, *Under Fire*: 26.

61. North, *Under Fire*: 27.

62. Thompson. *Political Scandal*: 213; Secord, *Honored*: 222, 316.

63. North, *Under Fire*: 32; Secord, *Honored*: 228; Carlisle and Golson, *Reagan Era*: 132.

64. Williams, *Political Scandals*: 39.

65. Secord, *Honored*: 200.

66. Williams, *Political Scandals*: 40.

67. Anderson, *Revolution*: 389; Schudson, *Watergate*: 178.

68. Williams, *Political Scandals*: 40; Carlisle and Golson, *Reagan Era*: 133; Secord, *Honored*: 296.

69. Secord, *Honored*: 280.

70. Williams, *Political Scandals*: 40.

71. North, *Under Fire*; 358; Secord, *Honored*: 311; Williams, *Political Scandals*: 40; Regan, *For the Record*: 26; Ledeen, *Perilous Statecraft*: 221.

72. North, *Under Fire*: 22.

73. Garment, *Scandal*: 205.

74. Williams, *Political Scandals*: 38.

75. *Ibid.*: 41; Anderson, *Revolution*: 400–401.

76. Anderson, *Revolution*: 402.

77. Secord, *Honored.*

78. Lou Dubose and Jake Bernstein, *Vice* (New York: Random House, 2006): 64.

79. Thompson, *Political Scandal*: 210; Schudson, *Watergate*: 165; Kyvig, *Age of Impeachment*: 241; Williams, *Political Scandals*: 42; Carlisle and Golson, *Reagan Era*: 133; Grossman, *Political Corruption*: 188; Regan, *For the Record*: 25.

80. Thompson, *Political Scandal*: 210.

81. Schudson, *Watergate*: 165.

82. North, *Under Fire*: 334.

83. *Ibid.*: 352; Kyvig, *Age of Impeachment*: 240; Ledeen, *Perilous Statecraft*: 40; Diggins, *Ronald Reagan*: 298; Carlisle and Golson, *Reagan Era*: 133.

84. Schudson, *Watergate*: 165.

85. Thompson, *Political Scandal*: 210.

86. Schudson, *Watergate*: 165.

87. North, *Under Fire*: 7; Dubose and Bernstein, *Vice*: 65.

88. North, *Under Fire*: 373; Secord, *Honored*: 326; Carlisle and Golson, *Reagan Era*: 134.

89. Kyvig, *Age of Impeachment*: 242.

90. North, *Under Fire*: 370.

91. Kyvig, *Age of Impeachment*: 242; Williams, *Political Scandals*: 43; Regan, *For the Record*: 35.

92. Williams, *Political Scandals*: 46.

93. Thompson, *Political Scandal*: 211; Carlisle and Golson, *Reagan Era*: 135.

94. Kyvig, *Age of Impeachment*: 242.

95. William S. Cohen and George J. Mitchell, *Men of Zeal* (New York: Penguin Group, 1988).

96. Secord, *Honored*: 329; Kyvig, *Age of Impeachment*: 243.

97. "The Iran-Contra Affair" *Congressional Quarterly Almanac* (Washington, DC: CQ Press, 1983, 423–436): 424.

98. Kyvig, *Age of Impeachment*: 244.

99. North, *Under Fire*: 5.

100. *Ibid*.

101. Kyvig, *Age of Impeachment*: 243–244; Carlisle and Golson, *Reagan Era*: 134; Schudson, *Watergate*: 166; Williams, *Political Scandals*: 43.

102. Thompson, *Political Scandal*: 213; Carlisle and Golson, *Ronald Reagan*: 135; Thomas Maxwell-Long, "White House Crisis Management," in Harry P. Jeffrey and Thomas Maxwell-Long, eds., *Watergate and the Resignation of Richard Nixon: Impact of a Constitutional Crisis* (Washington, DC: CQ Press, 2004, 95–111): 107.

103. Kyvig, *Age of Impeachment*: 246.

104. *Ibid*.

105. *Ibid*.

106. Maxwell-Long, "White House": 107.

107. Kyvig, *Age of Impeachment*: 247; Williams, *Political Scandals*: 44.

108. Williams, *Political Scandals*: 45.

109. Kyvig, *Age of Impeachment*: 247.

110. Williams, *Political Scandals*: 44.

111. Kyvig, *Age of Impeachment*: 248.

112. Thompson, *Political Scandal*: 213; Secord, *Honored*: 336–337; Schudson, *Watergate*: 166; Carlisle and Golson, *Reagan Era*: 135; "The Iran-Contra Affair" *Congressional Quarterly Almanac* (Washington, DC: CQ Press, 1983, 423–436): 426.

113. Fisher, "Independent Counsels": 65.

114. Williams, *Political Scandals*: 43.

115. Carlisle and Golson, *Reagan Era*: 135.

116. Dubose, Bernstein, *Vice*: 68.

117. Kyvig, *Age of Impeachment*: 251.

118. *Ibid*.: 250; Cohen and Mitchell, *Men of Zeal*.

119. Kyvig, *Age of Impeachment*: 251.

120. Williams, *Political Scandals*: 44.

121. Kyvig, *Age of Impeachment*: 253.

122. Williams, *Political Scandals*: 43–44.

123. Garment, *Scandal*: 211.

124. Kyvig, *Age of Impeachment*: 253.

125. *Ibid*.: 254–55; "The Iran-Contra Affair" *Congressional Quarterly Almanac* (Washington, DC: CQ Press, 1983, 423–436): 426.

126. Garment, *Scandal*: 209.

127. Williams, *Political Scandals*: 50.

128. Kyvig, *Age of Impeachment*: 256–257.

129. North, *Under Fire*: 16.

130. Kyvig, *Age of Impeachment*: 257.

131. Grossman, *Political Corruption*: 188.

132. Kyvig, *Age of Impeachment*: 264.

133. *Ibid*.: 262; Williams, *Political Scandals*: 51.

134. Timothy Naftali, *George H.W. Bush* (New York: Times Books, 2007): 154; Monica Crowley, *Nixon in Winter* (New York: Random House, 1998): 306; Kyvig, *Age of Impeachment*: 263.

135. Kyvig, *Age of Impeachment*: 263.

136. Secord, *Honored*: 347.

137. Fisher, "Independent Counsels": 65.

138. Secord, *Honored*: 348.

139. Williams, *Political Scandals*: 48.

140. Kyvig, *Age of Impeachment*: 262.

141. Thompson, *Political Scandal*: 214.

142. "North's Trial: A Year of Motions and Delays" *Congressional Quarterly Almanac* (Washington, DC: CQ Press, 1988, 560–567).

143. Kyvig, *Age of Impeachment*: 262.

144. Secord, *Honored*: 344; Anderson, *Revolution*: 409–410.

145. Williams, *Political Scandal*: 47.

146. Carlisle and Golson, *Reagan Era*: 136; "North Convictions Set Aside on Appeal" *Congressional Quarterly Almanac* (Washington, DC: CQ Press, 1990, 534–535).

147. Fisher, "Independent Counsels": 66.

148. Kyvig, *Age of Impeachment*: 245.

149. Schudson, *Watergate*: 175; Kyvig, *Age of Impeachment*: 245.

150. Alan M. Dershowitz, *Sexual McCarthyism* (New York: Basic Books, 1998): 26; Garment, *Scandal*: 198.

151. Cohen and Mitchell, *Men of Zeal*.

152. Carlisle and Golson, *Reagan Era*: 131.

153. Kyvig, *Age of Impeachment*: 236.

154. Cohen and Mitchell, *Men of Zeal*.

155. Kyvig, *Age of Impeachment*: 244.

156. *Ibid*.

157. Schudson, *Watergate*: 180.

158. Kyvig, *Age of Impeachment*: 258.

159. *Ibid*.: 259.

160. Williams, *Political Scandals*: 43.

161. Cohen and Mitchell, *Men of Zeal*.

162. Thompson, *Political Scandal*: 214.

163. Marion Just and Ann Crigler, "Leadership Image-Building: After Clinton and Watergate," *Political Psychology*, 21 (2000): 179–198, 196.

164. Russ Witcher, "The Media," in Harry P. Jeffrey and Thomas Maxwell-Long, eds., *Watergate and the Resignation of Richard Nixon: Impact of a Constitutional Crisis* (Washington, DC: CQ Press, 2004, 113–124): 123.

165. Thompson, *Political Scandal*: 214.

166. Regan, *For the Record*: 25.

167. Thompson, *Political Scandal*: 215.

168. North, *Under Fire*: 17.

169. Kyvig, *Age of Impeachment*: 232.

170. Schudson, *Watergate*: 181.

171. North, *Under Fire*: 11.

172. Kyvig, *Age of Impeachment*: 232.

173. Schudson, *Watergate*: 181.

174. Kyvig, *Age of Impeachment*: 250.

175. Schudson, *Watergate*: 181.

176. *Ibid.*: 182, 1235.

177. Secord, *Honored*: 271.

178. Williams, *Political Scandals*: 40.

179. *Ibid.*: 49.

180. Schudson, *Watergate*: 181.

181. Williams, *Political Scandals*: 56.

182. Kyvig, *Age of Impeachment*: 245.

183. Harry P. Jeffrey and Thomas Maxwell-Long, *Watergate and the Resignation of Richard Nixon: Impact of a Constitutional Crisis* (Washington, DC: CQ Press, 2004).

184. Schudson, *Watergate*: 178.

185. Williams, *Political Scandals*: 47.

186. Cohen and Mitchell, *Men of Zeal*.

187. Schudson, *Watergate*: 165; Secord, *Honored*: 314.

188. Schudson, *Watergate*: 173.

189. Jeffrey D. Schultz, *Presidential Scandals* (Washington, DC: CQ Press, 2000): 429.

190. James P. Pfiffner, "Presidential Character: Multidimensional or Seamless?" in Mark J. Rozell and Clyde Wilcox, eds., *The Clinton Scandal* (Washington, DC: Georgetown University Press, 2000, 225–255): 228; Sabato, *Feeding Frenzy*: 17, 171.

191. Sean Wilentz, *The Age of Reagan* (New York: Harper Collins, 2008): 307.

192. *Ibid.*: 310.

193. Sabato, *Feeding Frenzy*: 15, 157.

194. *Ibid.*

195. Garment, *Scandal*: 179.

Chapter 6

1. James P. Pfiffner, "Presidential Character: Multidimensional or Seamless?" in Mark J. Rozell and Clyde Wilcox, eds., *The Clinton Scandal* (Washington, DC: Georgetown University Press, 2000, 225–255): 228.

2. Michael Isikoff, *Uncovering Clinton: A Reporter's Story* (New York: Crown, 1999): 27.

3. Suzanne Garment, *Scandal: The Culture of Mistrust in American Politics* (New York: Anchor Books, 1991): 336. James B. Stewart, *Blood Sport: The President and His Adversaries* (New York: Simon and Schuster, 1996): 318.

4. David E. Kyvig, *The Age of Impeachment* (Lawrence: University Press of Kansas, 2008): 317.

5. Sewart, *Blood Sport*: 198.

6. Garment, *Scandal*: 337.

7. Mark Grossman, *Political Corruption in America* (Santa Barbara, CA: ABC Clio, 2003): 62.

8. Louis Fisher, "The Independent Counsel Statute," in Mark J. Rozell and Clyde Wilcox, eds., in *The Clinton Scandal* (Washington, DC: Georgetown University Press, 2000, 60–80): 76.

9. Stewart, *Blood Sport*: 118.

10. Robert Williams, *Political Scandals in the USA* (Chicago: Fitzroy Dearborn, 1998): 83.

11. Webb Hubbell, *Friends in High Places* (New York: William Morrow, 1997): 296; Fisher, "Independent Counsel": 68.

12. Stewart, *Blood Sport*: 427; Gene Lyons, *Fools for Scandal* (New York: Franklin Square Press, 1996): 85; Isikoff, *Uncovering Clinton*: 275.

13. Hubbell, *Friends*: 298–299.

14. *Ibid.*: 143.

15. Sean Wilentz, *The Age of Reagan* (New York: Harper Collins, 2008): 369.

16. Howard Kurtz, "The Hooker, Line and Sinker," *Washington Post*, September 4, 1996, B1.

17. Fisher, "Independent Counsel": 75; "Crash Claims Life of Sec. Brown; Kantor Takes Commerce Post" *Congressional Quarterly Almanac* (Washington, DC: CQ Press, 1996, 3-14-3-15).

18. *Ibid.*: 76.

19. Harriger, Katy J., "Special Prosecutors and Independent Counsels" in Harry P. Jeffrey and Thomas Maxwell-Long, eds., *Watergate and the Resignation of Richard Nixon: Impact of a Constitutional Crisis* (Washington, DC: CQ Press, 2004, 47–61): 58.

20. Dan E. Moldea, *A Washington Tragedy: How the Death of Vincent Foster Ignited a Political Firestorm* (Washington, DC: Regnery Publishing, 1998): 50.

21. Stewart, *Blood Sport*: 34.

22. Moldea, *Washington Tragedy*: 5; Stewart, *Blood Sport*: 34, 273.

23. Stewart, *Blood Sport*: 244.

24. Moldea, *Washington Tragedy*: 3–4.

25. Kyvig, *Age of Impeachment*: 318.

26. Moldea, *Washington Tragedy*: 2.

27. *Ibid.*

28. *Ibid.*: 4.

29. *Ibid.*: 68.

30. Isikoff, *Uncovering Clinton*: 36; Larry J. Sabato and S. Robert Lichter, *When Should the Watchdogs Bark? Media Coverage of the Clinton Scandals* (Washington, DC: Center for Media and Public Affairs, 1994): 8; Moldea, *Washington Tragedy*: 6, 146; Stewart, *Blood Sport*: 365; Lyons, *Fool*: 106.

31. Moldea, *Washington Tragedy*: 225.

32. *Ibid.*: 7.

33. Stewart, *Blood Sport*: 300.

34. *Ibid.*: 302.

35. Moldea, *Washington Tragedy*: 6.

36. Kyvig, *Age of Impeachment*: 318.

37. Sabato and Lichter, *Watchdogs*: 8.

38. Moldea, *Washington Tragedy*: 141.

39. *Ibid.*: 142.

40. *Ibid.*: 223; Stewart, *Blood Sport*: 422; Lyons, *Fool*: 83.

41. Moldea, *Washington Tragedy*: 10, 272.

42. Wilentz, *Age of Reagan*: 378; Moldea, *Washington Tragedy*: 14, 360.

43. Moldea, *Washington Tragedy*: 6; Stewart, *Blood Sport*: 311.

44. Howard Kurtz, *Spin Cycle: Inside the Clinton Propaganda Machine* (New York: Free Press, 1998), 53.

45. Stewart, *Blood Sport*: 73.

46. *Ibid.*: 79–81.

47. *Ibid.*: 77.

48. *Ibid.*: 73.

49. Michael Schudson, "Notes on Scandal and the Watergate Legacy," *American Behavioral Scientist*, 47 (2004): 1231–1238, 1232.

50. Wilentz, *Age of Reagan*: 329.

51. *Ibid.*: 330.

52. Stewart, *Blood Sport*: 245; *Schudson,* "Notes on Scandal": 1231.

53. Wilentz, *Age of Reason*: 330; Schudson, "Notes on Scandal": 1231–1232.

54. Stewart, *Blood Sport*: 250; Wilentz, *Age of Reason*: 330.

55. Stewart, *Blood Sport*: 251; "President Withdraws Guinier Nomination" *Congressional Quarterly Almanac* (Washington, DC: CQ Press, 1993, 307–308).

56. John B. Thompson, *Political Scandal: Power and Visibility in the Media Age* (Malden, MA: Polity Press, 2000), 188.

57. Wilentz, *Age of Reagan*: 376; Fisher, "Independent Counsel": 75.

58. Thompson, *Political Scandal*: 188.

59. Grossman, *Political Corruption*: 116.

60. Wilentz, *Age of Reagan*: 376.

61. Fisher, "Independent Counsel": 75; Grossman, *Political Corruption*: 116; Paul J. Quirk, "Scandal Time: The Clinton Impeachment and the Distraction of American Politics," in Mark J. Rozell and Clyde Wilcox, eds., *The Clinton Scandal* (Washington, DC: Georgetown University Press, 2000, 119–141): 133.

62. Kurtz, *Spin Cycle*: xix.

63. "'Travelgate,' FBI Files Spur Inquiry" *Congressional Quarterly Almanac* (Washington, DC: CQ Press, 1996, 1-47–1-49).

64. Wilentz, *Age of Reagan*: 331; Williams, *Political Scandals*: 67; Stewart, *Blood Sport*: 267; Kurtz, *Spin Cycle*: xix.

65. Stewart, *Blood Sport*: 265; Lyons, *Fool*: 136.

66. "White House Travel Office" *Congressional Quarterly Almanac* (Washington, DC: CQ Press, 1993, 317); "'Travelgate,' FBI Files Spur Inquiry" *Congressional Quarterly Almanac* (Washington, DC: CQ Press, 1996, 1-47–1-49).

67. Isikoff, *Uncovering Clinton*: 31.

68. Karen O'Connor and John R. Hermann, "The Courts: The Perils of Paula," in Mark J. Rozell and Clyde Wilcox, eds., *The Clinton Scandal* (Washington, D.C.: Georgetown University Press, 2000, 40–59): 44.

69. Isikoff, *Uncovering Clinton*: 57, 216.

70. *Ibid.*: 47.

71. *Ibid.*

72. Wesley O. Hagood, *Presidential Sex: From the Founding Fathers to Bill Clinton* (Secaucus, NJ: Citadel Press, 1998): 223–224.

73. Isikoff, *Uncovering Clinton*: 256.

74. Hagood, *Presidential Sex*: 205.

75. Isikoff, *Uncovering Clinton*: 226.

76. O'Connor and Hermann, "The Courts": 40.

77. Garment, *Scandal*: 333.

78. Gennifer Flowers, *Passion and Betrayal* (Del Mar, CA: Emery Dalton Books, 1995): 1.

79. *Ibid.*: 42.

80. Isikoff, *Uncovering Clinton*: 55, 255.

81. *Ibid.*: 225.

82. Lyons, *Fool*: 6.

83. O'Connor and Hermann, "The Courts:" 44; Hagood, *Presidential Sex*: 206–217; Garment, *Scandal*: 333; Flowers, *Passion*.

84. Lyons, *Fool*: 6; Monica Crowley, *Nixon in Winter* (New York: Random House, 1998): 320; Monica Crowley, *Nixon off the Record* (New York: Random House, 1996); John Anthony Maltese, "The Media: The New Media and the Lure of the Clinton Scandal," in Mark J. Rozell and Clyde Wilcox, eds., *The Clinton Scandal* (Washington, DC: Georgetown University Press, 2000, 195–210): 197; Kenneth T. Walsh, "Sex. Lies, and Major Headlines," *U.S. News and World Report,* January 28–February 4, 2008, 36–37.

85. O'Connor and Hermann, "The Courts": 44; Garment, *Scandal*: 334.

86. Sabato and Lichter, *Watchdogs*: 5, 10; Stewart, *Blood Sport*: 365.

87. Sabato and Lichter, *Watchdogs*: 38; Hagood, *Presidential Sex*: 219–222.

88. O'Connor and Hermann, "The Courts": 45; Kurtz, *Spin Cycle*: xix.

89. Kyvig, *Age of Impeachment*: 323; Isikoff, *Uncovering Clinton*: 7; Emily Van Tassel and Paul Finkelman, *Impeachable Offenses* (Washington, DC: Congressional Quarterly, 1999): 268.

90. Isikoff, *Uncovering Clinton*: 22, 9; Hagood, *Presidential Sex*: 226–228.

91. Lyons, *Fool*: 22, 24; Kyvig, *Age of Impeachment*: 323; O'Connor and Hermann, "The Courts": 45; Thompson, *Political Scandal*: 150; Stewart, *Blood Sport*: 386.

92. Sabato and Lichter, *Watchdogs*: 10; Hagood, *Presidential Sex*: 197.

93. O'Connor and Hermann, "The Courts": 45.

94. Isikoff, *Uncovering Clinton*: 18; Stewart, *Blood Sport*: 389.

95. Isikoff, *Uncovering Clinton*: 49.

96. *Ibid.*: 89; Wilentz, *Age of Reagan*: 380.

97. Kyvig, *Age of Impeachment*: 324; Van Tassel and Finkelman, *Impeachable Offenses*: 324.

98. Isikoff, *Uncovering Clinton*: 6.

99. Hagood, *Presidential Sex*: 229.

100. Stewart, *Blood Sport*: 421.

101. Alan M. Dershowitz, *Sexual McCarthyism* (New York: Basic Books, 1998): 15; Kyvig, *Age of Impeachment*: 326.

102. Kyvig, *Age of Impeachment*: 324; Isikoff, *Uncovering Clinton*: 111.

103. Kyvig, *Age of Impeachment*: 324.

104. O'Connor and Hermann, "The Courts": 47; Hagood, *Presidential Sex*: 229.

105. O'Connor and Hermann, "The Courts": 47.

106. Wilentz, *Age of Reagan*: 378.

107. Kyvig, *Age of Impeachment*: 324–325; Hagood, *Presidential Sex*: 230.

108. O'Connor and Hermann, "The Courts": 47; Hagood, *Presidential Sex*: 230; L. Darnell Weeden, "The President and Mrs. Jones Were in Federal Court: The Litigation Established No Constitutional Immunity for President Clinton," *George Mason Law Review,* 7 (1999): 361–389.

109. Hagood, *Presidential Sex*: 230.

110. O'Connor and Hermann, "The Courts": 47.

111. Wilentz, *Age of Reagan*: 378.

112. Kyvig, *Age of Impeachment*: 325; Robert J. Spitzer, "The Presidency: The Clinton Crisis and Its Consequences," in Mark J. Rozell and Clyde Wilcox, eds., *The Clinton Scandal* (Washington, D.C.: Georgetown University Press, 2000, 1–17): 5; O'Connor and Hermann, "The Courts": 48.

113. Leon Friedman, "Separation of Powers," in *Watergate and the Resignation of Richard Nixon: Impact of a Constitutional Crisis*, in Harry P. Jeffrey and Thomas Maxwell-Long, eds., (Washington, DC: CQ Press, 2004, 31–46): 45.

114. Wilentz, *Age of Reagan*: 378; Van Tassel and Finkelman, *Impeachable Offenses*: 268.

115. Isikoff, *Uncovering Clinton*: 141; Hagood, *Presidential Sex*: 232; Thompson, *Political Scandal*: 151.

116. Hagood, *Presidential Sex*: 242; Kyvig, *Age of Impeachment*: 327.

117. Isikoff, *Uncovering Clinton*: 107; Kurtz, *Spin Cycle*: 236.

118. Kathleen Willey, *Target* (Los Angeles: World Ahead Publishing, 2007).

119. Wilentz, *Age of Reagan*: 381.

120. Hagood, *Presidential Sex*: 246; Andrew Morton, *Monica's Story* (New York: St. Martin's Press, 1999).

121. Isikoff, *Uncovering Clinton*: 171.

122. Thompson, *Political Scandal*: 152; Kurtz, *Spin Cycle*: xiii.

123. Isikoff, *Spin Cycle*: 171.

124. Isikoff, *Uncovering Clinton*: vii.

125. Dershowitz, *Sexual McCarthyism*: 17; Isikoff, *Uncovering Clinton*: 268; O'Connor and Hermann, "The Courts:" 52; Maltese, "The Media": 195.

126. Thomas Maxwell-Long, "White House Crisis Management," in Harry P. Jeffrey and Thomas Maxwell-Long, eds., *Watergate and the Resignation of Richard Nixon: Impact of a Constitutional Crisis* (Washington, DC: CQ Press, 2004, 95–111): 109; Kyvig, *Age of Impeachment*: 328.

127. Maltese, "The Media": 197.

128. O'Connor and Hermann, "The Courts": 54.

129. Dershowitz, *Sexual McCarthyism*: 21; Kyvig, *Age of Impeachment*: 328.

130. Isikoff, *Uncovering Clinton*: 131; Kyvig, *Age of Impeachment*: 326.

131. O'Connor and Hermann, "The Courts": 53; Isikoff, *Uncovering Clinton*: 196; Thompson, *Political Scandal*: 152; Morton, "The Media": 96; Kyvig, *Age of Impeachment*: 327.

132. Van Tassel and Finkelman, *Impeachable Offenses*: 269.

133. Morton, *Monica's Story*: 10.

134. O'Connor and Hermann, "The Courts": 54.

135. Fisher, "Independent Counsel": 66.

136. Isikoff, *Uncovering Clinton*: 293, 313.

137. Hagood, *Presidential Sex*: 251; Kyvig, *Age of Impeachment*: 328; Mark J. Rozell and Clyde Wilcox, "The Clinton Presidency and the Politics of Scandal," in Mark J. Rozell and Clyde Wilcox, eds., *The Clinton Scandal* (Washington, DC: Georgetown University Press, 2000, viii–xxii): ix; Fisher, "Independent Counsel": 66.

138. Rozell and Wilcox, "The Clinton Presidency": ix.

139. Morton, *Monica's Story*: 10.

140. Isikoff, *Uncovering Clinton*: 314; Morton, *Monica's Story*: 16.

141. Fisher, "Independent Counsel": 70.

142. O'Connor and Hermann, "The Courts": 54; Isikoff, *Uncovering Clinton*: 265.

143. Kyvig, *Age of Impeachment*: 329; Morton, *Monica's Story*: 11.

144. Kyvig, *Age of Impeachment*: 329; Morton, *Monica's Story*: 11.

145. Dershowitz, *Sexual McCarthyism*: 22.

146. Kyvig, *Age of Impeachment*: 330; Van Tassel and Finkelman, *Impeachable Offenses*: 270.

147. Maxwell-Long, "White House": 109.

148. *Ibid.*: 109; Kyvig, *Age of Impeachment*: 330.

149. Rozell and Wilcox, "The Clinton Presidency": x.

150. Maltese, "The Media": 198; Hagood, *Presidential Sex*: 253.

151. O'Connor and Hermann, "The Courts": 55; Maxwell-Long, "White House": 109.

152. Van Tassel and Finkelman, *Impeachable Offenses*: 270; Bill Gertz, *Betrayal: How the Clinton Administration Undermined American Security* (Washington, DC: Regnery Publishing, 1999): 3.

153. O'Connor and Hermann, "The Courts": 55; Isikoff, *Uncovering Clinton*: 354.

154. Maxwell-Long, "White House": 108.

155. Kyvig, *Age of Impeachment*: 331; Dershowitz, *Sexual McCarthyism*: 193; Thomas A. Kazee, "The Congress: The Politics of Impeachment," in Mark J. Rozell and Clyde Wilcox, eds., *The Clinton Scandal* (Washington, DC: Georgetown University Press, 2000, 18–39): 23; O'Connor and Hermann, "The Courts,": 40; Thompson, *Political Scandal*: 155; Rozell and Wilcox, "The Clinton Presidency": x.

156. Kyvig, *Age of Impeachment*: 332.

157. Isikoff, *Uncovering Clinton*: 353.

158. Dershowitz, *Sexual McCarthyism*: 214.

159. Kyvig, *Age of Impeachment*: 331.

160. Rozell and Wilcox, "The Clinton Presidency": x.

161. Dershowitz, *Sexual McCarthyism*: 189.

162. Maxwell-Long, "White House": 109.

163. Rozell and Wilcox, "The Clinton Presidency": xi.

164. *Ibid.* xi; Kyvig, *Age of Impeachment*: 337.

165. Quirk, "Scandal Time": 125.

166. *Ibid.*

167. Dershowitz, *Sexual McCarthyism*: 34.

168. Rozell and Wilcox, "The Clinton Presidency": vii; Kyvig, *Age of Impeachment*: 311; Maxwell-Long, "White House": 109.

169. Rozell and Wilcox, "The Clinton Presidency": vii.

170. Kyvig, *The Age of Impeachment*: 346.

171. Kazee, "The Congress": 20.

172. Michael J. Gerhardt, "The Impeachment and Acquittal of President William Jefferson Clinton," in Mark J. Rozell and Clyde Wilcox, *The Clinton Scandal* (Washington, DC: Georgetown University Press, 2000, 142–170), 149.

173. Isikoff, *Uncovering Clinton*: 354; Rozell and Wilcox, "The Clinton Presidency": vii.

174. Fisher, "Independent Counsel": 72; Rozell and Wilcox, "The Clinton Presidency": ix; Gerhardt, "The Impeachment": 142.

175. O'Connor and Hermann, "The Courts": 55.

176. Stanley Renshon, "The Polls: The Public's Response to the Clinton Scandals, Part 2: Diverse Explanations, Clearer Consequences." *Presidential Studies Quarterly*, 32 (2002): 412–427.

177. Molly W. Andolina and Clyde Wilcox "Public Opinion: The Paradoxes of Clinton's Popularity," in Mark J. Rozell and Clyde Wilcox, eds., *The Clinton Scandal* (Washington, DC: Georgetown University Press, 2000, 171–194): 173.

178. *Ibid.*

179. *Ibid.*

180. Maltese, "The Media": 207; Gerhardt, "The Impeachment": 147–148; Jeffrey L. Katz and Jackie Koszczuk, "GOP's Recovery Strategy: Get Back to Legislating," *Congressional Quarterly Weekly Report*, February 13, 1999, 356–357; Gary C. Jacobson, "Impeachment Politics in the 1998 Congressional Elections," *Political Science Quarterly* 114 (1999): 36; Kazee, "The Congress": 19.

181. Kyvig, *Age of Impeachment*: 328.

182. Andolina and Wilcox, "Public Opinion": 174.

183. *Ibid.*

184. *Ibid.*: 173.

185. Gerhardt, "The Impeachment": 147–8.

186. Andolina and Wilcox, "Public Opinion": 173.

187. Diana Owen, "Popular Politics and the Clinton/Lewinsky Affair: The Implications for Leadership," *Political Psychology*, 21 (2000): 161–177:175; Kyvig, *Age of Impeachment*: 312.

188. Gerhardt, "The Impeachment": 148.

189. Jeffrey L. Katz, "Politically Charged Vote Sets Tone for Impeachment Inquiry," *Congressional Quarterly Weekly Report*, October 10, 1998, 2712–2715.

190. Marion Just and Ann Crigler, "Leadership Image-Building: After Clinton and Watergate," *Political Psychology*, 21 (2000): 179–198: 192.

191. Stephen Early Bennett, "Another Lesson about Public Opinion during the Clinton-Lewinsky Scandal," *Presidential Studies Quarterly*, 32 (2002): 276–292, 276.

192. Quirk, "Scandal Time": 125.

193. *Ibid.*: 126.

194. Kazee, "The Congress": 20.

195. Andolina and Wilcox, "Public Opinion": 175.

196. Just and Crigler, "Leadership": 191.

197. Gerhardt, "The Impeachment": 148; Rozell and Wilcox, ""The Clinton Presidency": x.

198. Mark Fischle, "Mass Response to the Lewinsky Scandal: Motivated Reasoning or Bayesian Updating?" *Political Psychology*, 21 (2000): 135–159, 136.

199. Just and Crigler, "Leadership": 192–193.

200. *Ibid.*

201. Owen, "Popular Politics": 161; Just and Crigler, "Leadership": 184; Fischle, "Mass Response": 135–136.

202. Andolina and Wilcox, "Public Opinion": 180.

203. Just and Crigler, "Leadership": 192–3.

204. *Ibid.*

205. O'Connor and Hermann, "The Courts": 40.

206. Dershowitz, *Sexual McCarthyism*: 221.

207. Isikoff, *Uncovering Clinton*: 13.

208. *Ibid.*: 58.

209. Gerhardt, "The Impeachment": 142.

210. O'Connor and Hermann, "The Courts": 57.

211. Spitzer, "The Presidency": 12.

212. Larry J. Sabato, *Feeding Frenzy* (New York: Free Press, 1991): 4.

213. Quirk, "Scandal Time": 123; Stewart, *Blood Sport*: 424.

214. Rozell and Wilcox, "The Clinton Presidency": vii; Quirk, "Scandal Time": 129.

215. Gerhardt, "The Impeachment": 142.

216. Dershowitz, *Sexual McCarthyism*: 34.

217. Rozell and Wilcox, "The Clinton Presidency": viii.

218. Spitzer, "The Presidency": 10.

219. Rozell and Wilcox, "The Clinton Presidency": xi; Stewart, *Blood Sport*: 425; Van Tassel and Finkelman, *Impeachable Offenses*: 271.

220. Rozell and Wilcox, "The Clinton Presidency": xi; Kazee, "The Congress": 20.

221. Spitzer, "The Presidency": 13.

222. *Ibid.*: 6.

223. *Ibid.*: 5.

224. Gerhardt, "The Impeachment": 143.

225. *Ibid.*: 160.

226. Spitzer, "The Presidency": 9.

227. Van Tassel and Finkelman, *Impeachable Offenses*: 267.

228. Dershowitz, *Sexual McCarthyism*: 27.

229. Sabato and Lichter, *Watchdogs*: 60–61.

230. Robert L. Bartley, "On Arkansas Sex, Not Inhaling, and Whitewater," *Wall Street Journal*, January 6, 1994.

231. Isikoff, *Uncovering Clinton*: 80.

232. *Ibid.*: 168.

233. Williams, *Political Scandals*: 63.

234. O'Connor and Hermann, "The Courts": 44.

235. Moldea, *Washington Tragedy*: 140.

236. Kyvig, *Age of Impeachment*: 319.

237. Stewart, *Blood Sport*: 63; Williams, *Political Scandals*: 64; Robert L. Bartley, *Whitewater: A Journal Briefing* (New York: Dow Jones and Company, 1992): 1.

238. Sabato and Lichter, *Watchdogs*: 7; Bartley, *Whitewater*: 1; Stewart, *Blood Sport*: 61.

239. Williams, *Political Scandals*: 64.

240. Stewart, *Blood Sport*: 62.

241. Thompson, *Political Scandal*: 189; Stewart, *Blood Sport*: 61, 88.

242. Moldea, *Washington Tragedy*: 140.

243. Stewart, *Blood Sport*: 87.

244. Bartley, *Whitewater*: 1.

245. Thompson, *Political Scandal*: 189.

246. Stewart, *Blood Sport*: 130.

247. *Ibid.*: 131; Lyons, *Fools*: 69.

248. Lyons, *Fools*: 70.

249. Stewart, *Blood Sport*: 93.

250. *Ibid.*: 94.

251. *Ibid.*: 95.

252. *Ibid.*: 102.

253. Hubbell, *Friends:* 112; Lyons, *Fool*: 35.

254. Stewart, *Blood Sport*: 103, 106; Thompson, *Political Scandal*: 189; Moldea, *Washington Tragedy*: 140.

255. Stewart, *Blood Sport*: 99. Williams, *Political Scandals*: 64.

256. Stewart, *Blood Sport*: 100; Moldea, *Washington Tragedy*: 140.

257. Stewart, *Blood Sport*: 110; Williams, *Political Scandals*: 66.

258. Bruce Ingersoll and Paul M. Barrett, "U.S. Investigating S&L Chief's '85 Check To Clinton, SBA-Backed Loan to Friend," *Wall Street Journal*, November 1, 1993.

259. Stewart, *Blood Sport*: 197.

260. Bartley, *Whitewater*: 1.

261. Stewart, *Blood Sport*: 137; Isikoff, *Uncovering Clinton*: 34; Lyons, *Fool*: 41.

262. Stewart, *Blood Sport*: 314; Bartley, *Whitewater*: 89, 110.

263. Hubbell, *Friends*: 113; Stewart, *Blood Sport*: 124; Kyvig, *Age of Impeachment*: 319; Moldea, *Washington Tragedy*: 140.

264. Stewart, *Blood Sport*: 197.

265. Bartley, *Whitewater*: 1.

266. Stewart, *Blood Sport*: 197.

267. Dershowitz, *Sexual McCarthyism*: 42; Bartley, *Whitewater*: 109.

268. Bartley, *Whitewater*: 1.

269. Dershowitz, *Sexual McCarthyism*: 43.

270. Stewart, *Blood Sport*: 142.

271. Dershowitz, *Sexual McCarthyism*: 42.

272. Thompson, *Political Scandal*: 189.

273. Sabato and Lichter, *Watchdogs*: 7.

274. Sabato and Lichter, *Watchdogs*: 7; Lyons, *Fool*: 43, 46; Thompson, *Political Scandal*: 191; Williams, *Political Scandals*: 65.

275. Thompson, *Political Scandal*: 190; Williams, *Political Scandals*: 66.

276. Kyvig, *Age of Impeachment*: 319.

277. Stewart, *Blood Sport*: 376.

278. Williams, *Political Scandals*: 68.

279. *Ibid.*: 69.

280. Sabato and Lichter, *Watchdogs*: 8; Van Tassel and Finkelman, *Impeachable Offenses*: 267.

281. Kyvig, *Age of Impeachment*: 320.

282. Williams, *Political Scandals*: 71.

283. Kyvig, *Age of Impeachment*: 321.

284. Sabato and Lichter, *Watchdogs*: 9; Stewart, *Blood Sport*: 423.

285. Williams, *Political Scandals*.

286. Kyvig, *Age of Impeachment*: 321.

287. *Ibid.*

288. O'Connor and Hermann, "The Courts": 52; Hagood, *Presidential Sex*: 251.

289. O'Connor and Hermann, "The Courts": 52S; Stewart, *Blood Sport*: 399.

290. Stewart, *Blood Sport*: 425.

291. Sabato and Lichter, *Watchdogs*: 8.

292. *Ibid.*

293. Williams, *Political Scandals*: 67.

294. Moldea, *Washington Tragedy*: 333.

295. Wilentz, *Age of Reagan*: 376.

296. Williams, *Political Scandals*: 76.

297. *Ibid.*: 75; "Panel Issues Whitewater Report" *Congressional Quarterly Almanac* (Washington, DC: CQ Press, 1996, I-46–I-47).

298. Williams, *Political Scandals*: 76.

299. Fisher, "Independent Counsel": 68; Williams, *Political Scandals*: 74; Stewart, *Blood Sport*: 430.

300. Williams, *Political Scandals*: 77; Fisher, "Independent Counsel": 69.

301. Thompson, *Political Scandal*: 189; Stewart, *Blood Sport*: 175.

302. Isikoff, *Uncovering Clinton*: 273.

303. Williams, *Political Scandals*: 74; Stewart, *Blood Sport*: 428.

304. Stewart, *Blood Sport*: 326.

305. Sabato and Lichter, *Watchdogs*: 7–8; Stewart, *Blood Sport*: 414.

306. Isikoff, *Uncovering Clinton*: 355.

307. Lyons, *Fool*: 140.

308. Kurtz, *Spin Cycle*: xix, 50; Wilentz, *Age of Reagan*: 369.

309. Grossman, *Political Corruption*: 46.

310. Isikoff, *Uncovering Clinton*: 169.

311. Hubbell, *Friends*: 117.

312. Grossman, *Political Corruption*: 45.

313. *Ibid.*: 46.

314. *Ibid.*: 45.

315. *Ibid.*: 46.

316. Kurtz, *Spin Cycle*: 63.

317. *Ibid.*: 63.

318. Grossman, *Political Corruption*: 45.

319. *Ibid.*: 46.

320. Kurtz, *Spin Cycle*: 154–155.

321. Isikoff, *Uncovering Clinton*: 169.

322. Kurtz, *Spin Cycle*: 156–160.

323. Grossman, *Political Corruption*: 47.

324. Gertz, *Betrayal*: 9, 84; Grossman, *Political Corruption*: 51.

325. Grossman, *Political Corruption*: 51.

326. *Ibid.*: 52.

327. Gertz, *Betrayal*: 84, Grossman, *Political Corruption*: 52.

328. Gertz, *Betrayal*: 85.

329. Grossman, *Political Corruption*: 52; Gertz, *Betrayal*: 85.

330. Gertz, *Betrayal*: 85.

331. *Ibid.*: 82.

332. *Ibid.*

333. Grossman, *Political Corruption*: 51.

334. *Ibid.*: 53.

335. *Ibid.*: 51.

336. *Ibid.*: 53.

337. Gertz, *Betrayal*: 86.

338. Grossman, *Political Corruption*: 53.

339. Gertz, *Betrayal*: 86.

340. *Ibid.*: 136.

341. *Ibid.*: 139.
342. *Ibid.*: 138.
343. *Ibid.*: 135.
344. *Ibid.*: 84, 4.
345. *Ibid.*
346. *Ibid.*: 5.
347. *Ibid.*: 3.
348. *Ibid.*: 5.
349. Dershowitz, *Sexual McCarthyism*: 198.

Chapter 7

1. Robert Williams, *Political Scandals in the USA* (Chicago: Fitzroy Dearborn, 1998): 89–90.

2. Ibid.: 115.

3. *Ibid.*: 116.

4. Susan J. Tolchin and Martin Tolchin, *Glass Houses: Congressional Ethics and the Politics of Venom* (Cambridge, MA: Westview Press, 2001): 13.

5. *Ibid.*: *Glass Houses*: 13–14.

6. Williams, *Political Scandals*: 91.

7. Mark Grossman, *Political Corruption in America* (Santa Barbara, CA: ABC Clio, 2003): 1; Tolchin and Tolchin, *Glass Houses*: 50; Williams, *Political Scandals*: 98; Frederick M. Kaiser, "Executive Investigations of U.S. Legislators: A Comparison of Abscam and the Land Fraud Schemes," *Police Studies,* 13 (1990): 14–25.

8. Grossman, *Political Corruption*: 3.

9. Williams, *Political Scandals*: 97.

10. John B. Thompson, *Political Scandal: Power and Visibility in the Media Age* (Malden, MA: Polity Press, 2000): 186.

11. Grossman, *Political Corruption*: 2.

12. *Ibid.*: 1.

13. *Ibid.*

14. Williams, *Political Scandals*: 97.

15. Grossman, *Political Corruption*: 2.

16. Thompson, *Political Scandal*: 186.

17. *Ibid.*

18. *Ibid.*

19. Grossman, *Political Corruption*: 1.

20. Thompson, *Political Scandal*: 186.

21. Grossman, *Political Corruption*: 2.

22. "Abscam Defendants Enter Prison" *Congressional Quarterly Almanac* (Washington, DC: CQ Press, 1983, 585–586): 585.

23. *Ibid.*: 3.

24. Kaiser, "Executive Investigations."

25. *Ibid.*

26. Myra MacPherson, *The Power Lovers* (New York: Ballantine Books, 1976): 313.

27. Tolchin and Tolchin, *Glass Houses*: 22.

28. David E. Kyvig, *The Age of Impeachment* (Lawrence: University Press of Kansas, 2008): 22, Tolchin and Tolchin, *Glass Houses*: 22.

29. Suzanne Garment, *Scandal: The Culture of Mistrust in American Politics* (New York: Anchor Books, 1991): 19; "An American Family in the Rockets' Red Glare," *American History,* 43 (June 2008): 74.

30. Garment, *Scandal*: 19.

31. *Ibid.*: 20.

32. *Ibid.*

33. Grossman, *Political Corruption*: 19; C. Vann Woodward, *Responses of the Presidents to Charges of Misconduct* (New York: Delacorte Press, 1974): 387; Tolchin and Tolchin, *Glass Houses*: 44.

34. Woodward, *Responses*: 387.

35. Grossman, *Political Corruption*: 20.

36. Tolchin and Tolchin, *Glass Houses*: 45.

37. Larry J. Sabato, *Feeding Frenzy* (New York: Free Press, 1991); 9; Garment, *Scandal*: 185.

38. MacPherson, *Power Lovers*: 206.

39. Dan Rather, *The Palace Guard* (New York: Warner Paperback Library Edition, 1975), 17, 200.

40. MacPherson, *Power Lovers*: 195.

41. Sabato, *Feeding Frenzy*: 9–10.

42. Grossman, *Political Corruption*: 157.

43. Stanley G. Hilton and Anne-Renee Testa, *Glass Houses* (New York: St. Martin's, 1998): 18; Michael Isikoff, *Uncovering Clinton: A Reporter's Story* (New York: Crown, 1999): 58; Garment, *Scandal*: 177; Grossman, *Political Corruption*: 157.

44. Garment, *Scandal*: 177; Grossman, *Political Corruption*: 157.

45. Grossman, *Political Corruption*: 157; Tolchin and Tolchin, *Glass Houses*: 77.

46. Grossman, *Political Corruption*: 157.

47. *Ibid.*: 158.

48. MacPherson, *Power Lovers*: 312; Grossman, *Political Corruption*: 158.

49. Sabato, *Feeding Frenzy*: 47.

50. Grossman, *Political Corruption*: 158.

51. *Ibid.*: 158.

52. *Ibid.*: 231.

53. *Ibid.*: 230.

54. Sabato, *Feeding Frenzy*: 19; Garment, *Scandal*: 176; MacPherson, *Power Lovers*: 188; Grossman, *Political Corruption*: 231.

55. Grossman, *Political Corruption*: 231.

56. *Ibid.*: 208.

57. Williams, *Political Scandals*: 96.

58. Grossman, *Political Corruption*: 153.

59. Tolchin and Tolchin, *Glass Houses*: 3.

60. Hilton and Testa, *Glass Houses*: 17.

61. Garment, *Scandal*: 66–69.

62. *Ibid.*: 37.

63. *Ibid.*: 237.

64. Sabato, *Feeding Frenzy*: 14.

65. Hilton and Testa, *Glass Houses*: 61–65.

66. Garment, *Scandal*: 186–187.

67. Sabato, *Feeding Frenzy*: 12.

68. Garment, *Scandal*: 181.

69. *Ibid.*: 181; Kenneth T. Walsh, "Sex, Lies, and Major Headlines," *U.S. News and World Report*, January 28–February 4, 2008, 36–37.

70. Nigel Cawthorne, *Sex Lives of the Presidents* (New York: St. Martin's Press, 1996): 2; Sabato, *Feeding Frenzy*: 14; Thompson, *Political Scandal*: 146.

71. Isikoff, *Uncovering Clinton*: 59.

72. Hilton and Testa, *Glass Houses*: 33.

73. Garment, *Scandal*: 194.

74. Sabato, *Feeding Frenzy*: 22.

75. Hilton and Testa, *Glass Houses*: 35.

76. *Ibid.*: 38.

77. Williams, *Political Scandals*: 95.

78. Sabato, *Feeding Frenzy*: 21; Williams, *Political Scandals*: 108.

79. Paul J. Quirk, "Scandal Time: The Clinton Impeachment and the Distraction of American Politics," in Mark J. Rozell and Clyde Wilcox, eds., *The Clinton Scandal* (Washington, DC: Georgetown University Press, 2000, 119–141): 132.

80. Williams, *Political Scandals*: 109; Tolchin and Tolchin, *Glass Houses*: 3.

81. Williams, *Political Scandals*: 11.

82. Thompson, *Political Scandal*: 109.

83. Williams, *Political Scandals*: 101.

84. Grossman, *Political Corruption*: 199; Tolchin and Tolchin, *Glass Houses*: 51.

85. David I. Thompson, "The Clinton Two vs. the Keating Five," *Wall Street Journal*, February 10, 1994.

86. Williams, *Political Scandals*: 102; Tolchin and Tolchin, *Glass Houses*: 51.

87. Grossman, *Political Corruption*: 82.

88. Larry Margasak, "Keating Scandal Left its Mark on McCain," *The (Canton, Ohio) Repository* March 24, 2008, A-3.

89. Grossman, *Political Corruption*: 201.

90. *Ibid.*: 82.

91. *Ibid.*: 8.

92. Williams, *Political Scandals*: 102; Tolchin and Tolchin, *Glass Houses*: 51; Grossman, *Political Corruption*: 201.

93. Grossman, *Political Corruption*: 168; "Scandals Plague Members in First Session" *Congressional Quarterly Almanac* (Washington, DC: CQ Press, 1991, 39–42).

94. Garment, *Scandal*: 340.

95. Williams, *Political Scandals*: 105.

96. Grossman, *Political Corruption*: 169.

97. *Ibid.*

98. Garment, *Scandal*: 342.

99. Williams, *Political Scandals*: 105.

100. Grossman, *Political Corruption*: 168.

101. *Ibid.*

102. Garment, *Scandal*: 342.

103. Grossman, *Political Corruption*: 286.

104. *Ibid.*: 287.

105. *Ibid.*: 286.

106. Tolchin and Tolchin, *Glass Houses*: 85; Mark Kirchmeier, *Packwood* (New York: HarperCollins West, 1995).

107. Tolchin and Tolchin, *Glass Houses*: 85.

108. Monica Crowley, *Nixon in Winter* (New York: Random House, 1998): 330; Kirchmeier, *Packwood*.

109. Thompson, *Political Scandal*: 146; Tolchin and Tolchin, *Glass Houses*: 85; "Packwood Accused of Harassment" *Congressional Quarterly Almanac* (Washington, DC: CQ Press, 1992, 52–53).

110. Crowley, *Nixon in Winter*: 330.

111. *Ibid.*

112. *Ibid.*: 333.

113. *Ibid.*: 330.

114. *Ibid.*: 332; Tolchin and Tolchin, *Glass Houses*: 87.

115. Crowley, *Nixon in Winter*: 333.

116. Kirchmeier, *Packwood*.

117. Hilton and Testa, *Glass Houses*: 10.

118. *Ibid.*: 173.

119. "Moseley-Braun Loses to Republican Fitzgerald," CNN, November 3, 1998; Associated Press, "Moseley-Braun Lashes Out at Columnist, Apologizes," CNN, September 9, 1998.

120. Hilton and Testa, *Glass Houses*: 176.

121. *Ibid.*: 177.

122. Williams, *Political Scandals*: 111.

123. Quirk, "Scandal Time": 132.

124. Hilton and Testa, *Glass Houses*: 112.

125. Tolchin and Tolchin, *Glass Houses*: 5.

126. *Ibid.*

127. Williams, *Political Scandals*: 112.

128. *Ibid.*: 113.

129. Hilton and Testa, *Glass Houses*: 89.

130. *Ibid.*

131. Hilton and Testa, *Glass Houses*: 90.

132. *Ibid.*: *Glass Houses*: 75.

133. *Ibid.*: *Glass Houses*: 79.

134. Alan M. Dershowitz, *Sexual McCarthyism* (New York: Basic Books, 1998): 205.

135. Hilton and Testa, *Glass Houses*: 9.

136. *Ibid.*: 78–80.

137. *Ibid.*: 23.

138. Dershowitz, *Sexual McCarthyism*: 25.

139. Hilton and Testa, *Glass Houses*: 9, 24; Kyvig, *Age of Impeachment*: 338.

140. Hilton and Testa, *Glass Houses*: 25.

141. *Ibid.*: 26; Dershowitz, *Sexual McCarthyism*: 25.

Chapter 8

1. David E. Kyvig, *The Age of Impeachment* (Lawrence, KS: University Press of Kansas, 2008): 200–201.

2. *Ibid.*: 366.

3. *Ibid.*: 5.

4. *Ibid.*: 13–14.

5. *Ibid.*: 23.

6. Mark Grossman, *Political Corruption in America* (Santa Barbara, CA: ABC Clio, 2003): 261.

7. Emily Van Tassel and Paul Finkelman, *Impeachable Offenses* (Washington, DC: Congressional Quarterly, 1999): 90.

8. Michael J. Gerhardt, "The Impeachment and Acquittal of President William Jefferson Clinton," in Mark J. Rozell and Clyde Wilcox, eds., *The Clinton Scandal* (Washington, DC: Georgetown University Press, 2000, 142–170): 154–155; Van Tassel and Finkelman, *Impeachable Offenses*: 86; Grossman, *Political Corruption*: 260.

9. Van Tassel and Finkelman, *Impeachable Offenses*: 91.

10. Kyvig, *Age of Impeachment*: 23.

11. Grossman, *Political Corruption*: 280.

12. Kyvig, *Age of Impeachment*: 23.

13. *Ibid.*: 24.

14. Grossman, *Political Corruption*: 255.

15. Van Tassel and Finkelman, *Impeachable Offenses*: 108.

16. Kyvig, *Age of Impeachment*: 25; Grossman, *Political Corruption*: 255.

17. Grossman, *Political Corruption*: 174.

18. *Ibid.*

19. Van Tassel and Finkelman, *Impeachable Offenses*: 115.

20. *Ibid.*: 86, 116.

21. Kyvig, *Age of Impeachment*: 25.

22. Van Tassel and Finkelman, *Impeachable Offenses*: 119.

23. Kyvig, *Age of Impeachment*: 30.

24. Suzanne Garment, *Scandal: The Culture of Mistrust in American Politics* (New York: Anchor Books, 1991): 20.

25. Kyvig, *Age of Impeachment*: 30; Grossman, *Political Corruption*: 316.

26. Grossman, *Political Corruption*: 13.

27. Van Tassel and Finkelman, *Impeachable Offenses*: 132.

28. Kyvig, *Age of Impeachment*: 30.

29. Van Tassel and Finkelman, *Impeachable Offenses*: 132.

30. Grossman, *Political Corruption*: 13.

31. Van Tassel and Finkelman, *Impeachable Offenses*: 133.

32. Kyvig, *Age of Impeachment*: 31.

33. Grossman, *Political Corruption*: 113.

34. Kyvig, *Age of Impeachment*: 32.

35. Grossman, *Political Corruption*: 114.

36. *Ibid.*: 113; Kyvig, Age of Impeachment: 32.

37. Grossman, *Political Corruption*: 215.

38. Van Tassel and Finkelman, *Impeachable Offenses*: 152; Grossman, *Political Corruption*: 215.

39. Grossman, *Political Corruption*: 215.

40. *Ibid.*: 216.

41. Van Tassel and Finkelman, *Impeachable Offenses*: 153; Grossman, *Political Corruption*: 216.

42. Grossman, *Political Corruption*: 216.

43. Van Tassel and Finkelman, *Impeachable Offenses*: 157.

44. Kyvig, *Age of Impeachment*: 33.

45. Grossman, *Political Corruption*: 280.

46. Kyvig, *Age of Impeachment*: 33.

47. *Ibid.*

48. Grossman, *Political Corruption*: 219.

49. Kyvig, *Age of Impeachment*: 70; Grossman, *Political Corruption*: 136.

50. Kyvig, *Age of Impeachment*: 71; Grossman, *Political Corruption*: 136.

51. Jeffrey D. Schultz, *Presidential Scandals* (Washington, DC: CQ Press, 2000): 366.

52. Kyvig, *Age of Impeachment*: 72; Grossman, *Political Corruption*: 136.

53. Kyvig, *Age of Impeachment*: 70.

54. Grossman, *Political Corruption*: 136.

55. Kyvig, *Age of Impeachment*: 76; Grossman, *Political Corruption*: 137.

56. Kyvig, *Age of Impeachment*: 76–77.

57. *Ibid.*: 83.

58. *Ibid.*: 78.

59. *Ibid.*: 81.

60. *Ibid.*: 82.

61. *Ibid.*: 76.

62. *Ibid.*: 82; Grossman, *Political Corruption*: 137.

63. Kyvig, *Age of Impeachment*: 83.

64. *Ibid.*: 85.

65. *Ibid.*: 90.

66. *Ibid.*

67. *Ibid.*: 91.

68. *Ibid.*

69. *Ibid.*: 92.

70. *Ibid.*: 87.

71. *Ibid.*: 88.

72. *Ibid.*: 93.

73. *Ibid.*: 88.

74. *Ibid.*: 94.

75. *Ibid.*: 95.

76. *Ibid.*: 88.

77. *Ibid.*: 89.

78. *Ibid.*: 95.

79. Gerhardt, "Impeachment and Acquittal": 83.

80. Kyvig, *Age of Impeachment*: 87.

81. *Ibid.*: 96.

82. *Ibid.*

83. *Ibid.*: 97.

84. *Ibid.*: 99.

85. *Ibid.*: 100.

86. *Ibid.*: 102.

87. *Ibid.*: 106.

88. Gerhardt, Impeachment and Acquittal": 83.

89. Kyvig, *Age of Impeachment*: 109.

90. *Ibid.*: 199.

91. *Ibid.*: 289; Grossman, *Political Corruption*: 154.

92. Kyvig, *Age of Impeachment*: 288.

93. Stanley G. Hilton and Anne-Renee Testa, *Glass Houses* (New York: St. Martin's, 1998): 121.

94. Kyvig, *Age of Impeachment*: 289.

95. Grossman, *Political Corruption*: 154; Van Tassel and Finkelman, *Impeachable Offenses*: 172; Kyvig, *Age of Impeachment*: 288, 290.

96. Kyvig, *Age of Impeachment*: 288.

97. *Ibid.*: 292.

98. Grossman, *Political Corruption*: 155.

99. *Ibid.*

100. Van Tassel and Finkelman, *Impeachable Offenses*: 172.

101. Grossman, *Political Corruption*: 154.

102. Van Tassel and Finkelman, *Impeachable Offenses*: 173; Grossman, *Political Corruption*: 156.

103. Kyvig, *Age of Impeachment*: 307.

104. Maurice Possley, "Operation Greylord: A Federal Probe of Court Corruption Sets the Standard for Future Investigations," *Chicago Tribune*, August 5, 1983; available at http://www.chicagotribune.com/news; accessed 7/19/2008.

105. Kyvig, *Age of Impeachment*: 269.

106. *Ibid.*: 270.

107. *Ibid.*

108. *Ibid.*

109. *Ibid.*: 271.

110. *Ibid.*

111. *Ibid.*

112. *Ibid.*

113. *Ibid.*

114. *Ibid.*: 272; Van Tassel and Finkelman, *Impeachable Offenses*: 168.

115. Gerhardt, "Impeachment and Acquittal": 154.

116. Kyvig, *Age of Impeachment*: 272.

117. *Ibid.*

118. *Ibid.*: 273.

119. *Ibid.*: 274.

120. *Ibid.*: 275.

121. Van Tassel and Finkelman, *Impeachable Offenses*: 168.

122. Kyvig, *Age of Impeachment*: 277.

123. *Ibid.*: 276.

124. *Ibid.*: 277.

125. Grossman, *Political Corruption*: 55.

126. *Ibid.*: 56.

127. Kyvig, *Age of Impeachment*: 260.

128. "Video Rentals Privacy" *Congressional Quarterly Almanac* (Washington, DC: CQ Press, 1988, 120–121).

129. Larry J. Sabato, *Feeding Frenzy* (New York: Free Press, 1991): 20.

130. Schultz, *Presidential Scandals*: 415.

131. Kyvig, *Age of Impeachment*: 305.

132. *Ibid.*

133. *Ibid.*: 278.

134. *Ibid.*

135. *Ibid.*: 279.

136. *Ibid.*

137. *Ibid.*: 280.

138. *Ibid.*: 280–281; Van Tassel and Finkelman, *Impeachable Offenses*: 180–181.

139. Kyvig, *Age of Impeachment*: 281.

140. *Ibid.*

141. *Ibid.*: 282.

142. *Ibid.*: 284.

143. *Ibid.*: 285.

144. Sean Wilentz, *The Age of Reagan* (New York: Harper Collins, 2008): 311.

145. Wilentz, *Age of Reagan*: 311; Timothy Naftali, *George H.W. Bush* (New York: Times Books, 2007): 124.

146. James P. Pfiffner, "Presidential Character: Multidimensional or Seamless?" in Mark J. Rozell and Clyde Wilcox, eds., *The Clinton Scandal* (Washington, DC: Georgetown University Press, 2000, 225–255): 232.

147. Wilentz, *Age of Reagan*: 311.

148. *Ibid.*

149. Monica Crowley, *Nixon in Winter* (New York: Random House, 1998): 323.

150. Michael Isikoff, *Uncovering Clinton: A Reporter's Story* (New York: Crown, 1999): 59; Garment, *Scandal*: 309.

151. Garment, *Scandal*: 313.

152. Wilentz, *Age of Reagan*: 311; Naftali, *George H.W. Bush*: 134; Garment, *Scandal*: 309; Michael Schudson, *Watergate In American Memory* (New York: Basic Books, 1992): 23; Crowley, *Nixon in Winter*: 323.

153. Alan M. Dershowitz, *Sexual McCarthyism* (New York: Basic Books, 1998): 102.

154. Naftali, *George H.W. Bush*: 134.

155. Wilentz, *Age of Reagan*: 312; Garment, *Scandal*: 311.

156. Garment, *Scandal*: 314.

157. *Ibid.*: 317.

158. Wilentz, *Age of Reagan*: 312.

159. *Ibid.*: 312; Naftali, *George H.W. Bush*: 134.

160. Isikoff, *Uncovering Clinton*: 59.

161. Kyvig, *Age of Impeachment*: 304.

162. *Ibid.*: 302.

163. *Ibid.*

Chapter 9

1. John W. Dean, *Worse than Watergate* (New York: Little, Brown, 2004): 25.

2. David Corn, *The Lies of George W. Bush* (New York: Crown, 2003).

3. Robert D. Novak,"Mission to Niger," *Washington Post* July 14, 2003, p. A 21; Valerie Plame Wilson, *Fair Game* (New York: Simon and Schuster: 2003): 270.

4. Dean, *Worse than Watergate:* 170.

5. Dean, *Worse than Watergate*: 171; Eric Alterman and Mark Green, *The Book on Bush* (New York: Penguin Books: 2004): 270.

6. Wilson, *Fair Game*: 141.

7. Alterman and Green, *The Book on Bush*: 270.

8. David E. Kyvig, *The Age of Impeachment* (Lawrence: University Press of Kansas, 2008); 369; Dean, *Worse than Watergate:* 173.

9. Kyvig, *Age of Impeachment*: 369.

10. *Ibid.*

11. *Ibid.*

12. Associated Press, "Valerie Plame's Lawsuit Dismissed," *USA Today,* July 19, 2007; Carol D. Leonnig, "Plame's Lawsuit Against Top Official Dismissed," *Washington Post* July 20, 2007.

13. Richard Leiby, "Valerie Plame, the Spy who Got Shoved Out into the Cold," *Washington Post*, October 29, 2005, C01.

14. Reuters, "White House: E-mails on firings may have been killed," April 11, 2007.

15. "GOP Senator Calls for Gonzales' Head," CNN, March 16, 2007.

16. Barton Gellman and R. Jeffrey Smith, "Report to Defense Alleged Abuse by Prison Interrogation Teams," *Washington Post,* December 8, 2004, A1.

17. Kyvig, *Age of Impeachment*: 370.

18. Seymour M. Hersh, *Chain of Command: The Road from 9/11 to Abu Ghraib* (New York: HarperCollins, 2004): 8; Jack Goldsmith, *The Terror Presidency* (New York: Norton, 2007): 119.

19. Mark Green, *Losing Our Democracy* (Naperville, IL: Sourvebooks. 2006): 167.

20. Hersh, *Chain of Command*: 1.

21. Alterman and Green, *The Book on Bush*: 101.

22. Hersh, *Chain of Command*: 7.

23. Green, *Losing Our Democracy*: 168.

24. Hersh, *Chain of Command*: 15.

25. *Ibid.*: 20.

26. Ibid,: 21.

27. *Ibid.*: 22.

28. "A Roll Call of Recent Abuse Cases," Associated Press, January 16, 2005, A09.

29. *Ibid.*; T.R. Reid, "Graner Gets 10 Years for Abuse at Abu Ghraib," *Washington Post,* January 16, 2005, A1.

30. Gellman and Smith, "Report to Defense".

31. Associated Press, "Rumsfeld Offered to Quit After Abu Ghraib," *Washington Post,* February 4, 2005.

32. Matt Apuzzo, "U.S. Asks to Rewrite official detainee evidence," *(Akron, Ohio) Beacon Journal* June 21, 2008, A-1.

33. Jack Huberman, *The Bush-Hater's Handbook* (New York: Nation Books, 2003).

34. Apuzzo, "U.S. Asks to rewrite": A-1; Matt Apuzzo, "Judge: Guantanamo Is Top Priority," *(Canton, Ohio)Repository* July 9, 2008, A-2.

35. Apuzzo, "Judge": A-2.

36. Huberman, *Bush-Hater's Handbook.*

37. Green, *Losing Our Democracy*: 192.

38. Corn, *Lies*: 205.

39. *Ibid.*: 206.

40. *Ibid.*

41. David Frum, *The Right Man* (New York: Random House, 2003): 236.

42. Alterman and Green, *The Book on Bush*: 254.

43. Kyvig, *Age of Impeachment*: 371.

44. Alterman and Green, *The Book on Bush*: 278.

45. Corn, *Lies*: 208.

46. Alterman and Green, *The Book on Bush*: 280.

47. Huberman, *The Bush-Hater's Handbook.*

48. Corn, *Lies*: 206; Alterman and Green, *The Book on Bush*: 284.

49. Alterman and Green, *The Book on Bush*: 284.

50. Corn, *Lies*: 208.

51. Alterman and Green, *The Book on Bush*: 254.

52. Corn, *Lies*: 209.

53. *Ibid.*: 208.

54. *Ibid.*: 266.

55. *Ibid.*: 268; Alterman and Green, *The Book on Bush*: 257.

56. Corn, *Lies*: 285.

57. *Ibid.*

58. *Ibid.*: 286.

59. *Ibid.*: 212.

60. Kyvig, *Age of Impeachment*: 373.

61. Ivor Van Heerden and Mike Bryan, *The Storm* (New York: Penguin Books, 2007): 98.

62. *Ibid.*:150.

63. *Ibid.*: 64.

64. *Ibid.*: 67.

65. *Ibid.*: 148.

66. Dave Montgomery, "HUD Secretary Jackson Quits," *Akron (Ohio) Beacon Journal,* April 1, 2008, A3.

67. Dean, *Worse than Watergate*: ix.

68. John B. Thompson, *Political Scandal: Power and Visibility in the Media Age* (Malden, MA: Polity Press, 2000): 31.

69. Robert Williams, *Political Scandals in the USA* (Chicago: Fitzroy Dearborn, 1998): 122.

70. Alan M. Dershowitz, *Sexual McCarthyism* (New York: Basic Books, 1998): 49.

71. James P. Pfiffner, "Presidential Character: Multidimensional or Seamless?" in Mark J. Rozell and Clyde Wilcox, eds., *The Clinton Scandal* (Washington, DC: Georgetown University Press, 2000, 225–255), 226.

72. Michael Isikoff, *Uncovering Clinton: A Reporter's Story* (New York: Crown, 1999): 351; Al Hunt, "L'Affair Clinton: A Press Scandal, not a Sex Scandal, *Wall Street Journal*, January 26, 1992.

73. Pfiffner, "Presidential Character": 226–227.

74. Williams, *Political Scandals*: 132.

75. Pfiffner, "Presidential Character,": 228.

76. *Ibid.*: 243.

77. *Ibid.*: 250.

78. Theodore H. White, *Breach of Faith: The Fall of Richard Nixon* (New York: Atheneum, 1975): 325.

79. Monica Crowley, *Nixon in Winter* (New York: Random House, 1998): 321.

80. Elizabeth Drew, *Richard M. Nixon* (New York: Times Books, 2007): xvi.

81. Susan J. Tolchin and Martin Tolchin, *Glass Houses: Congressional Ethics and the Politics of Venom* (Cambridge MA: Westview Press, 2001): 2.

82. Howard Kurtz, *Spin Cycle: Inside the Clinton Propaganda Machine* (New York: Free Press, 1998): 260.

83. Dershowitz, *Sexual McCarthyism*: 236.

84. Richard Secord, *Honored and Betrayed* (New York: John Wiley and Sons, 1992): 343.

85. Crowley, *Nixon in Winter*: 335.

86. *Ibid.*

87. Suzanne Garment, *Scandal: The Culture of Mistrust in American Politics* (New York: Anchor Books, 1991): 273.

88. Paul J. Quirk, "Scandal Time: The Clinton Impeachment and the Distraction of American Politics," in Mark J. Rozell and Clyde Wilcox, eds., *The Clinton Scandal* (Washington, DC: Georgetown University Press, 2000, 119–141): 139.

89. James B. Stewart, *Blood Sport: The President and His Adversaries* (New York: Simon and Schuster, 1996): 38.

90. Kyvig, *Age of Impeachment*: 311.

91. Michael Schudson, "Notes on Scandal and the Watergate Legacy," *American Behavioral Scientist*, 47 (2004): 1231–1238, 1234.

92. Joseph A. Palermo, 2004. "Politics, Public Opinion and Popular Culture," in Harry P. Jeffrey and Thomas Maxwell-Long, eds., *Watergate and the Resignation of Richard Nixon: Impact of a Constitutional Crisis* (Washington, DC: CQ Press, 2004, 17–29): 24.

93. Thompson, *Political Scandal*: 238.

94. Garment, *Scandal*: 296.

95. Myra MacPherson, *The Power Lovers* (New York: Ballantine Books, 1976): ix; Garment, *Scandal*: 259.

96. Michael Schudson, *Watergate in American Memory* (New York: Basic Books, 1992): 117.

97. *Ibid.*: 163.

98. Garment, *Scandal*: 291.

99. *Ibid.*: 295.

100. Williams, *Political Scandals*: 126.

101. Garment, *Scandal*: 262.

102. *Ibid.*

103. Williams, *Political Scandals*: 124.

104. MacPherson, *Power Lovers*: 77.

105. Mark Fischle, "Mass Response to the Lewinsky Scandal: Motivated Reasoning or Bayesian Updating?" *Political Psychology*, 21 (2000): 135–159; 154.

106. Thompson, *Political Scandal*: 235.

107. Garment, *Scandal:* 273.

108. Quirk, "Scandal Time": 132.

109. Katy J. Harriger, "Special Prosecutors and Independent Counsels" in Harry P. Jeffrey and Thomas Maxwell-Long, eds., *Watergate and the Resignation of Richard Nixon: Impact of a Constitutional Crisis* (Washington, D.C.: CQ Press, 2004, 47–61): 60.

110. White, *Breach of Faith:* 222.

111. Quirk, "Scandal Time": 119.

112. *Ibid.:* 139.

113. Williams, *Political Scandals:* 12.

Index